Christ, Society and the State

Brian T Trainor

Adelaide
2010

Text copyright © 2010 remains with the author.

All rights reserved. Except for any fair dealing permitted under the Copyright Act, no part of this book may be reproduced by any means without prior permission. Inquiries should be made to the publisher.

National Library of Australia Cataloguing-in-Publication entry

Author: Trainor, Brian.

Title: Christ, society and the state / Brian T. Trainor.

ISBN: 9781921511585 (pbk)

Subjects: Christian sociology.
            Christian ethics.
            Church and state.
            Christianity and politics

Dewey Number: 261.5

Cover design by Astrid Sengkey

An imprint of the Australasian Theological Forum Ltd
P O Box 504
Hindmarsh
SA 5007
ABN 90 116 359 963
www.atfpress.com

Contents

Introduction

Part One: Christ and Society

1. God and Society
Universal and Particular: Niebuhr and Walzer
The Universal in the Particular
The Universal in Particular Traditions: Gadamer
Absolute and Relative: H Richard Niebuhr and Reinhold Niebuhr
Conclusion

2. Christian Social Ethics
Christian Social Ethics: Principles and Practice
Church and Society
The Invisible Community of Holy Citizens
False Faith and Fanaticism
Separation or Political Engagement: Scriven and Hauerwas
Two Kingdoms: Martin Luther
Conclusion: Universal and Social Salvation

Part Two: God and Truth

3. Foucault, Truth and the Politics of Difference
Postmodernism and Truth
Politics and Truth

A Truth-oriented normative Foucault
Connolly, Butler and Ransom on Foucault's Normativity
Conclusion

4. Walzer, Communitarianism and Truth: Pluralism and Public Policy
Pluralism, Truth and Liberal Democracy: Walzer
Public Policy and Bosanquet's Truth-orientated communitarianism
The Need for Ethico-political consciousness
The State and the Family
Adultism and the Homosexual Family
Culturally Formative Religion and Public Prayer

5. Western Liberalism, Islam and the 'Vertical Truth' of our Common Humanity
Liberalism and its Critics
Against the 'particularist' Case for Liberalism
Universal Liberalism and Kekes's Conservatism
Universal Liberalism and the Clash of Civilisations
The Horizontal Exportation of Liberal Deomocracy and Christian Realism
Justice, the State and our Universal Humanity
Islam and our Way of Life

Part Three: Christ and State

6. The Ethical Theory of the State
  Introduction
  Pluralism, Behaviouralism and Postmodernism
  Geographical versus Geometrical Political Unity

Marxism, the Return of the State and 'Relative
  Autonomy'
State-government-citizen/subject: God-Pilate-
  Jesus/Son of God
Conclusion: Marxism and Bartelson's
  'Unicorn State'

7. Barth and the State
Introduction
The State, Angels and Demons
Principalities and Powers: The Single Flow of Authority'
  and the 'Twin Flows of Salvation'
Moltmann's Criticism of Barth
Herberg's Criticism of Barth
Conclusion

8. Statism and Totalitarianism
Bosanquet and 'Statism'
The Mutuality of Self and Society
Conclusion: Each Restless Human Heart

Part Four: The Holy Spirit, Law and the State

9. Hobbes, the Holy Spirit and Natural Law
Uplifting Law and the Holy Spirit
The Political Covenant and the Human Condition
Essence and Existence: Sovereignty and the
  Sovereign Power
Before and After the Political Covenant
Hobbes and the 'Person' of the State

10. Barth, Reformation Theology and Natural Law
Faith in, with, and of Jesus
Divine Justification and Human Justice

Barth and Natural Law
The 'Catholic' Natural Law Tradition and 'Protestant' Reformation Theology
Essence as 'For Us' and Against Sin: The 'Prescriptive Ontic'

11. Derrida, Foundational Violence and the Mystical Foundation of Authortity

Montaigne, Pascal and Kant
Derrida, Justice, Law and Force/Violence
Bartelson, Derrida and Hobbes: Architecturalism
The Condition of all Possible Justice
The Ordeal of the Undecidable
Political Critique

Bibliography

Index

Acknowledgments

Parts of this book draw on previously published articles. I wish to express my gratitude to *The Review of Politics* for permission to use 'The Politics of Peace; the Role of the Political Covenant in Hobbes's Leviathan', (47, 4, July 1985), to *Hobbes Studies* for permission to use 'Hobbes, Skinner and the "person" of the state', (xiv, 2001), to *Animus* for permission to use 'Statism and Anti-Juristic Moralism in Bosanquet's Political Philosophy', (7, 2002), to the *European Journal of Political Theory* for permission to use 'Back to the future; the Emancipatory essence of the State' (4, 4 October 2005), to *Philosophy and Social Criticism* for permission to use 'Foucault and the Politics of Difference', (29, 5, 2003) and 'The State as the Mystical Foundation of Authority' (32, 6, 2006), and to *Dissent* for permission to use 'Pluralism, Truth and Social Democracy' (Fall, 2002).

I wish to especially thank George Crowder (Politics: Flinders University of South Australia) and Mark Worthing (Theology: Tabor Adelaide) for their charity, patience and perseverance in reading and criticising this work and Heather Eaton (Tabor Adelaide) for her invaluable assistance in 'matters bibliographical'.

Finally, I wish to thank Michael Walzer (Editor: *Dissent*) for the helpful comments and suggestions he made prior to the publication of the *Dissent* article which, like the other articles mentioned above, reappears in a modified and extended form in this work.

To

The Immaculate Heart

of Mary

Introduction

The kingdom of God is among you
Luke 17:21

Man fully alive is the glory God seeks
St Ireneaus

My kingdom is not of this world
John 18:36

On January 19, 2004, at the invitation of the Catholic Academy of Bavaria, Jürgen Habermas and Joseph Ratzinger engaged in a public discussion in Munich on the topic 'The pre-political moral foundations of a free state'. Just as remarkable as the dialogue that took place on that day between these high profile figures is the fact that these intellectual 'antipodes' agreed to meet at all. In his foreword to the published version of their discussion, Florian Schuller points out that this remarkable event 'had its origin in impressions from outside the German linguistic sphere'.[1] He mentions that in Italy a 'very intensive, open and commit-

---

1. J Habermas, and J Ratzinger, *Dialectics of Secularization: On Reason and Religion* (San Francisco: Ignatius Press, 2006), 8.

ted discussion'[2] had been going on for years between the *credenti* (believers) and the *laici* (secular persons), between philosophy and religion, but that 'we in Germany seem to lack a common philosophical dialogue on the basis of different positions that are interested in each other (as in Italy) or structures that permit a plurality of world views to engage in a societally institutionalised yet completely free conversation on a high level of reflection (as in France)'.[3] It is hardly surprising, then, that Habermas's call in 2001 for secular society to acquire a new understanding of religious convictions and to acknowledge that these convictions pose a 'cognitive challenge' to philosophy caused a great stir.[4] It was as if a wall of separation had become, in an instant, a doorway to dialogue. My feeling is that we, in the English-speaking world, are more like Germany than we are like Italy and that we need to try our utmost to rise to the 'challenge to dialogue' that the 'Munich moment' poses. In this book, I attempt to rise to this challenge by contributing in a useful way to the broad domain of social and political theory, but I wish to approach this domain (and to look at a number of important topics and concerns within it) from a faith perspective and, in so doing, (i) to make a fruitful contribution to a dialogue between those 'within', so to speak, and those 'without' the realm of faith, (ii) to contribute to an 'intra-faith' dialogue between Christians who hold opposing views concerning the 'true' social and political significance of their faith and

---

2. *Ibid.*
3. *Ibid*, 11
4. *Ibid*, 10

(iii) to steer as judicious a course as I can between these two kinds of dialogue (*between* the *credenti* and the *laici*, and *within* the realm of faith), whilst duly acknowledging those areas and occasions when the two in effect merge into one.

Dialogue cannot take place between individuals or groups who are located in separate, hermetically sealed universes of discourse, between which an unbridgeable chasm or division exists. Now, the very fact that Habermas calls for secular society to acquire a new understanding of religious convictions suggests that, for him at least (and certainly for me), the terms 'secular' and 'sacred' do not depict such separate realms; what I hope to make clear in this book is that they are, in theory and in truth, (that is, 'really' but not always 'actually' or 'empirically') integral aspects of a single dynamic totality. The 'sacred' is, I maintain, the origin and end of the 'secular', and the 'secular' is, I hold, only truly and fully itself when suffused with the 'sacred', that is, when the relative autonomy exercised by ruling authorities, organisations and social groups within the secular realm are exercised in such a way that the 'sacred' (God, the Holy Spirit-in-us) is perfectly at home there, and when the Father, descending upon this realm through the authority of the Son, encounters in love the Spirit ascending in us. The 'sacred' enfolds, and ethically and spiritually constitutes, the 'secular', overcoming the sinful resistance it encounters in our secular realm and patiently (though at times with anger, expressed through prophets of every kind) bringing about life to the full.

When speaking of the sacred-secular distinction, there is, I believe, no harm in using representative symbols, in, for example, using 'priest' and 'king' to designate or symbolically represent the 'secular' and 'sacred' respectively, provided that we recognise that 'priest' and 'king' are both, in their different ways, temporal media of the 'sacred' in the secular realm and that ultimately the distinction between 'priest' and 'king' is a distinction between distinct types of service to the 'sacred', rather than a distinction between the 'sacred' (exclusively identified with 'priest') and something else again. Using (and suitably adjusting) the terminology of Bernard of Clairvaux, we may say that the sacred (God) 'reigns', whereas the secular authorities 'rule'. In this book I hold that the 'sacred' reigns through its presence in what I call 'the invisible community of holy citizens', by which I mean, not the visible church, but the body of citizens, including believers and non-believers, in whom the public spirit (properly recognised as the immanent, indwelling Holy Spirit) dwells. Citizens are 'holy' to the degree (i) that they come under the influence of the Spirit, 'anonymously' or otherwise, and (ii) that they live up to the designation 'people of God' in Revelation 21:3 ('Behold, the dwelling of God is with men. He will dwell with them, and they shall be his peoples, and God himself will be with them'). We need to bear in mind here Harlan Beckley's point that neither the church, nor any other collective agent, is 'a force for redemption in which divine justice is fully immanent'.[5] However, the church, reading the signs of the times and open to the socio-political promptings of the Spirit, has a special responsibility to try to be a visible and audible expression of this holy community and to join with all citizens of good will in helping to articulate its will.

All of this may be alternatively expressed by saying that the state is the 'sacred in the midst of the secular' or that it is the 'own self' of society as a collective person (the Holy Spirit co-present with us in our community). By referring to the state as 'the own self of society' (normally referred to in political theory as 'the moral person of the state'), I mean that the state is the real or true collective purpose of its citizens/subjects (spasmodically entertained in their minds but always an ever present operative ideal) to secure justice and the true good of all. Augustine tells us that the state is simply 'the generality of men united by the bond of common agreement',[6] but he makes it clear that it is an elevating and edifying Spirit-inspired agreement; it is in the spirit of the command to love God and our neighbour that Augustine finds 'the praiseworthy security of the state, for the best city is erected and safeguarded on no other foundation than the bond of faith and unbreakable concord. This happens when the common good is loved, when God is the highest and truest good, and when men

---

5. Harlan Beckley, Passion for Justice: Retrieving the Legacies of Walter Rauschenbusch, John A Ryan and Reinhold Neibuhr, (Louisville: Westminster/John Knox Press, 1992), 381.
6. *St Augustine Letters 131–164* in *The Fathers of the Church,* Volume 3 (New York: New City Press, 1953), 137:17.

love each other most sincerely because they love themselves for the sake of Him from whom they cannot hide the true sentiment of their hearts'. The sovereignty of justice and the common good should preside over our life as a political community; this is, in the words of Bernard of Clairvaux, 'no ordinary sovereignty', for it is the true sovereignty that presides over and calls to account the ruling authorities or, again more simply, it is the state. The 'sacred' *vis-à-vis* the 'secular' *is* the presiding authority of the will to justice and the common good (simultaneously a divine and an ideal collective social will) and it exercises a constant 'spiritual gravitational pull', so to speak, upon each political community. This spiritual/sacred authority is ultimate but indeterminate, the felt intimations of the 'sacred' in the midst of the 'secular', whereas the political and legal authority of actual, empirical sovereigns or rulers is penultimate but determinate, the sacred 'secularised' or the universal 'concretised'. The former type of authority is really 'authority-in-itself' or the ultimate Author, God the Father and it unleashes the sacred/spiritual 'power of Truth', whereas the latter simply exercises the 'power of force'. In his *Defender of the Peace*, Marsilius of Padua speaks in these terms, regarding the authority of the sacred (in his times and in his terms, the 'authority of the priesthood') as the 'authority of truth' which convicts and persuades, in contrast to secular political authority which is based on command and sanction, but a similar distinction between these two types of authority is found in John of Paris, in Martin Luther (the famous two kingdoms doctrine) and in the Salamanca school. In this book, the spiritual/secular authority of the 'priesthood of all citizens' (both the *credenti* and the *laici*) replaces, or serves as the functional equivalent in our times of, Marsilius's 'authority of the priesthood' or sacred authority. What this means, expressed in more personal terms, is that each of us has a responsibility (or even a kind of 'authority' as a citizen) to 'preside' over, whether or not we 'rule', our society, that is, to arrive at our own conception (i) of its origin and end, (ii) of what its true wellbeing consists in, and (iii) of the extent to which the actual, empirical political rule in our society matches up to its 'presiding spirit' or, in my terms, to the state. This applies to believers and non-believers alike.

It is not a consequence of this analysis and interpretation of the sacred-secular distinction that the visible church or Christian believers have no distinct role to play in civic and political life and that they must now fade imperceptibly into the 'invisible body of holy citizens', those conscientiously exercising the 'priesthood of all citizens'. Rather the church must attempt to be its voice and visible presence, and it has a special responsibility to do so for it symbolises the presence of the sacred in the midst of the secular and is uniquely placed (i) to issue to its political community a call to social repentance and (ii) to be a visible 'social light' that draws the surrounding society into its sacred truth. It is important for the church and its mission, not just to have a definite institutional presence in society but also a strong, clearly visible social presence that stands at a safe distance from its institutional presence and that casts a challenging 'light to its nation'. This is, I think, what Oliver O'Donovan has in mind when he says that the church 'never was, in its true character, merely the temple of the city; it was the promise of the city itself'.[7] Hence, whilst I would take issue with Stanley Hauerwas's rejection of 'the very idea that Christian social ethics is primarily an attempt to make the world more peaceable or just'[8] and his view that Christians, as such, should not bring their faith to bear when reflecting, as citizens, on social and political issues, yet at the same time I fully agree with his insistence that the Christian churches have been too ready and too quick to embrace the 'problems of Constantine' as their own. I hold that Hauerwas is right to insist that for Christians there is simply nothing more important, and more true to the essence of their faith, than forming a community of believers (generally a church) in which Christ's love, mercy and forgiveness is clear for all to see and which, by its witness and example, attracts those being saved to 'come and see'. He is surely incontestable in his claim that the first task of the church is not so much to act effectively or successfully in the world but to *be* the 'community of Christ' in the world, the practical 'corporate' manifestation of the love and truth of his kingdom. Hauerwas grasps a genuine aspect of our life as Christians in the world when he says that the church is not a sect but a counter-cultural colony living within and among a largely secular culture, and he correctly insists that the main task of the church is to *be* a transformed (or an 'ever *being* transformed') 'micro'

---

7. *The Desire of the Nations; Rediscovering the Roots of Political Theology* (Cambridge: Cambridge University Press, 2003), 285.
8. *The Peaceable Kingdom; A Primer in Christian Ethics* (Notre dame Indiana: University of Notre Dame Press, 1983), 99.

community of love and peace (a counter-cultural colony) within a largely secular society, rather than to *do* 'important' political things. In many ways, it is the 'social presence' of the church that is the true bearer (assuredly, it is the most effective bearer) of its spiritual/sacred authority. What I have in mind here is all of those socially visible Christian churches and communities (the Franciscans, the Salvos) who in any significant way resemble the community practices of the early post-resurrection Christians, those who sold their possessions, held all things in common, gathered daily as a group in the temple, 'enjoyed the good will and favour of all the people and thereby daily attracted others to their company' (Acts 2:43–47). In the case of these early Christians, we see that their 'social presence' was the light by which, and medium through which, the surrounding society was drawn into the heart of the sacred. Such communities are an anticipation of 'the holy city, the new Jerusalem, coming down out of heaven from God' (Revelation 21: 2), a city in which there is no temple 'because its temple is the Lord God Almighty and the Lamb' (Revelation 21: 22); they are a living testimony to society at large that the ideal is possible with God's grace. Thus, whilst the church must eschew the attempt to directly transform society by political means into a utopian 'macro' community of love and peace, it must nevertheless seek to indirectly (or non-politically but fundamentally) draw its society towards its divinely ordained perfection and it must have the courage and audacity to present itself as its (society's) own true soul.

Richard Niebuhr in his *Christ and Culture* notes that '[t]he effort to bring Christ and culture, God's work and man's, the temporal and the eternal, law and grace, into one system of thought and practice tends, perhaps inevitably to the absolutising of what is relative, the reduction of the infinite to a finite form, and the materialisation of the dynamic'.[9] In chapter two of this book I will be arguing that Niebuhr in this quote makes a very sound point, for it is indeed erroneous to 'absolutise the relative' in the sense of ascribing to what is merely relative qualities possessed only by the Absolute, but equally, I will argue, we need to acknowledge that the 'relative' only is what it truly is (or only can be what it truly is) in its proper relation to the 'Absolute'. Certainly, we need to be alert to the danger that (i) we might construe the 'Absolute' as, so to speak, 'absorbing' the 'relative' into itself in a false and distorting way that deprives it (the 'relative', the spatio-temporal realm) of its true character or that (ii) we might construe the 'relative' as attempting to contain the Absolute within itself, to *be* absolute itself, rather than to be the *medium* of the Absolute. The same problem or danger, namely that of absolutising what is only relative, is also raised by Lesslie Newbiggin in his book *Foolishness to the Greeks: The Gospel and Western Culture*. In that work he asserts that, as cultural beings, we are in culture as a fish is in water, and that the gospel itself is from beginning to end 'embodied in culturally conditioned forms'. At the same time he holds that the gospel 'calls into question all cultures, including the one in which it was origi-

---

9. *Christ and Culture* (New York: Harper Collins, 2001), 145.

nally embodied'.[10] If, however, the gospel is itself cultural 'through and through', then how, one may well wonder, can the gospel call each particular human culture to account or find a vantage point beyond culture from which to cast its critical light on particular human cultures? Broadly, my response to this question is to say (in chapter two) that whilst we should indeed acknowledge, as Newbiggin suggests, that human societies are cultural 'all the way down', we need to *also* acknowledge that human societies embody or 'concretise' universal values and that they are thus universal 'all the way down' too. It is the ever present *universality* of each human culture or the vertical relation each human culture has to the Divine (the 'Absolute') that enables the gospel to speak universally and critically to all human cultures. This 'real presence of the universal' doctrine holds that that what we might broadly and liberally call the *Ressourcement*/culture school (de Lubac, Troeltsch, von Bathasar, Ratzinger, Stassen, Newbiggin) is right to assert that the truths of faith cannot be transmitted in a cultural vacuum and that no cultural expression of the faith is 'absolute', since each exists for its time only. However, the 'real presence' doctrine also holds that what we might call the 'Rahnerian' universal/instrumentalist school is right to assert that the same constant truths of faith can and should be propositionally expressed in different cultural settings and that the 'absolute faith' (its unchanging universal truth) is universally

---

10. *Foolishness to the Greeks; The Gospel and Western* Culture (Grand Rapids: Eerdmans, 1986), 4.

present and may be propositionally expressed in different cultural embodiments.

In the first main part of this book (God and Society) I broadly take issue with what I regard as the curious and over-inflated 'fondness for the particular' (for difference, diversity, specificity, the concrete, the local) in western culture at the present time and its corresponding 'hostility towards the universal' (oneness, sameness, form), and I argue for a re-evaluation and rehabilitation of the 'universal'. In chapter two, for example, I argue that the 'finger' of unity (of the 'universal') points to 'particularity' (and to 'specificity' or the 'concrete') as 'its other', its necessary correlative, complement, and completion, and I show how Richard Niebuhr and Michael Walzer succeed in seamlessly incorporating into their work the truths emphasised both by the ('particularist', 'historicist', 'postmodern') *Ressourcement*/culture school and the ('universalist', 'supra-historical', 'modern') Rahnerian/instrumentalist school. In chapter three I show how a proper understanding of the 'universal/particular' relation in ethics and politics helps us to better deal with and elucidate the key issue in Christian social ethics, namely, the extent and type (or nature) of the church's responsibility for the proper ordering of society. I hold that we can gain very valuable assistance in dealing with this question by taking into account the full socio-political significance of the crucial ethical distinction between the 'right/just' and the 'good'. I hold that in the ethical consciousness the 'right/just' ('right' used in the sense of 'just') primarily consists in our *recognition* of the value of persons, whereas the 'good' consists mainly in our endeavours to *realise* values. Thus, when acting justly or when considering the requirements of justice, our primary concern is to act in conformity with our *recognition* or acknowledgement of the absolute value of persons as spiritual beings and the church has every right to speak its mind, whereas when it is a (mainly political) matter of *realising* value, in the form of the 'common good', the church, I suggest, needs to be considerably more circumspect, for we are dealing here with a delicate political version of von Balthasar's 'perichoresis of the transcendentals' (not just truth, beauty and goodness, but also the values of liberty, independence and equality) and whilst church members would assuredly agree on value-based political objectives when pitched at a sufficiently high level of generality (helping the poor, liberating the oppressed, etc), they are liable to diverge in liberal, conservative and socialist directions as soon as practical policy measures are proposed to achieve such objectives and to realise the common good in a concrete sense.

In this chapter (chapter three) I adopt the kind of Rahnerian position that has been strongly criticised by John Milbank and I defend Rahner against Milbank's criticism that he regards the 'social' as an 'autonomous sphere which does not need to turn to theology for its self understanding'[11] and that, as employed by 'Rahnerian integralists', theological beliefs 'tend to become but a faint regulative gloss upon Kantian ethics and a somewhat eclectic,

---

11. *Theology and Social Theory: Beyond Secular Reason* (Oxford: Blackwell, 1995), 208.

though basically Marxist, social theory'.[12] Milbank holds that the French version of integralism (Blondel, de Lubac) properly 'recognises the always finitely mediated character of participation in the supernatural',[13] whereas the German Rahnerian version fails to do so, but this is because he holds, erroneously as I shall argue, that there is an incompatibility between what he terms Blondel's 'supernatural pragmatism' and Rahner's 'foundational *praxis*'.[14] In this chapter (chapter three) I also argue that the conviction that Christians have a sacred duty to promote the wellbeing of society is broadly reflected in the writings of major Christian thinkers and theologians, not only in the case of mainstream Catholic social thought and the Reformed doctrine of 'the Lordship of Christ over all' but also, though to a lesser degree and with a strong realistic acknowledgement of the limitations imposed by our rebellious and sinful humanity, in the case of Luther's doctrine of the two kingdoms.

In the second main part of the book (God and Truth) I focus on truth, justice, goodness, common decency, unselfishness, integrity, etc, as values and virtues that belong to the whole of (our common) humanity. In the present postmodern climate, and especially in the light of Michel Foucault's devastating critique of 'Masters of Truth' and totalistic (Truth-revealing) metanarratives, it has become increasingly difficult to seriously believe that anything is 'good and true' or any goals or social visions

---

12. *Ibid.*
13. *Ibid*, 209.
14. *Ibid.*

worth striving for. Foucault took a strong stand against 'Truth' and warned us to be ever alert to what he called the 'main danger', by which he meant the latest 'regime of truth' expressing our personal or collective 'will to power' and parading itself socially, politically or culturally as a 'regime of Truth'. Now when Foucault speaks in this way, what he has to say is not without precedent in the Christian tradition, especially when Christian writers are contemplating the contrast between (the holiness of) God and (the corruption of) humanity or when they are reflecting upon what we might call the social and political equivalent of the view that 'free will avails for nothing but sinning'. Now, this Christian 'point of contact' with Foucault is real in one sense but illusory in another; it is real in the sense that all of us who believe in a 'God who saves' experience moments when we are acutely aware of the contrast between the holiness of God and our own sinfulness. However, it is illusory in the sense that for the 'soul being saved', it is the revelation of the majestic reality of God's Truth (His infinite love, mercy and beauty) that reveals the full depths and ugliness of our conceit and sinfulness (the truth of our 'egoity' and the 'worldly truths' it engenders and defends) as a 'contrast-effect'. In the case of Foucault, this contrast between our human truths and God's absolute Truth is entirely absent; his human (worldly) truths stand alone, without any 'constitutive' divine counterpoint or divine criterion.

In the present intellectual climate, those who entertain a social vision of any kind (socialist, feminist etc) are liable to be accused of entertaining Truth-inspired totalistic 'designs' upon their fellow human beings. Against this backdrop, I suggest in chapter four that the baby (Truth) has been recklessly thrown out with the bathwater (totalistic ideologies) and that we need to strenuously attempt to re-legitimise the quest for Truth. In this chapter I suggest that we need to keep the quest for Truth at the heart of our personal and 'civic' lives in the manner suggested by classical political theory. I also suggest that, as Christians, we should entertain an attitude of 'ecumenical graciousness' towards all Truth-metanarratives, and that we should be 'servants' rather than 'masters' of Truth as we pursue (both personally and collectively) our quest for 'the right, the good and the true'. In chapter five, I argue that the 'own self' to which I personally wish to be true is spiritually connected to the 'collective own self' to which we, as a society, wish to be true, and that the state (the public spirit or the 'collective own self of society') requires of us as citizens that we seriously endeavour to pursue public policy measures that are 'good and true' or as good and true as the limits of our human powers will allow. We are required, indeed, to form a truly (that is 'Truth-oriented') deliberative democracy whose procedures allow the 'collective own self of society' the maximum freedom of expression and realisation. To be a temple of the Holy Spirit is a privilege of society as a 'collective person' or 'body politic' and not just a privilege of individuals and of the gathered community of believers, so that it is to the Holy Spirit that we are ultimately referring when we refer to the 'public spirit' or to the 'collective own self' of society. Ultimately, it is the Holy Spirit that we serve in political life, though we are really, in a sense, only serving ourselves (our true interests). In this chapter I suggest that, as citizens, we must be seekers and servants of the Truth of our society, and then show that the relationship of public policy and the state (government) to Truth is inadequately portrayed by Walzer and Foucault but positively illuminated by Bernard Bosanquet. I hold that if Foucault, taken as representative of contemporary postmodernism, is the 'theoretical problem', then the 'theoretical solution' lies in the work of a theorist such as Bosanquet, taken as representative of traditional social philosophy and political theory and as a strong exponent of what I call 'the ethical theory of the state'. I explore the Truth-oriented communitarianism of Bernard Bosanquet and show how it provides a theoretical complement to (or perhaps an unwelcome metaphysical fulfilment of) Michael Walzer's communitarianism. In section (iii) of this chapter, I view the state as a form of what I call 'ethico-political consciousness', as a kind of 'collective subject' that pursues Truth in social and public life (the 'social promptings' of the Spirit) and that contributes thereby to what Barth refers to as 'the fulfilment of the State's own righteous purposes'.[15]

In this chapter (chapter five) I also argue that one of the most important 'righteous purposes' of the state is to preserve and support the (traditional) nuclear family as the basic unit of a single, unified society. We need to bear in mind that a liberal pluralist democratic society is still *one* society, a unity of differences which need to be constantly integrated and harmonised by a unifying will, and that it needs agreed-upon norms and a public philosophy or a

---

15. *Community, State and Church: Three Essays* (Gloucester Mass: Peter Smith, 1968), 171.

public orientation to the common good that is 'consensus seeking' and 'consensus generating'. This is what I try to provide in my discussion of the traditional nuclear family as the basic unit of society and also in my discussion of the homosexual couple as a family, and what Richard John Neuhaus has in mind when he speaks of the need for Christians to develop a mediating language through which religious language dealing with ultimate things can be used to elucidate social and political issues. Just as all citizens in a liberal pluralist community must continue the ongoing quest for unity-in-diversity (for a unifying will that blends together ever changing and proliferating differences), so too they must continue the ongoing quest for a 'public philosophy' or for a philosophy that is as 'public' and common as possible. Christians, I will suggest, should be fully themselves in contributing to this quest. They should make a strong religiously grounded contribution to public philosophy and, in so doing, try to touch the 'spiritual heart' and deepest convictions of all citizens. In this chapter, my broad concern is the same as Habermas's, namely to 'ask which cognitive attitudes and normative expectations the liberal state must require its citizens—both believers and unbelievers—to put into practice in their dealings with each other'.[16]

In his *The Desire of the Nations; Rediscovering the Roots of Political Theology*, Oliver O'Donovan has recently suggested that 'classic liberalism' is more sympathetic and

---

16. *Dialectics of Secularization: On Reason and Religion* (San Francisco: Ignatius Press, San Francisco, 2006), 23.

open than '[r]ecent reworkings of the tradition'[17] to the idea of a Christian society, or at least to an acknowledgement that it is important for the members of a society to engage in a common quest for truth. Likewise, in a number of comments made following the presentation of a paper by Kenneth Grasso at the Ethics and Public Policy Centre in May 1995, a succession of speakers emphasised what they saw as the importance of 'saving liberty from liberalism'. Grasso himself uses this expression. Sometimes, he says, 'liberalism' is used to mean a broad, practical political orientation in favour of the rule of law, limited government, constitutionalism, etc. and in this broad sense it predates modernity, whereas liberalism as a distinct political philosophy with a particular understanding of the individual and society and its own metaphysic, is a modern phenomenon, which, for the sake of clarity, he calls 'modernist liberalism'.[18] 'The task today', he says, 'is to save liberty—and liberalism in the first sense of the term—from modernist liberalism'[19]. Though not using this particular expression, it is clear that many of the speakers who commented on Grasso's work were likewise concerned to 'save liberty from liberalism'. Luis Lugo, for example states:

---

17. *The Desire of the Nations; Rediscovering the Roots of Political Theology* (Cambridge: Cambridge University Press, 2003), 221.
18. 'Man, Society and the State: A Catholic Perspective'/ Comments in *Caesar's Coin Revisited: Christians and the Limits of Government*, edited by M Cromartie (Grand Rapids: Eerdmans, 1996), 137.
19. *Ibid*, 139.

> We no longer have the liberalism of John Locke, who borrowed deeply from Christian sources, including Catholic sources, through the French Calvinists. The problem is that liberalism has sort of exhausted the very sources that sustained it and has come to the view that it no longer needs them. But once it jettisons them, it realises that it has no way to justify itself. That's what I see the Christian tradition doing: coming in to seek to rescue the best parts of liberalism from itself.[20]

In a similar vein, Paul Marshall states:

> I think that we allow liberals to claim credit for too much. One of the things that annoy me intensely about Rawls and Rorty—and there are many things-is their use of 'us' and 'we'. They are claiming all the goodies of Western history and of a constitutional or a limited state and saying, 'This is us, the Enlightenment and liberals, this is just *our* position'. They have no right to say that. The notion of 'liberal' as an expression is early nineteenth century. The notion of a constitutional order, of limited government, or a rule of law, vastly predates that. Liberalism is the product of

---

20. 'Man, Society and the State: A Catholic Perspective'/ Comments, in *Caesar's Coin Revisited: Christians and the Limits of Government*, edited by M Cromartie (Grand Rapids: Eerdmans, 1996), 129.

that, not the originator . . . It is trying to take something out of an older, Christian tradition of thinking about the state and make it independent. We should try to take this stuff back from the liberals by asking them to justify, in terms of liberal thought, where they think it originated.[21]

Finally, Glenn Tinder states:

> I think it may be a big mistake to make an enemy out of liberalism, in part because liberalism may be capable of being renovated. There are various kinds of liberalism. I wrote my master's thesis on Bernard Bosanquet and my doctoral thesis on Thomas Hill Green, two people who are rarely mentioned any longer. Both give a very different tone to liberalism than is found in John Stuart Mill. When we talk about liberalism as the enemy, we tend to foreclose the possibility of a renovation of liberalism, and we also tend to blind ourselves to who our real enemy is. If I had to say who I think the enemy is, I would use words like 'relativists,' or maybe 'nihilists,' or 'postmodernists,' or 'pragmatists': Richard Rorty represents something that is extremely dan-

---

21. 'Man, Society and the State: A Catholic Perspective'/ Comments, in *Caesar's Coin Revisited: Christians and the Limits of Government*, edited by M Cromartie (Grand Rapids: Eerdmans, 1996), 131–132.

gerous. My sense is that liberalism has been devastated by this real enemy, whatever we call it, whether postmodernism or anti-foundationalism or something else. Our primary enemy may be metaphysical, and our primary response may have to be metaphysical.[22]

I am generally sympathetic to the views expressed by these writers[23] and in chapter six of this book I set myself the task of trying to save liberalism in one sense (the earlier form of 'universal liberalism') from liberalism in another sense (the more recent development of 'particularist liberalism'). I argue that the attempt to justify the core institutions and cultural practices of 'our way of life'

---

22. 'Man, Society and the State: A Catholic Perspective'/ Comments, in *Caesar's Coin Revisited: Christians and the Limits of Government*, edited by M Cromartie (Grand Rapids: Eerdmans, 1996), 132–133.
23. In my *Justice and the State: On Liberal Organicism and the Foundations of Emancipatory Politics* (Quebec: World Heritage Press, 1998), I present what I call a 'liberal organicist' defence of emancipatory politics; it is liberal in that it emphasises the freedom and dignity of each individual, assigning indeed to each person an absolute significance, but it is also organicist in that it holds that we are social beings, that our identity is formed (we are 'who and what we are') in and through our relations with others and through sharing in the life of wider totalities or forms (the family, kinship groups, the community). Liberal organicism needs to be clearly distinguished from any form of holism or organicism which regards the individual as merely an aspect of (alone 'real') social totalities and has nothing in common with any form of liberalism which holds that individuals are the 'basic stuff' of society and that 'society' is indeed no more than a term for designating the variety of external relations pertaining between a number of (alone 'real') individuals.

in terms of the values of our common humanity is not a 'western prejudice' but a universal, sound and wholesome 'human prejudice'; it is one, moreover, that needs to be cultivated and properly (that is, critically) deployed, especially where 'inter-civilisational' matters are concerned. This involves the nurturing of what I call 'universal politics' or 'universal criticism', that is, a willingness on the part of a political community to subject its way of life and cultural practices to the critical judgment of the court of our common humanity (our 'universal' humanity). It is in the spirit of universal criticism, thus understood, that I defend 'western' (universal) liberalism against a variety of charges that have been directed against it, and argue that the kind of 'universal' liberal doctrine developed in the west and seen as indispensable to (Judaeo-Christian) western civilisation warrants serious consideration, not only by those already sympathetic to the liberal tradition but by everyone, including members of non-western Muslim societies often deemed to be 'non-liberal'. I will also argue that we need to do our utmost to ensure that our use of the expression 'our tradition' or 'our way of life' should not be used as an instrument of closure or separation from our universal humanity (from 'God-in-us-all') and that the great disadvantage of the kind of 'particularistic' defences of liberalism presented by John Rawls, Joseph Raz and John Gray is that they do just that, regarding 'our way of life' as somehow self-justifying, as beyond the reach of universal criticism. I also argue that Samuel Huntington's *The Clash of Civilisations; Remaking of World Order* is susceptible to a similar kind of critique.[24]

In part three of the book (Christ and State) we focus on the nature and role of the state. In chapter seven I argue that the kind of ethical-metaphysical theory of the state that we broadly associate with idealist political philosophy provides us with a theoretical account of the state that is both sound and insightful and that it is quite capable of withstanding the hostile criticisms to which it has been subjected in the twentieth century. According to this theory or approach, the state, as well as being a broad network of political and judicial institutions, is also, and more fundamentally and essentially, an ethical community or a 'living ethical reality' in whose name governments act and in whose name governments that fail to live up to their divinely ordained task of realising the public good (common interest) may be justly condemned. Another name for this 'living ethical reality', I contend, is the Holy Spirit or the 'angelic presence' of the Spirit in the socio-political realm. Having looked in this chapter at the state as the 'own self' of society as a 'collective person', I then look in chapter eight at Barth's version of the ethical theory of the state and his understanding of the state as an 'angelic power' or presence. I argue that Barth rightly insists that the rebellious powers and principalities have been created in and for God, that they do not belong to themselves, and that from the first 'they stand at the dis-

---

24. *The Clash of Civilisations and the Remaking of World Order* (New York: Touchstone, 1997).

posal of Jesus Christ'.[25] To the extent that these powers fall under the influence of 'the hosts of spiritual darkness' and attempt to exist in their own right and apart from God, they will be destroyed in their 'separateness', their bastardised form of existence, and re-integrated into God's creation (or restored to their true point and purpose in Christ). I then suggest that when reflecting upon this 'fading away' of the principalities and powers (in the sense of the spiritual forces of darkness), it is helpful to think in terms of the 'twin flows of salvation' from God to humanity (creation) and from humanity (creation) to God.

In chapter nine, I draw attention to the fact that Barth developed his ethical or righteous theory of the state as a critical response to the emerging totalitarian regime in Germany, for too often the ethical theory of the state associated with Green and Bosanquet is seen as a sinister harbinger of totalitarian tendencies, whereas the truth is the very opposite. As in the case of Barth's ethical/righteous theory of the state, the ethical theory of the state does not lead to, but stands firmly against and roundly condemns, totalitarian political ideologies. However, it has to be acknowledged that Bosanquet does make himself vulnerable to the charges of statism and anti-juristic moralism by his outright and, in my view, ill-considered rejection of the tradition of civil association, for it lends powerful practical and theoretical support to the juristic concern for justice and for solidly grounded individual rights. I argue

---

25. *Community, State and Church: Three Essays* (Gloucester Mass: Peter Smith, 1968), 117.

that, in order to avoid the charges of statism and totalitarianism, exponents of the ethical theory must do what Bosanquet failed to do and embrace the tradition of civil association as its true counterpart and completion.

Through the Scriptures, we are introduced to the idea that God (the Father) is somehow 'really' present (or is re-presented or has a 'face' or appearance/epiphany) in the world through his Son, Jesus Christ and we also have some idea what it might be like for God, through Christ and the Holy Spirit, to be present in the church (as Christ's body) or in the individual believer (as a temple of the Holy Spirit). However, we have very little idea—and an insignificant armoury of concepts to help us reflect upon and ascertain—what it might be like for God to be 'indirectly present' (again, being re-presented or having a 'face') in the political world of our experience through the state. The political theory of Thomas Hobbes can help us here, for he speaks in a very illuminating way of a 'person' of the state who is present in and through the collective will of those seeking peace and justice in good conscience, and when he does so, it certainly sounds as if he has in mind something like God's 'indirect presence' in the civil realm or the political counterpart (or analogue) of the presence of the Holy Spirit in the gathered community of believers. Exponents of the ethical theory of the state hold that a common moral purpose or unifying will informs our lives as citizens but this 'ethical unity of the state', as we may call it, received perhaps its strongest, most intellectually daring and most articulate expression in the work of Thomas Hobbes. He figures prominently in this final part of the book (The Holy Spirit, Law and the State) because in articulating this notion of a 'person' of the state, he assigns a redemptive role to law and to the universally operative 'spirit' of both natural and civil law. Perhaps more than any other political philosopher, he exhibits a very fine and subtle understanding of the ennobling and constructive role of law and in this respect, as I point out in chapter ten, Hobbes is at one with Reinhold Niebuhr's insistence that the civil laws of society, as 'the servants and instruments of the spirit of brotherhood', exercise a redeeming or uplifting influence on the citizen body. Hobbes is also illuminating and 'ecumenically valuable' because he is associated both with the (Catholic) natural law tradition and yet also with the (Protestant) Occamite, nominalist tendencies of the Reformation tradition and his work may thus serve, even today, as a bridge between the two.

Barth, of course, is well known for the antagonism he expressed towards the Catholic natural law tradition associated with Thomas Aquinas and towards the view that all persons, having been created in the image of God and with God's law written on their hearts, have at least a natural foundation or divine compass that points to God, or a kind of 'pathway to God' in their souls. However, I suggest in chapter eleven that whilst Barth, in his earlier work, is clearly out of sympathy with these Catholic 'natural law' views both rhetorically and substantively, yet we find that in his later work he appears to be out of sympathy rhetorically *rather than* substantively. I hold that the natural law tradition is not only consistent with Barth's later theology but may indeed be used to broadly support his 'theological politics' and more specifically, his theological account of the state. In this chapter I also (i) look at the strained relationship between the 'Catholic' natural law tradition and 'Protestant' Reformation theology in general, (ii) indicate whilst doing so that precisely the same strain has arisen more recently within Catholic theology itself and then (iii) suggest that, in a similar vein, there is actually a basic compatibility between apparently contending positions held (over the centuries) between Catholic and Protestant thinkers and held (more recently) within Catholic theological circles. I hold that whilst law as 'essence' or 'nature' may certainly be characterised descriptively or ontologically (in the 'Catholic' manner) as 'form' as opposed to matter, yet it is also the 'personal' voice of God addressed (in the 'Protestant' manner) to existential (sinful and rebellious) human matter *through* essence/form. Law in its truest sense simply *is* 'prescriptive form or essence'; it is the prescriptive claim exercised by the eternal and unfallen upon the temporal and fallen. The 'prescriptive essence', considered as prescriptive, is the voice of God as the mystical font of law entering our lives with authority; considered as essence, it is the uplifting Spirit constantly flowing through us and bringing our humanity to its proper fulfilment. Hobbes treats it as such, whereas Derrida regards it, not as ultimately emanating from its source in God at all, but from an originary or 'foundational' act of violence, as I show in the next chapter (chapter twelve).

True or legitimate political authority can have no truck with political violence, with the kind of murderous acts of foundational violence that established 'European America' and its laws ('European Australia' and its laws, etc) and yet, in a sense, the violence of sin and the sin of violence are deeply embedded in our fallen nature. We see all around us (and in us) the grotesque inevitability of violence (or so it seems at times) in a fallen world, and we are aware of God's absolute abhorrence of it, but we also know that God's hatred of sin is matched by his love for the sinner and his hatred of the violence in each of us (our sin) by his love for the (violent) sinner. In the light of this, what is the status of governments instituted and laws enacted by violent conquerors? In this chapter I wish to suggest that when Jacques Derrida contends that the ultimate font or origin (what he calls the 'mystical foundation of authority') of law is an originary or 'foundational' act of violence, this is tantamount to saying that God's blessing of a 'violent' people (what people is wholly innocent of violence?) implies God's blessing of their violence. I argue that Derrida is mistaken in holding that the ultimate font of (legitimate) political authority is a 'foundational' act of violence and that Hobbes is correct in holding that the state, as the collectivised will to peace and as 'authorised force', is the very antithesis of the rampant violence of the state of nature and of the kind of originary or 'foundational' violence of which Derrida speaks. Hobbes was a 'foundationalist' in the entirely proper sense that he believed that it was possible to trace the authority of law to its source in the 'person' of the state and to God as the author of nature, but I suggest in this chapter that Derrida and, more recently, Jens Bartelson fall prey to a curious, one-sided narrow view of 'foundationalism'. However, I also argue that Derrida is extremely helpful in drawing our attention to the violent foundations of political regimes and that we should employ his insights to draw a distinction between the empirical, historical *de facto* origins (causes) of political regimes and the (universal) ethical grounds or reasons for regarding them as legitimate (*de jure*) or illegitimate, just or unjust.

I also suggest in this final chapter that, despite his rejection of metaphysics, Derrida is implicitly metaphysical in his treatment of justice. He holds that what he calls 'impossible' and 'mad' justice is a kind of epiphany in the mind of the critical ethical observer (a kind of 'phenomenal' appearance in the critical, focused mind of real, incalculable 'noumenal' justice) and he speaks in almost 'Hegelian-Christian' terms of deconstruction as the permanent, circulating movement of the spirit of justice in human history, 'objectively' going about its business well before it happened to be called 'deconstruction'. Thus I suggest that the key reason for his apparent blindness to the presence of universal justice is that he calls it by another name (deconstruction). He asks us to banish from our minds the ghost of 'calculable, rule-associated justice' that induces in us a sense of illusory certainty and to allow *instead* the presence of 'incalculable universal justice', the mystical spirit of justice itself, to exercise a kind of sovereign freedom in our minds. This certainly resembles the way in which we Christians invite the Holy Spirit to be the sovereign lord of all aspects of our lives and thoughts. It comes, then, as no surprise to find that in using the language of deconstruction, Derrida is simply doing what the leading proponents of the Christian faith and western metaphysics, using the language of universalism (of reason, truth, justice and freedom), have always done. So understood, even against his wishes (though his wishes in this regard are by no means clear), Derrida's deconstructive (and divisive) wall of 'universal suspicion and separation' becomes instead both a bridge to, and an instrument of, the kind of common philosophical dialogue which Habermas and Ratzinger believe to be possible and which, I believe, their shared 'Munich moment' has indeed shown to be possible against all the odds.

Part One

Christ and Society

Chapter One

God and Society; Universal and Particular

And I heard every creature in heaven and on earth and under the earth . . . saying 'To him who sits upon the throne and to the Lamb be blessing and honor and glory and might for ever and ever!'
Revelation 5:13

'Respect for contextual, academico-institutional, discursive specifities, mistrust for analogies and hasty transpositions, for confused homogenisations, seem to me to be the first imperatives the way things stand today'[1] (Derrida 1990, p. 933). With these words, Jacques Derrida captures very well the spirit of our times, its 'fondness for the particular' (for difference, diversity, specificity, the concrete, the local) and its corresponding 'hostility towards the universal' (oneness, sameness, form, confused or oppressive homogenisations).[2] In this chapter I wish to take

---

1. 'Force of Law: The Mystical Foundation of Authority', in *Cardozo Law Review*, 11:5/6 (1990): 921–1045.
2. Interestingly, Derrida refers in this quote to 'the way things stand today' almost as a disinterested spectator or polite observer,

issue with what I regard as our curious and over-inflated 'fondness for the particular' at the present time and argue for a re-evaluation and rehabilitation of the 'universal'. What we might call this 'universal-particular' problematic is, I wish to suggest, at the heart of the question concerning whether or not it is possible to have a 'culture-free' or 'culture-neutral' expression of the same faith by articulating a series of propositions whose universal meanings transcend culture. This was the question raised by Pope John XXIII when, at the opening of the second Vatican Council, he called for a distinction to be made between doctrine that does not change and the constantly

---

whereas in fact, of course, over his extended career, he himself has made a profound contribution to the current intellectual antipathy to the 'universal'. As evidence of the 'particularist' turn in modern thought that Derrida has helped to bring about, we could point to Joseph Raz's claim that personal autonomy 'is a cultural value, that is, of value to people living in certain societies only' (*The Morality of Freedom*, [Oxford: Clarendon Press, 1986], 198), to Joseph Carens's view that the critical standards we apply universally are 'a feature of *our* morality' (*Culture, Citizenship and Community: A Contextual Exploration of Justice as Evenhandedness* [Oxford: Oxford University Press, 2000], 47), emphasis in original), to Samuel Huntington's conviction that imperialism is 'the necessary logical consequence of universalism' (*The Clash of Civilisations and the Remaking of World Order* [New York: Touchstone, 1997], 310) and, perhaps most notably of all, to Rawls's shift from a 'universalist' defence of liberalism in the 1970s in his *A Theory of Justice* (Oxford: Oxford University Press, 1971) to his 'particularist' defence of liberalism in the 1990s in his *Political Liberalism* (New York: Columbia University Press, 1993).

changing manner of its presentation or, we may say, between one and the same faith and its cultural articulation under a specific set of socio-historical circumstances. My response to this question is 'yes' and 'no'. In this chapter I will argue that it is not possible to have a 'culture-free' or 'culture-neutral' expression of the same faith by articulating a series of 'culture-transcending' universal meanings, but that it is nevertheless possible, and routinely possible (indeed normal), for one and the *same* 'universal' faith (and a number of crucial universal propositional meanings at the heart of that faith) to be expressed and to be fully present, so to speak, in a wide variety of *different* cultural forms. Even though it is not possible to achieve a culture free expression of the universal truths and meanings of a faith, yet the same universal meanings may be (and, indeed, routinely are) present in widely different cultural settings. I call this the doctrine of 'the real presence', by which I mean the real presence of the universal meanings and truths of one and the same faith in a variety of historical and cultural settings, or, more simply, the real presence of the same (universal) faith in a variety of (particular) cultures. Although no cultural expression of the faith is 'absolute', since each exists for its time only and is a means of expression of the faith for that time, yet by virtue of the fact that the 'absolute faith' (its unchanging universal truth) is universally present in different cultural embodiments, there is an *absolute aspect* of each living, culturally embodied faith; what we might call the 'transcendent meaning-in-itself' of faith lives in each such cultural embodiment. This 'real presence' doctrine holds that what we might broadly and liberally call the

Ressourcement/culture school (de Lubac, Troeltsch, von Bathasar, Ratzinger, Stassen, Newbiggin) is right to assert that the truths of faith cannot be transmitted in a cultural vacuum; they emphasise the truth that no cultural expression of the faith is 'absolute', since each exists for its time only. However, the 'real presence' doctrine also holds that what we might call the 'Rahnerian' universal/instrumentalist school is right to assert that the same constant truths of faith can and should be propositionally expressed in different cultural settings; they emphasise the truth that the 'absolute faith' (its unchanging universal truth) is universally present and may be propositionally expressed in different cultural embodiments.

In this chapter I also hold that the same 'universal-particular' problematic is at the root of what Stanley Grenz refers to as the 'devastating problem' that surfaces when we attempt to articulate a Christian vision in a postmodern context where communitarianism holds considerable sway. He formulates the problem in this way:

> The loss of universality seems to be inherent in any understanding that views the ethical life as integrally embedded in the life of the social group. Such a focus serves to highlight the multiplicity of communities and hence the diversity of ethical visions present in our world. This multiplicity, in turn, seems to lead us headlong into a communitarian pluralism. The multiplicity of community-based ethical visions appears to call into question any attempt to claim that one is somehow more

correct than the others. Rather than promoting the search for the one, universal human ethic, the various interpretative frameworks or theological visions seem to offer equally valid foundations for ethics in the postmodern context.[3]

I wish to suggest that the root of the problem Grenz here alludes to is the misplaced hostility directed towards the 'universal' at the present time and the erroneous belief that the requirements of universality or oneness (the 'quest for unity') are somehow at odds with the need to respect the diversity and multiplicity of community-based ethical outlooks. The kind of current depreciation of the 'universal' I have in mind may be illustrated by considering the following quotation from Glen Stassen.

> Only what is universal is true. This devalues all that is historically specific, all that is rich and concrete in religious faith, all that is the peculiar love (and joy) of human community. It reduces truth to a very thin, lowest common denominator, if such can be found. It drains concreteness from the ethics of Christ and reduces his teachings to a historically detached universal principle or two.[4]

---

3. *The Moral Quest; Foundations of Christian Ethics* (Downers Grove, Illinois: InterVarsity Press, 1997), 234.
4. GH Stassen, DM Yeager, and JH Yoder, *Authentic Transformation: A*

Stassen is here criticising the work of Richard Niebuhr who, he claims, pays a heavy price for succumbing to the lure of Kantian universalism and Kant's universal 'rationality detached from historical differences'). Stassen believes that Niebuhr abandoned the 'concretely real' in favour of an abstract, Kantian 'universal' point of view, and that his work suffers from the defects just mentioned (devaluation of the historically specific, of the richness of diversity, etc) but does, we need to ask, an acknowledgement of the role and importance of the universal have such dire consequences? I believe not. In this chapter I wish to show that the 'finger' of unity (of the 'universal') points to 'particularity' (and to 'specificity' or the 'concrete') as 'its other', its necessary correlative, complement, and completion. This will involve showing that whilst writers such as Richard Niebuhr and Michael Walzer certainly believe that there could exist a type of universality that does not negate the richness of particularity and difference, they are not at all deceived or mistaken in so doing.

Universal and particular; Niebuhr and Walzer

In our current postmodern intellectual *milieu*, the element of 'particularity' dominates our understanding of 'particular cultures'; it's as though we have been trained to see only their particularity and to obviate our intellectual gaze from the reality of the universal, from the dimension of 'the all-inclusive', from the universality of the Word of

---

New Vision of Christ and Culture (Nashville: Abingdon Press, 1996), 148.

God. This 'high visibility of particular cultures/invisibility of the universal' is highlighted by Lesslie Newbiggin when, in his book *Foolishness to the Greeks: The Gospel and Western Culture*, he notes that, as cultural beings, we are in culture as a fish is in water:

> There can never be a culture-free gospel. Yet the gospel, which is from the beginning to the end embodied in culturally conditioned forms, calls into question all cultures, including the one in which it was originally embodied.[5]

Now it is no doubt the case, as Newbiggin points out, that the gospel does call into question all 'particular' cultures but it is by no means clear how this can be so if the gospel itself is thoroughly suffused with culturally conditioned forms. Newbiggin raises this problem himself in a later work.

> [C]an we who are both Christian believers and also products of this collapsing Western post-Enlightenment culture . . . find a stance from which we can criticise our own culture? A recent writer in *Theology*, reviewing my book *Foolishness to the Greeks*, says bluntly that it is impossible. Trying to criticise one's own culture is, he says, like pretending to move a

---

5. *Foolishness to the Greeks; The Gospel and Western Culture* (Grand Rapids: Eerdmans, 1986), 4.

bus when you are sitting in it. We are what our culture has made us and we have to accept that fact. To appeal to the Bible is futile.[6]

This was precisely the problem faced by Ernst Troeltsch who, convinced that '[w]e are children of time, not its masters',[7] found himself veering more and more, though reluctantly and against his best instincts, towards a thoroughgoing historical and cultural relativism. The problem is certainly acute; if the gospel is itself cultural 'through and through' and if it is particular 'through and through', how can it call human cultures to account or find a vantage point beyond culture from which to cast its critical light on human culture?[8] My response would be to say that whilst we should indeed acknowledge, as Newbiggin suggests, that each human society is cultural 'all the way down', so to speak, we must also acknowledge that each human society is universal 'all the way down', right

---

6. *The Gospel in a Pluralist Society* (Grand Rapids: Eerdmans, 1990), 191.
7. 'Das Wesen des modernen Geist', in JL *Religion in History*, edited by JL Adams, (Minneapolis: 1991), 271.
8. Newbiggin (*The Gospel in a Pluralist Society* [Grand Rapids: Eerdmans, 1990], 197) holds that 'the answer to the complex questions about the relation of the gospel to human culture has to be a practical one and not merely a theoretical one' (*ibid*). I suspect that it is the other way around, or at least that our theoretical and practical endeavours must be equally matched but hopefully, he would agree that the response I provide in the main text provides a theoretical approach and direction that would prove fruitful in our endeavours to better understand the gospel/culture (universal/particular) relation.

into the interstices of its everyday life, its daily practices and routines. Human cultures are, in the main, concretisations of universal values; they attempt to embody universal values in everyday cultural forms and are legitimate (as judged by both internal and external commentators and critics) to the degree that they 'live out' these values, and illegitimate to the degree that they fail to do so. Each human culture, whether consciously or not, and whether expressed in its public rituals or not, is ever oriented to the Divine, just as God is ever oriented to and works within each human culture through its citizens, both individually and collectively, through the intimations of the Spirit. Thus whilst we are indeed ever on the 'bus of culture and history', we are not trying to move it forward as we sit in it; we are, rather, in the driver's seat, and are accountable to God for the direction in which our culture moves or fails to move. Thus whilst it is true, as Newbiggin asserts, that 'the way in which the gospel can challenge our culturally conditioned interpretations of it is through the witness of those who read the Bible with minds shaped by other cultures',[9] yet it is not, as Newbiggin appears to believe, the most important or even the only critical resource we have. The implicit, ever present *universality* of our culture—what we might call its vertical relation to the divine, to its transcendent source, to a divine beckoning from beyond itself—is the primary source of self-criticism (and of social and religious criticism) available to us and has been well grasped and understood by

---

9. *The Gospel in a Pluralist Society* (Grand Rapids: Eerdmans, 1990), 196–197.

Michael Walzer (minus the reference to the divine) and by Richard Niebuhr. I will briefly consider the reflections of each of these thinkers on the universal-particular relationship and the way in which they seamlessly incorporate into their accounts the truths emphasised both by the *Ressourcement*/culture school and the Rahnerian/instrumentalist school.

In his earlier work, Niebuhr was certainly acutely aware of the importance of particularity and historicity; the 'groundedness' and 'concreteness' of his earlier theological reflections on ethics, for example, is beyond question. In his *The Meaning of Revelation*, he holds that our 'reason is not a common reason, alike in all human selves, but one which is qualified by inheritance from a particular society',[10] that 'the time that is in man is not abstract but particular and concrete... the time of a definite society with distinct language, economic and political relations, religious faith and social organisations' and, finally, that 'language is always particular and historical, never general and static'.[11] However, Niebuhr certainly does not privilege 'universality' over against 'particularity, specificity and difference' for he consistently employs throughout his work a sense of 'universality' which is not hostile to 'particularity' or 'concreteness'. It is true that in *Meaning of Revelation* he invidiously compares the 'universal/abstract' with the 'concrete/particular' and speaks as if we are obliged to choose between the two, but he *also* embraces, even in this book, a sense of 'universality' which

---

10. *The Meaning of Revelation* (New York: Macmillan, 1967), 7.
11. *Ibid*, 10.

is perfectly consistent with—indeed presupposes—concreteness/ particularity. He states, for example, that since each person must inhabit a particular spatio-temporal society, so too every view of the universal must be 'from the finite standpoint of the individual in such a society'.[12] It would seem, then, that we each must view the (same) universal through the mediating prism of the historical. As historically conditioned creatures, we 'cannot describe the universal save from a relative point of view'.[13] To 'see' the universal, we must peer 'darkly' through the glass of our concreteness/particularity (our difference). For this reason he says that theology, like the church (and in the language of the church) must be 'directed toward the universal from which the church knows itself to derive its being and to which it points in all its faith and works'.[14] Despite Stassen's claims to the contrary then, we find that even in his earlier work, and especially in *The Meaning of Revelation*, Niebuhr employs the term 'universal' in what is clearly, for him, a very significant sense and—more importantly in the light of our present purposes—it is a sense which is, for him, perfectly compatible with an emphasis on historicity and concreteness.

What, then, we may well wonder, is this 'universal' of which Niebuhr speaks, in which he had such a profound faith, and which, apparently, imparts its life-giving spirit to each particular church across the span of history? It is, of course, God as the Universal or the One of whom he

---

12. *Ibid*, 15.
13. *Ibid*, 8.
14. *Ibid*, 15.

speaks more elaborately in his later work; it is the One beyond the many, the Source of all Being, the Universal who both transcends all particulars (the Father) and yet also pervades all particulars (the Spirit). When Niebuhr in his later work speaks in this manner of God as the One (Universal) beyond the many, and beyond all historical particularities, as he does in the two quotations that follow, this emphasis on his part on the transcendence of God (the Father) should not be viewed as in any way compromising his earlier emphasis on the historical concreteness of the Son's incarnation and the immanence of the Spirit in particularity/difference. In *Christ and Culture* Niebuhr writes:

> As Son of God he points away from the many values of our social life to the one who alone is good, from the many powers which men use and on which they depend to the One who alone is powerful; from the many times and seasons of history with their hopes and fears to the One who is Lord of all times and is alone to be feared and hoped for; he points away from all that is conditioned to the Unconditioned. *He does not direct attention away from this world to another; but from all worlds, present and future, material and spiritual, to the One who creates all worlds, who is the Other of all worlds.*[15]

---

15. *Christ and Culture* (New York: Harper Collins, 2001), 28. Emphasis added.

Niebuhr refers in a similar vein to the One to whom Jesus points in *Radical Monotheism and Western Culture.*

> When the principle of being is God—that is the object of trust and loyalty—then He alone is holy and ultimate sacredness must be denied to any special being. No special places, times, persons or communities are more representative of the One than any others are.[16]

Stassen regards such passages as illustrating that for Niebuhr 'God is the One beyond the many, the principle of being and the principle of value, and the Universal, *in a way that rejects the relative and the particular*',[17](emphasis added). However, in response to this criticism, we should note that in the first passage quoted above from *Christ and Culture*, the final sentence makes it clear that, as Christians, we are not to turn our attention away from this world and in the second passage from *Radical Monotheism and Western Culture*, Niebuhr merely duplicates Christ's words that the Father is alone good in an absolute sense and that this 'goodness itself' of the Father is always inadequately 'imaged' and represented in a fallen world. We should also note here that John Howard Yoder makes a similar criticism of Niebuhr, based on a similar misappre-

---

16. *Radical Monotheism and Western Culture* (New York: Harper, 1960), 52.
17. GH Stassen, DM Yeager, and JH Yoder, *Authentic Transformation: A New Vision of Christ and Culture* (Nashville: Abingdon Press, 1996), 175.

hension. He holds that Niebuhr's 'universal' is of such a kind or character that it, at best, hovers idly and abstractly above, and at worst, positively negates and rejects, the relative and particular[18] but neither author seriously attempts to show precisely why or how the kind of universality Niebuhr believed in involved this kind of rejection.

In the case of Michael Walzer, we find a similar understanding of the universal-particular relationship. In his *Thick and Thin: Moral Argument at Home and Abroad* he says that when he saw television images of people marching in the streets of Prague in 1989, carrying signs saying 'Truth' and 'Justice', he 'knew immediately what the signs meant—and so did everyone else who saw the same picture'. Moreover, he 'also recognized and acknowledged the values the marches were defending—and so did (almost) everyone else'.[19] In order to try to explain (the possibility of) this understanding and acknowledgement, Walzer distinguishes between thin (minimal) and thick (maximal) moral meanings, although he is careful to insist that minimalist meanings (universal justice or the idea of justice) are embedded in the maximal morality (particular, concrete norms of justice) of each human society.[20] It is because these universal terms (truth, justice) have different particurlarist meanings in each society

---

18. 'How H Richard Niebuhr Reasoned: A Critique of *Christ and Culture*', in *Authentic Transformation: a New Vision of Christ and Culture*, edited by GH Stassen, DM Yeager and JH Yoder (Nashville: Abingdon Press, 1996), 59.
19. *Thick and Thin: Moral Argument at Home and Abroad* (Notre Dame Indiana: University of Notre Dame Press, 1994), 1.
20. *Ibid*, 2–3.

that 'they resonate differently in Prague than their translations resonate in, say, Paris or New York'.²¹ Thus far, I believe, Niebuhr and Walzer would be in perfect agreement. It might seem, however, that Walzer parts company with Niebuhr in saying that when Czechs and Slovaks get down to the business of ascertaining what is the practical, common good for them (designing their own health care systems, etc.), 'they will not be universalists; they will aim at what is best for themselves, what fits their history and culture, and won't insist that all the rest of us endorse or reiterate their decisions'. Now Niebuhr would, I think, believe – and certainly I would wish to assert–that there is an important sense in which the practical work of the Czechs and Slovaks *is* universal (that is, in the sense that they are interpreting the ideas of Justice and Truth into the unique circumstances of their lives), but I am persuaded that if there is any disagreement here at all, it is merely linguistic; for Walzer, as we have seen, points out (i) that minimalist (universal) moral meanings are embedded in the maximalist (particular) morality of each human society, so that particularist moral meanings are also, at the same time, universal and (ii) when considering the relation between a (thin) set of universal principles and the manner in which they become embedded in specific historical circumstances, the 'idea of elaboration is better than adaptation' because 'it suggests a process less circumstantial and constrained, more freely creative; governed as much by ideal as by practical considerations'.²²

---

21. *Ibid*, 3.
22. *Ibid*, 4.

Now the reason why Walzer prefers 'elaboration' to 'adaptation' is that the latter term conjures up the idea of 'routine application', as if the policy decisions of each society were merely practical conclusions arrived at deductively (syllogistically) from universal moral premises; his point is that our human, political agency is crucially and creatively involved in interpreting—in his terms 'elaborating'—universal moral ideals into the circumstances of each society. All that I would add here is that the final result—each practical policy decision actually arrived at in implementing universal moral norms—is just as much 'universal' as it is 'particular'.

Walzer asks us to imaginatively enter into the world of the other (he calls this the method of 'reiteration') or, to use Stassen's expression, 'to walk in the shoes of another community'.[23] But how are we to do this? Certainly, it *is* possible for us to do this but *how* is it possible for us to transcend or get beyond our culture, our history, the world of our experience, to ever understand, let alone empathically grasp, the inner meaning and 'lived substance' of the practices of another society? Walzer seems to concede that we must appeal to 'universality' in some sense but the precise sense is not entirely clear in his work. Clearly, both he and Niebuhr believed or assumed that there could exist a type of universality that did not negate the richness of particularity and difference, but were they deceived or mistaken in so doing? Stassen believes that

---

23. GH Stassen, DM Yeager, and JH Yoder, *Authentic Transformation: a New Vision of Christ and Culture* (Nashville: Abingdon Press, 1996), 158.

a 'Kantian residue was always incipient in [Niebuhr's] thought', and that those who succumb to the lure of Kant's universalism and of his 'rationality detached from historical differences'[24] pay a heavy price for so doing. This is the kind of charge that the *Ressourcement*/culture school regularly brings against the Rahnerian instrumentalist school but must, we need to ask, an acknowledgement of the role and importance of the universal have such dire consequences?

The Universal in the Particular

In order to answer this question, let us consider two simple cases of the way in which a 'universal' inheres in, or is present in and through, its particulars.[25] Let us regard the universal 'justice' as, in broad terms, 'a willingness to give each his due or its due' and consider two series of acts that we would unhesitatingly regard as just. In the first series a man, let's say Martin Luther King, keeps a promise, that is, he leaves his home, drives his car to the bank, withdraws the money he promised to pay by a certain date, and then proceeds to pay his debt in good time. In the second series of acts, this same person travels from city to city in America, writes speeches, addresses rallies and talks to politicians, in order to try to bring an end to injustice and discrimination against American blacks.

---

24. *Ibid*, 148.
25. In this and the following paragraph. I have made use, in a modified form, of material which first appeared in my book *Justice and the State: On Liberal Organicism and the Foundations of Emancipatory Politics* (Quebec: World Heritage Press, 1998), 63, 65–66.

Clearly, both sets of successive, particular acts are different from each other but they are not 'entirely' different since the same universal (justice) pervades or informs the two sets of acts and, I would further suggest, makes their differences real and significant. If we consider these two sets of acts *purely* at the horizontal level, so to speak, and compare them, that is, if we try to ignore the unifying universal and concentrate only on the differences between the two sets of acts, we find that we have laid to one side not just the universal, the common denominator, but the *differences* as well; viewed horizontally, there are no differences between the two but, in effect, indifference, that is, two sets of particular acts that are entirely isolated and indifferent because cut off in thought from their universal. However, when we restore the vertical dimension to its proper place in our thoughts and relate each of these sets of particular acts vertically, so to speak, to *its* (and the same) universal, we not only restore the element of unity but we also abolish indifference and restore the aspect of *real* difference. Thus, the ultimate answer to the (Derridean) question—or at least to the question that should be asked of Derrida in relation to two such sets of particular acts that are said to be 'different' from each other—'different from what?' is simply 'different from *its* self or *its* universal'; we find that we are referred back ultimately to the 'containing' universal. However, the same, I maintain, holds true for the relation that obtains between 'just acts' as conceived of in our society and 'just acts' as conceived of in any other society. These two sets of 'just acts' are different from each other *as* different 'concretisations' or 'particularisations' of justice itself, that is, of the *same* 'containing' universal.

The foregoing analysis, though certainly holding that the universal is the source of significance and intelligibility, is not meant to suggest that the particular is somehow insignificant or unimportant. In our actual moral experience there is, I would suggest, a sense of 'descent', of the universal 'entering into' the particular (the Father's will eternally expressed and enacted through the Word,) and also of ascent, of the concrete and particular being drawn into the richness of a higher spiritual life, or of time being elevated at each instant into eternity. However, what this analysis does support us in saying is that the universal is, whereas the particular is not, significant and intelligible *in itself*. After all, it is perfectly possible and intelligible (and, I think, legitimate) to speak of justice-in-itself, the pure essence of justice or the meaning of justice, whereas it is not possible to divorce different and particular just acts from *their* universal without destroying their difference and particularity in the process and thus rendering them unintelligible. Still, it is important to note that we only grasp the presence of the 'universal' in and through the 'particular' and that the universal Word always comes to us 'enfleshed'. This is what Hans Urs von Balthasar has in mind when he says that the essence of Christianity does not 'hover like some abstract universal law over history and its changes, but rather expresses itself in the level of history in ever-new forms without being able thereby to call any one of these forms the absolute one'.[26] God's universal intent towards humanity as a whole, whilst self-identical and ever the same in principle and whilst eternal and unchanging in essence, can only be grasped by us as historically situated persons as we struggle to discern its specific, concrete implications for us in our particular cultural setting. God's 'eternal' intent towards humanity may well be perfectly clearly expressed in the universal command 'Love God and neighbour' but this divine command, whilst universally (and, in a sense, easily) apprehensible by all of humanity, only has real, heart-felt meaning as it becomes 'enfleshed' in our world and culture and as its Spirit enters into and elevates our cultural concepts and categories. As Stassen himself eloquently remarks, '[w]ithin our history, on our level, with our strife and differences, we hear God's truth. We can hear it nowhere else'.[27] However, what it is important for us to acknowledge is that, by virtue of actually *being* God's truth (or Truth), what we hear in our time and place is an emanation from a single source, a particular interpretation into our lives here and now of the same Universal Word that ever guides all of humanity. As such, as Rahner might insist, its universal meaning and truth (its absolute aspect, so to speak) can and should be propositionally expressed in our historical time and socio-cultural setting.

---

26. 'The Fathers, the Scholastics and Ourselves', in *Communio: International Catholic Review*, 24 (1997): 347–396.
27. GH Stassen, DM Yeager, and JH Yoder, *Authentic Transformation: a New Vision of Christ and Culture* (Nashville: Abingdon Press, 1996), 151.

It is worth dwelling for a moment on the expression 'a particular interpretation into our lives here and now of the same Universal Word', for it helps us to clarify the sense in which it is, and is not, proper to speak of our 'common human experience'. Fully acknowledging and bearing in mind the element of particularity (of difference, of 'this-ness', of *haecceitas*, of egocentricity or 'sociocentricity') in our experience in general, and especially in our moral experience, we can see that there can be no 'common human experience', if by this we mean an experience that is identical in form and content across a range of persons, historical periods and socio-cultural contexts. However, it is perfectly legitimate, proper and intelligible to speak of our 'common human experience' as a means of referring to the presence of the same self-identical universal (God's truth) *in* the particular values and beliefs of *our* community. If, peering analytically through the lens of our particularity, our 'this-ness', the universal that we 'see' seems pale and thin, as it does in the case of Hans Kung, for whom 'particularity' looms large (particular churches, particular historical contexts, particular ecclesiologies) and 'universality' virtually fades from view, or if we only find, to use Stassen's expression, 'a very thin set of abstract moral principles lacking in the richness and depth of what makes community and faith real',[28] then we have unwittingly divided or cut apart what should only be distinguished in thought; we have divided in an absolute, dualistic and violent manner the single, concrete whole of our actual moral experience, a concrete whole

---

28. *Ibid*, 146.

which, if its nature as a unified 'whole-of-differences' had been respected, could only have been separated in thought by us into its different, distinguishable aspects. In brief, we would have 'murdered to dissect'; we would have ruptured a concrete whole (of moral experience), a living, breathing integration of principle and practice, by abstracting the universal from its home in the particular, as if it could exist or have any sort of life apart therefrom. We can hardly be surprised then if we find ourselves with two corpses, a thin death-pale ethereal 'universal' and a set of differences/particulars drained of the vitality of *their* containing universal. Likewise, just as it is perfectly proper and intelligible to speak of our 'common or universal human experience', so too it makes sense to speak of our 'common religious experience', provided that we do not think, as George Lindbeck[29] does, of 'experience coming first and theology coming later', for every religious experience invariably presupposes universalist theological understandings or meanings, or, to put the same point the other way around, God's universal intent for all of humanity always comes wrapped or pre-packaged in historically and culturally specific terms; the 'universal' is 'always already' in the 'particular' and the latter in turn is unintelligible apart from its universal. Again it makes sense to speak, as Barth does, of the 'particularity' of the revelation of God in Jesus, provided that we recognise that Jesus, as the Word of the 'universal God', the God who is 'All-in-all', who is the unity and unifier (the unifying intent) of the diversity of the world, is the unique

---

29. *The Nature of Doctrine* (Philadelphia: Westminster Press, 1984).

expression of God's universal intent for all of humanity. ('For God so loved the world . . .')

The expression 'a particular interpretation into our lives of the same Universal Word' is also, I believe, useful when considering and evaluating Troeltsch's well-known two-volume work *The Social Teaching of the Christian Churches*.[30] At the end of his study he inquires as to whether or not his work teaches us 'something lasting and eternal about the Christian social ethos, which might serve us a guiding star for the present and for the future'[31] and his response is the five ideals or universal norms of individual personality, divine love, mutuality, active helpfulness and the realisation of the Kingdom of God. In Stassen's view, the latter are 'thin and abstract. They lack the richness and concreteness of Troeltsch's historical study'.[32] In a sense, this is perfectly true, but I would suggest that if these norms appear abstract and thin, it is only because they have been provisionally (and legitimately) abstracted in thought from their 'past particularities' as an aid to us in interpreting them into our 'present particularities'. The universal is fully present and really operative only in our concrete actions and through the religious-cultural norms that govern our concrete acts. The more the 'universal' is removed in thought from the (or 'its') 'concrete', the more abstract it inevitably appears,

---

30. (New York: Harper, 1960).
31. *Ibid*, Volume 2, 1004
32. GH Stassen, DM Yeager, and JH Yoder, *Authentic Transformation: a New Vision of Christ and Culture* (Nashville: Abingdon Press, 1996), 149.

for it has been removed, so to speak, (for analytic purposes or whatever) from where it truly belongs. Also, in Troeltsch's quest for 'the permanent ethical values which are contained within the varied history of the Christian social doctrines',[33] I would suggest that he was not, as Stassen argues, 'expecting true Christian norms to be universally maintained by the various churches throughout the centuries of church history'.[34] In the end, Troeltsch concedes that the only true Christian norms that can be identified as universally recognised must be something like the five universal norms or principles we have just mentioned. We must, indeed, surely acknowledge that no more concrete, specific norms can be identified across the span of history, for each generation of Christians confronts the task of interpreting these universal norms into the unique circumstances they encounter, and of finding more concrete, 'culture-specific' norms to mediate, so to speak, between the two. The 'tragedy of Troeltsch' is that he launched his public career as a kind of Rahnerian universalist, arguing that Christianity was absolutely valid, and finished it as a kind of '*Ressourcement* relativist' by becoming wholly entrapped in what he himself called the 'crisis of historicism', that is, by portraying Christianity as a contingent episode in European culture, as something that 'has grown up with us and has become a part of our

---

33. *The Social Teaching of the Christian Churches*, volume 2 (New York: Harper, 1960), 1004.
34. GH Stassen, DM Yeager, and JH Yoder, *Authentic Transformation: A New Vision of Christ and Culture* (Nashville: Abingdon Press, 1996), 149.

very being' and hence as a set of beliefs that *only* has 'validity for us'.³⁵ He failed to see that whilst Christianity is indeed only 'valid for us', it is so in a relativising sense that does not undermine its universality, that is, (i) in the sense that there is always a 'we' who accept the universal Word into our hearts, uniquely concretise it and culturally express it, a 'we' whose very being is 'relative' to the call of God specifically addressed to *us*, and (ii) in the sense that Gadamer had in mind when he spoke of *our* prejudices or 'biases of openness to the world'.³⁶ The universal Word is indeed, as we saw earlier, 'always already' concretised and culturally expressed in some form or another by those groups for whom, in whom and through whom, it is true and alive; it is true for them or relative to them. Our Christian life is also universally valid—and universally recognisable as such by any rational, ethical being—as a *bona fides* endeavour to realise and implement the five universal norms mentioned above in a specifically Christian way.

The expression 'a particular interpretation into our lives here and now of the same Universal Word' is also useful in helping us guard against the kind of false universality that Adolfo Percy Esquivel speaks of. In terms of our present discussion, this could be described as a 'universal' with a life or autonomous existence of its own,

---

35. Troeltsch, E, 1957, "The Place of Christianity among the World Religious" in *Christian Thought: Its History and Application, Meridian Books*, New York.
36. 'The Universality of the Hermeneutical Problem', in *Contemporary Hermeneutics*, edited by J Bleicher (London: Routledge and Kegan Paul, 1980), 133.

hovering idly above and entirely cut off from its differences. This 'containing' universal contains nothing but itself!

> We cannot agree with those of our brothers and sisters who seek to reduce the gospel to a message of false universality—bland tidings to all in the same tone that blissfully washes out the differences between rich and poor and speaks to us as if there is no difference between a rich Christian and a poor Christian. Such an insipid gospel can never be the leaven of resolute action for justice and the liberation of our people.
>
> We cannot resign ourselves to a church unity based on an abstract universality, on a colorless, odorless, and tasteless gospel of equality among all human beings that takes no account of social, economic, and cultural differences. Our love for the unity of the church must drive us forward together in search of a full gospel, a gospel read in its totality—not a mawkish message in which all differences vanish into thin air . . . This kind of unity would be the very contrary of the eschatological unity in fullness for which Jesus prayed.[37]

---

37. AP Esquivel *Christ in a Poncho* (MaryKnoll, New York: Orbis, 1983), 134.

If we acknowledge that it is our task to interpret God's Universal Word into our lives here and now or, alternatively expressed, that it is our task to enable the Universal Spirit to flow through our thoughts and various mediating norms into our world, and if we thereby sense the living, flowing integrated unity of our moral experience, then we will regard as futile any attempt to find a one-to-one correspondence between the concrete norms of different societies or even of one society at different times, and we will then be alert to the danger of confusing universality (or true universality) with the mere generality of a class (sometimes referred to as a kind of universality but, I would suggest, misleadingly so). Stassen, as we have just seen, holds, unfairly I believe, that Troeltch's quest for 'the permanent ethical values which are contained within the varied history of the Christian social doctrines'[38] is just such a futile attempt but what is at any rate beyond doubt, or so I wish to maintain, is that the only kind of universality, if such it may be provisionally called, that can emerge from such a quest, is what Bosanquet calls 'universality in spite of differences' and what I call 'horizontal, external universality', which really turns out, as Bosanquet has shown, to be the mere generality of a class. However, the kind of universality that is pertinent and important here and that 'answers authentically' so to speak, to our actual moral experience, is what Bosanquet, following Hegel, calls 'concrete universality' ('universal-

---

38. *The Social Teaching of the Christian Churches*, volume 2 (New York: Harper, 1960), 1004.

ity by means of the other') and what I would call 'vertical, internal universality'.[39]

---

39. Bosanquet notes that the endeavour behind the simple generalisation (all crows, despite their differences, are black, winged, animals etc) is to pursue an identity, a sameness, a kind of (horizontal) universality apart from differences:

> The generality is framed by attending to the common qualities of a number of individuals, and disregarding their differences. This procedure has two inevitable results; it prohibits the consideration of any world or structure of which the individuals before us are members, and by the same necessity it prohibits the consideration of the entire or concrete nature of any individual by itself (*The Principle of Individuality and Value* [London: Macmillan, 1927], 35).

He holds that if we insist upon construing identity as excluding difference/diversity, we will end up not with a living, concrete 'whole-of-parts/differences' but with what he calls a mere class or 'whole of repetition' and what I call inert, external horizontal duplication:

> A world or cosmos is a system of members, such that every member, being *ex hypothesi* distinct, nevertheless contributes to the unity of the whole in virtue of the peculiarities which constitute its distinctness. And the important point for us at present is the difference of principle between a world and a class. It takes all sorts to make a world; a class is essentially one sort only. In a word, the difference is that the ultimate principle of unity or community is fully exemplified in the former, but only superficially in the latter. The ultimate principle, we may say, is sameness in the other; generality is sameness in spite of the other; universality is sameness by means of the other (*Ibid*, 37).

This 'universality by means of the other' helps us to grasp how God's universal, identical, self-same intent for humanity may be expressed in and through the various value and belief systems of many different cultures. These diverse belief and value systems, though vastly different from each other—and indeed, 'incommensurable' when compared horizontally, as if some kind of one-to-one correspondence of beliefs/values/ethical practices across diverse cultures was possible—are yet the same (they have something vital in common) by virtue of their common source in the divine, in God's eternal Truth, or in God as the ultimate, enveloping universal. This is what O'Donovan has in mind when he speaks of the 'paradoxical truth about sameness and difference' in Christian theology, in diverse theological undertakings, and in each 'political hermeneutic', by which he means each interpretation of the universal word of Scripture into the variegated circumstances of our lives:

> Since no one context is the same as any other, no one theological undertaking will exactly mirror another; and yet as each enterprise takes seriously its own authorization in the Gospel of Jesus Christ, it will find that it is in a symbiotic relation to every other enterprise that does so. The Gospel is one Gospel, which has manifold implications for us as we believe and obey it. Theology is a manifold witness, which has a unified object on which it concentrates its witness. The 'political hermeneutic' is discovered and explored in a particular con-

text of discipleship; yet it does not belong to that context, nor is it the context that imposes it in the first place. It belongs to the Scriptures and is imposed by the exercise of reading the Scriptures.[40]

This is precisely what Bosanquet has in mind when he uses the expression 'universality by means of the other', what I have in mind by 'the vertical sense of universality' and what Niebuhr and Walzer have in mind when they reflect upon the universal-particular relationship. Certainly, the vertical sense of universality is what Walzer has in mind when he states that each human society is 'universal because it is human, particular because it is a society'.[41] He then explains as follows:

> Societies are necessarily particular because they have members and memories, members *with* memories not only of their own but also of their common life. Humanity, by contrast, has members but no memory, and so it is has no history and no culture, no customary practices, no familiar life-ways, no festivals, no shared understanding of social goods. It is human to have such things, but there is no singular human way of having them. At the

---

40. *The Desire of the Nations; Rediscovering the Roots of Political Theology*, Cambridge: Cambridge University Press, 2003), 21–22.
41. *Thick and Thin: Moral Argument at Home and Abroad* (Notre Dame, Indiana: University of Notre Dame Press, 1994), 8.

same time, the members of all the different societies, because they are human, can acknowledge each other's different ways, respond to each other's cries for help, learn from each other and march (sometimes) in each other's parades.[42]

This remarkable passage is as intriguing and ambiguous as it is insightful and path breaking, for it could be interpreted as meaning that 'humanity' or the adjective 'human' is 'universal' only in the (universality in spite of differences) sense that a class may be designated as universal. We have just seen that the unity or 'mere generality' of a class can only be achieved by ignoring or omitting significant differences. Now, if we invoke unity or universality in this sense to enable us to imaginatively enter into the world of another community, we will be trying to find a one-to-one correspondence between elements in our collective human experience and theirs, such that these elements may be described as 'the same' but most certainly we will succeed only in, to use Stassen's expression, reducing the rich experiences of the other 'to a universal principle or to exactly the same experience we have had'.[43] To invoke universality in this sense is to assume that human societies are related to each other in an inert, indifferent horizontal way. Perhaps, however, this is

---

42. *Ibid*, 8.
43. GH Stassen, DM Yeager, and JH Yoder, *Authentic Transformation: A New Vision of Christ and Culture* (Nashville: Abingdon Press, 1996), 158.

not the sense of universality that Walzer appeals to, or at least not the only sense. Perhaps he employs the adjective 'human' in the 'universal through its differences' sense, for Walzer (also) seems to be saying that our common humanity is the universal means or 'doorway' by and through which we are enabled to 'acknowledge each other's different ways, respond to each other's cries for help, learn from each other, and march (sometime) in each other's parades'.[44]

In this passage, Walzer seems to be precariously balanced between these two interpretations and, for this reason, he may be easily 'tilted' in one direction or the other. When he says, for example, concerning all human societies, that 'there is no reason to think that they are all heading in the same direction',[45] this could be interpreted as illustrating that Walzer favours 'universality' in the external, horizontal sense but it could, with equal plausibility, be interpreted simply as saying that the same universal can lead different societies in different directions. There is indeed no reason to think that all human societies are heading in the same direction but perhaps they are all attuned, in their own unique fashion, to the same (unifying) divine will, as the different members of an orchestra each take their lead from the one conductor. Could it be then (and would Walzer agree?) that just as the human body is a 'whole of parts/differences' which yet contains within itself other 'wholes of parts' (for example the liver,

---

44. *Thick and Thin: Moral Argument at Home and Abroad* (Notre Dame, Indiana: University of Notre Dame Press, 1994), 8
45. *Ibid*, 9.

the heart,) as microcosmic worlds within the enveloping macrocosmic world of the body as a whole, and just as the life of the liver may seem, at a superficial glance, to be remote from the life of the heart, so too our humanity or the 'world community' consists of a whole of parts/differences comprising the different human societies of our world as microcosmic worlds whose apparent distance and remoteness from each other is deceptive? Likewise, the vertical sense of universality is what Niebuhr has in mind when he speaks of 'the oneness of a will directed toward unity of all things in our world',[46] of 'the unity of life aspiring toward and impelled by an infinite purpose',[47] of 'the One who acts in all the many'[48] and of the limited, yet universal, standpoint of the Christian community as it peers through time into eternity, through particularity and difference into the enveloping universality of God and His Love:

> The standpoint of the Christian community is limited, being in history, faith and sin. But what is seen from this standpoint is unlimited. Faith cannot get to God save through historic experience, as reason cannot get to nature save through sense-experience. But as reason, having learned through limited experience an intelligible pattern of reality, can

---

46. *The Meaning of Revelation* (New York: Macmillan, 1967), 133.
47. *Ibid*, 134.
48. *The Responsible Self; An Essay in Christian Moral Philosophy* (New York: Harper, 1963), 173.

> seek the evidence of a like pattern in all other experience, so faith having apprehended the divine self in its own history, can and must look for the manifestation of the same self in all other events.[49]

Niebuhr's social analysis then does not rely on 'universality' in the external horizontal sense—he praises the early Christian Church precisely for *not* following 'the dictates of some common human conscience, unhistorical and super-social in character'[50]—but on universality in the internal, vertical, 'identity though its differences' or 'universality by means of the other' sense. Each community and generation of Christians must interpret the essential meaning of the life, death and resurrection of Jesus into its own unique socio-historical circumstances, as the *Ressourcement*/culture school rightly insists. God's Truth in Jesus Christ can only be real (real for *us*) in our time and place. As Niebuhr remarks, as historical beings, we can speak only of what we see 'through the medium of our history. We are in history as the fish is in water and what we mean by the revelation of God can be indicated only as we point through the medium in which we live'.[51] Again, as the following passage makes clear, Niebuhr, through his faith in special revelation (the incarnation of Jesus), has no difficulty in fully endorsing and embracing God's

---

49. RH Niebuhr, *The Meaning of Revelation* (New York: Macmillan, 1967), 63.
50. *Ibid*, 32.
51. *Ibid*, 36.

all-containing universal presence in the diversity (difference/particularity) of creation (the Father's will eternally expressed and enacted through the Word) and the single 'Spirit of Totality' that pervades the world as a whole, including each human community (the Holy Spirit that works within all actual unities, or 'wholes of parts', and ever draws them beyond themselves into the ideal unity willed by the Father):

> How revelation is revolution in religious knowledge may be indicated by reference to the ideas we have about divine unity, reality and especially goodness. The unity of deity which we anticipated in our hypotheses about deity is realised in the revelation of God in Christ. Beyond the many and conditioned beings for which and among which we lived, beyond eternal objects and ideas we have learned to posit one unconditioned being. We thought about a single principle which might serve as the source of the unities we find in our experience, but though the Father of our Lord Jesus Christ met that expectation he fulfilled it in another manner than we anticipated, and made necessary a change in all our thinking about the unity of the world. He met us not as the one beyond the many but as the one who acts in and through all things, not as the unconditioned but as the conditioner. The oneness of the person was the oneness of

a will directed toward unity of all things in our world.[52]

If we include 'all human communities' in Niebuhr's 'all things in our world', then we may say that it is only possible for them to attain mutual comprehension and sympathy with each other by conforming to the universal intent of the Father and by living the life of the Spirit, that is, by participating in the very life of the ultimate source of the unity enjoyed by each political community. Just as reason, as Niebuhr remarks, 'having learned through limited experience an intelligible pattern of reality can seek the evidence of a like pattern in all other experience; so faith having apprehended the divine self in its own history, can and must look for the manifestation of the same self in all other events'.[53] From this perspective, then, Walzer's method of reiteration appears not as a dyadic relation, involving simply (i) us and our world and (ii) the other's world of experience, but is a triadic relation involving (i), (ii) and, in addition, (iii) the enveloping (one and the same) universal Spirit.

The Universal in Particular Traditions: Gadamer

We can only step outside the boundaries of our world to imaginatively and empathically enter into the world of 'the other' by means of what Hans-Georg Gadamer called a 'fusion of horizons', though in light of our reflections

---

52. *Ibid*, 133.
53. *Ibid*, 63.

thus far on the (universal) gospel/word-(particular) culture relation, it will become clear, I trust, that Gadamer's notion of the 'fusion of horizons' is more useful and informative in helping us to understand our encounter with the 'culturally and religiously different', rather than our encounter with our own past, our tradition, or with the universal as it is embodied and expressed in our traditions. Gadamer regards our relation to our tradition as a 'fusion of horizons', as an intercourse or interweaving of the *near* horizon of the present in which we live and the *distant* horizon of the past or of the culturally different in which others live or have lived.[54] These horizons are not separate from each other. There is, he insists, no present horizon cut off from the past and there is no past horizon awaiting discovery and existing apart from the present. When, for example, we interpret from our vantage point (from within our near horizon or way of life) a text located in our distant past, both 'we' and the 'text' belong to the same tradition and the latter is always appropriated from the horizon of expectations engendered by this tradition. However, if the 'horizon of expectations' we inherit from our past and the 'pre-understanding' from our past horizon that is incorporated into our present horizon[55] are in essence the means whereby a tradition bears (or 'differences') the universal into the unique circumstances of our lives, then this 'bearing', 'conveying' or 'differencing' into our world should, I would suggest, be seen as a one-way flow of the universal into the particular (a hermeneutical

---

54. *Truth and Method* (London: Sheed and Ward, 1989), 306–307.
55. *Ibid*, 296–277.

'flow'), rather than as a two-way 'fusion of horizons' (a hermeneutical 'circle').

As the bearer, or 'historical conveyor belt', of universal meanings into the concrete (social, historical and personal) circumstances of our lives, a tradition is a kind of 'one-way flow'—time moves in only one direction—of the 'past' into our 'present', though of course it must be acknowledged that the characteristic concepts and categories of the tradition, and their modes of linguistic/cultural expression, are constantly being modified and adjusted by their encounter with the unique and highly particular features of our present. Interestingly, Gadamer calls an inherited pre-understanding a 'prejudice' and prejudice in this positive sense he sees as a 'predisposition to truth' but this is precisely what I have in mind (and perhaps too, I suspect, what Gadamer had in mind) by 'the universal in quest of *its* particular' in our time and place, or by 'the universal emanating from the heart of the tradition and struggling *through us*, its carriers, to extricate itself from its old particulars in order to incarnate itself in the new.' Gadamer says that we are each immersed in a tradition which provides us with prejudices or 'biases of openness to the world'[56] but he also says that prejudices are conveyed by language, that 'being which can be understood is language', that language not merely reflects 'our own being and all being' but is 'the living out of what it is with us' and is the (Heideggerian) 'dialogue which

---

56. 'The Universality of the Hermeneutical Problem', in *Contemporary Hermeneutics*, edited by J Bleicher (London: Routledge and Kegan Paul, London, 1980), 133.

we are'.⁵⁷ To be immersed in tradition and prejudice (in Gadamer's benign sense) is thus to be immersed in Being; prejudice is thus not simply our 'bias of openness to the world'⁵⁸ but also, and more importantly, our bias of openness to the transcendent, to the divine, to Being itself. For Heidegger, we gain access to Being through *Dasein* (and language close to actual existence), whereas for Gadamer this is achieved through tradition (and a language which faithfully expresses its life in us).

Prejudices are the divine as seen and as actually experienced from our unique (relative) point of view; they are 'universal meanings' or 'divine ideas' that have been thoroughly incorporated into a tradition in such a way that they fashion and form *our* bias of openness to the divine/the Absolute or the bias of openness of *our* form of being to Being. As Paul Ricouer says, for Gadamer 'belonging-to language provides the universal medium for belonging-to being,'⁵⁹ but we each, culturally and personally, 'belong to Being' from different angles of vision, so to speak; we are each vertically related to the divine, the Absolute, the agathon but we each stand horizontally at different points in history. For this reason we are, I think,

---

57. 'Hermeneutics and the Critique of Ideology', in *Hermeneutics and the Human Sciences*, edited by JB Thompson (Cambridge University Press, Cambridge, 1981), 86.
58. 'The Universality of the Hermeneutical Problem', in *Contemporary Hermeneutics*, edited by J Bleicher (London: Routledge and Kegan Paul, London, 1980), 133.
59. 'Philosophical Hermeneutics and Theology' in *Theology Digest*, 24/2 (1976): 154–164.

profoundly challenged not so much by the encounter of our tradition (our bias of openness to the divine) with radically new circumstances, as by the encounter of our tradition with another tradition, with an alternative bias of openness to the divine that initially strikes us as alien and unfamiliar. How can such an encounter *not* unsettle us? The mysterious realm of language, as Gadamer says, 'allows what is to come to expression'[60] and allows the divine to come to expression in and through us but language in which a real dialogue with the 'culturally and religiously different' takes place, can hardly fail to unnerve us. We have difficulty enough trying to grapple with the divine as we (narrowly) understand it in our own culture and way of life. However, if we have difficulties coming to grips with this 'semi-domesticated divine', how are we to cope with the wild, untamed divine that another tradition (or love in another, unfamiliar guise) confronts us with. An encounter of this kind, a genuine 'fusion of horizons' is as difficult and intimidating as it is necessary. Where and when such a dialogical encounter takes place, Gadamer's expression ('fusion of horizons') is alone adequate to convey the burgeoning growth in 'the human consciousness of the divine' that such a painful fusion generates.

In the preceding sections of this chapter, we have been concerned to ensure that when we are thinking of relations between the universal Word of God and particular cultures/traditions, universality should not be opposed

---

60. *Philosophical Hermeneutics* (Berkeley, California: University of California Press, 1976), 50.

to particularity/difference. By 'universality' we have not had in mind anything abstract or ethereal (abstract universality) but something concrete (concrete universality). Thus, we may well accept that, as Diane Yeagher remarks, Niebuhr's universalism (and Walzer's, Bosanquet's, etc) is 'quite remote from the myth of sweet reason's fixed and timeless findings concerning "nature, man and God"',[61] but it is not at all remote from the immutable truth that universal 'reason' (or, if one prefers 'sweet reason', or the 'mind and heart of God') is ever endeavouring to draw nature and humanity to their ideal fulfilment. We may thus say that the 'universal' draws the 'particular' into itself, and that the particular is true to itself as it is drawn fully into the life of the universal and as the embodiment of the universal. May we say the same thing of the 'absolute' and the 'relative'?

Absolute and relative: H Richard Niebuhr and Reinhold Niebuhr

In his *Christ and Culture*, Richard Niebuhr alerts us to the following danger:

> The effort to bring Christ and culture, God's work and man's, the temporal and the eternal, law and grace, into one system of thought and practice tends, perhaps inevitably to the

---

[61]. 'The Social Self in the Pilgrim Church' in *Authentic Transformation: a New Vision of Christ and Culture*, edited by GH Stassen, DM Yeager and JH Yoder (Nashville: Abingdon Press, 1996), 125.

> Absolutising of what is relative, the reduction of the infinite to a finite form, and the materialisation of the dynamic. It is one thing to assert that there is a law of God inscribed in the very structure of the creature, who must seek to know this law by the use of his reason and govern himself accordingly; it is another thing to formulate the law in the language and concepts of a reason that is always culturally conditioned.[62]

Niebuhr is of course making a very sound point here; it is indeed erroneous to 'absolutise the relative' in the sense of ascribing to that which is merely relative qualities possessed only by God, but equally, or at the same time, we need to acknowledge that the 'relative' only is what it truly is (or only can be what it truly is) in its proper relation to the 'Absolute'. Certainly, it is a mistake to try to bring Christ and culture, God's work and human work, the eternal and the temporal, into a 'once and for all' system of thought and practice, but it is desirable for the Christian to acknowledge that the presence of Christ in culture, of the eternal in the temporal, of the absolute in the relative produces a kind of constant, productive tension in the sphere of 'culture/time/the relative' towards fulfilment in 'Christ/the eternal/the Absolute'. Absolutising the relative in the way Niebuhr criticises certainly leads to the false 'infinitising of the finite' or to an improper

---

62. *Christ and Culture* (New York: Harper Collins, 2001), 145.

'materialisation of the dynamic' but the Godly effort to make 'time' the moving image of eternity, or to make the 'relative' the living vehicle of the Absolute under mundane circumstances, or to participate in and welcome the process whereby the infinite constantly draws the finite into itself, is to 'absolutise the relative' or to 'dynamise the material' in a perfectly proper, legitimate and wholesome way. The 'finite' is truly what it is, (and can be) by virtue of (i) its living relation to *its* Infinite, its vertical relation to God and (ii) through that relation, its horizontal relation to everything else. Again, too, Niebuhr is right to say that Clement and Aquinas are at fault to the degree that they may have wished, consciously or unconsciously, to impose a 'once and for all' pattern on God's will for humanity. He says that 'Clement's understanding of what is natural to man is often pathetically provincial. The hierarchical view of natural order in Thomas Aquinas is historical and medieval.'[63] However, we should note that for Aquinas and Clement in their time, as for us in ours, the task of Christianity and humanity alike is to make God truly present in time, without divinising the temporary vehicles of eternity beyond the blessed moment. We may hope that Clement and Aquinas experienced such blessed moments in their times. Hopefully, they acted and spoke as God required them to do and established or modified temporal institutions in their societies in accordance with His will; hopefully, too, to the extent that they may have stopped the 'moving image of eternity' in its tracks, He will be gracious in his mercy and forgiveness towards

---

63. *Ibid*, 145.

them—and towards us in our time. Like them, as Niebuhr says, we must not attempt a 'once and for all' formulation of the law but we must rather ponder a 'here and now' interpretation of the law into our present circumstances in the language and concepts of our culturally conditioned reason. Only if we, in our time, have seriously endeavoured to interpret the eternal law (divine reason) into our lives through the prism of our cultural language and concepts, can we use the term 'reason' in its full, proper ethical sense.

Niebuhr uses terms such as 'synthesis' and 'system' to characterise the way in which the 'Christ above culture' approach understands the relationship between the two (Christ and culture) but these terms would not, I think, be used or deemed to be appropriate by actual exponents of this approach. For the latter, the kind of relationship that ideally obtains between Christ and culture cannot be adequately conveyed or described by the (Niebuhrian) terms 'synthesis' or 'system'. It is entirely legitimate to show how ideas cohere in a single 'system of ideas' (an ideology) or how discrete physical entities form parts of a mechanical system (a mechanical device) but the language and (spatial) mental imagery of 'synthesis' or 'system' in no way elucidates the way in which the divine is instantiated in our human affairs. Since what we are trying to understand is the way in which the eternal is present in the temporal, the universal in the concrete, or the Absolute Truth in relative 'truths', expression such as 'instantiation', 'embodiment', 'concrete expression' etc are much more appropriate than 'system' or 'synthesis'. Perhaps, at all times, we are concerned with the coherence of our experience but there is still a major difference between (i) the mind's quest for unity or synthesis (truth) and (ii) the endeavours of the human will to unify experience or to rid our experience of self-contradiction (goodness). Christ is to culture, not as one part of a system or synthesis is to another, but as eternity is to time, as grace to law, as form to matter, as idea to concrete lived reality. Thus whilst Niebuhr is right to remind the exponent of this approach (whom he misleadingly calls the 'synthesist') that 'all human achievement is temporal and passing',[64] yet we must take care here, as Niebuhr also acknowledges, lest we fail to assign to the 'temporal' and the 'passing' their proper value. The whole of earthly creation, after all, is temporary and passing, as are our lives but that is not to say that these things—created things, our lives—are of no value at all. The presence of God in time and above all, of course, the incarnation of Christ, the Word, in time, point in the completely opposite direction. A moment in time which God's presence has made holy is forever holy and no good deed is ever lost, worthless or forgotten, despite the evanescence of its appearance on the 'plane of time', for it exists or subsists eternally in the mind of God. However, God expects us to move on, to leave the holy moment in His memory. However precious or significant the moment may have been for us personally, or collectively as a family or nation, we must not seek to recapture it (remember Lot's wife!). Yahweh *was* there then but *is* now here; the moving image of eternity has moved on, and so too must we. At this point we turn our attention

---

64. *Ibid*, 146.

to the work of Reinhold Niebuhr, who has reflected upon the same problems and themes as his brother Richard and whose contribution is no less valuable.

We have seen that universal, absolute principles of justice (or natural law) are present as what we might call 'orienting principles' amidst the contingencies and historical relativities of human existence. When thus present in an actual historical society, these principles serve to orient or draw that society towards justice, that is, towards a recognition of the absolute value (and hence of the inalienable rights) of all its citizens or towards a genuine, harmoniously related, socio-political 'whole-of-parts'; as orienting principles of justice, they are unifying, that is they draw the 'social mind' ever closer to the 'social ideal' or to what Reinhold Niebuhr refers to as the spirit of brotherhood. This 'orienting presence' (or 'critical presence') of absolute principles of justice needs to be distinguished from the 'embodied presence' (the concrete realisation) of these principles in the legal operations of an actual human society. Having drawn differences towards an integrated social harmony by their orienting, critical unifying presence, these principles then become historically embodied in the operating rules of justice in a given society. As Reinhold Niebuhr remarks, '[t]he definitions arrived at in a given community are the product of a social mind. Various perspectives upon common problems have been merged and have achieved a result, different from that at which any individual, class or group in the community would have arrived'.⁶⁵ However, what this means, I wish to suggest, is that the absolute is, or may be, present in the relative (an historically continent set of legal rules). Niebuhr himself concedes as much when he speaks of a 'distinction between ideals of justice and their embodiment in historical or "civil" law',⁶⁶ by which he means a distinction between 'pure' laws of nature or eternal principles of justice and their relative approximation to conditions in the real world, or to what he calls the 'pressures and counter-pressures in a living community'.⁶⁷ Now, if universal, absolute, 'pure' principles of justice may become embodied in historical or civil law in this relative or approximate sense, then the 'absolute' may likewise be said to be truly present in the 'relative and contingent' in the same sense. Thus as well as the 'unifying and orienting presence' of principles of justice in a human society, constantly subjecting its structures and its civil law to the test of critical scrutiny, there is also their 'real and operative presence' in its structures and civil law.⁶⁸ Wherever, and to the ex-

---

65. *The Nature and Destiny of Man: A Christian Interpretation*, volume 2 (London: Nisbet & Co Ltd, 1944), 58.
66. *Ibid*, 263.
67. *Ibid*.
68. Thomas Hobbes in the seventeenth century argued that the laws of nature were commanded by God and that the authority or presence of natural law fully inhered in civil laws designed to bring about the peace, security and communal wellbeing intended by natural law. He is perhaps the strongest exponent of the view that the Absolute may be fully present in the contingently determined laws of a society. The intimacy of the relation between natural law and civil law is laid out most succinctly by Hobbes as follows:

tent that, universal principles of justice are embodied in civil laws and social policy, then they are, to use Reinhold Niebuhr's terminology, 'the servants and instruments of the spirit of brotherhood in so far as they extend the sense of obligation towards the other, (a) from an immediately felt obligation, prompted by obvious need, to a continued obligation expressed in fixed principles of support; (b) from a simple relation between a self and one "other" to the complex relations of the self and the "others"; and (c) finally from the obligations, discerned by the individual self, to the wider obligations which the community defines from its more impartial perspective'.[69]

Niebuhr says that in these three ways 'rules and laws of justice stand in a positive relation to the law of love'[70] but this, in my view, is tantamount to saying that in so far as eternal, absolute principles of justice are present in the

---

> The law of nature, and the civil law, contain each other, and are of equal extent. For the laws of nature . . . in the condition of mere nature . . . are not properly laws, but qualities that dispose men to peace and obedience. When a commonwealth is once settled, then are they actually laws, and not before; as being then the commands of the commonwealth; and therefore also civil laws . . . Civil and natural law are not different kinds, but different parts of law; whereof one part being written is called civil, the other unwritten, natural.
>
> *Leviathan* in *The English Works of Thomas Hobbes*, volume 3, edited by W Molesworth (London: J Bohn, 1839), 253; *Leviathan*, edited by R Tuck (Cambridge: Cambridge University Press, 1996), 314.

69. *The Nature and Destiny of Man: A Christian Interpretation*, volume 2 (London: Nisbet & Co Ltd, 1944), 257.
70. *Ibid*.

temporal, relative civil laws of a state (empirical laws of justice), then the 'absolute' (the law of love) is positively expressed, embodied and present in the relative and particular (the contingent civil law). Barth is well known for constantly reminding us that the divine 'No' is in reality a divine 'Yes', that the apparent negativity God expresses towards us in his firm moral prohibitions is always to our real benefit, like hedges along a roadway that 'constrain' us from going astray, and Niebuhr makes precisely the same point with regard to the justice immanent in the civil law which, he insists, is designed for our betterment and draws us deeper into the orbit of love. He warns us against 'the error of excluding rules of justice from the domain of love' and rightly takes Emil Brunner to task for holding that the role of politics and law is of secondary importance and that, in Brunner's words, the 'one thing that matters is to do what can be done only from the standpoint of faith, namely, to love our neighbour "in Christ", and to serve him in any way we can . . . It is supremely important to emphasise the truth that what is decisive always takes place in the realm of personal relations and not in the political sphere, save where we are concerned with preserving the whole order from a general breakdown.'[71] This criticism of Brunner is, I think, sound and incisive[72]

---

71. *The Divine Imperative: A Study in Christian Ethics* (Philadelphia: Westminster Press, 1957), 223.
72. A similar criticism may, I think, be made of Helmut Thielicke, at least to the extent that he believes that fundamental change of the social order is a by-product of the changing of persons and their individual lives. It may well be true, as he says, that the 'changing of persons will necessarily mean the changing of the order'

but Niebuhr fails to realise that if love (absolute and divine) can be present in and through rules of justice and if the absolute or 'unconditioned' may be—indeed, routinely is—present in a society in and through such rules, then he is mistaken in asserting that the relative and contingent character of these rules of justice 'refutes the claim of their unconditional character, made alike by Catholic, liberal and even Marxist social theorists'.[73] The absolute *is* present in the contingently determined laws of a society and also in the minds of its citizens *to the extent that* they respect, routinely obey and enter into, the uplifting spirit of the civil law, that is, to the extent that they are receptive to what Niebuhr refers to as 'rules and principles of justice, slowly elaborated in collective experience'.[74]

In line with the preceding analysis, I would hold that laws and systems of justice that genuinely reflect the universal (absolute) principles of justice have a strong positive relation to Niebuhr's 'spirit of brotherhood'. When Niebuhr maintains that such operating legal systems 'have a negative as well as a positive relation to mutual love and brotherhood' and 'contain both approximations to and contradictions of the spirit of brotherhood',[75] it is important to note that by 'contradictions' here he has in

---

(*Theological Ethics, Volume 2: Politics* [Grand Rapids: Eerdmans, 1979], 645), but it is equally true that legislation designed to secure the right ordering of society can exercise major and uplifting effects on the lives of individuals.

73. *The Nature and Destiny of Man: A Christian Interpretation*, volume 2 (London: Nisbet & Co Ltd, 1944), 262.
74. *Ibid*, 258.
75. *Ibid*, 261.

mind 'the sinful element in all social reality', for he insists that laws and systems of justice are 'merely approximations in so far as justice presupposes a tendency of various members of a community to take advantage of each other, or to be more concerned with their own weal than with that of others'.[76] The critical and entirely valid point being made here by Niebuhr is that empirical rules of justice or civil laws contradict, challenge and constantly endeavour to bring to order our sinful and selfish nature, but surely this means that the 'challenging tension', so to speak, is between the law of love and empirical systems of justice on the one hand and our wayward sinful nature on the other. This, after all, is the gist of his criticism of Brunner. Niebuhr's use of the term 'approximations' in this particular context to mean the way in which civil laws can only partially succeed in modifying our selfish desires is, I think, misleading and inappropriate. I would suggest that we should *only* speak of civil laws 'approximating' natural law when we have in mind either the critical/orienting presence and impact of the latter on the former or the ever changing concrete embodiment/presence of the latter (natural law) in the former (civil law).

When Niebuhr speaks of the embodiment of ideals of justice in historical or civil law,[77] he appears, as we noted earlier, to implicitly acknowledge that the absolute or eternal may be truly present in a temporal and relative system of civil law, with the consequence that 'universal reason' may be said to be present at least in the law as

---

76. *Ibid*, 261.
77. *Ibid*, 263.

reflective of eternal principles of justice, if not in the minds of selfish, partisan citizens. However, this is precisely what Niebuhr appears to deny when he says that '[t]here is no universal reason in history, and no impartial perspective upon the whole field of vital interests, which compete with and mutually support each other'.[78] He would thus seem to deny us the opportunity to speak either of the 'real presence' of universal reason in the civil law of a state or of its 'intended or hoped for presence' in the minds of its citizens. We are likewise forbidden to distinguish between what I would call the 'informed or ordered contingent' as opposed to the 'merely contingent' (contingency cut adrift or isolated). Acknowledging that systems of justice are *intended* to bring the realm of the contingent, including our unruly passions and partial interests, within the fold and limits of impartial reason, we may say that to the extent that they succeed, the contingent, partial, self-interested character of our individual viewpoints is ordered, informed and elevated by the higher unity of the spirit of brotherhood, whereas to the extent that they fail, the contingent and historical (along with our assorted partialities) remain 'merely so' or unaffected by the grace of the law. We should also note here that the fact that, as Niebuhr says, there is 'no impartial perspective upon the whole field of vital interests' of a society in no way excuses us from being guided and motivated by the ideal of impartiality and from acknowledging that 'the impartiality of universal reason', even if it constantly hovers beyond the grasp

---

78. *Ibid*, 261.

of our ever tainted partial reasoning, is nevertheless a crucial regulative ideal in our ethical reflections. We must each do our utmost to discern what the impartiality of universal reason requires of us, personally or collectively, in each situation of personal or social complexity, even as we acknowledge the power of pride and partiality to mar our judgments in these difficult cases and Ratzinger's point that 'reason has a wax nose'. Niebuhr reminds us that such 'rules of justice as we have known in history have been arrived at by a social process in which various perspectives have been synthesised into a more inclusive one'[79] but this would not have been possible unless we as citizens were capable, if not of achieving a 'wholly transcendent' and infallible standpoint, at least of partly transcending (and reflectively appraising 'from a distance') our partiality and pride and also of recognising (admittedly with acute difficulty, for here pride really rebels and deceives) the depth and full extent of our partiality when it is revealed to us by our fellow citizens.

Conclusion

Each human culture and tradition feels the lure of ideal perfection expressed in Jesus' high calling that we must not judge, but must forgive and heal our neighbour; that we must deliver justice, preach the gospel and call for repentance and discipleship; that we should engage in non-violent transforming initiatives to correct existing evils;

---

79. *Ibid*, 262.

and that we should love our enemies, serve one another and pray fervently and often for the coming of the kingdom. Problems arise, however, as soon as an attempt is made to characterise these scripturally based norms in a particular way, as 'universal' for example, as opposed to 'concrete' and 'historical', or as 'formal' as opposed to 'substantive', but if we follow, as I suggest we should, RM Hare in regarding the formal principle of ethics as 'Treat all other human beings with equal dignity and respect',[80] then we will designate the scripturally based norms outlined above not as formal (or merely 'definitional', merely stipulating what in general it means to be ethical, simply outlining a universal form that prescribes no specific, substantive content) but as substantive (requiring, that is, certain sorts of reasonably definite and specific sorts of actions that fall within the formal definitional boundaries and proscribing any actions that clearly breach these boundaries). However, whilst these norms are substantive, as opposed to formal, it would be a profound error, I submit, to designate them as concrete *as opposed to* universal. Though with some reservations, I would describe these norms as universal, substantive and concrete. (Admittedly, as applied to these norms, the term 'substantive' is, I believe, more concise and appropriate than 'concrete', for the latter term, unlike the former, carries, for me at least, the connotation of 'definite action actually required here and now to be done'. My feeling is that the adjective 'concrete' more properly applies not so much to ethical norms *per se* as to 'ethical norms as enacted' or to estab-

---

80. *Moral Thinking* (Oxford: Clarendon Press, Oxford, 1981).

lished ethical practices or customs, but I can also see that there is no great harm, and even some clear advantages, in referring to these norms, as they actually govern the lives of certain communities, as 'concrete'.)

Jesus certainly intended the norms of scripture to be (horizontally) universal, to be listened to with an open heart and accepted by all (and at all times and in all cultures), and so we may regard them as 'ideally universal'; they are, we might say, 'actually universal' within the life of real Christian communities, though no doubt stretching the moral imagination of the members of such communities to the very limit of human (perhaps superhuman) capacity.[81] No doubt, as abstracted from the concrete

---

81. Richard Niebuhr sees this more clearly than any other Christian writer and yet many authors hold, erroneously I believe, that he privileges 'universality' over against particularity, specificity, concreteness and difference. For example, Joseph L Allen ('A Decisive Influence on Protestant Ethics', in *Christianity and Crisis*, 23-25 November 1963, 217) and John C Bennett ('Ethical Principles and the Context', Presidential Address, *Yearbook of the American Society of Christian Social Ethics* 1960–61, 112 ff.) both reflect upon what they see as the puzzling absence of concrete moral principles from his writings and Diane Yeager ('The Social Self in the Pilgrim Church' in *Authentic Transformation: a New Vision of Christ and Culture*, edited by GH Stassen, DM Yeager and JH Yoder [Nashville: Abingdon Press, Nashville, 1996], 97) holds that his writings 'are notably empty of any particular concrete suggestions, beyond the call for a contrite heart, as to how this flawed and aching world might be repaired.' In a similar vein, John Howard Yoder (*Authentic Transformation: a New Vision of Christ and Culture*, edited by GH Stassen, DM Yeager and JH Yoder [Nashville: Abingdon Press, Nashville, 1996], 42) also complains that there is a 'vacuity about moral substance' in Niebuhr's *Christ and Culture* and Elizabeth Bounds ('Why Have We

moral experience of Christian life, these norms will seem to acquire the inert, ethereal 'the same across all time and space' quality of horizontal universality but as concretely integrated into our moral experience as Christians, and when felt as the will of the Father and the inner presence and prompting of the Spirit, these norms are (vertically) universal and 'descend' into our inner world with both ordering and uplifting power and, to use CS Lewis's expression, as 'lords that are certainly expected'. Each culture must respond to the lure of the divine perfection (to the divine criterion) as best it can, by *inter alia* stretching its time-bound 'collective/public reason' to its fullest capacity. Each 'us' (each society and tradition) must make its culture (and especially its inherited prejudices, in Gadamer's sense) an ever more effective prism or medium of the divine (of Being), so that Being—the Spirit of truth working through the concepts and categories historically embedded in our culture and tradition—can in turn find expression in us through the ever inadequate, ever changing, but always indispensable 'prism of culture'. Objec-

---

gathered in This Place?; A Critical Evaluation of Selected Theories of Community', PhD dissertation, Union Theological Seminary, New York, 1993, 100ff) is persuaded that for Niebuhr, '[e]specially in his later writings, the particular historical community became more and more abstract until it seemed to disappear behind a universal society and a universal generalized other, nature and Nature's God.' In a similar vein, Lonnie Kliever (*H Richard Niebuhr* [Waco: Word, 1977], 145–170) holds that the absence of specificity in Niebuhr's ethics was considered to be a serious weakness both by some of his closest followers as well as his sternest critics.

tively and ideally, there exists at all times and places a true and proper relationship between humanity, nature, society and God. However, this is not a timeless or eternal relationship that might be grasped as it truly is by a perceptive human insight in time, but rather a timeless, ideal relationship that constantly draws the actual, historically embedded relationships of each human generation and society into itself. As we shall see in the next chapter, this ideal relationship is not directly knowable or 'cognisable' by the human mind, especially in any 'once and for all' sense, but yet its universal 'ethical presence' ever guides (redemptively informs) the relations actually obtaining throughout history between God, humanity, society and nature. We constantly inhabit the Platonic metaxy, the shadow land; we live in the cave of time but it is a place, not of unrelieved darkness, but of intensifying light. Far from being hermetically sealed off from eternity, the temporal cave is a place where eternity ever makes its presence felt. To use Richard Niebuhr's phrase, 'the eternal is now'.

Chapter Two

Christian Social Ethics

The church never was, in its true character, merely the temple of the city; it was the promise of the city itself.
Oliver O'Donovan, *The Desire of the Nations*, 285

The best contribution of religion is precisely not to be ideologically predictable or loyally partisan.
Jim Wallis, *God's Politics*, xx

And we are witnesses to these things, we and the Holy Spirit whom God has given to those who obey him.
Acts 5: 32

'All pieties to the contrary notwithstanding, it is possible that "Christian social ethics" is an incoherent phase, and because the pieties press upon us so forcefully at present, we have all the more reason to examine this question with care'.[1] This challenging and thought-provoking remark

---

1. DM Yeager, 'The Social Self in the Pilgrim Church' in GH Stassen, DM Yeager, and JH Yoder, *Authentic Transformation: A New Vision of Christ and Culture* (Nashville: Abingdon Press, 1996), 91.

by Diane Yeager puts the issue before us in a very stark and confronting manner. Perhaps the phrase 'Christian social ethics' is no more or no less coherent than 'Christian mathematics' or 'Christian geology' and should thus be abandoned in the interests of clarity of thought. I wish to suggest that the real issue before us here is the *nature* of the relation between the 'universal' and the 'concrete', between universal norms and ethical practice, or between moral principles/ideas and their implementation. I will argue that this relationship is indirect (and non-derivative) rather than direct (and derivative) and that, *as a consequence* the substance of Christian social ethics cannot be definitively and abstractly worked out for all time but must be interpreted by Christ's followers into their unique, complex and ever changing circumstances.

Christian social ethics; principles and practice

We may take Christian social ethics to mean the practical, social, economic and political 'intimations' of, broadly and generally, Christ's injunction to 'love God and neighbour' or, more narrowly and specifically, of Christ's more precise ethical injunctions as revealed in Scripture (feed the poor, turn the other cheek etc) but, whether conceived of broadly or narrowly, the practical intimations are always a matter of interpretation in accordance with prevailing circumstances. This is because the relationship in the moral sphere between universal norms/principles and actual moral judgment or practice is not one of derivation; it is indirect rather than direct, a matter of 'intimation' rather than of strict, logical (direct) deduction, and this is so whether we are thinking of ethical norms/principles in general or of norms/principles that we regard as specifically Christian. The relation between (Christian) moral norms/principles and (Christian) acts/practices is not comparable to the relations of strict deducibility that obtain in logic and mathematics. (All men are mortal; Socrates is a man therefore Societies is mortal). What FH Bradley has to say in the following quotes from his *Ethical Studies* concerning the principle/act relation in morality in general, is just as true of 'Christian morality'.

> I am not forgetting that we act, as a rule, not *from* principle or with the principle before us, and I wish the reader not to forget that the principle may be there and may be our basis or our goal, without our knowing anything about it.[2]

> In practical morality no doubt we *may* reflect on our principles, but I think it is not too much to say that we *never* do so, except where we have come upon a difficulty of particular application. If anyone thinks that a man's *ordinary* judgment, 'this is right or wrong,' comes from the having a rule *before* the mind and bringing the particular case under it, he may be right; and I can not try to show that he is wrong. I can only leave it to the reader

---

2. FH Bradley, 1988, *Ethical Studies* (Oxford: The Clarendon Press, 1988), 69.

> to judge for himself. We say we 'see' and 'feel' in these cases, not we 'conclude'. We prize the advice of persons who can give us no reasons for what they say. There is a general belief that the having a reason for all your actions is pedantic and absurd. There is a general belief that to try to have reasons for all that you do is sometimes very dangerous.[3]

In a similar vein, the fact that Christians in their day-to-day enactment of their beliefs generally do not have their Christian principles consciously and reflectively before their minds at all times means, or at least ideally means, that these principles have become constitutive of their existence and have become deeply interwoven into the fabric of their everyday lives; it certainly does not mean that they are not guided or influenced by them.

Perhaps another way of saying the same thing would be to say that the moment of 'deducibility' comes at the very end of (and is often only a small part of) our moral reflections. More often than not in our ethical life, we are faced with the difficulty of trying to work out which ethical principle more truly, properly and appropriately applies in *this* situation. For example, it often happens that when a loved one appears to be close to death, relatives and medical staff find it difficult to decide in specific cases whether the principle 'Preserve life at all costs' or the principle 'Allow a natural death' properly or appro-

---
3. *Ibid*, 194–195.

priately applies. However, even in the less dramatic and more mundane circumstances of everyday life, we often find ourselves reflecting upon which principle is relevant to a particular situation. As several principles fleet across our minds and we attempt to weigh the claims of each to be relevant to *this* situation, it could be said that our moral judgment is part of a reflective process whereby a particular principle indirectly 'weaves its way', through our thoughts into action in the world. Having thus (circuitously and indirectly) staked and won its claim to be enacted, it may then be (directly) enacted without further ado. Once we have ascertained which principle is relevant, appropriate and 'right' in a particular situation, it is usually just a question of 'applying' it or acting upon it, almost indeed as a matter of simple, deductive logic. (I judge this to be the relevant principle in this situation; it follows, therefore, that I ought to . . .)

One would normally expect those interested in Christian social ethics to be vitally interested in issues such as social justice or third world poverty but Hauerwas believes that these are the very things that *Christian* social ethics should not be concerned with because 'once such questions are made central for determining an agenda for a social ethic, we feel the pull of natural law as an essential feature of Christian ethics'.[4] (1983a, p. 99). To those who believe that 'in matters of social ethics there must

---

4. S Hauerwas, *The Peaceable Kingdom; A Primer in Christian Ethics* (Notre dame, Indiana: Notre dame Press, 1983), 99.

be moral generalities anchored in our social nature that provide the basis for common moral commitment and action',[5] (1983a, p. 99), he replies that 'I am in fact challenging the very idea that Christian social ethics is primarily an attempt to make the world more peaceable or just. Put starkly, the first social ethical task of the church is to be the church –the servant community' (1983a, p. 99). My response to Hauerwas would be to note that the universal ethical principle 'all human beings ought to endeavour to make the world more peaceful and just' is, when thus stated, a 'mere' universal. However, it may be called an 'abstract' or 'bare' universal, *only* in the sense of 'urgently needing to be acted upon in specific, concrete ways' and *not* in the sense of being irrelevant to practice. This call to concrete action is at the same time a call to acknowledge the universal aspect of ethics and it is what lies behind what Hauerwas refers to as the 'pull of natural law'. It is a 'holy' call and, far from being resisted, its life giving intimations should be warmly embraced. Admittedly, it is a call or pull on our common humanity, rather than a specifically Christian call or pull, but it is also a call of the 'Father of all' on our common humanity and it is the Holy Spirit that enables us to respond to it in good faith. We should then, as Christians and not just as ethical human persons, as specifically Christian believers as well as generically human persons, treat this call with the utmost seriousness and reverence. Laying aside Hauerwas' reservations, we must acknowledge the profound 'for-each-otherness' of universal ethics, which expresses

---

5. *Ibid.*

the 'will-for-us-all' of the Father, and Christian (social) ethics, which expresses the 'will-for-us-as-Christians' of his Son. Whilst we should acknowledge that Hauerwas is right to hold that 'as a Christian people there is literally nothing more important that we can do'[6] than to be the people who as Church hear and enact the Gospel of Jesus, this in no way negates the responsibility of Christians to be concerned for the poor, not just as citizens of their society or as members of the Father's human family, but as disciples of Jesus. Christian social ethics sets believers the clear and definite task of discerning or hearing the 'vertical' call (unique but no less 'universal' for being so) of the Father to the society and wider world to which they belong, even if this is a task that they share with all of the Father's family.

Christ provided us with clear cut, concrete norms and Christian social ethics thus provides us with very definite guidelines, but we should not forget that these norms are, as we noted in the last chapter, just as 'universal' as they are 'concrete'; they are 'universal' as reflected upon, and 'concrete' as actually acted upon; they are universal, and even abstract and ethereal, as they fleet across our minds and jostle with each other in their claims for relevance and appropriateness in the particular situations that we confront, but they are each 'concrete' as judged appropriate to the precise circumstances we encounter in a particular case. The fact that 'concrete', used in an ethical sense, connotes 'directly relevant to practice' lulls us into the comforting illusion that moral choice is easier than it

---

6. *Ibid*, 100.

actually is, whereas in fact, all too often, we are at a loss to know *what* (universal/concrete) norm to apply and *when* to apply it. We know, for example, that Christ proclaimed liberty to captives and uncompromisingly condemned the oppression of the poor. The Christian is to help the poor, set them free, and not oppress them. However, what all of this means in practice is not as clear as it is in principle. What, for example, are we as Christians, or as 'holy citizens', supposed to do or say when a government in a rich, industrial western society proposes to make welfare payments to the poor conditional, that is, to insist that the rights of welfare recipients are conditional upon the fulfilment on their part of their responsibilities towards society. In Australia, the fact that the unemployed have been required to show evidence of having searched long and hard for a job, to attend periodic interviews and to meet other requirements as a condition of receiving unemployment benefits, has been interpreted by some as punishing the poor, as blaming the victims of poverty instead of really helping them, but by others as liberating the poor from dependency upon the state, as opening the door to freedom, dignity and independence. Clearly, the issue of how the poor can best be helped and how their liberty and independence can best be enhanced is one that requires our careful and discriminating attention but the difficult challenges we face in such cases are caused, it must be remembered, not by the absence of concrete (and universal) Christological norms but by their very forceful and 'competitive/cajoling' presence in our minds.

Church and society

We may further develop our understanding of Christian social ethics by considering Niebuhr's reflections on the kind of relation that in his view should ideally obtain between the church and society. In his essay 'The Attack upon the Social Gospel'[7] he distinguishes between (i) the goals and objectives of the church (Is, for example, the wellbeing of society as well as spiritual wellbeing of the individual, a proper object of Christianity's mission?) and (ii) the strategies or means used to secure them. Concerning the former (goals and objectives), he holds that persons stand directly and individually before their God and that the church's concern for the spiritual wellbeing and salvation of individuals will always be a crucially important concern. However, he rightly maintains that the issue of social salvation is, or should be, just as important for us today as it has been in the history of the Jewish people. Concerning the latter (strategies or means), he distinguishes between the direct and indirect means available to the church in pursuing its social objectives ('social salvation'). What he calls a religiously direct strategy is one that the church can pursue without reference to or without the assistance of mediating agents or institutions. If the church's efforts to bring about social justice and alleviate human misery are to be truly Christian and truly effective and transformative, it must make its own direct analysis of the problems that loom large in the so-

---

7. HR Niebuhr, 'The Attack upon the Social Gospel', in *Religion in Life*, 5/2 (1936): 176–181.

cial landscape and 'spiritually diagnose' these problems in terms of false faith and pervasive idolatry. Niebuhr is convinced that, in the final analysis, social problems are the effect of social sin, which in turn is due to the fact that the citizen body has falsely idolised or absolutised something other than the true absolute, that is, God, and so the church, pursuing 'the social equivalent of the evangelical strategy'[8] must prophetically call for society to repent. Holding that the life of the body politic can be just as infected by false faith and idolatry as the life of the individual, he is clear that in both cases repentance is a precondition to the 'born again' experience that transforms or, as he put it in an earlier work, '[t]he road to unity is the road to repentance'.[9] 'Men', he holds, 'will be ready for no radically new life until they have really become aware of the falsity of the faith upon which their old life is based'.[10] (1936, p. 180). Niebuhr's fondness for this strategy is due to the fact that it duly acknowledges and takes properly (for Christians) into account 'the priority of God—not as a human ideal, or the object of worship, but as the moving force in history—who alone brings in His kingdom and to whose ways the party of the Kingdom of God on earth must adjust itself'.[11] For Niebuhr, the direct or, one could almost say, the 'paradigmatic' role of the Church in pursuing its social mission (social salvation) is to seek 'the

---

8. *Ibid*, 181.
9. HR Niebuhr, *The Social Sources of Denominationalism* (New YorK: Meridian Books, 1929), 284.
10. HR Niebuhr, 'The Attack upon the Social Gospel', 180.
11. *Ibid*, 181.

adjustment of human ways to the way of God as revealed in Jesus Christ'.[12]

In his 'The Responsibility of the Church for Society' Niebuhr specifies three crucial functions of the Christian community. Firstly, it is the apostolic function of the church 'to proclaim to the great human societies, with all the persuasiveness and imagination at its disposal, with all the skill it has in becoming all things to all men, that the centre and heart of things, the first and last Being, is utter Goodness, complete love';[13] as part of this role, it must preach the necessity of social repentance. Secondly, it is the pastoral function of the church to 'take an interest in political and economic measures or institutions'[14] because of their impact in the lives of individuals; 'if the individual sheep is to be protected, the flock must be guarded'[15] and so, in fulfilment of its pastoral function, Niebuhr proceeds to endorse the religiously indirect strategy of supporting 'all those measures of large–scale relief and liberation which the times call for'.[16] Finally, it is the pioneering function of the church to be 'that part of the human community which responds first to God-in-Christ and Christ-in-God';[17] by its right response to Christ, it should model the kind of response that the whole com-

---

12. *Ibid.*
13. HR Niebuhr, 'The Responsibility of the Church for Society', in *The Gospel, the Church and the World*, edited by KS Latourette, Interseminary Series, book 3 (New York: Harper, 1946), 127.
14. *Ibid*, 129.
15. *Ibid*, 129.
16. *Ibid.*
17. *Ibid*, 130.

munity should adopt. The church is to be a representative of the larger culture and society, of which it forms an integral part, and it is to lead the community spiritually by first discerning God's will for it; it is the first 'to obey Him when it becomes aware of a new aspect of His will'.[18] Two key questions that arise from Niebuhr's analysis are: (i) Does the church have the kind of pioneering role that he ascribes to it and how we are to understand this role and (ii) Is the identification of false faith and idolatry as root causes of social problems the exclusive, unique and distinctive function of the church, that is, is it a hallmark only of Christian social analysis?   In order to answer the first question I believe that it is important, as a preliminary move, to reflect briefly upon the social and political significance of the distinction within the ethical realm between the 'right' and the 'good'.

The familiar distinction between the 'right/just' and the 'good', I wish to maintain, provides us with a principle that enables us to distinguish between proper and improper realms of Church involvement in the social and political arena. This distinction has of course been discussed at great length,[19] but for our present purposes it will be sufficient to point out that in the ethical consciousness the 'right/just' ('right' used in the sense of 'just') primarily consists in our *recognition* of the value of persons, whereas the 'good' consists mainly in our endeavours

---

18. *Ibid*, 131.
19. See, for example, BT Trainor, *Justice and the State: On Liberal Organicism and the Foundations of Emancipatory Politics* (Quebec: World Heritage Press, 1998), 25–31.

to *realise* values, more precisely, to realise absolute value through the prism of the familiar, and relative, human values. (By 'absolute' and 'relative' what I have in mind is a distinction between that which is absolutely valuable or good and that which is good in its place or of value only under, or relative to, certain circumstances. For example, we regard love or loving oneself and others as good unconditionally and without qualification, whereas we regard friendship, or the spending of time with a friend, as good in its place and, correspondingly, as bad when over indulged.) When acting justly or when considering the requirements of justice, our primary concern is to act in conformity with our recognition or acknowledgement of the absolute value of persons as spiritual beings and children of God. Where matters of justice are concerned, then, it is a question of *recognising* or acknowledging each person, born or unborn, as a distinctive centre of consciousness and of 'spiritual initiative' in the universe and the church has every right to speak its mind, whereas when it is a (mainly political) matter of *realising* value, in the form of the 'common good', the church needs to be considerably more cautious and more prone to silence (non-involvement), for whilst church members would assuredly agree on political objectives when pitched at a sufficiently high level of generality (helping the poor, liberating the oppressed, etc), they are liable to diverge in liberal, conservative and socialist directions as soon as concrete policy measures are proposed to achieve such objectives and to realise the common good in a concrete sense.

Certainly, then, an important implication of the distinction between the right and the good in the ethical realm (or at least of the understanding thereof here proposed) is that the role of the church in social and political affairs must be largely confined to the realm of 'right' (justice) and that the church, *as church*, does not have a significant role to play in the realm of 'the good' (the common good). In the latter realm, Christians, as individuals, have a significant role to play, but if the official, institutional church attempts to exert an influence in this realm, the effects are likely to be unfortunate, counter productive and even positively harmful and 'scandalous'. Consider, for example, the case mentioned earlier of whether or not a proposal to introduce conditional welfare payments (such as forcing the unemployed to work in order to receive government financial support) helps or hinders, liberates or represses, the poor. What precisely is in the 'common good' or 'public interest' in such a case is extremely difficult to determine and judgments, even when made in good faith, are still liable to diverge. We are dealing here, after all, with a delicate political version of von Balthasar's 'perichoresis of the transcendentals' (not just truth, beauty and goodness, but dignity, liberty, independence and equality) so that Christians will inevitably find themselves on opposite sides of the debate on this issue. However, their disagreement with each other should be as individual citizens rather than as Christians. In such delicate—and quite typical—cases where what the common good requires is complex and extremely difficult to discern, and where Christians, along with their fellow citizens, are liable to diverge in their political judgments, the church as an institution should refrain from taking an 'official' position; it is simply not its proper role to do so. If

God had ordered the world in such a way that one could easily, straightforwardly, directly and 'deductively' apply biblically based norms to each and every situation, then it might, perhaps, have been a proper role of the church to take a positron on such issues, but God, I would suggest, has so ordered the world that such fine and intricate decisions as to what constitutes the public interest need to be made by citizens or voters, by Christians as citizens and voters, and by governments formally endowed with the requisite authority to execute their clear responsibilities in such matters. The church, in passing 'official' judgment in such cases, would clearly be going beyond its proper role and function.

The Invisible Community of Holy Citizens

Turning now directly to the question raised by Niebuhr's analysis (Does the church have the kind of pioneering role that he ascribes to it and how we are to understand this role?) I wish to suggest that what Niebuhr refers to as the pioneering function of the church could be just as appropriately referred to (indeed, in certain respects, could be *more* appropriately referred to) as the pioneering function of 'the invisible community of holy citizens', by which I mean the body of citizens in whom the public spirit dwells. This is because, as Harlan Beckley points out, neither the church nor any other collective agent is 'a force for redemption in which divine justice is fully immanent'.[20] Likewise, I would suggest that when Barth holds in a similar vein (i) that '[t]he light which falls from the heavenly polis upon the earthly ecclesia is reflected in the light which illuminates the earthly polis from the earthly ecclesia, through their mutual relation'[21](1968, p. 135), and when he holds (ii) that whenever the state acts against its true nature, the church 'through its intercession . . . represents the only possibility of restoring the state and saving it from ruin',[22] (1968, p. 140), the kind of pioneering function that he here ascribes to the Church could, rather, be more appropriately regarded as the pioneering function of this same 'invisible community of holy citizens'. Thus, whilst it is certainly a function of the church, rather than of this invisible holy community, to seek 'the adjustment of human ways to the way of God as revealed in Jesus Christ',[23] yet it is also the responsibility of Christian members of this body, working co-operatively with its non-Christian members as fellow citizens, towards this same goal, but there is no guarantee that they will reach agreement (either with one another as Christians or with one another as fellow citizens), and it is certainly better for them to disagree as citizens doing their best (along with their fellow citizens as members of

---

20. H Beckley, Passion for justice: Retrieving the Legacies of Walter Rauschenbusch, John A Ryan and Reinhold Neibuhr (Louisville: Westminster/John Knox Press, 1992), 381.
21. Barth, K 1968 *Community, State and Church: Three Essays*, (Glouchester, Mass: Peter Smith, Gloucester, 1968), 135.
22. *Ibid*, 140.
23. HR Niebuhr, 'The Attack upon the Social Gospel', 181.

the body of holy citizens) to exercise their all too human (and all too fallible) judgments in complex socio-political affairs, rather than as Christians who claim to have some kind of special, infallible insight into God's plans for humanity.

The citizens of a political community, in so far as they are open to and motivated by its public spirit and are concerned for its common wellbeing, call upon a 'common grace' and are a 'holy community'. O'Donovan is, I believe, thinking along the same lines when, reflecting on 1 Peter 2:13–17, he holds that the institution of secular government 'belongs to humankind as such, so that the common grace of God, rather than his saving purposes, forms the foundation of secular authority.[24] We are inclined, I believe, to use the term 'public spirit' too casually and unreflectively, not recognizing, as we should, that it is not only a holy spirit but a manifestation (an angelic presence) within a particular political community of *the* Holy Spirit immanent in all of creation but especially in our most unselfish and community-minded pursuits. Moreover, this (public) spirit is present in the minds and hearts of citizens in their disagreements as well as their agreements, perhaps indeed *more so* in their disagreements than their agreements. This is so for all citizens, though we may hope that Christians will exhibit the humanity of their Lord in an exemplary manner through listening intently and empathically to their political opponents and

---

24. O O'Donovan, 2003, *The Desire of the Nations; Rediscovering the Roots of Political Theology* (Cambridge: Cambridge University Press, 2003), 149.

in acknowledging the strengths as well as the weaknesses of their arguments. In this way the Spirit of Truth will be present between them and those with whom they disagree, and the Spirit will be empowered to move—'to find its own way,' to use Niebuhr's expression[25]—*through* the process of discussion and dialectical interchange. All of those concerned with the handling of temporal affairs in a Godly manner, 'whether or not the consciousness of grace becomes explicit',[26] are guided by the 'spirit of truth' and, in their empathic openness to each other, allow (anonymously or non-anonymously) the Absolute to flow into the socio-political realm and enable love and mutual understanding to become 'an "emergent", a potentiality in our situation which remains unrealised so long as we try to impose our pattern, our wishes, upon the divine creative process'.[27] To be under the influence of the Spirit in this way is not, we need to remember, the privileged monopoly of Christians. We must accept then, I believe, that the Church as such should not play an ongoing, routine role in publicly discerning the common good and should be cautious and circumspect about offering its judgment on the day-to-day affairs of government, but this diminished role for the church in the 'realm of the good' (or at least its diminished role in determining the day-to-day political good) is counterbalanced by its importance and,

---

25. HR Niebuhr, 'Faith, Works and Social Salvation', in *Religion in Life*, 1 (1932): 429.
26. HR Niebuhr, *The Purpose of the Church and its Ministry* (New York: Harper, 1956), 26.
27. HR Niebuhr, 'The Only Way into the Kingdom of God', in *Christian Century*, 49, (1932): 447.

ideally, its centrality (i) in forming, sustaining, elevating, developing and re-invigorating the public spirit (in being a light to its nation in a broad generic sense) and (ii) in the 'realm of right/justice'.

It is mainly in this realm (of right/justice) that the church needs to exercise the kind of apostolic, pastoral and pioneering functions ascribed to it by Niebuhr. In matters of justice/right, a religiously direct strategy is both possible and highly desirable. Our churches should, I believe, form a Christian coalition calling upon our western societies, as an urgent matter of justice, to acknowledge our collective social sin in allowing the liberty and respect due to the individual to degenerate into license and exploitation, in allowing the trade in pornography to diminish our respect for each other as sexual beings, in legally permitting the death of countless aborted babies (Every abortion stops a tiny, innocent heart beating), in failing to guarantee the right of children to be raised by their own, two natural parents. If the conventional evangelical strategy is the call to individual conversion through repentance (Repent and believe the Gospel), then a political platform of this kind, oriented to justice in its deepest divine sense, would constitute in our time 'the social equivalent of the evangelical strategy' of which Niebuhr speak. This platform rests upon a truth or 'knowing' deeply embedded in the religious consciousness but apparently fading from the wider social consciousness, namely awareness that each individual without exception possesses absolute significance as a child of God from the moment of conception to the point of death. Where, in a particular social situation, the question can be meaningfully, convincingly or plausibly posed 'Is it *right* for a child of God to be treated in this way?', then the church, as church, has a crucial social role to play and a sacred obligation to raise its voice in the public sphere.

The church claims to 'know deeply', to be a light to the nations and defender of justice, because as the bride of Christ, it represents the One who, by right, rules the entire universe, who is the true Lord of the political. What makes the visible church, in truth (and despite its empirical sinfulness), the bride of Christ, (and as a result the representative of God's truth for each society), is *its being so in the eyes of Christ*; this means that the church ever has the task of bridging the gap between 'ought' and 'is', between what it ultimately and truly (ontologically) is and what it empirically is, so that it may, at last, become empirically what it is in (its) truth. It is not just that Christ sees what the church 'can be'; rather, it is his very 'seeing' (his Word upon us that yearns to achieve its purpose in us) that draws the visible sinful church ever closer to what it is in truth, so that the church (or each church) in turn can draw its socio-political universe closer to what it is in truth. This is the divinely ordained political role of the church as God's holy people, as those who worship Jesus and rely upon his grace. However, there is another sense of 'God's holy people' that we need to take into account, that is, 'God's holy people' as the invisible holy community of which we have just spoken, for the universal love of the Father also draws sinful humanity as a whole ever closer to what it is in truth, to the 'holy destiny' of which its heart is always more or less aware, and the movement of humanity towards that holy destiny and divine calling (the response, however large or small, of each human heart to it) is also a movement of God's holy people. The 'political' is thus a realm in which 'God's holy people' operates in two senses and in two 'sanctuaries'. However, this means that the church, as well as being a light to the nations and drawing humanity into itself, into its heart (Christ), must also allow itself in humility and trust to be drawn into the 'holy' heart of humanity (the Spirit, the Father) so that *all* of God's people may at last be openly and visibly seen as the Father sees them, as 'one and holy', so that it may become a transparent fact rather than an ideal principle of distinction that 'a king [secular authority] bears the image of God, a bishop [the church] the image of Christ', and so that God may at last be openly seen as All-in-all.

In the meantime, in a practical, mundane political sense, we are left with the problem of distinguishing the proper role of the church from the proper role of this invisible holy community. Certainly, we are often dealing here with a matter of degree and of difficult and delicate judgement, for it is often unclear in particular cases where the dividing line lies between (i) the church's legitimate concern for issues of justice and for the spiritual tone of society, and (ii) an improper concern (bordering on 'interference') on the part of the church with the day-to-day business of governments attempting to deal with complex, finely balanced issues (compulsory work for the dole, etc) without being burdened by high-sounding pontifical pronouncements from church representatives that fail to take properly into account the details and complexities of the political cases in question.

False faith and fanaticism

Concerning the second question that arises from Niebuhr's account (is the identification of false faith and idolatry as root causes of social problems the exclusive, unique and distinctive function of the church?), I wish to suggest that the identification of false faith and idolatry as the root causes of our social ills is an important, even necessary, function of the church but not its exclusive function, and that it is a core, integral element, but not a distinctive hallmark of Christian social analysis. This is because the latter (or at least Christian social analysis of the type commended by Niebuhr) is characterised by its strong opposition to extreme and eschatologically oriented forms of radicalism and thus it has a lot in common with conservatism and postmodernism, both of which oppose, even if for quite different reasons, the kind of penchant for absolutisation (the secular equivalent of Niebuhr's 'idolatry') and for 'grand' theorizing exhibited by radicalism. For Niebuhr and, I would hope for Christians generally, both the ideal and practical task of each and every human society is at all times and places precisely the same, namely to move 'nearer my God to Thee'. Christians are interested in bringing about real social progress and in making the world a better place than they found it, but Niebuhr is careful to distinguish this kind of meliorism, or 'elevation drawn from above', from (historical) progress as understood by the radical eschatologists of Marxism and Fascism and, we could add today, of radical Feminism and radical right Liberalism. Niebuhr's expression 'lifting up' or 'elevating' (I would add 'ascending') helps us to grasp the difference between the two. As Christians, in all we say and do, we hope to rise 'nearer my God to Thee'; it's as if, in our experience, the 'descending deontology' of the law and the prophets facilitates our ever fuller integration (our elevation or ascension) into the divine life of Christ. We are drawn from above; eternity has descended into time that we might ascend into eternity. The 'end', so to speak, is ever (vertically) above us, whereas for radicalism it is always (horizontally) ahead of us, ever receding before us into a Utopian future. The Christian believes that, through God's grace and redeeming power, everything will be drawn together in unity in eternity; the radical (Marxist, Feminist, Nazi, etc) believes that, through the destruction of insidious forms of social/national restraint (capitalism/ the 'bourgeois' family, sexism/the 'patriarchal' family, the sinister world wide web spun by international Jewry), everything will come together in time (in Communism, an androgynous Utopia, the Third Reich etc) when every form of oppression will pass away and a new, ideal world will emerge. The Christian life is one of rising, falling, and of being lifted up and redirected when we fall; the radical's life is one of progress in the sense of steadfast movement, generally through historically determined stages, along the plane of time to a culminating point of perfection when Utopia dawns. The Christian recognizes God-in-Christ as the absolute, as the ultimate source of all value, of all that is good; the radical absolutises a single value and wrecks untold havoc in so doing. As the Nazi absolutises the good of the nation and the brave new world order that he dreams of ushering into existence, he demonizes those deemed to be undermining the new world about to be born and proceeds, equipped with the armour of righteousness, to exterminate them. As the Marxist absolutises equality and struggles to bring about a new Communist world order, he demonizes all counter revolutionaries devoted to liberty and free enterprise and proceeds to exterminate them (the Kulaks).

Now what I have called 'false absolutisation' and fanaticism, Niebuhr would call 'false faith' and idolatry. He is right, I believe, to hold that sound Christian social analysis must employ concepts and categories of this kind to diagnose the ills of society and the fiercely attractive intellectual temptation (the 'glamour of evil') to which the mind of the extreme radical is particularly prone. However, whilst eschewing the kind of religious language I have used to articulate what I would regard as the 'basics' of Christian social analysis, and preferring, I would expect, to use my more secular terminology rather than Niebuhr's more explicitly religious language, advocates of conservatism and postmodernism would strongly agree with these fundamentals of Christian social analysis, so that, though integral to a Christian outlook upon society, yet they are still not distinctively or uniquely Christian.

For Niebuhr, to realise the Kingdom, both in oneself and in the world, is a matter of conversion, of turning away from sin and towards God's goodness. All regeneration, whether personal or social, is ultimately spiritual; it is the work or accomplishment of the Spirit operating in and through us. Niebuhr is not interested in a new law but in a new, or renewed spirit. Similarly, it is not, for him, the role of the Christian to promote a new order or a distinctive moral and political agenda but rather to 'elevate' the values, institutions and practices already operative in the community or, rather, to see them in the divine light which reveals them as they truly are. God, the origin of all, draws all to himself as the final end of all, and reveals to us, caught between 'source' and 'summit', the harmony (the 'nisus' or 'will' to integrative unity) operating though all things. We live in a world in which God, the source of value and truth, draws every truly lived human value and all the finest accomplishments of the human spirit into their final home or resting place in the bosom of the Father. Ever caught up in this spiral, our task is to realise the good (absolute value) through the prism of our relative human values. It is to draw the existing values and practices of our society towards their final good in God. Our task is to be both wholesome and holy. It is to bathe time in the light of eternity or, to use Niebuhr's expression, it is to generate a 'holy worldliness'.[28]

Separation or Political Engagement: Scriven and Hauerwas

At this point we need to consider how the broad (Niebuhrian) understanding of Christian social ethics that we have outlined so far in this chapter is able to withstand the kind of criticism directed against it by Stanley Hauerwas and Charles Scriven. To begin with, the latter (Scriven) has argued that the current society and its idolatrous practices is not amenable to 'transformation from within', since such an effort to convert could only end in defeat

---

28. HR Niebuhr, 1944, 'Towards a New Otherworldliness', in *Theology Today* 1/1 (1944): 81.

and capitulation. Scriven argues that Niebuhr's rejection of Anabaptist separatism was ill-founded, for far from being a turning away from the sinful realm of culture and politics, the Anabaptist strategy involved, rather, a profound act of political engagement:

> Anabaptist witness addressed social and political structures as well as individuals. It spoke judgment upon rulers and institutions while upholding an alternative form of social life as a way of changing the world. This was a form of political engagement. Anabaptists believed that the Bible requires such engagement, and I am saying they were right.[29]

Diane Yeagher describes the disagreement between Niebuhr and Scriven in the following way:

> Scriven reads the relationship of the Christian community to that of culture as fundamentally antagonistic; it is the mission of the church to identify false value and evil behaviors and to substitute true values and right behaviors in their place, creating an alternative social space in which the good may flourish. This program of substitution is, in Niebuhr's view, antithetical to conversion. Conversion has as its model redemption by incarnation; by

---

29. C Scriven, 1988, *The Transformation of Culture* (Scottdale: Herald, 1988), 170.

patiently entering into the world as it is and
by bringing out its potential for the good, we
heal it of its corruption.[30]

I believe that the 'Anabaptist witness' is in truth a very profound 'form of political engagement' but for it to really be so, for it to present a constant challenge to the wider society and draw it (vertically) closer to Christ, it must be in a strong tension-filled relationship to that wider society, separate from it physically but united to it spiritually by the disturbing truth of the opposing ideal it proclaims and lives out. However, if it is to speak Christ's truth to the wider society, surely the Anabaptist witness must not disparage whatever fragments of truth are already there. I am not saying that this kind of disparagement is actually or automatically a part of the Anabaptist witness; far from it, but the way in which Scriven presents his radical separationist strategy makes it extremely difficult to focus on whatever good there may be in society and culture. There is, for Scriven, a major clash between Christ and culture, between the *true* values of the Church and the *false* values in society and the world, but he regards this as matter of *a priori* conviction rather than as a matter of discriminating empirical judgment in each particular case. His approach is far too close to the radical tendency to see the current institutional and cultural order as irredeemably infected with 'false' or even 'evil' values (for example, the capitalist value of liberty or the sexist value of male authority) and hence as needing to be replaced, through a

---

30. D M Yeager, 'The Social Self in the Pilgrim Church', 102.

revolutionary transformation, by a new order permeated by 'true' values (equality, co-operation, androgynous humanity etc). This 'horizontal' substitution of 'repressive falsity' by 'liberating truth' contrasts with Niebuhr's 'vertical elevation' of existing values by seeing them in relation to their source in the mind, heart and will of God, and it is, I believe, this 'vertical elevation' which is the key feature and crowning glory of the Anabaptist witness.

Turning now to Stanley Hauerwas; we earlier noted his challenge to 'the very idea that Christian social ethics is primarily an attempt to make the world more peaceable or just'[31] and his view that Christians, as such, should not bring their faith to bear when reflecting, as citizens, on social and political issues. However, by distinguishing between two senses of 'God's holy people', by distinguishing between the Christian church on the one hand and Christians as citizens on the other, and by clarifying the distinctive roles of each as we have attempted to do in this chapter, we are able to take issue with his view that the faith of Christians should be 'publicly silent' in the way he suggests, whilst agreeing that the Christian churches have at times been too ready and too quick to embrace the day-to-day 'problems of Constantine' as their own and to make 'authoritative' judgements on those problems that have been entirely inappropriate, unhelpful and counterproductive. Christians, as citizens, assuredly should, *pace* Hauerwas's insistence to the contrary, face up to the 'Constantinian question' of how power can be used in an ethically and socially responsible

---

31. S Hauerwas, *The Peaceable Kingdom; A Primer in Christian Ethics*, 99.

manner for the good of all but the same does not hold true for the Church which, whilst it has a responsibility to draw public attention to the ways of God and to ensure as far as possible that the public spirit is a holy spirit, must at the same time keep a respectful distance from matters requiring complex and finely balanced political judgements (for example a hard choice between two sound political goods). Too often pastors undermine the unity of their own congregations by attempting to formulate a 'church' position on social and political issues concerning which there is legitimate disagreement among Church members and when official church leaders do the same with very public pronouncements on such issues, serious damage may be done to the unity of the body of Christ as a whole.

Hauerwas believes that instead of focusing on Jesus as Lord and Saviour and proclaiming the specific truth claims of the faith, modern mainline Christianity has sought to accommodate itself to an increasingly secular culture, and especially to the leading intellectual ideas of the time. He holds that theologians and religious thinkers have been anxious to show that 'the modes of argument and conclusions reached by philosophical ethicists are no different from those reached by ethicists working with more explicit religious presuppositions' and that therefore the 'task of Christian ethics, both socially and philosophically, was not revision but accommodation'.[32] The difficulty with the whole enterprise of translating religious truth into a non-theological idiom, so enthusi-

---

32. *Ibid*, 31.

astically entered into by modern mainline theologians, is that 'once such a translation is accomplished, it becomes very unclear why they need the theological idiom in the first place'.[33] Paradoxically, he points out, the attempt of modern theologians to make Christian theology relevant to the modern world, and especially to the concerns of the modern academy, has merely reinforced the conviction of secular academics that theology has nothing of its own to say and can be simply ignored. He summarises as follows;

> 'The more theologians seek to find the means to translate theological convictions into terms acceptable to the non-believer, the more they substantiate the view that theology has little of importance to say in the area of ethics'.[34]

His response to this predicament is to say that modern Christianity must at last give up its obsessive attempt to find common ground with contemporary secular culture and intellectual trends and acknowledge that it is a mistake for Christians to try to turn their faith into a civil religion.

My personal response to Hauerwas would be as follows. It is of course unacceptable to attempt to make Christianity a civil religion if by this is meant the universal imposition of our faith on all citizens in a particular

---

33. *Ibid*, 30.
34. *Ibid*, 31–32.

jurisdiction, but that is not to say that we should not attempt to sustain and/or create a *'civic* religion or culture', meaning by 'civic religion' a set of commonly held tenets which bind together (*religio*) all citizens in such a way that social unity (society) is possible; every citizen should, indeed, constantly endeavour to sustain and/or create a 'civic religion' (less contentiously, a set of beliefs and values to which all citizens should subscribe). As a citizen, I have a responsibility to contribute to the ongoing task of sustaining or of creating (or recreating) a 'civic religion' in this less contentious sense but this means integrating my Christian faith into my civil and political practice in a particular way; it means that when I express my Christ-based views on abortion, euthanasia, divorce, gay marriage, etc, I must do so in such a way as to establish as many points of commonality with my fellow citizens as possible. I must do so with the purpose and hope that by entering into public debate and offering public/universal reasons for my position I will ultimately contribute to the emergence of a broad, ideal consensus on these issues. Certainly, my theological convictions (my faith) are important to me and I believe that the more I am able 'to find the means to translate theological convictions into terms acceptable to the non-believer', the better.

Hauerwas takes exception to the attempt to link our faith and theological convictions to what he sees as non-Christian philosophical and social perspectives which denature them, but if we take socialism as an example of the kind of socio-political perspective he has in mind, we can readily see that a political perspective of this kind is neither 'Christian' nor 'non-Christian' but might be more aptly (and certainly less sinisterly) described as 'a-Christian'; that is, it is a possible socio-political perspective which Christians might, or might not, choose to adopt, in whole or in part, under particular circumstances. When on a particular occasion socialism (or liberalism, or . . .) does indeed seem to resonate with their faith, or to flow from their faith into the form of a 'political disposition for our time', this sense of resonance (of eternity flowing through faith into time) will no doubt induce them to seek common cause with non-religiously inspired socialists, but all of this will surely *confirm* their theological convictions and their relevance, rather than providing a reason for abandoning them as redundant. When Christians interpret the gospel into their own life and times, they are in fact implicitly developing their own 'practical theology' and too much should not be read into any 'points of contact' that are thereby established with secular political ideologies. For a non-Christian socialist to say to his Christian socialist friend 'Your Christianity is redundant! Why not simply be a socialist?' would be to fail to grasp that, whilst they both share a common concern for the poor, the Christian also has a concern for 'Christ-in-the-poor' or for the 'face of Jesus' in each poverty-stricken, marginalised person. For Christians, the practical 'theological task' is to recognise and serve Christ in others and the test of the soundness of one's 'in the world' theological convictions is always this 'sight test' or 'recognition test', the challenge of 'seeing' the truth of Christ's presence in others and acting accordingly. Now, under certain circumstances, this may involve adopting a broadly socialist political strategy (one's 'being a socialist' in at least a temporary sense) but under other circumstances (or for others confronting the same circumstances but persuaded that a different political strategy is required), this may involve adopting a broadly liberal or conservative political strategy (one's 'being a liberal' or 'being a conservative' in at least a temporary sense). A preferential concern for the poor certainly has a strong scriptural warrant but so too does a concern for human freedom and autonomy, for the dignity and rights of the individual, for the requirements of social order and stability, etc. Only by conscientiously applying this test (the 'sight test' or' recognition test') in a properly self-critical and 'self-sceptical' spirit can we hope to avoid the illicit pursuit of our own ends on the pretext of serving others or the illicit promotion of the advantage of one social class (one's own or one's 'adopted' class) at the expense of another. This 'good faith' test is all that we have.

The position I have adopted here could be broadly described as 'Rahnerian' and it has been strongly criticised by John Milbank, who holds that Rahner and those sympathetic to his version of 'integralism', regard the 'social' as an 'autonomous sphere which does not need to turn to theology for its self understanding'.[35] Milbank, we need to note, is just as favourable as Rahner to Vatican Two's embrace of what has been called the 'integralist revolution', which means, as he says:

---

35. J Milbank, *Theology and Social Theory: Beyond Secular Reason*, (Oxford: Blackwell, 1995), 208.

> the view that in concrete historical humanity there is no such thing as a state of 'pure nature': rather, every person has always already been worked upon by divine grace, with the consequence that one cannot analytically separate 'natural' and 'supernatural' contributions to this integral unity.[36]

However, he holds that, as employed by Rahnerian integralists, theological beliefs 'tend to become but a faint regulative gloss upon Kantian ethics and a somewhat eclectic, though basically Marxist, social theory'.[37] To this I would reply that the 'social' properly enjoys autonomy in its own sphere (up to a point, Yves Congar's 'distinction of planes' between ecclesial-clerical and lay-secular types of action is analytically sound and appropriate) but at the same time its autonomy is penultimate and relative (i) in the sense that it is conditional upon exhibiting a proper respect for widely accepted notions of justice, for the natural law of societies and nations (for God's law in the case of Christians and theists) and (ii) in the sense that it must acknowledge that the legitimating origin and end of the secular is the sacred, that the 'rule' of the secular authority is under the 'reign' of the good (and of 'God as the good'). We may perhaps summarise by saying that the secular (the 'social') is penultimately rather than ultimately autonomous, or relatively but not absolutely autonomous. Thus, using Gelasian terminology, even

---

36. *Ibid*, 206.
37. *Ibid*, 208.

though the institutional human church has no *auctoritas*, yet being ever oriented to God, and as an institutional sign of the sacred (the font of *auctoritas*) in the midst of the secular, it rightly exercises a special influence on the executive *potestas* of the *imperium*, of whose origin and end it is a constant reminder. Likewise, (i) every Christian (in full awareness) and every citizen (in full awareness or anonymously) is to be a living, personal sign of the sacred in the midst of the secular and (ii) every Christian ruler or politician (in full awareness) and every government official (in full awareness or anonymously) is to be an earthly representative that bears the *auctoritas* that truly belongs to the sacred into the midst of the secular. Now, the unceasing 'flow' of the sacred into the 'secular' does not simply take place through the medium of the institutional church or religiously inspired socio-political acts of believers but through political institutions ordained by God and by the Spirit-directed acts of all men of good will. Thus, what Milbank, in my view, fails to understand is that there are times when what he calls a 'true theology of the political' largely coincides in practical or 'action' terms with a 'true or sound ethico-theoretical analysis of the political'. Theology always has its own 'transcendental reasons', but where they fortuitously coincide with the 'immanent reasons' of the political, there is no cause for embarrassment, alarm or concern that a 'true theology of the political' is being sacrificed.

Milbank holds that the French version of integralism (Blondel, de Lubac) properly 'recognises the always finitely mediated character of participation in the supernatural',[38] whereas the German Rahnerian version fails to do so. This is because he holds, erroneously in my view, that there is an incompatibility between what he terms Blondel's 'supernatural pragmatism' and Rahner's 'foundational *praxis*'.[39] Even what is foundational (natural law, reason, 'constants' of human nature) must be differentially expressed in or 'differenced' into each culture and always has a distinctive historical colouring. Moreover, it is questionable whether Blondel does indeed propose a truly Copernican, de-centred universe. Whilst there is without doubt a strong existential and postmodern 'feel' about Blondel's work, it does not anticipate in any way the deliberately de-centering work of Foucault, for whom the 'universal' almost appears at times to be anathema, thereby allowing the 'de-centred particular' and the 'de-universalised difference' to dominate and distort his intellectual landscape. Milbank himself points out that 'like Hegel, Blondel associates the metaphysical moment, the acknowledgement of an infinite ground for finite reality . . . with a concrete act of expression whose power of interpreting the rest of finitude discloses to us the "universal"'[40] but this 'universal' is not without what we might call a 'centering' or integrating effect. Likewise, the new perspective or creative synthesis of each finite act is ultimately grounded in the (one and the same and hence, in a sense, 'centripetal') infinite. Blondel's version of historicism, it is not important to note, is not a recipe

---

38. *Ibid*, 209.
39. *Ibid*, 209.
40. *Ibid*, 212.

for 'centrifugal' chaos, for as each single, unique intellect confronts in its actions the infinite power of illumination outside itself, it is drawn in harmony towards every other intellect.[41]

If Hauerwas and Milbank takes exception, mistakenly in my estimation, to the attempt to link our faith and theological convictions to what they see as non-Christian philosophical and social perspectives which de-nature them, O'Donovan takes exception to the attempt to sunder our faith and theological convictions from our political commitments. He rightly holds that there is a clear scriptural mandate for the 'preferential concern' of Christians for the poor and that Christians sympathetic to socialism (or to liberation theology) should openly acknowledge and warmly embrace the fact that there is a strong theological mandate for their concern. However, he is, I think, mistaken in holding that one way in which the socialist sympathiser or liberation theologian can avoid the charge of pursuing a merely sectional interest, of merely promoting 'the class advantage of the poor'[42] is by taking up 'the cause of the poor as a theologically given mandate'.[43] The problem here, I would suggest, is that there simply is no straightforward divine justification (no clear 'perpendicular descent' from on high) for *any* political strat-

---

41. M Blondel, *Letter on Apologetics and History and Dogma*, translated by Alexander Dru and Illtyd Trethowan (London: Harvill, 1964), 175–179.
42. O O'Donovan, *The Desire of the Nations; Rediscovering the Roots of Political Theology* (Cambridge: Cambridge University Press, 2003), 10.
43. *Ibid*, 11.

egy, let alone a religiously or ideologically inspired one. It is quite true that there is a clear scriptural mandate for our concern for the poor but then there is an equally clear scriptural mandate for our concern for the freedom and dignity of the individual (liberalism) and for social order and stability (conservatism). Thus, Christian citizens sympathetic to any of these political standpoints are not in any way advantaged *vis-à-vis* their non-Christian fellow citizens; for, rather than being informed by a straightforward scriptural/divine mandate which speaks with perfect clarity into *this* situation, they too, like the latter, find themselves confronted by (what is for Christians) a 'cacophony of divine voices' between which they must prayerfully discern in order to decide, in fear and trembling, what is the best political course to follow, or what recognising and serving Christ in others really means in a practical political sense. We must acknowledge that there simply is no privileged epistemic position that would allow us to know with certainty what to do politically. Our problem is that we know both more and less than we need to know for 'true' political action—'more', because there is an abundance or superfluity of sound ethical principles and biblical mandates/criteria that we can draw upon in order to know or to judge what needs to be done politically either in general, in the form of a guiding political outlook or in more specific day-to-day decision making; and 'less', because this very embarrassment of riches shrouds in uncertainty our attempts to know with conviction what needs to be done.

A useful summary of the position I have outlined on Christian social ethics would be to say that the primary socio-political task of the Christian is, or should be, to recognise and serve rather than to evangelise and save, whereas the primary task of the Church is to form a Jesus-centred community that is distinct from the world but which attracts the world through the light of Christ that it shines forth, and no-one, surely, speaks more truly and insightfully of this critically important task of the church than Stanley Hauerwas. 'As Christians we believe we not only need a community, but a community of a particular kind, to live well morally. We need a people who are capable of being faithful to a way of life, even when that way of life may be in conflict with what passes for 'morality' in the larger society'.[44] He holds that 'Christianity is an invitation to be part of an alien people who make a difference because they see something that cannot otherwise be seen without Christ'.[45] In such communities or churches, Christ's real, explicit, openly acknowledged presence in the gathered body of believers is celebrated and worshipped, but Hauerwas fails to acknowledge Christ's real, implicit, anonymous, 'practical' presence (common grace) in the service of the organised body of citizens to the poor. Hauerwas then is surely right in asserting that the problems, difficulties and dilemmas associated with the day-to-day exercise of Constantinian power are not directly the concern of the church (though the church as a 'corporate citizen' has a right and responsibility to speak out on issues of justice, the rights of the unborn, etc., and

---

44. S Hauerwas, *The Peaceable Kingdom: A Primer in Christian Ethics*, 35.
45. S Hauerwas, and M Williamson, 1989, *Resident Aliens: Life in the Christian Colony*, (Nashville: Abingdon Press, 1989), 24.

to constantly endeavour to raise the 'spiritual tone' of society) but he is surely mistaken in suggesting that they are not the problems of Christians as Christians or as Christian citizens and that they can therefore be 'safely handed over with a clear conscience to liberal Constantinians and well meaning intellectuals in policy institutes and universities who are only too willing to manage the world in a "good" way'.[46] Likewise, he is surely right to take issue with Reinhold Niebuhr's view that the kingdom of God never manifests itself concretely but 'is always an ideal that stands over against any possible realisation in history'[47] and with Niebuhr's dismissal of those who adopt the 'love perfectionist', non-violent way of Jesus as sectarians who withdraw from the socio-political struggle for justice. It is important to note here that 'love perfectionism' is a *living* ideal, one that really animates God's holy people (the church) and that, in so doing, serves to not only set a socio-political criterion for the wider society but also to draw the wider society towards (and into) its holy self (God-self). The church, despite the sinfulness of its all too human members, is nevertheless called to be the visible community that embodies the divine ideal through the grace of Christ and that thereby attracts not only those individuals being saved (as Hauerwas would

---

46. S Hauerwas, 'A Christian Critique of Christian America' in C Reynolds and R Norman, *Community in America: The Challenge of Habits of the Heart* (California: University of California Press, 1988), 263.
47. R Niebuhr, quoted in P Stallsworth, 'The Story of an Encounter,' *Reinhold Niebuhr Today* edited by RJ Neuhaus (Grand Rapids: Eerdmans, 1989), 114.

no doubt agree) but the whole of society as a 'collective person' responding to God's call. Hauerwas is assuredly right to insist that the single most important task of the church is to bear faithful witness to the teachings of Jesus and to live out his 'hard sayings' in communities of believers, and that believers must never regard this faithful witness of Christian communion as secondary to their political involvements as citizens, however important they may be. However, Hauerwas does not entirely escape from Niebuhr's criticism, for whilst it is true, as he suggests, that love perfectionism (self-sacrificial love for each other that does not count the cost) is 'not an option for the few, but incumbent on all Christians who seek to live faithfully in the kingdom made possible by the life, death and resurrection of Jesus',[48] Christian churches that try to concretely manifest Christ in the world would be rightly seen as unloving and unconcerned if their members were seen to be indifferent to society's own efforts in the same direction (the genuine wellbeing of the body of citizens).

Christian ethics enjoins both political and pastoral concern for our neighbour but it also enjoins the formation of communities (churches) where Christ's counsels, 'hard sayings' and the example of the early Christian believers (Acts 2:43–45) can be lived out more fully and effectively and under the more immediate sovereignty of the Spirit. It is to be fervently hoped that within the bounds of the church, and guided by the presence of the Spirit, the sense of being 'ethically obliged or enjoined' fades into the background as members of the congregation 'have eyes

---

48. S Hauerwas, *The Peaceable Kingdom; A Primer in Christian Ethics*, xvi.

only for Jesus' and breathe in the presence of His Spirit. This, no doubt, is what Hauerwas has in mind when he says that the point of Christian ethics is not so much to *do* anything in particular but to *be* something in particular, though it would, I believe, be more apt and accurate to say that the 'language of ethics', of duty and service, is more appropriate for the Christian 'in the world' (in the pastoral and political sense), whereas the 'language of being' (of being a community 'resting' in the Lord and ever oriented to Him) is more appropriate for the church as Christ's corporate body in the world but not of it. Still, the point that Hauerwas is making here is extremely important and all the more so in the present context for it is one that is in danger of being overlooked by Christians who become passionately involved in pastoral ministries or political missions.[49] Let me summarise what I take to be its most important practical ramifications.

What all Christians should acknowledge (and live out in practice) is that there is simply nothing more important,

---

49. Concerning this danger, Gary Dorrien states the following: 'Social Christianity since the generation of Rauschenbusch and Mathews has often downplayed the question of religious truth . . . Rauschenbusch rarely mentioned the resurrection of Christ . . . Christian ethicists have too often assumed that the crisis of modern Christianity can be resolved if Christianity can be translated into a sufficiently compelling social vision. At a time when large numbers of Americans have no religious background at all, this assumption is more untenable than ever. Christianity must be more than the underpinning of an attractive social philosophy or politics if it is to become a living faith for unchurched religious seekers.' G Dorrien, *Soul in Society: The Making and Renewal of Social Christianity* (Minneapolis: Fortress Press, 1995), 373.

and more true to the essence of their faith, than forming a community of believers (generally a church) in which Christ's love, mercy and forgiveness is clear for all to see and which, by its witness and example, attracts those being saved to 'come and see'. These believers must love one another in a real and not a nominal sense, which means that they must know each other in a real and not just a nominal sense. A large congregation must contain within it something like 'house churches' or at least groups of believers small enough to live out something like the 'Acts Two life' (Acts 2:43–45) under modern conditions. ('And all who believed were together and had all things in common; and they sold their possessions and goods and distributed them to all, as any had need.') Hauerwas is surely incontestable in his claim that the first task of the church is not so much to act effectively or successfully in the world but to *be* the 'community of Christ' in the world, the practical 'corporate' manifestation of the love and truth of his kingdom.[50] He here echoes John Howard Yoder's belief that 'the primary social structure through which the gospel works to change other structures is that of the Christian community',[51] Helmut Thielicke's convic-

---

50. In a similar vein, Gary Dorrien holds that the church of the kingdom 'seeks to incarnate the way of Christ' and 'does not worry about finding a respectable place in society, but lives by its own dynamic', though he also wholeheartedly supports the view (I am much more cautious) that the church (as such) should seek to 'transform society into Christ's reign of justice and peace.' G Dorrien, *Soul in Society: The Making and Renewal of Social Christianity*, 371.
51. JH Yoder, *The Politics of Jesus* (Grand Rapids: Eerdmans, 1972), 157.

tion that the 'changing of persons will necessarily mean the changing of the order'[52] and Jim Wallis's insistence that the church's biblical identity is that of 'a new community which is a sign of the kingdom in history, an alien society of God's people whose life and action is intended to play a prophetic and decisive role in the world'.[53] A body of believers must assuredly be a light that illuminates and strengthens the 'best' of its world but that also exposes, and pierces with the 'sword of offence' the 'worst' (the darkness) of current secular culture; the purity of their life in the Spirit and their identification with the poor and marginalised (especially the vulnerable unborn) will assuredly be an offence *to* their fellow citizens and they must be prepared to enter into redemptive suffering *for* their fellow citizens. Each Christian and Christian church is called upon not just to be sympathetic to the poor and marginalised or to make loving gestures in their direction but to really *share* their pain, to be 'compassionate' in the literal sense of 'suffering with' and, as expounded in black and womanist theology, to thereby honour Christ as divine co-sufferer and redeemer. In the words of Jacquelyn Grant, 'God is in solidarity with the struggles of those on the under side of humanity'[54] and in the words of James Gustafson, Christ 'knows and feels

---

52. H Thielicke, *Theological Ethics, Volume 2: Politics* (Grand Rapids: Eerdmans, 1979), 645.
53. J Wallis, *Agenda for a Biblical People* (New York: Harper & Row, 1976), 143.
54. J Grant, J 1989, *White Women's Christ and Black Women's Jesus: Feminist Christology and Womanist Response* (Atlanta: Scholars Press, 1989), 209.

the pain and suffering of the world . . . in which the oppressed remain shackled in the chains of indifferent and tyrannical social orders'.[55] Redemptive suffering is neither to be sought nor shunned, for it is simply inevitable in so far as we and our world remain unredeemed and subject to sin, sickness and death; it is not a form of quiet resignation to an oppressive *status quo,* for there can be no suffering on Christ's behalf without the soul being 'transformed into Christ' and without this 'personal' liberation bearing fruit in a movement of the 'being transformed' soul towards 'social' liberation (a rejection of oppression in all its forms, social, cultural, political, etc).

Hauerwas then grasps a genuine aspect of our life as Christians in the world when he says that the church is not a sect but a counter-cultural colony living within and among a largely secular culture. He is right to insist that the primary task of the church is to *be* a transformed (or an 'ever *being* transformed') 'micro' community of love and peace (a counter-cultural sect) within a largely secular society, rather than to *do* 'important' political things. However, if the church must not directly attempt by political means to transform society as a whole into a utopian 'macro' community of love and peace, it must nevertheless seek to indirectly (or non-politically but fundamentally) transform its society by having the courage and audacity to present itself as its true soul, by ever drawing it towards its true self, and by persisting unrelentingly in its Christ-assigned task of making society as loving, as just,

---

55. JM Gustafson JM 1974, *Theology and Christian Ethics* (Philadelphia: Pilgrim Press, 1974), 88.

as inclusive, and as close to Utopia (to the Kingdom) as possible.

Two kingdoms: Martin Luther

With regard to the kind of responsibility that Christians have for the proper ordering of society (should Christians avoid the secular realm and the kingdoms of this world in favour of a focus on Christ's spiritual kingdom of grace?), I have held that Christians have a sacred duty to promote the wellbeing of society and to take their civic and political responsibilities very seriously, and I wish to further suggest that this conviction is broadly reflected in the writings of major Christian thinkers and theologians. Certainly this is true in the case of mainstream Catholic social thought and the Reformed doctrine of 'the Lordship of Christ over all' but it is unclear whether or not Luther's doctrine of the two kingdoms constitutes a major exception. It has to be acknowledged that, as expounded in the Ansbach Decree of 1935, the Lutheran state churches used the two kingdoms doctrine to justify a position of neutrality towards the German National Socialist dictatorship, in contrast to the Confessing Church, which, in the Barmen declaration, used the doctrine of the lordship of Christ to justify resistance to Hitler. The historical fact that German Lutherans used this doctrine to justify a position of 'political quietism' and non-resistance to Nazism is beyond dispute, and yet Gerhard Ebeling,[56] a leading

---

56. G Ebeling, *Wort und Glaube* 111, (Tubingen: J CB Mohr, 1975), 575f.

Lutheran scholar, holds that one of the 'most trivial distortions' of Luther's doctrine is to suggest that by it 'the world is released from its dependence on God, and faith from responsibility from the world' and this certainly suggests that it is in line with, rather than an exception to, the broad Christian consensus on this issue. My suggestion here is that whilst it must be acknowledged that historically the two kingdom doctrine has tended to foster in Christians a sense of 'political quietism based on political realism' (given the corrupt sinful nature of our humanity, the governing authorities are doing a laudable job if they only succeed in establishing and preserving basic social order), yet it is also important to recognise that the doctrine is not entirely without critical, potential and that it is unconcerned with, rather than by its nature opposed to, a more constructive Christian engagement with politics and culture. Thus whilst I would agree that this doctrine, however interpreted, 'does not motivate world-transforming hope',[57] yet on the interpretation I will here present it may motivate (and, more importantly, does not oppose) significant social and political involvement. Certainly, it can inspire hope that, despite the limitations imposed by our rebellious and sinful humanity, *real good* may and must be effected (by Christian and non-Christian alike) in the social and political universe and this real good should not be demeaned by comparing it invidiously with the radical transformation which can be effected in the soul through Christ's grace and forgiveness.

---

57. J Moltmann, *On Human Dignity; Political Theology and Ethics* (London: SCM Press, 1984), 76.

It should be noted, to begin with, that the spiritual kingdom of Christ and the secular kingdom of the world are both opposed to the kingdom of darkness, so that we perhaps need to speak, as U Duchrow has pointed out,[58] of a 'three kingdoms doctrine', or of a coalition of two against the spiritual kingdom of darkness. We need to think in terms of an alliance of two spheres against a single foe. What these allied spheres or coalition partners share is a 'common interest' in restraining Satan's power in this fallen world and restoring God's creation, as far as possible, to its original fullness and goodness; ideally, the distinctive role that each has to play in pursuing these goals complements the role of the other. Certainly, Luther intended the 'two regiments' to mutually limit and complement each other. The strategic means and goals of this coalition are clear; the world (the *regnum mundi*) is to be opposed in so far as it is under the influence of Satan (as Prince of the world in this 'fallen' sense) who undermines its true life and being in God and Christ, but the world as God's original and good creation is to be thereby uplifted, restored and redeemed. The true being and life of God is thus pitted against the anti-being and anti-life (the constant death-wish) of Satan and his minions and in this momentous struggle between good and evil, life and death, being and anti-being, God and Satan, at all times the church and the state stand resolutely on God's side in the heat of battle.

---

58. U Duchrow, Christenheit und Weltverantwortung. Traditionsgeschichte und systematische Struktur der Zweireiche-lehre (Stuttgart: E Klett, 1970), 526.

When considering the view that the two kingdom doctrine exercises a politically 'quietist' or socially conservative influence, it is important to bear in mind that the doctrine distinguishes between the manner in which God 'directly' rules his spiritual kingdom through the faith of those who believe in Jesus and the manner in which he 'indirectly' rules the *regnum mundi* though the civil laws of the state.[59] Now there is certainly no doubt that this doctrine is bound to lead in practice to a profound respect for the civil authorities and a strong regard for the civil law but it need not be an unhealthy respect. It is perfectly understandable that the positive laws of the state, when viewed as expressions or instruments of God's law (or as 'concretisations' of natural law considered as God's law) would be held by Christians in high regard but then it would be equally understandable if Christians used this doctrine to oppose the civil authority when, in their judgment, the civil laws of a particular jurisdiction actually went against or undermined God's law or blatantly failed to regard the state, the family and the economy as God's ordinances for humanity. The same doctrine could then be used as a critical tool against the civil power or even as a means of resistance to it, as in the case of the Nor-

---

59. Moltmann provides us with the following neat summary of the way in which the two kingdoms doctrine operates in the lives of believers: 'It appears that God has set Christians within his two regiments, so that the Christian as Christ person and world person is a citizen of two kingdoms, of the gospel and of the law. In the spiritual regiment God rules through Christ and faith. In the worldly regiment God rules through the law without Christ.' J Moltmann, *On Human Dignity; Political Theology and Ethics*, 72.

wegian Bishop Berggrav who actually used the two kingdom doctrine to oppose the Nazi regime. Article 16 of the Augsburg Confession makes it plain that faith becomes effective through love, that holy scripture requires the Christian to make God's ordinances (the state, the family, the economy) arenas for acts of love, and that the state is meant to be a means whereby—and the realm of the 'political' is meant to be an arena in which—'the eternal righteousness of the heart' is expressed:

> The gospel teaches an eternal righteousness of the heart, but it does not destroy the state or the family. On the contrary, it especially requires their preservation as ordinances of God and the exercise of love in these ordinances.

Here the Augsburg Confession could be seen as offering grounds for critically opposing governments in liberal democratic societies that fail to support or preserve the family as an ordinance of God.

We should note too at this point in the discussion that what Richard Niebuhr has called the 'Christ-against-culture' view of the Christ-culture relation is not necessarily a politically quietist or conservative viewpoint. This outlook or approach certainly insists that, whether or not it is the responsibility of Christians to attempt to transform culture, it is certainly their duty to avoid being 'transformed' (that is, deformed or debased) by it; correspondingly, this approach stresses the duty of the Christian to abandon the 'world' (in the sense, it is important to note, of the 'flesh and the devil' and not in the sense of God's created order) and to 'come out from among them and be separate'. However, this surely does not mean that those who espouse this position feel that they ought to eschew any attempt to convert the world, or to infuse secular society with Christian values, or that they should ignore the Lord's command (to engage with the world, to read the signs of the times, etc) and the Lord's example (freely mixing with sinners and tax collectors). My suggestion here is that the term 'separate' in the Scriptures has both a literal (spatial) meaning and a spiritual ('non-spatial') meaning. Christians are not to compromise their integrity but are, rather, to be separate from the world in the sense of avoiding occasions of sin and being constantly aware of the wiles of the devil. Separation in this spiritual sense is an absolutely imperative strategy at all times, even when—perhaps, especially when—Christians are actively engaged in confronting or converting the world, for the sinful world we wish to transform is as much in us as it is in the (external) world and we thus need to be ever vigilant and cautious. However, the call to be separate is not just a cautionary spiritual note or a reminder of our vulnerability to sin but is also a call to be separate in a literal, physical sense. Our endeavours to be at all times separate in the spiritual sense need to be undergirded and supported by our being regularly 'separate from the world' (in Hauerwas' counter-cultural colony) through our attendance at regular church services. There is then no incompatibility between the Lord's command to serve the poor and fight against injustice and the scriptural call to be separate, for the latter provides us with the means (both the permanent spiritual 'strategy' and the regular spiritual sustenance and support from our fellow believers) to effectively achieve the former.

Likewise, it is important to note here that a (radical) commitment to social justice is perfectly compatible with a ('politically quietist', conservative) respect for our culturally conveyed Christian tradition, for the latter requires us to transmit and conserve the best of our cultural heritage, including its most socially just and inclusive aspects. Admittedly, on the one hand, a concern for preserving our inherited social heritage is more likely, on the whole, to lead us to be wary in our attitude towards schemes for the transformation of society along radical lines and towards the possibly destructive ill effects of what appear to be progressive social ideas; but, on the other hand, in a case where our tradition clearly endorses a strong sense of social responsibility for the poor and condemns their unjust treatment, and where that sense has been lost in cultural transmission, then in such a case the conservative (though hardly 'politically quietist') concern for tradition or for its 'restoration' may become virtually indistinguishable from the radical desire for social transformation. There is here a 'tension of difference' between these two viewpoints but at the same time no permanent or ultimate incompatibility between the two. Likewise, there is no irreconcilable distance or division between what Richard Niebuhr calls the 'Christ-of-culture' approach to the Christ-culture relation and what he calls the 'Christ-against-culture' approach, for exponents of the former approach use the term 'culture' to refer to the elevating 'best' that our social heritage has to offer, whereas exponents of the latter viewpoint use the term 'culture' to refer to the degenerate depths (the 'worst') that our society and culture may descend to.

Niebuhr holds that there is a major contrast between Luther's 'dualistic' approach (the kingdom of God, mercy and grace, as against the kingdom of the world, of wrath) and the 'Christ-of-culture' approach. However, the contrast here is, I think, severely overdrawn. The kind of 'Christ-against-culture' comments that Luther makes should be seen, I would suggest, as together constituting a cautionary note, as an invitation to keep our feet on the ground whilst our eyes are fixed on the stars. Certainly, Luther says in his *The Freedom of a Christian*, 'From faith flow forth love and joy in the Lord, and from love a joyful, willing and free mind that serves neighbour willingly and takes no account of gratitude and ingratitude, of praise or blame, of gain or loss',[60] whereas in his pamphlet *Against the Robbing and Murderous Hordes of Peasants* he tells us that a prince or lord must remember that 'he is God's minister and the servant of his wrath to whom the sword is committed for use upon such fellows ... Here there is no time for sleeping; no place for patience or mercy. It is the time of the sword, not the day of grace'.[61] Thus we are to understand and accept that there are two kingdoms, one the kingdom of God (a kingdom of 'grace and mercy'), the other the kingdom of the world (a kingdom of 'wrath

---

60. M Luther, *The Freedom of a Christian,* in HT Lehmann and HJ Grimm (eds), *Luther's Works,* volume 31, (Phildadelphia: Fortress Press, 1979), 367.
61. M Luther, *Against the Robbing and Murderous Hordes of Peasants* edited by HT Lehmann and RC Schultz, *Luther's Works,* volume 46 (Phildadelphia: Fortress Press, 1967), 52–53.

and severity'). Certainly, then, there are two kingdoms, as Luther points out, but is he not merely stating here what any Christian would readily assent to? If Luther is to be deemed 'dualistic', then so too must Christianity as a whole. However, we need to be cautious here. The distinction between the two kingdoms is relative, rather than absolute; the two are significantly related to each other as 'saving' (God's kingdom) and 'to be saved' (the world). Moreover, Luther makes it clear that the prince or lord is enjoined to act in the world *as God's minister* and as the instrument of God's wrath and justice, which of course sounds severe and, indeed, *is* severe, but which, as directed to the ultimate wellbeing of sinful humanity and as the only route to that wellbeing, is perhaps 'mercy' in a profound sense, a 'divine' sense in which justice and mercy merge into each other. What the believer enjoys as a participant and member of God's kingdom of grace and mercy (God's spontaneous, 'natural' sin-free presence in the heart of a true, if sinful, believer), God must enjoin in the kingdom of the world (His 'enforced' presence in a world in need of law, grace and redemption). The world is wayward, ever oriented away from God and towards sin, but divine justice calls sin by its proper name and condemns it through the laws of the prince. As wielded by the prince, the sword of justice transforms neither individuals nor society; indeed it can do no more than contain the raging sinful lion in each human heart and force it into a resentful obedience through the fear of retribution, of punishment for civil wrong-doing. However, the prince's sword of justice clears a pathway and opens a channel for the flow of divine grace, thereby providing a space or opportunity for the inner transformation of individuals and, perhaps even, of whole societies. In the space cleared by the prince's sword, the kingdom of God can secure a foothold in the kingdom of the world in a battle that takes place in each human heart, not excluding those being redeemed.

It is hardly surprising, in light of the above, that Luther was mainly interested in personal rather than in social transformation and that, as Niebuhr remarks, Christians such as Martin Luther 'tend to think of the institutions of culture as having a largely negative function in a temporal and corrupt world'.[62] At the same time, however, Luther would have seen it as the responsibility of each believer to make the tone and temper of social and political life as Christian as possible. The battle against the kingdom of the world is to be waged on all fronts, in the 'outer' public world as well as the 'inner' private world. It was, no doubt, for this reason that Luther urged fellow believers to be involved in political activities as part of their service to God and neighbour. Here, I believe, Luther follows St Augustine, who holds that we should not regard God's glorious city and the earthly city as separate and mutually repellent—they both have 'our world' and its welfare in view—but that we should, rather, regard 'loving goodness' as the principle, theme and essence of the in-breaking Kingdom of God, and regard 'sinful pride' as the presently orienting principle and dominant theme of the kingdoms of this fallen world. (CS Lewis reminds us

---

62. HR Niebuhr, HR 2001, *Christ and Culture* (New York: Harper Collins, 2001), 193.

that, living in this world, we are in 'enemy occupied territory'.) I believe that this is what St Augustine has in mind when he contrasts the glorious city of God with the earthly city, for whilst he speaks at times as if God's city is to be exclusively identified with love and justice ('There is not any justice in any commonwealth whatsoever but in that whereof Christ is the founder and ruler'[63]) and as if the cities of the world are to associated with sin, evil and injustice (The earthly city 'hates a just peace of God and builds an unjust one for itself',[64]) yet where an earthly city acknowledges God as its 'highest and truest good', there 'the common good is loved' and 'men love each other most sincerely because they love themselves for the sake of Him from whom they cannot hide the true sentiments of their hearts'.[65] (*Letters 131–164*, Letter 137, par. 17, p. 34). For Augustine, as for Luther, the rulers and subjects of such a city (their lives, their thoughts, their private worlds, their collective world, their shared public realm) are the scene or site where a spiritual battle rages between the kingdom of light (God's total loving intent towards us and for us) and the kingdom of darkness (Satan's totally destructive intent towards us). Our world, the world of our experience, though claimed by Satan as his own and of which he is *de facto* 'Prince' through our sins (hence the highhanded behavior of 'earthly' rulers), does not belong

---

63. St Augustine, *De Civitate Dei* (Harmondsworth: Penguin, 1972), 2 Chapter 21.
64. *Ibid*, 19, chapter12.
65. St Augustine, 1953, *St Augustine Letters 131–164* in *The Fathers of the Church*, volume 20 (New York, 1953), letter 137, paragraph 17, 34.

to him ultimately but belongs *de jure* to God (hence the cries of the prophets against the oppression of the poor). As Reinhold Niebuhr incisively remarks,[66] the 'theological view that the spiritual and private world was virtuous and that the physical realm was self-seeking and that it was always so, obscured two important points. It obscured the residual self-regard in the personal and interpersonal realm, and also the residual sense of justice in the collective and political realm'.

We do indeed live in two kingdoms (God's kingdom and a human kingdom) but they are not hermetically sealed or separate for both are present (and contending for total victory) in this world—in my world, the world of my personal experience and the world of our collective experience as citizens. It is with this in mind that it is perfectly true to say that the rulers of this world lord it over their subjects (sin makes Satan powerful in this world) and that it is not to be so in God's kingdom (Matthew 20:25–26), but it is also true to say that the highhanded behavior of earthly rulers is soundly condemned by the values of the in-breaking kingdom of God. Indeed, if the prophets of the Old Testament so forcefully insisted that the proper role of government is to promote the common good and protect the poor, how much more so is this the case in the new order of grace initiated by Christ's victory? In brief, God requires us to respect and obey our earthly rulers but also to radically oppose injustice; one requirement should not be seen as silencing the other and neither requirement

---

66. R Niebuhr, Man's *Nature and his Communities* (London: Geoffrey Bles, 1966), 40.

is absolute. Both need to be taken into account when trying to discern God's will, which alone has an absolute claim on our lives. This is, I think, what John Knox had in mind when he replied to a query about the apparent incompatibility between his critique of royal authority and the scriptural injunction in Romans 13:

> The power in that place is not to be understood as the unjust command of men but the just power wherewith God has armed his magistrates and lieutenants to punish sin . . . And what harm should the government receive if the corrupt affection of ignorant rulers be moderated and bridled by the wisdom and discretion of Godly subjects so that they would not do violence to any man?[67]

Conclusion: universal and social salvation

Finally, the distinction we have made between 'saving' (God's kingdom) and 'to be saved' (the world) raises the difficult question of what precisely is to be saved. Can we hope and expect that all individuals and all societies are to be saved in the end and are ultimately destined to enter into the fullness of the life God (universally) intended? If Saint Paul hoped that the Jewish people 'as a whole' would be brought to salvation (Romans, 11:26), may we not entertain the same hope for every nation and people?

---

67. J Knox, *The History of the Reformation of the Church of Scotland*, volume 2 (Edinburgh: Robert Bryson, 1644), 282.

Niebuhr discusses these possibilities when he considers what he calls the conversionist or 'transformationist' approach to the Christ-culture relation. Those who view the latter in this 'conversionist' fashion see history as the temporal stage or scene for the dramatic and ongoing intervention in our everyday human affairs by the eternal God. The notion of eternity is here meant to evoke 'less the action of God before time and less the life with God after time and more the presence of God in time'.[68] The task of the Christian conversionist is not just to pass on the best of our social heritage or to contain the power of sin in our personal and social lives or to prepare ourselves for the joys of eternity beyond time, but, as well as all of these things—or perhaps, rather, with all of these things in mind—to live constantly with 'the divine possibility' of a transformed personal and social life and with the hope of the universal salvation of all humanity. Niebuhr provides us with the following summary:

> The conversionist with his view of history as the present encounter with God in Christ, does not live so much in expectation of a final ending of the world of creation and culture as in awareness of the power of the Lord to transform all things by lifting them up to himself. His imagery is spatial and not temporal; and the movement of life he finds to be issuing from Jesus Christ is an upward move-

---

68. HR Niebuhr, *Christ and Culture* (New York: Harper Collins, 2001), 195.

ment, the rising of men's souls and deeds and thoughts in a mighty surge of adoration and glorification of the One who draws them to himself. This is what human culture can be –a transformed human life in and to the glory of God.[69]

It is in the work of FD Maurice that we find the conversionist theme most clearly, consistently and persuasively elaborated. He was a strong universalist, taking issue with those who held that Christ's love and salvation was only for some and not for humanity as a whole, and with those who, whilst confessing that they belonged to a guilty race, nevertheless wished for a separate pardon. He thoroughly investigated all phases of human culture—social customs, political systems, languages, economic organizations—and was convinced that 'there is no phase of human culture over which Christ does not rule, and no human work which is not subject to his transforming power over self-will'.[70] For Maurice, the transformation of each individual and of society as a whole from self-centredness to love of the other in and through Christ was, despite the deforming influence of sin, a real, universal and ever present divine possibility.

Niebuhr holds that each appearance of this universal conversionist motif in Christian history is accompanied and undermined by a kind of 'exclusivist' shadow or undercurrent; thus, for example, Saint John in his fourth

---

69. *Ibid*, 195–196
70. Quoted in *ibid*, 227.

Gospel speaks of universal salvation, of God sending his Son 'into the world, not to condemn the world, but that the world might be saved through him' (John 3:16) and, at the same time, of God's 'exclusive' concern for the few; 'I have manifested thy name to those thou gavest me out of the world . . . I am praying for them: I am not praying for the world . . . They are not of the world, even as I am not of the world' (John 17:6, 9, 16). Again, we have Saint Augustine speaking about human solidarity in sin and salvation and, at the same time, Niebuhr reminds us, of the damned who are predestined to eternal punishment.[71] It would be neither possible nor appropriate, at this stage, to consider the many examples of this tension between 'universalism' (salvation for all and the unity of the human family; the salvation of humanity, rather than of separate persons) and 'exclusivism' (salvation for the few and an unbridgeable gulf between the elect and the damned) but my general view is that Niebuhr presses the tension between these two motifs too far, indeed to the point of outright contradiction, and that it is possible to take a less conflictual view. For example, given that the distinction between the two kingdoms (God's kingdom and the kingdom of the world) is relative, rather than absolute, and that the two are significantly related to each other as 'saving' (God's kingdom) and 'to be saved' (the world), it would be entirely reasonable and plausible to suggest that Saint John in the second quote above was telling us of a famous occasion when Christ, in his prayer, was focused on 'those being saved', rather than on those

---

71. *Ibid*, 208.

'yet to be saved'. No doubt, in the final analysis, we must concede that a strong element of tension remains in the gospels between these great themes but what we should, I believe, be prepared to acknowledge is that the gospels are at least clear in setting forth what we might call a 'universalism of divine intent' or a 'universalism of real possibility'. This, to me at least, is the uncontestable core of the conversionist case. In principle, or in terms of broad theory, we should see Christ's death as intending the salvation of all, of every person that has ever lived and will ever live, and in terms of our Christian practice right here and right now, we should see that the cross makes the salvation of all a *real* practical possibility. What else do we need to see or know in order to effectively serve the Lord? It is not for us to know who will be saved and who, if anyone, will be lost. All that matters, or that should matter to us right here and now, is that we should be striving our utmost to realise the universal salvation that the heart of God yearns for and to both hope for and work for the personal *and* social transformation that Christ has made possible.

Part Two

God and Truth

Chapter Three

Foucault, Truth and the Politics of Difference

Of the gods we believe, and of men we know, that by a necessary law of their nature they rule whenever they can.
Thucydides, History of the Peloponnesian War, Book 5, chapter 105

When Sir Humphrey Appleby in the BBC series 'Yes, Prime Minister' was told that he (Sir Humphrey) was suspected of being a spy, his response to the Prime Minister was that he couldn't possibly be guilty because 'a spy believes in things... in "good causes" and I don't believe in anything!' His response provides us with a useful way of characterising the major paradigm shift in western culture that has recently taken place. In the 60s and 70s it was still intellectually permissible, and even commendable, to believe in 'good causes', in socialism or feminism for example, but in the 80s and 90s, due in the main to the increasing intellectual ascendancy of postmodernism, relativism and social constructionism, 'good' causes rapidly lost their intellectual respectability; they were generally portrayed by postmodern critics as hopelessly enmeshed with totalistic 'Truth-revealing' meta-narratives, as attempts to foist rigid conceptual grids upon the living richness and diversity of social reality, and as the work of 'masters of Truth' whose spurious knowledge claims merely reflected their own 'will to power'. In the present 'postmodern' climate, and especially in the light of Foucault's devastating critique of the latter (masters of Truth), it has become increasingly difficult to seriously believe in anything or to entertain a social vision of any kind, for one thereby exposes oneself to the charge of harboring Truth-inspired totalistic tendencies towards one's fellow human beings. Against this backdrop, I wish to focus in this second main part of the book on truth, justice, goodness, common decency, unselfishness, integrity, etc, as 'true' values and virtues that belong to the whole of (our common) humanity. I wish to suggest that, both in our personal lives and in our lives as citizens of the state, we should be servants and seekers of Truth and that we should do our utmost to re-legitimise the quest for Truth– that is, for the 'good and the true'. It is true that postmodernism must be applauded for its incisive critique of the 'totalising tendency' of the quest for Truth, especially when fuelled by passionate ideological conviction, but at the same time its forthright rejection of Truth itself has had disastrous social consequences and serious deleterious effects on our personal lives and in the realm of public policy. Over the last two decades or so, the baby (Truth) has been recklessly thrown out with the bathwater (totalistic ideologies) and the consequences have been sorely felt in society, in the personal lives of individuals and in the welfare service professions, especially, of course, in the writings and professional practice of those who have enthusiastically embraced postmodernism.[1] Hence, in this chapter I will (i) outline some key postmodern tenets, (ii) suggest that we need to keep the quest for Truth at the heart of our personal and 'civic' lives in the manner suggested by Barth and classical political theory, (iii) show that there is actually some textual basis for the claim that Foucault may, in certain respects at least, be regarded as a 'Truth-oriented' political thinker in the classical tradition of political theory, (iv) discuss the views of William Connolly, Judith Butler and John Ransom on Foucault as a Truth-oriented defender of liberal democracy and the 'politics of difference', (v) argue why we should entertain an attitude of 'ecumenical graciousness' towards all Truth-metanarratives, and finally (vi) suggest that we should be 'servants' rather than 'masters' of Truth as we personally and collectively pursue our quest for 'the right, the good and the true'.

Postmodernism and Truth

Postmodernists either out-rightly reject, or exhibit an extremely skeptical and unsympathetic attitude towards, what they term 'modernity', which is usually understood as embracing a belief in science, in the usefulness, productivity and reliability of the empirical method and, finally,

---

1. These are fully explored in B Trainor and H Jeffreys *The Human Service Disciplines and Social Work: The Foucault Effect* (Quebec: World Heritage Press, 2003).

in progress, individuality and universal rights. Regarding themselves as 'post-metaphysical' or 'post-philosophical', they reject the notion that Truth—again, in the sense of 'the good and the true'—orients our thoughts, that it is the origin and end of human thinking and that it exercises a kind of constant 'gravitational pull' on the human intellect as 'its other'. Reality is deemed to be socially constructed and reason, truth, science are viewed as cultural constructs or biases. What is sometimes deferentially referred to as 'Science' should, they hold, be more appropriately described as 'western' or 'eurocentric' science, since it is a cultural construct of the west. Postmodernists are firm in their belief that there is no outside world beyond the reaches of the mind which is better grasped or understood by the concepts of western science than in any other way. In whatever way we grasp the world (social, external, legal etc), we do so—and only can do so—by means of the cultural concepts available to us. Thus our concepts only have 'truth-value' within our cultural milieu; any suggestion that our language and thoughts might 'truly' correspond to a world that lies beyond our thoughts and words is firmly rejected. Reality is linguistic through and through; there simply is no extra-discursive, extra-linguistic reality existing beyond thought and which lies 'out there', waiting to be grasped by our thoughts and words. We should, postmodernists hold, no longer think in terms of the centrality of the 'knowing, thinking subject', which exercises a kind of mastery over the world it subjects to its 'knowing gaze'. Rather, we should acknowledge the centrality and reality of the culture which encircles and immerses us, and which, in a sense, *is* us, for it constitutes us as the individuals (more properly, the assembly of diverse subject positions) that we are.

It is, I think, unfortunate that postmodernists refuse, on postmodern principle to consider the possibility that culture might itself be a prism of Truth. Foucault, for example, was intrigued by what he called 'the games of Truth and error through which being is historically constituted as experience'[2] but these 'games' are not of course for Foucault dialectical moves in and towards Truth, and he certainly did not regard the historically conditioned (for him, *only* historically conditioned) 'Truths' of a particular time and place as social or cultural expressions of Truth itself. Rather, his 'truths' and the 'games of Truth' that produce them are the socio-linguistic mechanisms through which various 'wills to power' operate in the world; indeed they are, for Foucault, the major normalising means through which the disciplinary power of the human service professions (social work, psychiatry, education, law, etc.) 'manufactures' individuals.[3] He would insist that these professions do not deal with pre-existent, 'real' individuals; rather, the 'individual' is socially and professionally 'constructed' by means of the terms, techniques and categories employed by the professional disciplines. Our hope, or what we might call the 'natural' hope

---

2. M Foucault, *The Use of Pleasure* (New York: Random House, 1985), 6.
3. M Foucault, *Discipline and Punish: The Birth of the Prison* (Harmondsworth: Penguin, 1977), 170. In his *Discipline and Punish: The Birth of the Prison*, Foucault states that 'discipline "makes" individuals; it is the specific technique of a power that regards individuals both as objects and as instruments of its exercise.'

of professionals, is that the use of their professional concepts serves to both elucidate in some sense what really and already exists (the individual client or group prior to professional intervention) and also to ethically inform, or further develop in a constructive manner, what already exists. However, it is precisely this hope that a Foucauldian postmodernism undermines by regarding a society's way of life as *only* a social construction (which of course, in a sense, obviously and tautologically is) and not *also* as the prism of Truth or the societal-cultural medium through which Truth finds expression with varying degrees of adequacy in different cultures. Again, this hope is dashed by the postmodern *a priori* conviction or assumption that cultural expressions and beliefs are to be understood solely in terms of the 'will to power' of dominant groups whose interests they always and only represent, for it renders futile our efforts to distinguish as best we can between those cultural expressions which reflect, to whatever extent, the 'will to power' of dominant groups and those which reflect, in the main, the collective 'will to Truth' of a political community; indeed, in postmodern terms, the very attempt to make these distinctions when formulating social policy is itself no more than an expression of a sectional 'will to power'.

Foucault, then, took a strong stand against 'Truth'. He was also clear in his warning that we need to be ever alert to what he called the 'main danger', by which he meant the latest 'regime of truth' parading itself socially, politically or culturally as a 'regime of Truth'. Now when Foucault speaks in this way, what he has to say is not without precedent in the Christian tradition, especially when Christian writers are contemplating the contrast between (the holiness of) God and (the corruption of) humanity. Barth, for example, states: 'I certainly can will—yes, in fact, only too well—but I cannot accomplish the good. How could I, since my very willing is, as that of a deceived deceiver, corrupt?'[4] and Niebuhr notes that what he calls Christian dualists of the Lutheran type call attention to 'the lust for power and the will of the strong which rationalises itself in . . . social arrangements. In monarchies, aristocracies and democracies, in middle class and in proletarian rules, in Episcopal, Presbyterian and Congregational polities, the hand of power is never wholly disguised by its soft glove of reason . . . ', as, for example, when it sanctions, through the ethical legitimacy conveyed by the institution of private property, 'the great seizures of alien possessions, as when it protects the settler in his rights over lands taken from Indians'.[5] Niebuhr is here referring us to what we might call the social and political equivalent of the view that 'free will avails for nothing but sinning' and it certainly reminds us of Foucault's endless 'games of truth and error through which being is historically constituted as experience'.[6]

Now, this Christian 'point of contact' with Foucault is real in one sense but illusory in another. It is real in the

---

4. K Barth, *Community, State and Church: Three Essays* (Gloucester, Mass: Peter Smith, 1968), 93.
5. HR Niebuhr, *Christ and Culture* (New York: Harper Collins, 2001), 156.
6. M Foucault, *The Use of Pleasure* (New York: Random House, 1985), 6.

sense that not just dualistic (in Niebuhr's sense) Christians but all of us who believe in a 'God who saves' experience moments when we are acutely aware of the contrast between the holiness of God and the sinfulness of humanity and more especially between the humility and truthfulness of God and our well nigh constant human attempts (i) to convince ourselves that, despite our 'minor' faults, we really are 'nice people', (ii) to hide from ourselves our craving for recognition and the violence of our anger when we feel that the recognition due to us has not been forthcoming and (iii) to cover our insatiable will to power with a suitable ethical embellishment that enables us to righteously, even religiously, take from others what is rightly theirs and to kill them if they resist. However, it is precisely at those moments when we recognise at last that the 'truths' we defensively grasp to shield ourselves from divine redeeming grace are really self-serving lies and that we stand condemned before the holiness of God, that we most fully experience the reality and unsurpassable beauty of God's Truth. Thus two revelations take place simultaneously; the revelation of the full extent of the corruption of our unredeemed humanity, of our violence and will to power, of the self deception at the heart of our self justification *is at the same time* the revelation of God's infinite love, mercy and beauty, so that the 'two' revelations are perhaps only distinct aspects of a single revelatory event.[7] Needless to say, in the case of Foucault,

---

7. It is important that what is here distinguished should not be separated. As Christians approach the throne of grace and sense the inadequacy of the 'truths' by which they have hitherto lived in

this contrast between our human truths and God's absolute Truth is entirely absent; he is able to discern the viciousness of our vanity and 'will to power' but is unable to see that this very discernment on his part is a gift of divine grace and not just his own insight.

Politics and Truth

Likewise, Foucault is unable to see that the ultimate justification of the institutions of liberal democracy—and, as we shall shortly see, of the 'politics of difference'—lies in its relationship to Truth. Unless the process of government in a liberal democracy is communal, deliberative and Truth-oriented, and unless its style of government exhibits a unifying rather than a unitary type of universality, it is not a true democracy at all but merely its

---

a world without God, their feelings may well be reflected in the words of the well known poem:
> Turn your eyes upon Jesus
> Look full in his wonderful face
> And the things of earth will grow strangely dim
> In the light of his glory and grace

However, as divine grace takes possession of the soul it also liberates the intellectual and aesthetic faculties and reveals to the newly awakened soul God's world in its positive, created being, a world suffused with the goodness and beauty that originally flowed into it from the finger of God at the time of creation and that rushes to meet the soul being redeemed.
> Heaven above is softer blue
> Earth around is sweeter green
> Something lives in every hue
> Christless eyes have never seen.

shadow. Barth's strong opposition to 'unitary' universality and endorsement of the 'unifying' universality of the (reconciling) word oriented to Truth is precisely what is needed for the defence of democratic institutions. In the following passage Barth shows the importantance of he 'unifying' word as the medium of Truth.

> The church sees itself established and nourished by the free Word of God—the Word which proves its freedom in the Holy Scriptures at all times. And in its own sphere the church believes that the human word is capable of being the free vehicle and mouthpiece of this free Word of God. By a process of analogy, it has to risk attributing a positive and constructive meaning to the free human word in the political sphere. If it trusts the word of man in one sphere it cannot mistrust it on principle in the other. It will believe that human words are not bound to be empty or useless or even dangerous, but that the right words can clarify and control great decisions. At the risk of providing opportunities for empty, useless and dangerous words to be heard, it will therefore do all it can to see that there is at any rate no lack of opportunity for the *right* word to be heard. It will do all it can to see that there are opportunities for mutual discussion in the civil community as the basis of common endeavours. And it will try to see that such discussion takes place openly. With

all its strength it will be on the side of those who refuse to have anything to do with the regimentation, controlling, and censoring of public opinion. It knows of no pretext which would make that a good thing and no situation in which it could be necessary.[8]

What Barth here assumes, and what both citizens and public representatives routinely take for granted in their everyday political discussions, is an understanding of thought as a kind of 'other-directed' orientation or movement of mind towards its objects, a movement guided or 'enveloped' by Truth itself as its motivating origin and eliciting end, its pioneer and perfector. As I argued in an earlier work,[9] it is important to understand that 'thought', in being ever oriented beyond itself to its world of objects, is a point of transition between its origin and end in Truth. Our constant hope, both in our personal and political life, is that the movement of our thoughts is towards Truth itself, that truths as they appear to us in thought—or what is relatively or perspectivally true for us—are also 'true' in a more fundamental sense, that is, really true or at least movements towards Truth in this absolute sense. In spelling Truth with a capital 'T,' my intention is to distinguish the ultimately from the merely relatively true[10] and to

---

8. K Barth, *Community, State and Church: Three Essays*, 176–177
9. *The Human Service Disciplines and Social Work: The Foucault Effect*, 16–17.
10. I here follow the advice and procedure of AE Taylor who in his *Elements of Metaphysics* [(London: Metheun, 1961), 20] states that 'to meet the kind of criticism which finds it humorous to jest at the

highlight, and also to take the first steps towards justifying, the endeavours of politicians to ensure that, as far as possible and allowing for human frailty and fallibility, the things they do and the policies they pursue really are good and true, or at least as 'good and true' as possible; my intention is to insist that personal or political values, when properly employed, may be, and even routinely are, aspects or instances of value itself (value 'appearing' to the open and ethically sensitive 'civic' mind in a manner or form relative to its current circumstances and concerns), that political 'rationalities' may be, and even routinely are, aspects of reason itself (reason likewise 'appearing' to the reflective public mind in the form of policies and techniques designed to meet particular human needs) and that the truths of the human sciences we enlist in the service of humanity may be, and even routinely are, aspects of Truth itself or, what I think is to say more or less the same thing, that they are valuable and reasonable under the circumstances of their usage. That thought is ever in quest of its true home and proper mode of functioning in the universe, finding which it senses itself to be on the road to Value, Truth and Reason, and that the human person is the medium of the absolute (Truth, Reason and Value as they are mundanely realised through the medium of human thought and consciousness) are 'foundational' truths for our personal and civic life which it is important

---

expense of those who "take consolation from spelling Reality with a big R," may I once and for all say that when I spell Reality thus, it is simply as a convenient way of distinguishing the ultimately from the merely relatively real.'

to uphold and to strongly defend against Foucault's opposing view.

A Truth-oriented, normative Foucault?

At this point, however, we need to acknowledge that there are times when Foucault, despite his strong and repeated 'anti-Truth' pronouncements, actually seems to be quite prepared to use the kind of normative, dialectical, Truth-oriented language and approach that Barth employs and which broadly reflects the approach of traditional or classical political theory to which Foucault (apparently) took exception. For example, Foucault makes it clear in 'Truth and Power' that he regards as obsolete the privilege once claimed by 'left' intellectuals to speak 'in the capacity of master of Truth and justice' and to arrogantly proclaim their supposed insights concerning what he calls the 'just-and-true-for all'[11] and yet in his *Remarks on Marx*, he also says that once we 'shut the mouths of prophets and legislators: all those who speak *for* others and *above* others', then at that moment the complexity of the socio-political problems we face 'will be able to appear in its connection with people's lives; and consequently, the legitimacy of a common enterprise will be able to appear through concrete questions, difficult cases, revolutionary movements, reflections, and evidence'.[12] Here we find Foucault

---

11. M Foucault, 'Truth and Power' in *Power/Knowledge: Selected Interviews and Other Writings 1972–1977*, edited by C Gordon (New York: Harvester Wheatsheaf, 1980), 126.
12. M Foucault, *Remarks on Marx: Conversations with Duccia Trombadori*,

adamantly refusing, on the one hand, to 'prescribe solutions' and yet on the other hand asserting, the legitimacy of solutions or policies that emerge as a result of a *bona fide* grappling with the real complexity of the concrete problems that intimately affect the lives of people. In the light of his anti-metaphysical aversion for 'Truth' and his strict avoidance of any appeal to normative criteria to justify social policies or political solutions, one could surely be forgiven for wondering at this point what Foucault means here by the term 'legitimacy'. It certainly looks as if it means something like 'just-and-true-for-all' concerned in the kind of common enterprise he has just described, and as if it means that the kind of direction taken and solutions or policies proposed appear thoroughly justified from the perspective—the only one that counts—of all those concerned to grapple patiently, realistically and co-operatively with the unavoidable complexity of real, everyday problems. Also, precisely because this kind of 'common enterprise' does seem to have a certain *prima facie* legitimacy, it also looks as if its direction and solutions could *not* be said to automatically involve contributing, as Foucault puts it, to 'the functioning of a determinate situation of power that to my mind must be criticised'.[13]

We are then surely entitled to raise, or at least to begin to speculate about, the possibility that perhaps Foucault was not quite so adamant, after all, in his opposition to 'Truth' (the Truth that is Christ, the surging Life of the

---

translated by RJ Goldstein and J Cascaito (New York: Semiotexte, 1991), 158–159.

13. *Ibid*, 157.

Spirit and the universal love of the Father) and that whilst he certainly condemned totalistic, unitary, theory-driven, 'Truth-driven' and 'top-down' theoretico-deductive systems of thought, he actually applauded and supported open, pluralistic, flexible, 'emergent', 'Truth'-enfolding 'bottom-up' modes of theorising. If so, we would have to say that alongside the Foucault who disbelieves in 'Truth', we now find a radical, activist Foucault who ardently desires to participate (with Barth) in the process whereby the Truth emerges or 'grows' into the clear light of day. Perhaps, we might even say that the former Foucault is an illusion and that the latter, the more 'Christ-friendly' Foucault, is the real Foucault. After all, it certainly seems that in commending the kind of 'common' enterprise that emerges from a vital contact with the complexities of real life problems and in condemning the kind of 'common' enterprise pursued by totalistic regimes or political parties, Foucault has in mind some kind of 'genuine' or 'true' or 'just' common-ness which serves as a criterion of legitimacy and even 'Truth'.

The suggestion that such a 'Truth oriented, justice-seeking, genuinely normative Foucault' really exists is strongly supported by the fondness he displays in his 'Two Lectures' for disqualified or subjugated knowledges. He tells us that the key role served by the genealogical project is 'to entertain the claims to attention of local, disqualified, illegitimate knowledges against the claims of a unitary body of theory which would filter, hierarchise and order them in the name of some true knowledge and arbitrary idea of what constitutes a science and its objects'.[14] Now this account of subjugated knowledges in the 'Two Lectures' surely dovetails perfectly with, and further elucidates his account of, emergent, concrete (and hence 'truly legitimate') ascending reason in his *Remarks on Marx*, for it would certainly seem that the genealogical method, in entertaining the claims to attention of local, disqualified knowledges, serves as the instrument or weapon of a legitimising reason ('Reason'?) that emanates or ascends from the everyday lives of ordinary individuals but which can only find expression, realisation or effective politicisation if it is able to successfully oppose or deconstruct the descending totalistic 'reason' illegitimately enshrined in a unitary body of theory which would filter, hierarchise and order them in its name. As Ransom points out, Foucault's fondness for these liberated particles of knowledge 'appears to involve their isolation from any cycle of Truth and power'[15] but in that case we have surely no option but to regard the unearthing or the liberating appearance of these 'monads of knowledge' as illuminative moments of Truth, as a kind of epiphany or 'ascending emergence' of Truth itself before our momentarily unsullied knowing/receiving minds. Given that these monads of knowledge are unassociated with forms of power—admittedly, as Ransom says, 'a striking discovery in the age

---

14. 'Truth and Power' in *Power/Knowledge: Selected Interviews and Other Writings 1972–1977*, 83.
15. JS Ransom, *Foucault's Discipline: The Politics of Subjectivity* (London: Duke University Press, 1997), 99.

of disciplines and power/knowledge'[16]—it might even be possible for us to regard the process of their emergence, their liberated and liberatory 'emanation', as the bearer of Truth and being into our lives. It should be noted at this point that Foucault also speaks in *The Care of the Self* [17] and in 'An Aesthetics of Existence'[18] in such a way as to give the impression that morality is a kind of suffocating, 'syllogistic' web that descends from hegemonic heights to stifle ethics, or ethical conduct, construed as a kind of inner source of Truth (or even 'Truth') that ascends from within each of us, or at least struggles to ascend against the intense pressure of normalisation.

Despite his opposition to global and radical 'grand theory', there are even grounds, I would submit, for asserting that Foucault is *not* opposed to grand theory if it is of a suitably, non-totalistic, kind. If we consider, for example, the very striking contrast he draws between the Marxism of the Parisian students in May 1968 and the Marxism of the Tunisian students in March of the same year, it is clear that he had the utmost contempt for the highly developed theoretical formulations of the different Marxist camps in Paris, the conviction of each that it had 'caught' or ensnared the Truth in the web of its theoretical system and the unrestrained willingness of each to pronounce anathemas on the others, and the utmost respect for the Marxism of the Tunisian students, which was the-

---

16. *Ibid.*
17. M Foucault, *The Care of the Self* (New York: Pantheon, 1986).
18. In *Politics, Philosophy, Culture: Interviews and Other Writings, 1977–1984*, edited by L Kritzman (London: Routledge, 1988).

oretically underdeveloped; in fact, it could be said to be not developed at all, in the sense that it did not attempt to devise a comprehensive, theoretical scheme or net which, possessing the concepts and categories necessary to catch or represent the whole totality of Truth in a single theoretico-deductive system, could then be applied syllogistically to the concrete situation at hand. It would, rather, be truer to say that the Tunisian students drew inspiration and theoretical support from a Marxism that was suitably tailored to the real exigencies and injustices of the time and that became transformed through this intimate link with 'practice' into a flexible instrument of political struggle. On Foucault's account, there can be little doubt that Marxist concepts and categories answered directly to the needs of that struggle. He said that what happened in Tunisia was

> something absolutely different from all that muttering of political speeches and debates that occurred in Europe . . . [E]veryone was drawn into Marxism with radical violence and intensity and with a staggeringly powerful thrust. For those young people, Marxism did not represent merely a way of analyzing reality; it was also a kind of moral force, an existential act that left one stupefied. And I felt disillusioned and full of bitterness to think of how much of a difference there was between the way Tunisian students were Marxists and

what I knew of the workings of Marxism in
Europe (France, Poland, etc)[19]

Again, in his reflections on his Tunisian experience, we find Foucault returning to the theme of 'innocence of power', its profound legitimacy, its awesome power to convey a pure and unchallengeable authority to act on behalf of Truth against injustice. Foucault of course does not himself use the expression 'on behalf of Truth' but he does not recoil from describing the actions of the Tunisian students as 'a true political experience'[20] and one is left wondering what else he could possibly mean by 'true' on an occasion such as this when he seems to be telling us that he stared 'Truth and Goodness' itself directly in the face. He asks pointedly 'What on earth is it that can set off in an individual the desire, the capacity, and the possibility of an absolute sacrifice without our being able to recognise or suspect the slightest ambition or desire for power and profit?' and he answers without the slightest hesitation 'This is what I saw in Tunisia'.[21]

What Foucault seems to be struggling to say here, but what his anti-metaphysical bias prevents him from saying, is that there is something grander or greater than 'grand theory' and that is the Truth itself, or the purity, innocence and awesome authority of the Truth. No doubt, grand theory claims to be grand because of the privileged rela-

---

19. *Remarks on Marx: Conversations with Duccia Trombadori*, 135–136.
20. *Ibid*, 134
21. *Ibid*, 136.

tion to Truth that it claims, but what grand theory needs to acknowledge is that it can never be more than Truth's temporary expression and, moreover, that it is only an aspect of Truth that it temporarily expresses. At any rate, Foucault seems to acknowledge that grand theory still has a role to play in our political experience but that it needs to be duly humbled and to be flexibly related to concrete circumstances and to dovetail with 'theorising' of the more patient, empirical, documentary type that he holds is so necessary and fruitful. This being so, we are entitled, I believe, to make one further, daring suggestion, namely that it is not altogether implausible to suggest that Foucault was not against 'essentialising' or essences *per se* but that he was, rather, opposed to abstract conceptions of the human essence that play a key but oppressive role in the 'difference denying' descending thrust of unitary, theoretico-deductive reasoning.

Taking our cue from James Bernauer's work *Michel Foucault's Force of Flight*[22] in which he identifies a 'negative theology' in Foucault that sets itself the task of exposing the inveterate human tendency to regard as 'the human essence' whatever form our being happens to assume at any given time, it seems plausible to suggest that for this 'normative Foucault', every such essentialisation is partially false, inevitably limited, unduly dismissive of other aspects of the human essence that it claims to conceptually grasp in its entirety, and ever in need of further dialectical elaboration to allow these other, different aspects

---

22. J Bernauer, J 1990, *Michel Foucault's Force of Flight* (London: Humanities Press International, 1990).

a 'surface of emergence'. It is when such a conception of the human essence becomes 'scientifically' intertwined in a power/knowledge circuit and descends 'from above' with destructive force to silence all differences within the purview of its regime of Truth that the play of differences through dialectical elaboration and integration from below, is subverted and the 'politics of difference' is rendered unattainable.

Despite the fact that in his writings as a whole normative positions and norm-based moralities are generally regarded as (more often 'seen through', transformed into or reduced to) mere instruments of power or 'ethical embellishments' designed to give an aura of legitimacy to particular wills to power, Foucault himself, as we have seen, appears to be offering us his own normative position, or what certainly looks like a normative stance and outlook. Thus, when commentators find in his work a core of 'genuine normativity' which provides the ethical backbone of his work as a whole and the supportive structure or form for a 'politics of difference', they are not, *pace* David Ransom's contrasting view, making an implausible or unjustifiable imputation. We have already mentioned Bernauer's suggestion that what Foucault actually targets is the inveterate human tendency to (falsely) essentialise, which suggests that our ongoing ethical task is to 'de-essentialise' and perhaps to 're-essentialise' in the form of a dialectical correction and elaboration. One normally thinks of this ongoing dialectical process as 'Truth'—oriented (that is, having Truth as its origin and end) rather than as 'Life'-oriented but perhaps Gilles Deleuze is saying something similar—or thinks that Foucault is saying something similar—when he suggests that Foucault's ongoing resistance to biopower is inspired by the vital power of life. At any rate, Deleuze holds that there is an idea of 'life' in Foucault's work that is ethically and spiritually significant. 'When power becomes bio-power, resistance becomes the power of life, a vital power that cannot be confined within species, environment or the paths of a particular diagram. Is not the force that comes from outside a certain idea of life, a certain vitalism, in which Foucault's thought culminates? Is not life this capacity to resist force?'.[23] Thus we could say, following Deleuze, that political movements that 'patiently ascend' or 'surge upwards' with a force and power (of life or Truth itself) comes from intimate contact with ordinary life 'below' are legitimate, genuinely normative and thoroughly justified. It is true that Foucault speaks at times as if he is content to simply argue for what we might call 'mere procedural legitimacy', that is, to hold that political regimes are legitimate to the extent that they procedurally allow for ongoing agonistic struggle. Hence we can well understand Leslie Paul Thiele's remark that 'Foucault's political project is founded on the valorisation of struggle'[24] and Jon Simmons' assertion that 'Foucault's object is to maintain 'the openness of agonistic relations'[25] and that his 'conceptualisation of power relations as agonistic im-

---

23. G Deleuze, *Foucault* (Minneapolis: University of Minnesota Press, 1988).
24. LP Thiele, 'The Agony of Politics: The Nietzschean Roots of Foucault's Thought', in *America Political Science Review*, 84 (1990): 918.
25. J Simmons, *Foucault and the Political* (New York: Routledge, 1995), 4.

plicitly includes a regulative principle for the assessment of political regimes'.[26] However, it should be noted that Foucault seems to be *also* saying that a substantive, and not merely procedural, legitimacy attaches to those social and political movements that have been vitalised by their contact with, and exhibit a real concern for, the lives of ordinary people, especially those silenced by heavily solidified patterns of domination.

Connolly, Butler and Ransom on Foucault's normativity

Perhaps, then, we should, after all, regard Foucault as a Truth-oriented ('Christ-friendly'), life affirming ('Spirit-friendly') justice-seeking ('Father-friendly) normative thinker who should be accorded his rightful place of honor in the 'great tradition' of political theory and as a champion of 'liberal democracy' and 'the politics of difference'. I use these two expressions virtually interchangeably because the ongoing ethical/normative task confronting politics (its self-constitutive task, so to speak) *is* the unifying or synthesising of differences or the dialectical elaboration and integration of differences. Postmodernism is, I believe, seriously mistaken in adopting a profoundly suspicious attitude towards this ethical task and towards moral principles and normative positions as such, generally dismissing them as mere ethical embellishments of real, underlying social struggles or as mere instruments of power, or 'wills' to power. In its emphatic rejection of

---

26. *Ibid*, 86.

what we might call 'genuine' normativity or authentic ethico-political prescriptions in favour of a construction of normativity as an instrument or ethical embellishment of power, postmodernism *opposes* unity (the inherently universalising and unifying dimension of politics) *to* diversity (the 'differences' which it is the proper function of politics to systematically integrate).

William Connolly[27] and Judith Butler[28] are two authors who are forthright in their claim that we find in Foucault the kind of genuine and substantive normativity necessary to undergird the liberal democratic state and the 'politics of difference', and it is for precisely this reason that John Ransom, who is convinced that there is no basis for ascribing a normative position to Foucault, subjects their work to special critical scrutiny.[29] With regard to

---

27. W Connolly, 'Beyond Good and Evil: The Ethical Sensibility of Michel Foucault', in *Political Theory*, 21 (Aug 1993): 365–389; W Connolly, *Political Theory and Modernity* (Ithaca: Cornell University Press, 1995). Ithaca.
28. J Butler, *Gender Trouble: Feminism and the Subversion of Identity* (New York: Routledge, 1990); J Butler, 'Gender Trouble, Feminist Theory and Psychoanalytic Discourse', Feminism/*Postmodernism*, edited by LJ Nicholson (New York: Routledge, 1990).
29. Other authors who, though in varying degrees, rely upon an appeal to a 'normative Foucault' to support a 'politics of difference' are Anna Yeatman in *Postmodern Revisionings of the Political* (New York: Routledge, 1994); Jane Flax 'Beyond Equality: Gender, Justice and Difference', in *Beyond Equality and Difference*, edited by G Bock and S James (New York: Routledge, 1992); Mark Bevir in 'Foucault and Critique: Deploying Agency Against Autonomy', in *Political Theory*, 27 (February 1999): 65-84; and Iris Young in *Justice and the Politics of Difference* (Princeton: Princeton University Press, 1990).

the 'politics of difference', Ransom makes two important points or claims; firstly, that it relies on normative and humanist notions and, secondly, that precisely because it does so, it lacks discriminatory power, is far too vague and ambiguous to be of much use, and may lead us to accept the unacceptable, to accept, for example, skinhead culture as part of the tapestry of difference and hence as acceptable and unobjectionable. I agree with his first point—and so, too, presumably would Butler, Connolly and the 'normative Foucault'—but not the second. With regard to the charge that the 'politics of difference' might incline us to be lenient in our attitude to objectionable forms of 'difference', it should be noted here that Ransom also upbraids the 'politics of difference' for serving up no more than a version of liberal pluralism 'spiced up with a heavy salting of deconstructive rhetoric'.[30] However, if we accept, as I believe we should, Ransom's suggestion here that the 'politics of difference' and the politics of liberal pluralism are substantively identical, even if expressed in quite different terms, then the 'politics of difference' is indistinguishable from, and in no way inferior to, liberal pluralism in its profound and unswerving respect of

---

In my *Justice And The State: On Liberal Organicism and the Foundations of Emancipatory Politics* (Quebec: World Heritage Press, 1998), 87–88, I have suggested that Young's account of the 'politics of difference' is particularly enlightening and that it helps us to more clearly grasp that the 'finger' of difference invariably 'points' to unity as 'its other.'

30. *Foucault's Discipline: The Politics of Subjectivity*, 121

the rights of the individual and in the uncompromising character of its rejection and thorough delegitimation of any objectionable forms of difference which might threaten to undermine these rights. With regard to the charge that the 'politics of difference' is too vague and ambiguous, we need to recollect here Foucault's account in *Remarks on Marx* of the way in which a unitary, totalising reason descends in imperious (top-down) fashion on emerging differences, effectively suppressing their emergence, for in that account he would seem to be offering a version of the 'politics of difference' which possesses precisely the kind of discriminatory power which Ransom believes it lacks. A 'normative Foucault'-style 'politics of difference' clearly condemns the unjust and oppressive effects of descending, hegemonic reason and its assorted regimes of Truth and valorises liberated and liberating differences that emerge from the uncaptured soul of everyday life.

Now Ransom might reply that this version of the 'politics of difference' still 'shares the same difficulties with other normative and vaguely humanist notions: it is too ambiguous' and 'does not tell you enough about the political context of one's decisions and alliances'[31] but surely this betrays a serious misunderstanding of the character of the ethico-political norms that operate in liberal pluralism and the 'politics of difference', and of the manner and mode of their operation. We need to note here that whilst these norms do, admittedly, possess an element of formality and universality, yet it is a formality 'ever in quest of'

---

31. *Ibid*, 107.

its material political context or a universality 'unceasingly seeking' its concrete realisation. Just as, through our ordinary personal moral judgments, the universal norms of morality find concrete expression or realisation, so too it is by means of our collective political judgment that the universal norms of liberal pluralism or the 'politics of difference' find their effective concrete embodiment. Ethico-political judgment and personal moral judgments are identical in requiring a consciousness or reflective medium—either collective/political or personal—to translate or consciously carry 'form' into its appropriate 'matter' or practice. Ethical judgment is always a matter of deciding, or of agonised reflection upon, which particular principle or type of norm is relevant, or most relevant and appropriate, in a particular case—is justice or mercy, individual freedom or community welfare, more relevant or appropriate in *this* case?—so that norms indirectly determine our actions, both personal and collective, *through* our decisions; it is never a matter of simple, deductive inference, and yet Ransom appears to believe that a 'politics of difference' is vague and ambiguous if it fails to provide such a syllogistic or deductive procedure for making political decisions. RM Hare once remarked, half in jest yet making a serious point, that 'if we could establish a formal, *a priori* (and yet somehow synthetic) principle, and then deduce maxims from it to govern our conduct, we should have succeeded in finding a set of moral principles to guide our lives without making up our own minds about a single moral question'.³² He also spoke of the unwillingness to make moral decisions as the 'oldest and most ineradicable vice of moralists'³³ but perhaps anti-normative political theorists, especially in this postmodern age, are also highly susceptible to this particular vice. Certainly Ransom, here echoing the 'anti-normative Foucault', appears to believe that a normative and humanist 'politics of difference' is only acceptable if it can provide the ethico-political equivalent of the kind of 'formal, *a priori* (and yet somehow synthetic) principle' of which Hare speaks, whereas what the 'politics of difference' in fact requires is that policies and political decisions be framed *in accordance with* its guiding principles, that is, the age-old tenets of liberal pluralism, not that they must be shown to be deducible from these principles.³⁴

The main problem of course with the normative, activist, liberating Foucault that we have examined thus far

---

32. RM Hare 'Universalizability', in *Aristotelian Society*, 55 (1955): 295–302.
33. *Ibid*.
34. In his 'Universalizability', 302 Hare states concisely what we, as individual persons or as a collective/ political agent, need to do to bring the ethical universal and concrete circumstances into fruitful intercourse when he says: 'We steer a middle course between the hide-bound inflexibility of the man who knows what he ought to do in a new situation even before he has properly considered its special features, and the neurotic indetermination of the man who cannot ever make up his mind what he ought to do, even in comparatively familiar situations, because he is never satisfied that he has exhausted their infinite particularity. The latter can learn nothing from experience; the former stops learning too early.'

is that this 'normative (Trinity-friendly) Foucault' implicitly relies upon a relation to Truth which he explicitly and very forcibly rejects and disparages, so that as soon as we endeavour to render this normative, implicit Foucault more visible and explicit, we find that we run the risk of destroying the anti-metaphysical and anti-God Foucault that we know so well and who constantly springs out at us from the pages of his work. This implicit or normative (God-friendly) Foucault is like a deep undercurrent that only occasionally rises to the surface to 'directly' threaten the familiar or 'mainstream' (God-resistant) Foucault, or like a dark un-Foucauldian 'persona' which has been banished to the recesses of his mind but which continues to constantly haunt his work and which occasionally escapes from its banishment to make its holy presence more forcibly felt. Foucault, I believe, never ceased to be haunted or 'pursued' by the 'holy specter' of Truth; it was a 'ghost' (a redeeming angelic presence) that he could never quite exorcise. Just as we are 'tempted' by the Spirit to rise to new heights of fullness and glory, so too was Foucault 'tempted' by the specter/Spirit of Truth and by the fullness of life the Spirit offers. If banished from his mind and thoughts, it nevertheless found a home elsewhere, in his soul or heart perhaps, for it continued, I believe, to inspire his most passionate political commitments and his quest for 'new forms of politicisation'. However that may be, I would suggest that we cannot take this normative (implicit and 'spectral') Foucault too seriously, since this Foucauldian 'persona' was never explicitly 'owned' or acknowledged by Foucault himself, but that we *must* treat with full or 'unconditional' seriousness what he clearly and explicitly states, charitably assuming that he was simply unaware of the reliance of his political activism on a version of Truth. Thus whilst I hold, *pace* Ransom, that it must be acknowledged that there is *some* textual basis in Foucault's work for the claim that he was a genuinely normative theorist who could provide an ethical scaffolding for the 'politics of difference' project, I nevertheless agree with Ransom's view that the latter, especially when considered as a normative or ethico-political project, is profoundly anti-Foucauldian and that the general tone and tenor of his work is adamantly (perhaps *too* adamantly) anti-normative, anti-metaphysical, anti-God and therefore 'anti' the project of providing a genuine normative underpinning for the 'politics of difference'.

Ultimately, the very notion of a 'politics of difference' collapses into incoherence unless it is acknowledged that the 'finger' of unity or, more precisely, of the unifying universal, points in quasi-Hegelian fashion to 'difference' as 'its other', its necessary correlative, its complement, even its completion. Not only does Foucault refuse to make such an acknowledgment but he actually opposes unity *to* difference. What the 'politics of difference' requires is a 'Barth-ian dialectical web of Truth' in the sense of an interweaving web or tapestry of differences that form a true harmony or living unity and which enables each part or difference to be itself, to find its true place and role in the whole and to live out its true destiny, i.e. its 'Truth' and its destiny as part of the whole. However, what Foucault offers us is not a universal web of Truth that envelopes its differences but, rather, an endless succession of 'games of truth and error'[35] or, alternatively, of life and death struggles by 'difference' *against* 'unity' (the unifying social or political universal). Whereas those who enter into the spirit of the 'politics of difference' play the 'game of Truth', or what we might call the divine/ontological game in which Being (the very life of God, the Spirit) historically realises itself (constitutes itself in time) in and through the living, experienced truths and differences of each spatio-temporal world (of the individual, family, society), Foucault's 'flat and empirical' method transforms the *milieu* of truth/Truth, of truths moving towards or away from Truth, into a horizontal succession of dead, inert, wholly mundane and insignificant 'truths'; in this way, Foucault literally tears into disconnected pieces the interweaving fabric of 'unity-in-diversity' that the 'politics of difference' regards as ideal and attempts to construct (or reconstruct as the case may be). There is simply no sense in Foucault's work of a meaningful 'play of differences', no sense of each difference being integrally and significantly related to what it is different from, no sense, in short, of the unifying function exercised by the universal through this very 'play of differences'. Taking Foucault's own definite anti-normative pronouncements seriously, it seems then that we must accept that the 'politics of difference' is profoundly anti-Foucauldian, as Ransom has so strongly insisted.

Although I have suggested that throughout his career, Foucault endeavoured, though not quite successfully,

---

[35]. M Foucault, *The Use of Pleasure* (New York: Random House, 1985), 6.

to exorcise the 'spectre of Truth', still I certainly would not suggest that this is a reason for disregarding or minimising in any way the significance of his anti-normative pronouncements. We have to take Foucault at his 'explicit' word and as we have seen, the great strength of Ransom's analysis of Foucault is that he does precisely that. Thus, even though I think that Ransom is much too severe on critics who search out and find a 'normative' Foucault, I think that he is correct to insist that Foucault is explicitly and frequently 'anti-normative' and that the 'politics of difference' must, in the end, be judged to be anti-Foucaultian. Unfortunately, however, or at least so it appears from my point of view, Ransom then proceeds to draw the conclusion that since the 'politics of difference' claims to cohere with the anti-normative tone and tenor of Foucault and postmodernism but in fact does not, and since it surreptitiously appropriates postmodern terms and concepts whilst rejecting the anti-foundational, anti-normative stance of postmodernism, it should therefore be abandoned. No doubt, a lot depends here on what we mean by postmodernism and I have argued at length elsewhere that a genuinely normative postmodernism is by no means self- contradictory.[36] However, even if we grant, in deference to Ransom, that Foucault's work and postmodernism in general are unequivocally anti-normative, it would by no means follow that the 'politics of difference' should be abandoned; what would follow is that a defence for the 'politics of difference' would have to be

---

36. BT Trainor, *The Origin and End of Modernity: Reflections on the Meaning of Post-modernism* (Quebec: World Heritage Press, 1998), 1–8.

sought elsewhere, in an unapologetically normative (and ultimately theological) form of political theory that clearly understands that political life actually consists in the ongoing quest, prompted by the Spirit, for a unifying synthesis of differences or 'diversities' (the 'common good'). This quest is the vital pulse, the 'life and soul' or the ongoing 'political substance' *of* the forms and procedures of liberalism and democratic pluralism. Thus we can agree with Ransom that behind the 'politics of difference' there lurks the 'familiar notions of democratic pluralism and justice'[37] or, alternatively expressed, that the former (the 'politics of difference') is the matter or substance of which the latter (procedural democratic pluralism) is the form. We can also agree that the vision of justice that informs the 'politics of difference' is 'the basic liberal pluralist version we all learned about in a first year political philosophy course'.[38] However, we must insist that Ransom's claim that the 'politics of difference' is liberal pluralism 'spiced up with a heavy salting of deconstructive rhetoric'[39] is very misleading, or at least it is misleading if taken in the negative, dismissive sense that Ransom clearly intends. Of course, it must be conceded that if the liberal usage of postmodern terms and concepts by advocates of the 'politics of difference' serves as no more than window dressing, it does little to advance the cause of tolerance, diversity, rights and pluralism, but the work of Connolly and Butler surely shows that it actually deepens our ap-

---

37. *Foucault's Discipline: The Politics of Subjectivity*, 120.
38. *Ibid*, 121.
39. *Ibid*.

preciation and intellectual grasp of the full meaning of terms and concepts ('tolerance' 'diversity' 'rights') that had perhaps become jaded, or whose moral force had been seriously diluted, by their over-familiarity and over-usage in our political language. What I would suggest then, is that advocates of the 'politics of difference' need to use Foucault's work as he himself suggested, that is, as a 'philosophical toolbox', for they can find therein elements of genuine normativity which actually serve their ends extremely well. In this way, they gain access to a rich treasure house of ideas which may be selectively used in defence of their cause. In brief, if I might borrow a phrase from Mark Bevir, they need 'to use Foucault rather than interpret him',[40] for this approach to his work allows them to take full advantage of the 'spectral' (God and Truth-oriented) Foucault whose rare but brilliant appearances (his insights are simply blinding at times) lend such powerful support to the 'politics of difference' when properly (that is, theologically) understood.

Conclusion; Meta-narratives and Servants of Truth

In an earlier work[41] I noted that a brief comparison of today's youth with youth in the 1960s highlights the enormous cultural difference we have traveled in a remarkably short period of time. In the 1960s, young people either felt a deep sense of alienation and fought against what they saw as obsolete and repressive (capitalist/individu-

---

40. 'Foucault and Critique: Deploying Agency against Autonomy', 80.
41. *The Human Service Disciplines and Social Work: the Foucault Effect*, 65.

alistic/materialistic) truths in the name of Truth itself, or else they saw the same truths (liberalism, individualism, material progress) not as redundant but as expressive of Truth itself. However, whatever their relation to the then dominant values, young people at the time generally lived in a cultural ambiance of Truth. In contrast, western youth at the present time is currently exhibiting a strong strain towards 'anomie', that is, towards a 'condition of relative normlessness'. The rash of suicides and of mental depression in our young people is largely due, I would suggest, *not* to a lack of ability or willingness on their part to embrace societal norms, values and ideals, but to the felt emptiness (and 'impossibility') of life in a social vacuum; that is, in a social world *without* norms, values and ideals and without meaning, metanarratives and grand ('Truth') theorising. This suggestion presupposes, but also goes beyond in a significant respect, Durkheim's insistence that the suicide *rate* is a social fact requiring a social explanation; it is at one with Durkheim in acknowledging the need in all of us for a sense of social integration in our lives, but goes further in suggesting that we all, but most especially our young people, *also* need the social and political groups and institutions to which we belong to be (or at least to seriously claim to aspire to be) worthwhile, sound, good and true, that is, to be vital sources of meaning in our lives and to provide cultural pathways to Truth. 'Social integration' is certainly important for human health and happiness but so too—again, for our youth especially—is 'Truth integration' or the sense that our lives as individuals, family members, professionals, citizens, etc, (i) are meaningfully related to 'the good and the true' and (ii), though culturally unique, are nevertheless defensible from the standpoint of our common humanity. It's as if a 'mushroom' generation of youth has somehow sprung overnight into existence. This generation, or a substantial portion thereof, has not grown steadily and surely in the soil provided by inherited cultural traditions, with their evolving understanding of 'the good and the true'. All too many young people at the present time have not experienced traditions that bear significantly on their minds, hearts and sentiments, traditions whose core values and beliefs they are invited to endorse, but which they can challenge, modify or cast into new forms. Rather, many young people of this generation have sprung rootless into existence, have been presented with no 'live' options, no pathways to 'the good or true' and have been left or 'abandoned' to their own devices by their parents' numbing fear of 'normalisation', that is, of 'imposing' their values on their own children. Intellectual and cultural signposts to the Truth seem to be largely absent in the lives of our youth; many, perhaps even most, hear only the deafening sound of silence, for their cultural wellsprings have all but run dry and no longer even claim to convey the 'living water' of encultured Truth. In short, they live in a world where the 'vacuum of Truth' is the 'main danger'. In such a world, Foucault's strong anti-Truth stand (implicitly of course, an anti-Christ stand) is part of the problem rather than part of the solution, for far from encouraging the emergence of a world in which our youth can live and breathe, it actually impedes the birth, or re-birth of an intellectual scene positively bursting at the seams with signposts to the Truth and overflowing with meta-narratives vying for their attention. But what exactly are meta-narratives? Why are they so important and why does the significance of life suddenly seem to shrivel up when they disappear from the cultural and intellectual landscape?

A meta-narrative is a story that provides an account of, and thereby attempts to explain or elucidate, how the humanity of each of us interweaves with the humanity of all of us. In so doing, it links the 'story' of our/my origin and destiny to the 'story' of the origin and destiny of our universe as a whole. Thus understood, the divine/historical drama of human salvation recorded in the bible is the grandest meta-narrative ever told. Marxism and Feminism, each of which tells the story of how we exit from an era of darkness (capitalist or patriarchal) and progress towards (or stumble into) the ultimate light or Truth of our world, are perhaps the most well known 'secular' examples. Whatever may be said against them—and a great deal has been said against them, and said truly, by Foucault and others—they at least have the great redeeming feature of being Truth-oriented, of linking the truths and meanings of everyday life with Truth and Meaning as such. In this way, they attempt to 'tell it like it is', to show how the meaning of our lives interweaves with, and is intimately connected to, the meaning and significance of the universe as a whole. In brief, a meta-narrative tells the story, including the twists and turns, of the collective movement of our humanity in and towards Truth and thus, explicitly or implicitly, in and towards Christ.

Now, it is my contention that we are as much in need of such meta-narratives today as ever we were; indeed, we are *more* in need of them, for there is much more danger today than in the past that individuals in their various pursuits—the editor of a union newspaper, the teacher in an experimental elementary school or the young lawyer working for a civil rights lobby group—may each feel that they are 'on their own', that perhaps, after all, they are just pursuing their own 'private' interest or hobby (what turns them on); they may even feel that the form of social engagement they have each chosen is really an expression of their own 'will to power', as Foucault would say, and not part of a wider, genuinely progressive and emancipatory social movement. Thus, the fact that intellectuals in general, and Left intellectuals in particular, have rightly abandoned any claim to be 'masters of Truth' in no way lessens, but actually increases, their ongoing responsibility to be 'servants of Truth', that is, to develop their own meta-narratives and to play a central and constructive role in the formation of an intellectual culture characterised by its 'ecumenical graciousness' towards meta-narratives in general. However, as well as cultivating such a sense of 'ecumenical graciousness' towards all meta-narratives, they also need to critically analyse the truth claims of each in turn in order to pinprick their pretensions and exaggerated claims, and in order to distil the precise aspect of Truth that each contains. Curiously enough, it is in the performance of this critical role in relation to meta-narratives (as distinct from an outright, anti-Truth dismissal of the latter) that postmodernism, and especially Foucault, is able to offer us invaluable assistance and real insight.

If postmodernism may be justly accused of throwing the 'baby of Truth' out with the bath water (totalising ideologies), we need to make sure that our search for Truth doesn't bring the dirty water back into the bath tub. We must acknowledge that Truth is a collective quest to be pursued, most certainly, with passion and enthusiasm, but at the same we must be careful not to succumb in the course of this pursuit to the 'totalising temptation' to set ourselves (or those of 'our persuasion') up as 'Masters of Truth'. It is important to note at this point that for Christians to seek God's Truth in our time and place in a political sense is not to aspire to be such 'Masters of Truth' or to engage in 'holy politics'; it is, quite simply, to do what all citizens must do, namely, to continuously make judgments in good faith concerning 'what is for the common good of society', or, in religious terms, 'what is God's will for society'. All such judgments, whether personal or collective, and however arrived at (through, for example, what Christians may take to be intimations of the Spirit) are invariably fallible. What we feel are the intimations of the Spirit (either 'public' or 'holy') may not in fact be so. As Pope Benedict XVI is fond of saying, 'reason has a wax nose' or as his predecessor Pope John Paul II once remarked, the Holy Spirit moves through earthen vessels; in the human heart of each such vessel, it is just as likely to be met by rocks of resistance ('I/we already *know* where the Spirit is leading') as by a truly listening ear that patiently and humbly seeks God's will through dialogue with those in whom the Spirit dwells and through whom the Spirit speaks, that is, one's fellow citizens. Whether believers or not, they are 'holy citizens' or 'anonymous Christians', if one prefers Rahner's expression; 'holiness' in this context has nothing to do with one's *credo* but with the degree of one's openness to the Spirit (again, holy or public) in and through others. Of the non-believers, it may be said that, like Cyrus, they should serve the Spirit of the Lord, though they know not his name (Isaiah 45:1, 4–6), by listening to his quiet voice in the heat of public debate, but believers must do likewise and refrain from using their *credo* in an obnoxious (and anti-Christian) way to set themselves up as 'Masters of Truth', those who already *know* with perfect assurance what God's will is in public affairs in each specific context, and who can therefore indulge in good conscience in 'holy politics' (in an invidious sense) or in what Stauffer once called 'the metaphysical glorification of policy';[42] in contrast, for Christians as 'servants of Truth', it (one's *credo*) is relevant, *not* as a way of infallibly 'knowing' God's will in the public realm but in nourishing the believer's inner motivational strength, in providing ethical boundaries (or 'side-constraints') for public policy, and as an impetus to seek God's will in the shared wisdom of all of humanity 'at its best'. Christian citizens as 'servants of Truth' do not regard their religious convictions or faith as providing some kind of unique and inerrant access to public or political 'Truth' but, like James Gustafson's 'Christian participant', are, rather, 'one partner among many in the human conversation that will give some determination to the ways in which men use their technical and political powers, their resources and

---

42. E Stauffer, *Christ and the Caesars*, translated by K and R Gregor Smith (Philadelphia: Westminster Press, 1955), 127.

talents in the development of history and society toward humane ends'.[43]

The greatest antidote to the 'totalising' temptation to set ourselves (or those of 'our persuasion') up as 'Masters of Truth' is the cultivation of a self-critical spirit. Now, no-one has done more to foster such a spirit and to undermine the false pretensions of 'Masters of Truth' and 'grand theorists' than Foucault. His withering critique of 'experts'—those who 'know it all' and can confidently and 'scientifically' show us the way—certainly helps us to become humble 'servants of Truth' and to endeavour to eradicate from ourselves the intellectual traits (arrogance, and a false sense of certainty) of these discredited 'Masters' and 'experts'. (A seeker and servant of Truth must constantly resist the temptation to act as a 'Master of Truth', whereas the latter has the illusory assurance of false certainty and is, in a sense, 'beyond temptation.') The kind of personal and professional 'humility' that is appropriate for us as 'servants of Truth' is well described in Foucault's portrayal of his own role as an intellectual.

> My role is to address problems effectively, really: and to pose them with the greatest possible rigor, with the maximum complexity and difficulty, so that a solution does not arise all at once because of the thought of some reformer or even in the brain of a political party. The problems that I try to address, these

---

43. *Theology and Christian Ethics*, 85.

perplexities of crime, madness and sex which involve daily life, cannot be easily resolved. It takes years, decades of work carried out at the grassroots level with the people directly involved; and the right to speech and political imagination must be returned to them . . . I carefully guard against making the law. Rather, I concern myself with determining problems, unleashing them, revealing them within a framework of such complexity as to shut the mouths of prophets and legislators; all those who speak for others and above others. It is at that moment that the complexity of the problem will be able to appear in its connection with people's lives; and consequently, the legitimacy of a common enterprise will be able to appear through concrete questions, difficult cases, revolutionary movements, reflections and evidence.[44]

Foucault here offers us what might appear to be a 'conservative' formula for resisting the simplifying and totalising tendencies of radical ideologies but his commendatory reference to 'revolutionary movements' indicates that his work is conservative in a true Burkean sense (Edmund Burke's conservatism of 'real experience' led him to support the American Revolution) rather than in a reactionary sense or in a way that opposes beneficial social change. At any rate, whether 'conservative' or not, the benefits to be

---
44. *Remarks on Marx: Conversations with Duccia Trombadori*, 158–159.

gained from the kind of full immersion in the real problems of everyday life that Foucault commends are surely beyond dispute and his critique of the 'knowing gaze' of experts and 'masters of Truth' certainly paves a humble pathway along which public representatives and those in positions of civic authority may not only walk side by side with each other but also with (and *for*), rather than above (and in the 'scientifically' assessed interests of) their fellow citizens. Moreover, just as the absoluteness and unassailable certainty of the 'knowing gaze' must be set aside, to be replaced by the provisionality and tentativeness of the genuinely 'attentive ear', so too the data (or truths) of the human and social sciences employed in the formation of public policy, though important and relevant, must not be allowed to operate in the process of policy formation as premises in a syllogism from which 'what is to be done' can be scientifically 'deduced' by 'Masters of Truth', but must be treated, instead, as background factors whose influence and meaning in the lives of individuals need to be assessed on a case by case basis.

In summary, Foucault is the leading theorist who, perhaps more than any other, has contributed to the current 'anti-Truth' cultural climate and his work constitutes the intellectual 'main danger' to the health and wellbeing of our society in general but most especially of young people seeking meaning and significance in their lives. However, although he has thrown his full intellectual weight against the very notion of 'Truth', he is at the same time the theorist who is most valuable and insightful in providing us with the kind of practical orientation necessary for a 'servant and seeker of Truth'. My own view is that Foucault is substantively and theoretically 'wrong' concerning 'Truth' but methodologically and practically 'right' concerning how we should proceed in practical terms towards what he would regard as legitimate (his expression) personal and political ends and what I would *further* regard as the Truth of ourselves and God's will for our political community. In brief, my suggestion is that we should decisively reject the substantive and theoretical Foucault who takes his stand against 'Truth' and warmly embrace the practical and methodological Foucault who recommends a full immersion into the real, personal and social problems of everyday life. In the next chapter I shall argue that if, in the formulation of sound public policy in the name of and at the behest of the state, Foucault is the 'theoretical problem', we need to look to the work of a thinker such as Bosanquet, taken as a representative voice of traditional social philosophy and as a strong exponent of the ethical theory of the state, for a 'theoretical solution' and as a 'theoretical advance' on the communitarianism of Michael Walzer.

Chapter Four

Walzer, Communitarianism and Truth:

Pluralism and Public Policy

My veil is my strength
Muslim woman

How am *I* to live? How are *we* to live as members of enveloping collective entities (our family, local community, society)? Is the 'own self' to which I wish to be true somehow connected to the 'own self' to which you, or perhaps we (again as a family, society etc) wish to be true? Is public policy, at its best, the ideal and highly desirable expression of such a 'collective own self' or is it, rather, the case that public policy conceived of in this way (as the realisation of the collective own self or as the pursuit of our authentic common good) constitutes a threat to the 'liberalism' of liberal democracy and to the freedom and diversity of lifestyle that we associate with modern multicultural society . . . and in what way, if at all, is the state relevant to how we answer these questions? My contention in this chapter is that the state, by virtue of what it is (our collective 'own self'), requires of us as fellow citizens that we seriously endeavour to pursue sound public policy measures, that is, measures that are 'good and true' or as good and true as the limits of our human powers will allow. We are required, indeed, to form a truly (that is 'Truth-oriented') 'deliberative democracy' whose procedures allow the collective own self the maximum freedom of expression and realisation. Since not just the single individual, but society as well, is a temple of the Holy Spirit, and since the state is a kind of 'collective own self' to which we, as fellow citizens, ought to be (collectively) true in much the same way as a man is under a solemn obligation to be true to his own self, then it is, I wish to suggest, to the Holy Spirit that we are ultimately referring when we refer to the 'collective own self' of society. Hence, my personal quest for the truth of my self (or of my 'own self') inevitably involves me in a quest for the truth of my society, that is, for the authentic common good of the socio-political whole I share with others, and this quest, pursued in good faith, is 'the state in action' or 'the Holy Spirit expressed through collective human action'. Having argued in the last chapter that we should be seekers and servants of Truth (that is, instruments of the Spirit) both in our lives as individuals and as citizens, in this chapter I discuss the reservations of Michael Walzer to such a suggestion. Finally, I consider the relationship of public policy—as an instrument of the state conceived of in the theological manner I have commended in this book—to Truth and show that Walzer and Foucault inadequately grasp, whereas Bosanquet positively illuminates, this relationship. I hold that if Foucault, taken (even if somewhat against his will) as representative of contemporary postmodernism, is the 'theoretical problem', then the 'theoretical solution' lies in the work of a theorist such as Bosanquet, taken (again, perhaps somewhat against his will) as representative of traditional social philosophy and political theory and as a strong exponent of what I call 'the ethical theory of the state' (see chapter eight). I will explore the Truth-oriented communitarianism of Bernard Bosanquet and show how it provides a theoretical complement to (or perhaps an unwelcome metaphysical/ theological fulfilment of) Michael Walzer's communitarianism, and also try to address the fears of postmodernists who have reservations about the idea of social universals informing 'their' differences. In the final sections of the chapter, I look at how the state, as a form of what I call 'ethico-political consciousness', operates (or, as I believe, should operate) in the civic and pursuit of Truth in social and public life, especially concerning the family, the homosexual family and culturally formative religion.

Pluralism, Truth and Liberal Democracy; Walzer

'I want to talk as a philosopher today—a practical and engaged philosopher. I won't argue for particular policies, but I also won't remain at the level of abstract principles. If philosophy is to engage with politics, it had better be political, not metapolitical philosophy'.[1] With

---

1. M Walzer, 'Pluralism and Social Democracy', in *Dissent* (Winter 1998): 47.

these words from the beginning of Michael Walzer's article 'Pluralism and Social Democracy', and with Michel Foucault's insistence that we should immerse ourselves with patience and persistence in problems of everyday life, most readers would no doubt feel a strong sympathy, but I wish nevertheless to introduce a note of caution. It is certainly fine and unexceptionable to aspire to be 'practical and engaged philosophers' but only if being such a philosopher is not compared invidiously with being a speculative, metaphysical or Truth-oriented philosopher. We need to keep our minds open to the distinct possibility that an 'engaged philosophy' may well be *both*, that is, practical and, at the same time metapolitical, metaphysical and Truth-oriented. It wasn't that long ago, after all, that the term 'praxis' was used in leftist circles to highlight the intimacy (the symbiotic 'innerness') of the link between meta-political or metaphysical (Truth-oriented) philosophy and political practice. However, Walzer seems at times to suggest that metaphysical or Truth-oriented reflections on political practice merely hover idly above 'real political life' and that they can be safely and innocuously dispensed with.

Certainly, we are all interested in sound reflection upon political practice; we all wish to avoid idle abstractions and forms of 'philosophising' that do not relate meaningfully to everyday political life. Moreover, it must be admitted at the outset that the suggestion that reflection upon political life needs to be Truth-oriented if it is to be sound and productive runs immediately into a major obstacle. It may seem that any suggestion that intellectuals in general, and left intellectuals in particular, should be explicitly and unashamedly 'Truth-oriented' would merely invite the kiss of death, for reasons that Walzer makes all too clear. He points out that we no longer 'admire people who make themselves organs of historical necessity, instruments of an all-powerful party, disciples of a sectarian leader, ideological or religious zealots'.[2] This of course is perfectly true and the main reason, it must be frankly admitted, why we no longer admire such people is that they were 'Truth-oriented' thinkers. However, we need to be more precise about what lies behind our distaste for such persons. The simple fact that, like Marx, they were Truth-oriented and that they (or their leading intellectual lights) articulated grand Truth narratives of world historical proportions should *not* be held against them. The Left is just as much in need of grand Truth narratives today as it was in Marx's day. The reason for our current distaste for those thinkers should not be that they were Truth-oriented *per se* but that they were Truth-oriented in the wrong way. They saw themselves as 'Masters of Truth' who could speak with supreme confidence from their lofty and enlightened positions to those still shackled in the 'darkness of the cave' below. However, the fact that their intellectual arrogance now stands fully revealed to our retrospective gaze should not blind us to the all-important fact that, empirically, the 'darkness of the cave' still exists. Families and communities are breaking up; poverty is still very much with us and large sections of our youth are in suicidal despair. To eschew the role of 'master of Truth' does not excuse us from the

---

2. *Ibid.*

task of being 'seekers of Truth'. Even in a liberal pluralist society—indeed, I would argue, especially in a liberal pluralist society—we need to be 'seekers and servants of Truth' who extensively and rigorously criticise each other's Truth meta-narratives in order to shed as much light as we can on the real (true) reasons for the forms of oppression still being experienced in the 'darkness of the cave'. Only in this way can we find the best public policies and, at the same time, be true to the state as our 'collective own self' and as the Holy Spirit 'prescriptively present' in our midst.

The importance of Truth and our profound need for Truth in a liberal pluralist society may be highlighted by considering the old Jewish proverb quoted by Michael Walzer. 'You are not bound to finish the work, but neither are you free to give it up'.[3] Walzer uses this proverb to highlight the tensions and paradoxes in our attitudes as free citizens of a pluralist society towards the projects we have inherited from the previous generation(s). He points out that without projects 'so central to our lives that we were prepared to impose them on our children, the freedom to choose (or refuse) would be very nearly meaningless'.[4] He insists that what is crucial for freedom is the capacity to exit from groups, for whatever reason, and find a 'new' home, so to speak, in alternative associations. However, as he says, 'this freedom to come and go requires that there be somewhere to come from and go to; it requires a genuine pluralism, a diversity of groups with

---

3. M Walzer, 'Pluralism and Social Democracy', 47.
4 *Ibid*.

members who are engaged, entangled, committed, hard at work'.⁵ Walzer is deeply concerned that the freedom, individuality and mobility of modern society engenders the risk that if individuals 'move so fast and in such numbers that [society's] groups and associations cannot sustain an inner life and if they experiment so casually that they are not marked by the experience, the freedom to move and experiment will become less and less significant'.⁶ Hence he believes that it is of the utmost importance, both for freedom itself and for our personal and collective health and happiness, to 'create and re-create stable social settings—families and communities—that produce strong individuals and provide them with seriously and interestingly different possibilities'.⁷

Thus far has Walzer carried forward the 'work' but to carry it further forward, we need to ask what it is precisely that makes a possibility 'seriously and interestingly different'. Let us consider the case of a young man who is reared in a stable, devout and deeply spiritual Jewish household. Having reached the age where he can fully exercise his own independent judgment, he owes it to his family, his community, the wider (pluralist) society, but, above all, to himself, to critically reflect upon the faith-filled upbringing he has received. As a consequence, he may come to realise that he has lived his life up to this point in a rich spiritual atmosphere (or in what we might call a 'cultural ambiance of Truth'), and that he has been

---

5. *Ibid*, 48.
6. *Ibid*.
7. *Ibid*.

privileged to experience the rich spiritual inheritance of a religious, Truth-oriented home; or perhaps he may feel, as a consequence of his critical reflections, that the Truth that he has inherited and wishes to live by needs to be expressed differently by his generation and that he has important 'work' to do; or, perhaps again, he may come to believe that what was portrayed to him as the living inheritance of Truth is in fact a grand deception. Obviously, it is only when such a point is reached that secular humanism, atheism, Buddhism, the 'gay lifestyle', Christianity, etc., fully emerge in his mind as 'seriously and interestingly different possibilities', having lain latent, so to speak, up to this point in his life, in his pluralistic social environment. The end result of all this is of course completely unpredictable. He may become a Buddhist monk or begin experimenting with a gay lifestyle to discover the truth of himself—the 'own self' to which he wishes to be 'true' and to which we, as his fellow citizens in a liberal pluralist society, wish him to be true. However, whatever choices he makes, he is subject, I submit, to what we might call the 'Sartrean imperative', that is, that 'in legislating for ourselves, we legislate for all humanity'. Both he and we are answerable to the higher court of our common, universal humanity. What Walzer says of 'solidarity', that it is something that people experience separately and differently,[8] can be likewise said of 'Truth'. Standing before the court of humanity, this young Jewish man must believe that the 'Truth' legitimates his singular personal choice by speaking to him in its unique voice. This 'verti-

---

8. *Ibid*, 51.

cal' relation to Truth, as we may call it, is crucial. Thus, we may say that in the case of this young man, and perhaps also in the case of all of us, his truths and solidarities (of family, community, association) are empirically or 'horizontally' acquired but that they must be legitimated and confirmed 'vertically' through this relation to Truth. Walzer is correct to insist that solidarity 'must have its local and particular sites' and that ' it is built from the ground up'[9] but it is also true that the empirical (horizontal or inherited) solidarities and truths that we experience need to be confirmed and enlivened 'from the top down', from their 'divine *arche*' for we can hardly take our values as families, associations or as a society at all seriously unless we believe (even in fear and trembling and against the resistance of doubt) that they are legitimated or 'blessed' by Truth itself (by Christ who is Truth) and that our 'local site' is a local embodiment of the Truth of our common humanity, a site where the Spirit reigns.

Likewise, Walzer's expression 'the singular, universal, political community' needs to be understood 'vertically' as well as 'horizontally'. He points out that this singular community requires a host of particular associations. 'The one', he says, 'depends on the many, the many on the one. This isn't a vicious circle; it is the deep structure of democratic politics itself'.[10] However, this is not the deepest structure (or the 'highest heights') of democratic politics itself, for the 'oneness' of the singular universal community possesses legitimacy and authority only as

---

9. *Ibid.*
10. *Ibid*, 53.

the expression, representation or 'face' of a higher unity whose many names (the unity of the 'general will', of the 'public interest', of the 'moral person of the state', of God, of Truth, of the Absolute, of the living Word, of the Spirit, of the 'world soul') direct our attention, each in their different ways, to the ultimate font of authority and legitimacy. The key point is that whilst the singular political community must indeed be universal in Walzer's sense (that is, it must possess the empirical or horizontal unity of order and government), it also needs to be universal in another 'vertical' sense, that is, in being a particular embodiment of universal Truth or in being acceptable to the higher court of our universal humanity. This latter kind of overarching ethico-political universality is important for it ensures that a particular group within a political community may raise the cry of oppression against the (merely) horizontal universality of the government of the day—against, for example, a universal (horizontal) political community that endorses slavery.

I now wish to suggest how an explicitly Truth-oriented approach provides support to the kind of social criticism so strongly commended by Walzer. He points out that the task of social criticism is to identify examples of social tyranny and long standing oppressive practices and to call them by their proper name, that is, 'to say that *this* is social tyranny'.[11] But how is social criticism to execute this task? If the kind of unity that exists in social groups or in society as a whole is merely of the empirical or horizontal kind, and if there is no higher unity (of Truth) which

---

11. *Ibid*, 52.

this empirical unity is meant to, but all too often fails to, express, then social criticism is simply impossible; all social criticism, we need to recollect, implicitly involves standing apart from a social group or practice in order to criticise it from a different (higher? better?) vantage point. To illustrate this point, let us take Walzer's own example of a longstanding oppressive practice that he wishes to subject to social criticism (and to 'proper naming'), that is, the denial of education to their women members by religious or cultural associations. What I hope to show, by considering this example, is that the foundation (in Truth) of social criticism is also the basis (or the 'ethico-political substance') of a genuinely open and free pluralist society.

Let us say that a particular Muslim group in a liberal pluralist society believes that it is perfectly right and proper for its female members to be denied any formal or public education. Such a group, I wish to suggest, can defend itself in either a 'vertical, Truth-oriented' manner or in a 'horizontal, empirical' manner. A merely horizontal defence of its belief would consist in saying that, as a matter of simple (empirical) fact, the belief is universally accepted by all members of the group, including its women, that it is essential to the group's sense of identity and solidarity, and that in a democratic pluralist society whose procedures are governed by tolerance and respect for 'group rights', it is not obliged to say any more than this in its defence. In contrast, a vertical defence would claim that the belief is justifiable before the court of our common humanity by arguing, for example, that a woman finds her ultimate fulfilment (the Truth of who she really is) in motherhood and that only the kind of informal education provided by every day family life is needed. Now the key characteristic of this latter line of defence is that it is a Truth-oriented defence that, simply by virtue of being Truth-oriented, automatically renders itself susceptible to social criticism and to arguments emanating from other perspectives and points of view—to, for example, the argument that formal education for women may enhance, rather than undermine, their mothering role. Thus the vertical defence is open to and invites, whereas the horizontal defence is closed to and repels, genuine social criticism. Now, I would suggest that a society characterised only by an empirical (horizontal) series of groups, each 'hugging' its own 'private' (to the group) truth which it regards as beyond the reach of social criticism, can hardly be described as a *genuinely* pluralist society. The free play of Truth-oriented discussion, and open communication between groups and individuals in a free flowing 'dialectic of Truth', are integral to the inter-group life of a democratic pluralist society. The key point here is that genuine pluralism and Truth-oriented social criticism go together, even if the two are in perpetual tension. (What group does not secretly harbor the desire to shield its truths, which it hopes are expressions of Truth itself, from probing social criticism which might suggest otherwise?)

It is also important to note that genuine social criticism cuts both ways, has no favourites, and always has surprises in store. Consider, for example, the case of a Muslim woman who says, not just to her Muslim sisters (within her 'private' group) but to all women and men 'A woman's veil is her strength'. This too, is a form of social criticism, though moving in the opposite direction. The danger, however, is that it might be too readily (that is, too easily and painlessly) dismissed as a merely private, horizontal 'truth' peculiar to a particular group, with the result that the kind of tension it *should* introduce into the inter-group life of a pluralist society is thereby circumvented. What this Muslim woman is entitled to from the wider society and its various groups is (i) the recognition that a serious 'Truth' claim is being advanced and (ii) the honesty and courage of a 'vertical' response, especially, perhaps, from those who insist most strenuously against our hypothetical Muslim group that 'All women have a right to a formal education'. A conceivable reply to the Muslim woman might proceed along the following lines. 'It may be true that modesty in female dress and behavior does indeed convey a sense of strength and enables a woman to enjoy a certain 'freedom from sexuality', even a real freedom to be her own person, but even if this is so, modesty can have various cultural expressions of which the veil is only one'. However, whatever reply is offered, the key point is that it should be a vertical, Truth-oriented response; the 'spirit' of both pluralist democratic society and of social criticism requires no less. This is made clear in Bernard Bosanquet's Truth-oriented communitarianism which, as I shall show in the following section, provides a theoretical advance upon, and complement to, Michael Walzer's communitarianism, and addresses the fears of postmodernists who have concerns about what they see as the 'totalising' implications of social universals.

Public Policy and Bosanquet's Truth-oriented communitarianism

In Bosanquet's work, as in classic political theory in general, there is an appreciation, both sound and profound, of two distinct aspects of the 'political', that is, firstly, its aspect as a 'particular' being in-formed or enveloped by its 'universal' (the state, the enveloping ethical self of society and of our universal humanity finding concrete expression in our socio-political world) and, secondly, its aspect as a 'universal', in-forming its 'particulars' or 'differences' (the distinctive social groups 'made one' by the embrace of the political universal). These two distinct aspects of the 'political' are what I call the 'twin flows of the universal' or the two pathways of (universal) Truth; two channels of social or common grace. However, the analytical illumination once provided by this classical distinction has certainly been obfuscated in recent times in the discipline of political theory, if it has not entirely faded from view. There can be little doubt, for example, (i) that the success in recent times of political communitarianism has severely attenuated the discipline's sense of each socio-political whole as an *'enveloped particular'*, as legitimate and truly itself when enveloped or 'held' in the light of its universal (that is, the state, especially considered as the instrument or form of our universal humanity finding authentic expression in our political universe and bringing our social humanity to its God-intended fullness) and (ii) that the success of postmodernism and poststructuralism has likewise undermined the discipline's sense of the socio-political whole as an *'enveloping universal'*, one that holds its differences within the embrace of its unity. It is important to recognise and reflect upon the state as both an 'enveloped particular' and as an 'enveloping universal', as the twin flows of the Absolute (the *agathon*) into socio-political life.

A real strength of the ethical theory of the state and of classic conception of the socio-political whole is that it is 'non-claustrophobic', 'non-solipsistic', and 'non-constrictive'. For example, Bosanquet's socio-political whole, considered as a 'particular', freely and naturally inhales the spirit of its enveloping universal and it is this that makes his 'communitarianism' very different from—and also, I would suggest, far superior to—the modern forms of communitarianism which have evolved under the shadow of Wittgenstein. The latter's famous tenet that all 'forms of life' are ultimate implicitly denied the 'ultimacy of God' or the divine grounding of all that is and led to the view that each socio-political whole or form of life is, in effect, self-justifying, or not justifiable at all and subsists in its own hermetically sealed universe of discourse or 'social prison', without recourse to any appeal to a wider world or to an enveloping universal to justify itself. For Bosanquet, 'humanity' was such a universal. He would have held, paraphrasing Sartre, that each human society, in legislating for itself, legislates for all humanity or, in different terms, that our universal humanity expresses itself in—and figuratively 'flows' into—a rich variety of socio-political embodiments. With regard to the moral world inhabited by the members of a particular socio-political whole, he states that

> its special form of good life, being a moral consciousness, is not merely a self-contained habit of conduct in the members of a group, but is an attitude and moral outlook which, though existing in them, has for its object the whole world, and is determined by the view and spirit which the group has evolved for itself, implying its conception of the best thing for the world.[12]

What Bosanquet refers to as 'devotion to humanity as a best', and what we might refer to in new creationist terms as the God-intended fullness of our humanity, is the ever present criterion, final court of appeal and source of justification, of each human society or, alternatively expressed, it is the divine, universal 'light' which enlightens and guides the unique pathway to Truth pursued by each society. Assuredly, then, the socio-political realm for Bosanquet is not, as it is as a general rule for modern communitarians, a self-enclosed realm. Each society is, for him, a distinctive particularisation of our (universal) humanity; the latter is not a universal which represses differences, or which stands abstractly and idly above them, but is an 'operative', 'active' or 'concrete' universal (a 'live' spiritual/ethical idea) which enables each human society in which its spirit (the Spirit, the Absolute) lives to make its distinctive and 'true' contribution to humanity as a whole; that is, to 'respond' to the unifying universal

---

12. B Bosanquet, Social and International Ideals: Being Studies in Patriotism (London: Macmillan, 1917), 199.

(the flow of our universal humanity) with the rich diversity it always intends. Though a 'fellow communitarian', Bosanquet would only stand, in Michael Walzer's words, 'in the cave, in the city, on the ground' provided that what he found there was acceptable from 'an objective and universal standpoint',[13] namely the standpoint of our universal humanity.[14]

Bosanquet's political theory, then, serves as a counterpoint and corrective to modern communitarianism as it

---

13. M Walzer, *Spheres of Justice: A Defence of Pluralism and Equality*, (New York: Basic Books, 1983), xiv.
14. In my *Justice and the State: On Liberal Organicism and the Foundations of Emancipatory Politics* (Quebec: World Heritage Press, 1998), 136, I note that most modern communitarians appear happy to endorse the belief, as expressed in Walzer's earlier work, that 'one must either "stand in the cave, on the city, on the ground"—that is, in a realm of particulars divorced from *their* universals—or "walk out of the cave, leave the city, climb the mountain, fashion for oneself an objective and universal standpoint"—that is, enter a realm where universals are divorced from *their* particulars'. In the case of both the political communitarianism and social constructionism of the present time, members of human societies are locked in their caves: their 'homes' become their prisons. One could perhaps say that for Bosanquet, too, reality is socially constructed but this, I think, is a misleading expression when applied to Bosanquet's position, for if his reality is socially constructed, it is constructed in a unique way that makes a crucial difference, that is, it is constructed in and by the light of our common humanity and in the spirit exuded by the traditions and institutions of its 'form of life'; it is a spirit in, but not just in, the form of life, for it is also universal. Hence, it would, I think, be preferable when analyzing Bosanquet's work to use the expression 'socially particularised or concretised' rather than 'socially constructed', in order to avoid the sense of arbitrariness and 'criterionlessness' evoked by the latter expression.

developed under the shadow of Wittgenstein but it also serves a similar function in relation to 'political' postmodernism and poststructuralism as they have developed under the shadow of Foucault. The import of Bosanquet's work for us today is that it contains a reflective and very powerful account of the socio-political whole and the twin aspects of its universality. He provides us with a particularly fine sense (i) of the 'social' and 'political' as 'particular'; that is, as each of these realms is informed from 'without', so to speak, by the Truth of our universal humanity, and (ii) of the 'social' and 'political' as 'universal'; that is, as universals each of which informs and 'unifies' its particulars or differences 'within', and of the way in which these two aspects complement each other. Thus we are able to grasp that the socio-political whole is both informed and informs, unified 'from without' by the bond of the universal (our universal humanity) and unifying its own inner diversity, flowed into or permeated by the river of our common humanity and itself a civil/political universal flowing into its particulars or the diversity of *its* aspects by means of the integrative, deliberative political process. However, as we come increasingly under the sway of postmodernism, we seem to find ourselves in a curious world, one in which particulars or elements of diversity seem to be increasingly cut off from *their* universals; indeed, the disassociation between the two may be so far advanced that even this language of 'in-forming universals' may now appear to many readers as alien and even as menacing and 'totalistic'. We seem to be increasingly reluctant to investigate, probe, discuss and criticise claims concerning the true or authentic social universals that should inform our lives, as the postmodern suspicion of the universal as such intensifies. For example, the monogamous, two (natural) parent family, as an ordering social universal (claimed to be true and socially beneficial) has been dismissed (recklessly and precipitately?) by feminists as 'patriarchal' and by gays and lesbians as 'heterosexist'. We seem to be entering into a world where universals as such are viewed as inherently and necessarily repressive. We seem, in other words, to be losing 'sociopolitical consciousness' altogether.[15] Needless to say, this renders almost impossible the task of public policy, to say nothing of the everyday political task of organising social life or 'life in common'.[16]

---

15. Many readers will have heard the jibe that psychology 'first lost its soul, then its mind and, finally, it lost consciousness'. The jibe was no doubt intended to be amusing, though with a hard, critical edge designed to provoke serious reflection about the condition and evolution (or devolution) of the discipline. There is not, so far as I am aware, a similar jibe directed at the disciplines of social philosophy and political theory, but perhaps there should be. Though less amusing and more cumbersome by far, the present theoretical state of affairs positively invites a jibe such as 'socio-political theory first lost its soul, (its sense of the 'universal' flowing into the socio-political whole, as 'particular'), then its mind (its grasp of the socio-political whole, as 'universal', flowing into its 'differences/particulars') and, finally, it lost socio-political consciousness altogether.
16. In *The Human Service Disciplines and Social Work: The Foucault Effect* (Quebec: World Heritage Press, 2003), 47–51, I show the extent of the problems generated for public policy by using the social constructionist language of Foucaultian postmodernists to indiscriminately characterise social universals as totalistic or repressive. I argue that when it comes to the 'professional crunch,' that is, when

important decisions affecting the lives of people in crucial ways need to be made, the language of social constructionism is not particularly helpful. For example, in her *Contested Territory: Sexualities and Social Work*, edited by AS Chambon, A Irving and L Epstein (New York: Columbia University Press, 1999), O'Brien states that she 'found that in social work publications about youth and sexuality since the mid-1980s, the authors typically constitute sexuality as an object of scientific knowledge and themselves as experts in that knowledge' (132–33). However, by constituting sexuality as an 'object of scientific knowledge,' it turns out that O'Brien merely means that these authors 'frequently employ statistics concerning the sexual activities of young people' (133). With these studies and this kind of evidence in mind, O'Brien states that 'the procreative activities of teenage women are constituted as dangerous, both to themselves and to society' (136). However, I counter by suggesting that those who disregard or attempt to diminish the significance of these facts must take full responsibility for the policy consequences of so doing. To say, for example that 'the procreative activities of teenage women are constituted as dangerous' is to suggest that those activities are in themselves innocuous and free of health risks to teenage mothers and their children, but that for some mysterious or moralising reason they have been 'constituted as dangerous' by powerful authoritative experts who descend upon them with their 'scientific sword'. I then insist (as a citizen, I think that I here have the right to insist) that if human service professionals and academics under the sway of Foucault feel that they must continue to use the language of social constructionism by saying, for example, that certain empirical studies constitute or construct a type of behavior as dangerous, ill-advised, beneficial or whatever, then they should at least pose the simple and direct question 'Is this type of behavior properly, appropriately or truthfully constituted as dangerous, beneficial or whatever?' It is important to stress here that human service professionals and all those involved in the formulation of public policy must do their utmost, that is, they are professionally obliged and obligated as citizens, to make a sound (or as sound and reflective as possible) judgment concerning what is truly dam-

The Need for Ethico-political Consciousness

Public policy, I have argued, positively requires the use of social universals, but they also require, especially in liberal democratic societies characterised by sharp internal divisions of opinion on policy issues, what I shall call 'ethico-political consciousnesses. In this section, in the course of explaining what I mean by this expression, I will explore the Truth-oriented communitarianism of Bernard Bosanquet and show how it provides a theoretical complement to (or perhaps an unwelcome metaphysical fulfilment of) Michael Walzer's communitarianism, and also try to address the fears of postmodernists who have reservations about the idea of social universals informing 'their' differences. I will present Bosanquet's explanation as to how a universal (social, ethical or familial) can 'descend' upon its differences without de-naturing or destroying them or how it is possible for a social policy (or politically mandated universal) to legitimately intrude, through the agencies of government, upon the lives of free individuals and freely formed groups (legitimately conceivable, as we shall see, as *its* individual citizens, *its* groups or *its* particulars/differences).

In *The Philosophical Theory of the State*, Bosanquet presents a very powerful argument to the effect that the task of justifying self-government or of defending liberal society/government is simply impossible without the notion of the 'self' or 'will' or 'person' of the state. Liberal

---

aging or beneficial for clients, client groups and indeed society as a whole under the prevailing socio-historical and cultural circumstances.

self-government presupposes such a (collective) self; it is implicit in the experience of self-government—in its possibility and actuality. By reviewing political theories current at the time, he shows that if the 'self' is understood simply as the 'private self' or as an isolated 'particular' uninformed by its 'universal', and if 'government' is identified with the 'not-self', as a 'universal' totally separate from the private self (rather than as the universal aspect *of* the self), then self-government simply becomes chimerical. He holds that there is a common-ness, a universality or 'a positive unity throughout the selves that compose a society'[17] and he characterises that unity as a 'self' (a 'common self' or co[m]-unity) or 'will' (a general will or common good). He understands the 'self' in 'self-government' to 'stand for the whole sovereign group or community, which is usually called "self-governing", as opposed to a subject state'[18] and insists that this 'self' must be understood and grasped as a reality in order to be able to justify 'the acceptance of what is done by the public power as an act of the whole community'.[19] His most crucial point, I think, is this; if the latter (the whole community) is not a self of some kind, one which collectively embraces—and in doing so, partly constitutes—the selves of its individual members, then the expression 'community as a whole' simply becomes shorthand for 'all (other) individuals' and an act performed in its name is not the

---

17. B Bosanquet, *The Philosophical Theory of the State* (London: Macmillan, 1965), 72.
18. *Ibid*, 71.
19. *Ibid*.

act of a free citizen body but is at best a necessary evil committed by some individuals against others in the interests of order, or, at worst, simply an act of tyranny. To posit, with Bosanquet, a universal or communal self oriented to the Truth of our common or universal humanity (our fulfilled humanity) is not to suggest that its 'voice' or intimations in public affairs are always or even normally clear and distinct; it is only to say that this voice and these intimations become more luminous and more easily 'heard', the more widely the channels of communication and dialogue are kept open, the more conscious members of a political community are of their mutual participation in a 'communal self" or way of life and the more genuinely sensitive they are to the views, needs and concerns of each other. This is what I mean by 'ethico-political consciousness', for as it exists in the minds of the members of a political body, it is both an ethical virtue to be cultivated and at the same time a key ethical requirement of political unity; it is the 'ethical substance' in and through which Bosanquet's 'communal self' lives, moves and has its being and it is the ground or wellspring of the 'public' in public policy; it is, in brief, the state as the ethical font of sound public policy and legitimate political action.

Ethico-political consciousness involves a sensitive appreciation, hopefully ever deepening in each of us of the manner in which the particular agenda (social, political, cultural) we pursue (or the agenda pursued by 'our' group/class/party etc) impacts upon, coheres with, supports or undermines, the *prima facie* reasonable and legitimate hopes and expectations of other members (individual or group) of the same political community or state, and places a heavy demand upon citizens to be constantly sensitive to the needs of the political body as a living whole or unity of parts. Looked at in another way or from the angle of Truth, the core of ethico-political consciousness is a humble recognition that our 'truths' may be merely our own and not, as we are too quick to suppose, the voice of Truth itself or of God speaking to us with perfect clarity! Where ethico-political consciousness prevails, and to the extent that discussions aimed at discerning Truth's intimations in social and political matters is genuinely dialectical (and not what Plato would call an exercise in 'eristics'), the Truth (the angelic presence of the Holy Spirit) is afforded the opportunity to make its presence felt.

To argue, as I have done, that the socio-political universal, is the integrative, reflective process whereby the 'common' or 'universal' informs, flows through or unifies *its* particulars or the diversity of *its* aspects or components, and that each 'difference' in a social whole is an 'enveloped difference', or a difference subsumed under and contained by its social universal, is to highlight the *unity* of the socio-political body and its ethical substance, its ongoing ethical task (the task or duty of 'ethico-political consciousness') of unifying or reconciling differences within its self (its 'communal self', as Bosanquet would call it). As I pointed out in the last chapter, a worthwhile and fruitful 'politics of difference' must take on the task of showing how a 'unity-in-and-of-differences' is possible, rather than pitting the one against the other, although it would then find itself in precisely the same position, and assuming precisely the same posture, as classic political theory. In essence, the 'political' is an ongoing, organised unity-of-differences, even though an actually existing socio-political whole may, contrary to its essence, in fact degenerate into a 'totalising' unity which tyrannises and represses its differences. The problem with the 'politics of difference', as currently understood and practiced by its proponents, is its tendency to deify or absolutise 'differences' at the expense of a 'unity' which is not so much de-absolutised as demonised and seen as a dangerous, threatening presence to be forever expelled from the world of differences—a task which is never quite achieved, for this world continues to be haunted by the banished ghost of unity. Certainly, we need to challenge the almost casual identification or equation at the present time of universality with repressiveness, authority with authoritarianism, the living in-forming presence of the universal with a purely destructive or negative intent; only by doing so can we then engage in the by no means easy task of distinguishing between a 'true' (in the sense of 'appropriately selected and employed') universal that informs *its* diversity and a 'false' (in the sense of 'inappropriately selected and applied') universal that overrides or eliminates differences, or between authoritarianism as the seemly veneer of authority used to justify the will of one or of some being forced on the rest, and authority as a genuine emanation from the heart and mind of God or the true communal self.[20]

---

20. I have a particularly self-serving reason for highlighting the *unity* of the socio-political body, its ongoing ethical task of unifying or reconciling differences within its self (its 'communal self') and the foundational ('wellspring') role of 'ethico-political consciousness'

Only a common consciousness of our membership of a single political community and a sensitive appreciation on our part of the requirements of 'ethico-political consciousness' can avoid the 'culture wars' that some regard, with a morose fatalistic resignation, as almost endemic

---

in social and political life in general and in social policy and social work in particular. In my *Gender, the Marriage Contract and the State; The Role of Promise Keeping in the Conjugal Body Politic* (Quebec: World Heritage Press, 1998), I argue that the state is a third party to each marriage contract, that it has a clear responsibility to support the traditional, heterosexual marital unit as its basic social unit and that it should protect both the interest of children in marriage and their right to be raised by their own, two, natural parents in a stable, loving environment; no child, I argue, should ever have to say 'my dad is a sperm donor'. This is 'my truth', which I naturally think reflects, echoes and expresses Truth itself. Clearly, however, this puts me immediately at odds with feminists who hold to the 'counter-truth' that the family is the oppressive stronghold of a patriarchal society and that a fully human, liberated society cannot be attained until the chains of sexism and patriarchy are sundered, and also with gays who put forward the 'counter-truth' that the nuclear family is the heart and bastion of a homophobic society and that only by challenging and destroying homophobic assumptions can we create a society that is free in a real sense for all its citizens. However, I venture to suggest that the proposals I make in the book are truly (in the sense of expressing Truth) in the public interest, that is, in the interests of the political community of which I and my gay and feminist opponents are equal members and whose communal 'self', as Bosanquet would say, we share. If I must find myself at odds with my fellow citizens, then I much prefer to do so as a member of a world we share, as one who disagrees with others about the good of our world or about which 'truths' reflect Truth itself, but who shares a common concern to arrive at the best possible collective judgment concerning what is indeed best and truly valuable for our political community.

or as a kind of 'necessity' in modern, pluralistic societies. The very notion of 'culture wars' suggests, or at least strongly suggests to me, that the combatants have abandoned the common world, our shared 'political' world, one in which authentically social policies can be formulated in the best interests of society as a whole and have set up separate worlds or fortresses which are *absolutely* different from each other and are pitted against each other, so that any kind of real communication across the barricades becomes impossible. Words convey meanings which circulate solipsistically in each of their opposing worlds; only their respective battle cries are loud and vicious enough to cross the abyss between them. A 're-birth' of universality or common ethico-political consciousness would not eliminate the sources of division with which we are all too familiar at the present time. In a liberal, plural society, there will no doubt always be groups identified with distinctive views and positions, and there may well be opposing camps. However, this does not render untenable or unattainable the project of engaging in public policy that is genuinely 'public', that is, *truly* in the public interest, or of pursuing social policies that are *really* socially beneficial, for where the spirit of the social whole still enlivens the minds of its members to some degree, there is always hope that divisions may be transformed into complementary aspects of the social whole and that 'absolutised' differences to be converted into relative and significant differences. This at least is the object or task of public policy and it is by no means a hopelessly idealistic one, for we need to bear in mind that opposing social groups or camps differ *significantly* from each other—an 'absolute' difference, I maintain, is not a difference at all; the expression collapses into incoherence[21]—and that this 'tension of differences' within a common, shared life can always generate a creative and productive movement towards unity and Truth; it is a 'unifying tension', a unity ever breaking apart into unrelated differences under the pressure of constantly changing circumstances but ever in search of its self. Again, this 'unifying tension of differences' might be described as the tension inherent in a 'developing unity', for even as it falls apart in the face of emerging 'differences' it can no longer contain, it is at the same time always reconstituting itself in a more comprehensive and inclusive manner and in this way always achieving a different relation to Truth and perhaps ever closer approximations to Truth. Paradoxically, it might be described as an ever-disintegrating, ever re-integrating unity. Thus the 'unifying tension of differences' of a political community may be understood (theoretically) as 'unity in quest of itself' and understood (theologically) as the Spirit working through us as citizens, drawing us through common grace into a deeper social unity and harmony. In a more practical, experiential sense, it is the source of the dynamic energy that feeds the ethico-political consciousness of its members and fuels the process of (re-)unification, the ongoing socio-political journey in and towards Truth.

---

21. This point is explained and explored further in my *Justice and the State: On Liberal Organicism and the Foundations of Emancipatory Politics* (Quebec: World Heritage Press, 1998), 63–65.

In the end, dreams and visions are to be shared, whatever the cost and pain involved, and however heated the disagreement generated by the different visions of the social good entertained by gays, feminists, traditionalists, neo-traditionalists etc. It is disagreement of this kind that has led many to believe that the quest for the 'best life' or for the true or authentic good of a political community (its origin and end in Truth) is a futile one and that the kind of differences we encounter are simply irreconcilable, but if we take seriously our common membership of a single political community, then we will insist that the differences between us are, as I said earlier, significant rather than absolute, that is, brimming with the tension of an emerging unity, and we will persist, both as citizens and as public representatives, in our quest for a genuine unity in-and-of these differences. A free society affords its citizens the opportunity for free ranging discussion and offers a forum or public medium in which differences are given the fullest possible rein and allowed to reconcile and 'find' themselves in unity. At the same time of course, this very freedom equally allows the emergence of acrimonious disunity and seemingly irreconcilable differences but hopefully the appearance of divisive conflicts will not destroy, but rather renew, the conviction that, even in the heat of conflict, unity lies at the heart of difference, that there is a hidden complementariness-of-differences which it is the civic task of ongoing *bona fides* discussion to reveal. Consider, for example, the case of abortion. It may for example become clear that we, as a society, ought to be passionately 'pro-life' *and* 'pro-choice', the former (pro-life) in recognising that a pregnant woman is 'pregnant with child' and that the term 'fetus' simply denotes 'a child considered from a strictly biological or medical point of view', and the latter (pro-choice) in recognising that a woman must not be forced to bear a child that has been forced upon her, as in the case of rape; might it not then be possible (in this way or in some other way as yet unimagined) for the feminist pro-choice voice and the traditionalist pro-life voice to each find their proper place in an emerging social harmony? Or consider the case of gays and the traditional heterosexual family. Surely it is possible, in a liberal democratic society, for gays to be different whilst at the same time publicly affirming the (heterosexual/traditional) family as the basic unit of society. (Homosexual men and women emerge from such heterosexual unions and love their heterosexual parents with as much passion as their 'straight' brothers and sisters.) Finally, in the 'war over the family', surely it is not unrealistic to hope that the principle 'Children ought to be reared, as far as possible, by their own two natural parents' might emerge as a unifying social universal. Perhaps, then, we need to remind ourselves that the state, as the angelic presence of the Spirit ever in our midst and ever guiding our thoughts to the good, is always close at hand, and ever ready to find practical expression in reconciling acts and policies. Perhaps, too, it is not so foolish or wildly idealistic to hope for the emergence of a renewed and re-invigorated ethico-political consciousness which can transform the 'scandal of division' into a unifying synthesis of different aspects and visions of 'the good' itself.[22]

---

22. In her *Inessential Woman: Problems of Exclusion in Feminist Thought*

This hope is not chimerical but is soundly based. The 'Munich moment' that we spoke about at the start of this book has already happened; it is not a dream. Habermas and Ratzinger[23] have already bravely walked into a new 'post-secular' world and invited the rest of us to do likewise. This hope is not chimerical because the world of western liberal democracy is moving in a new direction, one that Habermas and Ratzinger strongly support and attempt to understand, even though its final destination is by no means clear. Currently, we are witnessing a highly significant departure from the 'old' model of liberal society that championed a sacred-secular *divide*, where the state was (*only*) a neutral umpire with a deliberately cultivated attitude of 'studied public indifference' to the 'inner life' of the vast host of (private) associations that it was obliged to impartially regulate, and a transition to a 'new' post-secular model of liberal society that champions and promotes a sacred-secular *distinction* (a complementary unity of distinct aspects), where the state is obliged to rethink itself and become (*also*) the state *of*

(Boston: Beacon Press, 1988), 182, Elizabeth Spelman provides us with a vital clue as to how we might proceed with hope in the midst of conflict when she invites us to distinguish between tolerating and welcoming someone's opinion. To merely tolerate an opinion or viewpoint is to fail to genuinely consider it as a serious critique of one's own position. Though toleration is good as far as it goes, yet if I just tolerate you, I am not prepared to be challenged by you or to really change myself. I am not prepared to listen to you and leave the 'door of friendship ajar'; instead, I am simply concerned to avoid making you my enemy.

23. J Habermas, and J Ratzinger, *Dialectics of Secularization: On Reason and Religion* (San Francisco Ignatius Press, 2006).

its society; the post-secular liberal state is embedded in and part of its society, rather than floating above it with an attitude of studied indifference to the inner life of its citizens and associations. The key task of this emerging post-secular liberal state is to be the unifying principle that pervasively informs all aspects of its society. As in the case of the 'old' secular liberal state, the 'new' post-secular liberal state will continue to maintain an impartial neutrality on questions of world views, allowing each to bloom without interference, but it will also seek, with hope and confidence, for threads of unity between them. With this same hope in mind, we will proceed in the next section to look at the state's role and responsibilities with regard to the family in general and then, in the following section, at the 'homosexual family' in particular, before considering the role of culturally formative religion in public life in the final section.

The State and the Family

Barth holds that 'the Christian community shares common interests with the world and its task is to give resolute practical expression to this community of interest';[24] 'the civil cause (and not merely the Christian cause) is also the cause of the one God',[25] so that Christians must 'apply themselves to the same task with non-Christians

---

24. K, Barth, *Community, State and Church: Three Essays* (Gloucester, Mass: Peter Smith, 1968), 159.
25. *Ibid*, 160.

and submit themselves to the same rule'[26] and thereby contribute to 'the fulfilment of the State's own righteous purposes'.[27] One of the most important 'righteous purposes' of the state, as I shall argue at length, is to preserve and support the (traditional) nuclear family as the basic unit of a single, unified society. We need to bear in mind that a liberal pluralist democratic society is still *one* society, a unity of differences which need to be constantly integrated and harmonised by a unifying will, and that it needs agreed upon norms and a public philosophy or a public orientation to the common good that is 'consensus seeking' and 'consensus generating'. This is what I will try to provide in my discussion of the traditional nuclear family as the basic unit of society and also in my discussion of the homosexual couple as a family, and what Richard John Neuhaus has in mind when he speaks of the need for Christians to develop a mediating language through which religious language dealing with ultimate things can be used to elucidate social and political issues. He holds that

> [i]n our several traditions there are rich conceptual resources for the development of such a mediating language—whether concepts be called natural law, common grace, general revelation, or the order of creation, that such notions will help to elucidate the good that as

---

26. *Ibid*, 159.
27. *Ibid*, 171.

citizens we seek in common and that it is a mistake to argue that the interests of good democracies are best promoted by avoiding the question of the good.[28]

He insists, on the contrary, that the kind of democracy we live in 'becomes a political community worthy of moral actors only when we engage the question of the good' and that as we disagree about what should be the chief constituents or guiding themes of our social philosophy, 'at least we would know what we are disagreeing about, namely, different goods by which we might order our life together'.[29] Certainly, just as all citizens in a liberal pluralist community must continue the ongoing quest for unity-in-diversity (for a unifying will that blends together ever changing and proliferating differences), so too they must continue the ongoing quest for a 'public philosophy' or for a philosophy that is as 'public' and common as possible or again, in circumstances where a community is threatened with rupture, for a set of ideas that will hold it together and hold chaos at bay until a more truly unifying will can (re)-emerge. Christians, I submit, should be fully themselves in contributing to this quest; they should

---

28. RJ Neuhaus, 'Nihilism without the Abyss: Law, Rights and Transcendent Good', paper delivered at a conference on Religion and Law in 1985 at the Catholic University Law School and cited in Stanley Hauerwas, 'A Christian Critique of Christian America', in *Community in America: The Challenge of Habits of the Heart*, edited by CH Reynolds and RV Norman (Berkley: University of California Press, 1988), 257.
29. *Ibid.*

make a strong religiously grounded contribution to public philosophy and, in so doing, try to touch the 'spiritual heart' and deepest convictions of all citizens. They will thereby unite in spirit, I believe, with early American communitarian ideals, with John Dewey's understanding of democracy as a 'great community' of shared values and of politics as the task of continually re-creating the public sphere, and with modern communitarianism, but they will part company with John Courtney Murray's hard and fast distinction between politics/law and religion/faith.[30]

It may be objected that the recommendation that the state should support the nuclear family in the sense of positively preferring the 'married' nuclear family 'lifestyle', is unsound, impractical and simply out of touch with the realities of a late twentieth century society. Has

---

30. JC Murray, We Hold These Truths; Catholic Reflections on the American Proposition (New York: Sheed and Ward, 1960). John Murray insists that the American constitution prescribes law, not dogma, and that it sets out articles of civil peace that Americans are obliged to respect and obey, rather than articles of religious faith to which they are expected to subscribe. However, he presents the law/faith distinction, I believe, in too dichotomous a fashion, for law is never self-authenticating but always requires justification by an appeal to public principles (faith-based or non-faith based) and considerations beyond the realm of law itself. When citizens offer their own justification of a law or constitutional article designed for public consideration and consumption, they thereby contribute to the ongoing task of articulating a public philosophy and if they happen to be Christian, their justification is in fact a mediating position that is informed by faith but is directed towards the enacting of laws designed to realise the common good.

not the nuclear family long since ceased to be the norm in our society and if we regard it as ideal in some sense, does it not follow that sole parents and their children must be deemed to be members of 'deficient families'? Moreover, is it not perfectly acceptable in a tolerant, culturally diverse society for homosexual couples to form families, either by means of the reproductive technologies currently available or through adoption?[31] Obviously, these are vitally important questions, but our efforts to answer them seem to me to be seriously hampered, rather than helped, by the currently fashionable thinking with regard to the complex issues they raise. This 'orthodoxy' may, I believe, be fairly summarised as follows.

It is widely held today that it is a mistake to regard the nuclear family as 'normative', or as representing some sort of ideal for humanity as a whole, for we know that it is just one of a vast number of family types that one finds in an endless variety of socio-cultural and historical settings. Moreover, to talk of the nuclear family, or indeed of any other kind of family or social arrangement, as being 'ideal' or 'the norm' is misconceived and inappropriate, because it attempts to make all families conform to a narrow, rigid stereotype, stifles diversity and impedes the emergence of new, innovative and creative family forms. To regard the time-bound social unit known as the nucle-

---

31. I have previously tackled the vexed question of homosexuality and the family in an earlier work [*Gender, the Marriage Contract and the State* (Quebec: World Heritage Press, 1998)], but I present my argument again in a modified form later in this chapter as an example of public argumentation accessible to all as rational citizens.

ar family (and more popularly known as 'mum, dad and the kids') as a 'real' family, not as just a possible model or form of the family but as the *only* one, is to cast a slur on sole parents and the children they valiantly struggle to raise. It is also widely held today that, since everyone knows that the single most important ingredient in child rearing is the love and care that committed parents provide, and that homosexual couples are just as capable of providing loving care to children as heterosexual parents, then there is no reason why children should not be raised by homosexual couples—or, at least, there is no good reason, but only superficial objections motivated by either blatant or thinly disguised homophobia.

With regard to the first question, which concerns the 'normativity' of the nuclear family, it is important to distinguish clearly between the descriptive sense of 'norm' employed in the question 'Is the nuclear family still the empirical or statistical norm at the present time or is there, rather, as a matter of (empirical and statistical) fact, a wide diversity of family types in our society today?', and the prescriptive, moral-evaluative sense of 'norm' employed in the question 'Is the nuclear family the norm, i.e. the *desirable* form and pattern of family living in our society and, if so, would it not be better to cultivate a wide variety of (socially approved or normatively legitimate) family types to replace the normative ascendancy of the nuclear family?' Obviously, the first of these two questions concerning the 'empirical/descriptive normativity' of the nuclear family can only be answered by referring to the relevant statistical data. However, the second, more complex and demanding question concerning the desirability or 'ethical/prescriptive normativity' of the nuclear family can best be answered, I believe, by briefly reflecting upon the historical origins of this modern family form.

Outside of modern, affluent, large-scale industrial societies, there is a whole host of vastly different marriage patterns and child-rearing practices, though generally speaking, these widely diverse practices are functionally linked to the survival needs of the small scale, traditional communities in which they are embedded. However, once a critical point of affluence is reached in any of these societies, one finds that the hold of traditional social practices (polygamy, arranged marriages, etc), which were essentially geared to survival, tend to decline and to be replaced by freely formed nuclear families. Whereas in pre-industrial societies there is a pressing necessity for marriages to be arranged for primarily practical, economic purposes, in modern, industrialised (or industrialising) societies, young 'marriageable' people are generally free to marry whomsoever they please, though the exercise of this free choice is frequently influenced by the advice of concerned parents. Thus, economic affluence facilitates or engenders the wish of young people to choose their own, lifelong, exclusive marriage partners (polygamy, in particular, seems to be unable to survive conditions of affluence) and to rear their own 'love-children' that is, the progeny of their freely chosen intimacy. I am not of course suggesting that monogamous nuclear families (and extended families of which the nuclear family is the readily identifiable 'core unit') are to be found *only* in more affluent societies, for the nuclear family form predominates *both* in affluent and non-affluent societies.[32] However, I do wish to stress that a high degree of autonomy in choosing one's spouse for a lifelong, monogamous family union does seem to be found *only* in more affluent societies.

This brief account of the historical conditions associated with the emergence of the freely-formed nuclear family is, hopefully, a non-contentious, even pedestrian one, but my own, no doubt more contentious, view is that conditions of affluence generate not just a 'freer' but also a more 'natural' society. If we define 'natural' for the purposes of this discussion as 'that which comes (freely and spontaneously) of itself under appropriate conditions', then I would suggest that the desire of young marriageable persons to enter into a lifelong, exclusive relationship with their freely chosen marriage partners is eminently 'natural', and springs spontaneously from the human heart when conditions are ripe. That this desire should surface in history where affluence facilitates its emergence should not, I believe, surprise us in the least; nor should we be surprised to find that polygamy and formally arranged marriages, once regarded as normal, socially acceptable and certainly as 'not unnatural', come to be regarded in more affluent circumstances as out rightly 'unnatural', that is, as artificially impeding 'what comes of itself'. Also perfectly natural in this sense is the desire of spouses to provide a stable environment or structure in which to rear and care for their children. Thus, I wish to

---

32. GP Murdock, 'The Universality of the Nuclear Family', in *A Modern Introduction to the Family,* edited by NW Bell and EF Vogel (New York: Free Press, 1968).

contend that the freely-formed nuclear family is not simply natural, but that it is the most perfectly and eminently natural of all family forms. However, what is *also* natural (though this is a point that is seldom considered at the present time) is that children should wish to be raised in an atmosphere of love and loyalty provided by their *own* parents. This is not to say that those non-affluent societies where children are not reared primarily or exclusively by their parents and immediate kin, are to be condemned as 'unnatural'; it is, rather, to say that such child rearing practices, though acceptable under conditions of subsistence, tend to be experienced as 'unnatural', once conditions of affluence begin to erode their point and functionality for survival. Thereafter, 'what comes of itself' is a desire on the part of parents to raise their own children and a corresponding and complementary desire on the part of children to be raised by their own parents and immediate kin. I would contend, then, that the child-rearing practices that characterise the modern nuclear family are not only natural but that they are the most perfectly or eminently natural of all child-rearing practices. (I should perhaps note at this point that the 'liberation' enjoyed by members of more affluent societies from the functional necessities of subsistence is by no means an unqualified 'good', for affluence, in facilitating greater individual freedom, also affords more opportunities for the irresponsible exercise thereof.)[33]

---

33. AO Hirschman, 'Rival Interpretations of market society: Civilizing, destructive or feeble?', in *Journal of Economic Literature*, 20 (1982): 1463-84 and Charles de Secondat Montesquieu, *The Spirit of the*

These considerations strongly support the desirability of the *form* of the nuclear family (mum, dad, kids), though I hasten to add that this single form can 'in-form' a wide diversity of family types. They also support the 'normative ascendancy' of the nuclear family, by which I mean not just the view that the nuclear family is, as a matter of fact, widely recognised as desirable, but also the conviction that it is a *good* thing (socially beneficial, in the interests of 'best practice' child-rearing, etc) that it is widely recognised as such, and that it would be a *bad* thing if it wasn't accorded this widespread recognition. One is tempted to ask at this point 'Who *really* doubts it?' The

---

Laws, translated and edited by AM Cohler, BC Miller and HS Stone (Cambridge: Cambridge University Press, 1989), provide an extensive discussion of the positive and negative effects of the increasing individual freedom facilitated by economic development and widening economic opportunities. Montesquieu (338) states that 'it is almost a rule that everywhere there are gentle mores there is commerce, and everywhere there is commerce, there are gentle mores' and notes that commercial affluence 'polishes and softens barbarous mores, as we see everyday'. JJ Rousseau, *The Social Contract and Discourses* translated by GDH Cole, (London: Everyman's Library, 1973), 240, provides an exposition of the contrary view that luxury 'corrupts at once rich and poor . . . and sells the country to softness and vanity'. Finally, D Burchell provides an illuminating contrast between those, such as Montesquieu, Karl Marx and Adam Smith, who saw commerce, specialisation and the division of labour as a stage through which human societies pass on their way from barbarism to civilisation and those who believed that 'the progress of luxury in society was a vice which tended to undermine the springs of civic virtue'. 'Civic Virtue, Civil Advice: Genealogies of Citizenship and Modernity', in *Political Theory Newsletter*, 6/1 (April 1994): 26.

vast majority of sole parents don't doubt it; they would much prefer not to be sole parents and would be either bemused or insulted if it was suggested to them that they had deliberately chosen the 'sole-parent family lifestyle'. Some are angry and resentful because they feel that they have been wrongly abandoned by their spouse; some are guilty because they feel that they have left their spouse for reasons which, in retrospect, appear flimsy and ill considered; and others, again, have left because the pain of ongoing conflict and hurt was just too much to bear. Only rarely, however, is sole parenthood a consciously and deliberately chosen lifestyle 'option', and this is hardly surprising. Anyone who takes the time to listen to sole parents will know that raising children on one's own is incredibly difficult, time consuming, lonely and emotionally draining. It is also 'impractical' in a sense understood only too well by sole parents, for being 'sole', they cannot be in two places at once (with one child in hospital, for example, and with another who needs to be driven to school). Sole parents are, of course, to be commended for their steadfast perseverance and for their sacrificial love of their children; however, those who know what it is really like to be a sole parent, generally don't recommend it and precisely because they do know what it's like, strongly *support* the normative ascendancy of the nuclear family.

The strongest challenge to the normative ascendancy of the nuclear family comes from quite a different source, that is, from the widespread view that it is perfectly legitimate and unexceptionable for stable homosexual couples to use modern reproductive technologies and surrogacy to have their own families, since what children need, first and foremost, is to be raised with love and care or, as is more frequently said, in a 'loving environment'. Admittedly, it is no easy matter for us to say precisely what we mean by 'a loving environment' but this much at least can surely be said with some degree of certainty. Love wishes the best for, and acknowledges the authentic needs of, its 'object', and wishes whoever or whatever it loves to develop in accordance with its own nature. However, loving a child, I maintain, *means* acknowledging that the child's natural wish and deepest need is to be raised, where possible, by its own natural parents; indeed, I would go further and insist that it also means according recognition and respect to a child's *right* to be born into a family comprised of its *own* parents, that is, into a loving environment which the parents should spontaneously and naturally offer, and which the child wishes to spontaneously and naturally receive. Under modern conditions of affluence, there is no good reason why this right should not be respected, and love *demands* that it be respected.

Consider the case of a child, raised by two women in a lesbian relationship, who says 'My dad is a sperm donor'. I maintain that the rights of such a child are being flouted. Perhaps this seems too harsh, especially when we consider that the homosexual couple involved may desperately and sincerely want to have and rear a family. Still, the unalterable fact remains that it is the right of a child to intimately know its own parents, and respecting this right involves denying their own wishes in the matter. If to love a child means doing all that can possibly be done to meet its needs, then in this case love requires the painful sacrifice—which is also, I believe, required of many heterosexual couples in a similar situation—of *not* having a child.

Adultism and the Homosexual Family

Whenever couples (heterosexual or homosexual) insist upon realising their desire to have a family by using reproductive techniques in a way that flouts the rights of the 'children-to-be-born', they are, I believe, properly describable as 'adult-ist'. What I call 'adultism' is in many respects more sinister and deplorable than other unsavory -isms, such as racism or sexism, for it negates the interests and rights of those who are least capable of looking after themselves or of raising their voices in articulate protest. Until recently, 'adultism' has been a vice exhibited, not by homosexuals, but almost exclusively by heterosexuals who abort their children and divorce each other. The 'right' to abort is a right exercised by adults against children; it negates not only their interests but their very lives, and disallows any pleas on their behalf. This right demands 'the silence of the lambs'. (It is often paraded as the woman's 'right' but it is just as much the man's 'right', for most women want to love, not to abort, their children, and it is frequently because the father does not want his child to be born that the mother 'agrees' to the abortion). Likewise, whilst some divorces are justifiable in the best interests of the children involved, many, if not most, take place as a result of a decision by one or both parents to put their own personal 'needs' (often more aptly described as 'whimsical wishes') above the needs of their family and children.

In one sense (and, I believe, in essence), adultism is simply the willingness exhibited by certain adults to negate the interests of their children in their own, or what they perceive to be their own, interests, or to disregard the rights of children when they conflict, or appear to conflict, with their own alleged rights. However, just as racists seldom see themselves as being racist, or sexists as being sexist, because they see the world through an ideological prism which renders innocuous what would otherwise be grasped by the non-ideologically tainted moral consciousness as simply wrong or selfish, so, too, adultists avail themselves of an ideology which casts an aura of propriety over their own adultist actions and attitudes and an aura of impropriety (of 'political incorrectness' or 'ideological un-soundness') over the views of their opponents. Thus, for example, with the assistance of a feminist-adultist ideology, the right to abort ceases to be an infringement of the rights of the child, but becomes instead the liberating means whereby women escape from their biological destiny and achieve equality with men (though as I suggested earlier, it is often the means whereby men avoid accepting responsibility for the consequences of their 'intimate' sexual acts); and, correspondingly, opposition to abortion comes to be characterised, not as a defence of children's rights, but as 'anti-choice', 'anti-women's rights', 'anti-equality', 'patriarchal', 'chauvinistic', 'sexist' etc. Likewise, however, we find that the currently emerging adultist variety of 'gay ideology' endorses the 'right' of homosexual couples to have a family by means of reproductive technology as a legitimate lifestyle choice, and regards any opposition to this 'right' as homophobic, anti-gay, based on narrow, traditional, heterosexual modes of thinking etc, Unfortunately, this kind of highly charged adultist rhetoric leaves no room for a dispassionate consideration of, and can scarcely be said to encourage fruitful and free-flowing discussion concerning, what really *is* in the best interests of children.

The question of the desirability of homosexual couples forming families by adopting children is of course an entirely different one. With regard to this issue, I would suggest that heterosexual couples are preferable to homosexual couples as adoptive parents, for the following reasons. We, as a society, wish the best for our children. Under today's conditions of affluence and freedom, it is possible for us to wish, and to realistically expect, that our children will develop into mature adults who will experience a depth of intimacy which is mirrored in the unity of sexual intercourse and that issues in the birth of a child—who is then reared by our 'children' (now husbands and wives!) as their very own. This is, at the very least, an important part of what we mean by 'the best' for our children. Now, if we really desire that every child should have the opportunity to experience the best that we can offer, then we need to recognise that the 'heterosexual' nuclear family offers a vital human experience (part of the *best* that human life can offer), which it alone can provide. There is no good reason, as far as I can see, why our children, as they grow to maturity, should not *expect* the best, or why they should settle for anything less. The intimacy and stability of family life should not be regarded as some kind of 'ideal', as a 'lofty' condition that can only be attained by a fortunate or saintly few, but as a good and wonderful thing to be realistically hoped for and earnestly expected. However, the 'best' for our children won't just happen. It is important that they be provided with appropriate role models; they need to actually experience a mum and dad interacting with each other as husband and wife. If we wish, as we certainly should, the adopted child to grow into a mature adult who will be able to experience a depth of intimacy with a freely chosen spouse and to 'co-create' a new human life ('their' new life), and if we further wish the adopted child to experience successful husband-wife role modeling which enables the child, in turn, to become a good parent, then the heterosexual nuclear family *alone* meets the child's requirements. If, for whatever reason, it is not possible for children to be reared by their own parents, then they should be raised in a manner which approximates the nuclear family model as closely as possible. It does not matter in the least, incidentally, whether or not adopted children are, or turn out to be, homosexual or heterosexual. Homosexuals love their mums and dads just as much as heterosexuals do, and very few, to my knowledge at least, regret having had the experience of a mum and dad who loved them dearly. What does matter is that every child should have the real, lived experience of a mum and dad, so that they will have the opportunity, as well as the wherewithal and the role modeling, to do and to be the same. What also matters is whether or not homosexual acts and relations are intrinsically wrong, for those who believe that they are, understandably feel that the kind of modeling provided by homosexual parents would likewise be wrong. The concern is a serious one, but in my view, it is advisable, at the present time and in the current climate, to avoid getting bogged down in what would surely be a sterile exchange of moral opinions ('homosexual acts and relations are simply wrong' versus 'They're perfectly okay'), rather than a fruitful discussion in which real communication takes place. Thus I have tried to show that, whether or not homosexual acts and relations are wrong, the kind of role modeling provided by homosexual couples is certainly inappropriate, if, as we should, we wish the adopted child to experience our human nature 'at its best'.

Finally, it is important that we continue to privately reflect upon and publicly debate the true meaning of 'family' and what is in the best interests of our children. However, the process of ongoing discussion is in no way helped when the charge of 'homophobia' is directed against anyone who suggests that children would be disadvantaged by being raised by homosexual parents. We must endeavour to keep the focus upon 'What is, or isn't, good for children?', rather than 'what is or isn't homophobic?' If representatives of homosexual groups feel that the latter question must be asked, in this connection or in any other, they should at least admit the difficulty involved in answering it. I would suggest that 'homophobic attitudes' are not quite as easy to identify as some representatives of gay groups appear to think, and for reasons which they themselves should understand very well. One often hears it said that 'where one homosexual (or black, or woman, or aboriginal person) is degraded, all are degraded'. Now, in one sense, what is being said is plainly ridiculous. How can the bashing of a gay person in New York have anything to do with, or be related in any significant way to, a gay male sunning himself on Bondi beach in Sydney? Are not the two incidents totally disconnected? One answer to this question, true enough so far as it goes, would be to say 'in space and time, perhaps yes'. However, given that we belong to one humanity and that we do so, not just as 'separate' individuals but as members of families, groups, nations, races, etc, then the answer is that these incidents *are* connected. What is really being said here is that where one human being is degraded, we are all degraded, for we share in one and the same universal humanity. It is right and proper when one homosexual person is bashed and degraded, for every other fellow human being to feel degraded as well (maybe 'co-degraded' would be a better word), to express their concern, and to help in any way possible. However, there are many who hold that the homosexual act is itself degrading, unnatural and dehumanising, and that where one homosexual person is degraded, we are all co-degraded, and that we should all be concerned. Of course, representatives of the gay community will disagree, and say that the concern is misplaced, but let them at least concede that it is well meant and that it is not, or at least not necessarily, homophobic for it is based upon a belief in our common humanity, which is, it should be noted, a crucially important 'emancipatory' belief or principle.

The state, then, should not recognise long term homosexual couples as 'families', for to do so would be to regard 'homosexual families' and 'heterosexual families' as equally legitimate from the 'public' point of view, and this, as we have just seen, would not be in the public interest. I would also strongly urge that whatever definition of the 'family' we come up with (and which we expect the state to 'operationally' and to enshrine in public policy) it must, at the very least, be non-adultist and have the welfare of children as its clear and central focus. On the presumption that coming into earthly existence in the first place and being reared by their own natural parents is integral to the 'welfare of children', homosexual couples simply do not fall within a child-focused understanding of the family. This is not to deny that a homosexual couple, 'at its best', is like a heterosexual couple or family, 'at its best', in certain important respects; the homosexual couple, like the heterosexual couple, may love each other purely and unselfishly and may express that love tenderly in sexual intercourse. Likewise, the homosexual couple may be just as committed to the unconditional care of each other as the husband and wife of a family, and precisely because they do resemble families in this respect, long term homosexual couples should be entitled to a carer's allowance, if such an allowance is made available to family members. (Indeed, in my view, long term homosexual couples are *more* like a family than a deliberately childless couple whose childlessness is a matter of 'ideological' conviction, for the latter are opposed *in principle* to child bearing whereas the former are unable *in fact* to have children.) Still, however pure and unconditional the love of the homosexual couple for each other, it is in no sense 'overflowing'; the 'site' of their sexual intimacy is not a 'sacred site' from which new life emerges. There is no link between sex and life, between the bedroom and the kindergarten; rather, the relationship is wholly 'inward' and private to the two individuals involved. Now, it was partly in recognition of this purely private character of the sexual relations of homosexuals that many western governments originally decided to decriminalise private homosexual acts between consenting adults, but this 'asocial', 'afamilial' character of their sexuality still holds good as a reason for not regarding the homosexual couple as a family.

Culturally Formative Religion and Public Prayer

To speak as Neuhaus does of 'a religiously grounded public philosophy'[34] as distinct from 'a religiously grounded contribution to public philosophy' is, I think, inappropriate in modern liberal democracies where citizens do not share a common faith. However, to speak, as Neuhaus also does, of 'culturally formative religion'[35] is, I believe, perfectly appropriate and unexceptionable, for it is the responsibility of *all* citizens in a liberal democratic society to be 'culturally formative'. This is also what Paul Tillich[36] has in mind when he speaks of culture providing the forms through which religion is contemporaneously expressed but of religion also helping to provide culture with substance. For Christians this means, on the one hand, attempting to integrate crucial Christian beliefs

---

34. RJ Neuhaus, 'The Real John Dewey', in *First Things* 19 (January 1992): 54.
35. RJ Neuhaus, *The Naked Public Square: Religion and Democracy in America* (Grand Rapids: Eerdmans, 1984), 220.
36. P Tillich, 'The Church in Contemporary Culture', in *World Christian Education*, second quarter (1956): 41–43.

relevant to society's wellbeing into the 'collective conscience', but also, on the other, recognising that it is the right and responsibility of other citizens with radically different beliefs (gay activists, radical feminists, etc) to do the same. Certainly, if by 'liberal' we understand a person who 'cannot take his own side in an argument' and hence chooses a political 'silence' or non-participation which never offends, then neither the Christian nor the gay citizen should be 'liberal' in this non-committal, nonjudgmental sense (Pilate's 'washing of the hands'). When Michael Novak holds that respect for the transcendence of God and freedom of conscience are better served by a 'reverential emptiness' at the heart of society than by 'a socially imposed vision of the good',[37] he veers dangerously close to being 'liberal' in this invidious, noncommittal sense. His 'reverential emptiness' is really an 'empty universal', an abstraction hovering idly above the socio-political world, whereas what we require in a liberal democratic society is the type of universal judgment that informs, enfolds and unifies differences; we need a reverential orientation to the 'spirit of unity' and to its promptings within ourselves, as well as persistence in the ongoing quest for a socially articulated (as opposed to socially imposed) vision of the good. However, if Pilate's posture of publicly 'washing the hands'—and of thereby ensuring that responsibility and guilt for difficult public choices lies elsewhere—is unacceptable to both the Christian and gay *citizen*, so too, though for different reasons, is American

---

37. M Novak, *The Spirit of Democratic Capitalism* (New York: American Enterprise Institute/Simon & Schuster, 1982), 68–69.

moral majoritarianism. To the extent that the Christian Right in America is intent upon politicising their private beliefs, eschewing public debate on these beliefs and regarding them as immune to public criticism as 'God's will for America', then, as Neuhaus points out, they are not contributing in any way to the emergence of a genuinely public philosophy or consensus. If to be 'liberal' in the sense we have just spoken of is to be non-participatory in principle, that is, to have an open mind permanently suspended above the world of political judgment as a matter of principle,[38] then moral majoritarianism, though decisive in judgment and willing to be substantively involved in the process of political decision-making, is nevertheless against the spirit of participation and public debate.

Whatever the reader may think of the arguments presented in this chapter concerning the nuclear family, homosexual marriage etc, hopefully it will at least be acknowledged that they constitute an exercise in 'public reason' in the sense that they do not rely upon metaphysical or religious convictions liable to be held by only a minority of citizens. This 'practical' claim accords with the more theoretical claim I make in chapter seven that the ethical/metaphysical account of the state, though obviously metaphysical, is yet not metaphysical in a 'deep' or sectarian sense that is liable to give offence or engender reasonable resistance. My claim in that chapter is that the ethical theory of the state is not, in the sense that worries liberals, a metaphysical theory. This is the kind of claim

---

38. K Chesterton once remarked that the purpose of an open mind, like that of an open mouth, is to close itself firmly on something.

made by Martha Nussbaum[39] concerning her 'thick vague' theory of the good life for human beings and I would like to briefly refer to her theory at this point because I am making precisely the same claim for similar, though not quite identical, reasons. Nussbaum holds[40] that to count as worthwhile or 'fully human', a person's life must include certain 'central functional capacities', such as being able to think and reason, to have adequate food and shelter, to laugh play and enjoy recreational activities, etc. This conception or account of the human good, she maintains, is 'thick' in so far as it designates certain crucial human ends requiring fulfilment if a life is to be describable as (fully) human but it is also 'vague' in that it provides only an 'outline sketch' of the good life, the details of which 'admit of many concrete specifications'.[41] In formulating her 'thick vague' theory of the good life, Nussbaum has in mind the concern entertained by Rawls that a substantive conception of the human good is liable to be sectarian and divisive because it is based upon contested metaphysical claims concerning the ultimate nature of human beings. Rawls was particularly concerned that a metaphysical

---

39. M Nussbaum, 'Aristotelian social democracy', in *Liberalism and the Good*, edited by RB Douglass, G Mara and HS Richardson (New York: Routledge, 1990), 217.
40. M Nussbaum, *Women and Human Development: the Capabilities Approach* (Cambridge: Cambridge University Press, 2000), 79–80.
41. M Nussbaum, 'Aristotelian social democracy', 217. One is reminded here of Barth's 'analogical/concrete' use of a list of examples 'to illuminate the analogical but extremely concrete relationship between the Christian gospel and certain political decisions and modes of behavior', *Community, State and Church: Three Essays*, 179.

claim that arose from a particular religious perspective could reasonably be rejected by those who did not share it but, Nussbaum insists, her 'thick vague' conception of the good life 'is not, in the sense that worries liberals, a metaphysical theory . . . peculiar to a single metaphysical or religious tradition'.[42] Her 'thick vague' theory, she contends, does not begin with an abstract speculative account of human nature but with conceptions of humanity found in actual 'myths and stories from many times and places, stories explaining to both friends and strangers what it is to be human rather than something else'.[43] Moreover, we find, she holds, that there is a 'great convergence across cultures in such storytelling, and its singling out of certain areas of experience as constitutive of humanness' which 'gives us reason for optimism that if we proceed in this way, using our imaginations, we will have, in the end, a theory that is not only the parochial theory of our own culture, but also a basis for cross-cultural attunement'.[44]

I hold that the ethical/metaphysical theory of the state likewise begins not with abstract speculations on our humanness, society or the state, but with our everyday mundane experience of life in our families and political communities, reflection upon which reveals to us the presence and role of the state in our lives. I also hold that this theory, like Nussbaum's 'thick vague' theory of the human good, is not metaphysical in a way that would concern Rawls and liberals generally. At the same time, however, there is,

---

42. M Nussbaum, 'Aristotelian social democracy', 217.
43. *Ibid.*
44. *Ibid*, 218.

I believe, in public life a certain 'metaphysical minimum' that cannot and should not be dispensed with. I have in mind here certain minimal metaphysical beliefs to which the state, as a state, should be committed in the interests of the 'unity of identity' or the 'felt sense of unity' of its people. Often what serves to unite a people is its common past or, in the case of many western countries, their common Christian heritage. Where a people's deep sense of who they are as a people (or nation) is intimately tied up with their religious heritage, the state is, I believe, justified in acknowledging their core metaphysical beliefs, the constitutive role of these beliefs in forming a sense of common identity in the citizen body and the importance of reflecting these core beliefs in public ceremonies.

I will use as an example the issue of whether or not the Lord's Prayer should be said on certain public occasions (special school events, the opening of parliamentary sessions, etc) in western societies. I believe that this practice should be continued (or re-introduced, as the case may be), even when some of those present at the public event in question believe neither in God or in the Lord, and subscribe neither to the metaphysical minimum (God exists) nor to the religious minimum (Jesus is Lord).[45] To say that the state, in the interests of its unity of identity, is justified in representing this metaphysical minimum in public life does not mean that it will be publicly enforced or used

---

45. It should be noted here in passing that the 'religious' or Christian content of the Lord's prayer is practically zero, for it is a prayer *of* the Lord present on this earth, not a prayer *to* the Lord (of Christians) and hence is eminently 'prayable' by any believer in God.

as a test of loyalty; all that it means, in practice, is that (i) those who, in good conscience (*in foro interno*) cannot subscribe to such inherited core (metaphysical/religious) beliefs or collective sentiments should (minimally) exhibit tolerance and (preferably and ideally) show respect to those who do, by silently acknowledging (*in foro externo*) the role of these beliefs in forming the collective sense of identity that they share with their fellow citizens; and (ii) that those who, in good conscience, can and do subscribe to such inherited core (metaphysical/religious) beliefs or collective sentiments should, on appropriate occasions, publicly, actively and verbally acknowledge the role of these beliefs in forming the collective sense of identity that they share with *all* of their fellow citizens, and should (minimally) exhibit tolerance and (preferably and ideally) show respect to those who do not subscribe to them. Consider the case of a small Christian minority in a predominantly Muslim society. They would have no difficulty in subscribing to what I have called the 'metaphysical minimum' but could not subscribe to the 'religious minimum', that is, to a public, active and verbal acknowledgement that Mohammed is Allah's greatest prophet. In this case the formula of 'tolerance/respect' just outlined would come into play. Concerning the metaphysical minimum, tolerance and mutual respect are clearly (and 'universally') the order of the day.

Chapter Five

Western Liberalism, Islam and the 'Vertical Truth' of Our Common Humanity

Humanity, the characteristic and essential mode of man's being, is in its root fellow humanity. Humanity, which is not fellow-humanity, is inhumanity.'

Karl Barth, *Church Dogmatics* 111/4, 117

We generally like and value what we know well—our families, our friends, our culture, our 'way of life'—and generally feel that these likes are beyond criticism; they simply are what they are, and are part of who we are. Moreover, just as we feel free to like or dislike apples without involving our conscience in the matter, so too we feel that there is no need to justify what we feel instinctively comfortable with. In such cases, most of the time, 'live and let live' seems a reasonable motto to adopt, but there are certain occasions when it is not appropriate at all, when indeed we actually expect other people to value what we value and to be surprised and disappointed if they do not. As I suggested in the last chapter, we expect everyone—not just our family and friends and those who share our way of life but everyone—to value truth, justice, goodness, common decency, unselfishness, integrity, etc. These are divinely implanted values and virtues that belong to the whole of humanity. They *ought* to be prized by us all. In this chapter I wish to show that the acknowledgement that these divinely implanted values (referred to in more secular terms as a transcendent moral order) are universally present in humanity has important implications (i) for the manner in which we do, and should, reflectively approach political theory in general, western liberalism in particular, and the self-understanding of the Christian west and (ii) for how we answer the questions: Is Christian civilisation universally defensible? Is it merely a western prejudice?

I will argue that it is perfectly permissible and legitimate to attempt to justify the core institutions and cultural practices of 'our way of life' but that any such attempt, in order to be successful or plausible, must be an exercise in 'universal politics' or 'universal criticism', that is, a defence presented openly and transparently before the court of our common humanity. In the spirit of universal criticism, I wish to defend 'western' Liberalism against a variety of charges that have been directed against it, and to argue that the kind of liberal doctrine developed in the west and seen as indispensable to (Judaeo-Christian) western civilisation warrants serious consideration, not only by those already sympathetic to the liberal tradition but by everyone, including members of non-western Muslim societies normally deemed to be 'non-liberal'. Thus, my intention is to present a 'universalist' rather than a 'particularist' defence of the key tenets of Liberalism. I will also argue that we need to do our utmost to ensure that our use of the expression 'our tradition' or 'our way of life' should not be used as an instrument of closure or separation from our universal humanity or as a means of denying the 'ultimacy' of God, and that the great disadvantage of the kind of 'particularist' defences of liberalism presented by John Rawls, Joseph Raz and John Gray is that they do just that, regarding 'our way of life' as somehow self-justifying, as beyond the reach of universal criticism and the divine criterion. I also argue that Samuel Huntington's *The Clash of Civilisation; Remaking of World Order*[1] *is susceptible to a similar kind of critique.*

Liberalism and its Critics

Broadly, Liberalism holds that each of us should be free to pursue the good as we see it, and that the state should be as neutral as possible towards the variety of conceptions of the 'good life' entertained by its citizens. At first glance, as even the critics of Liberalism readily admit, this is an intuitively appealing viewpoint but upon further scrutiny, the critics allege, a cardinal weakness is that the state, thus viewed, is required to rank one good or value, namely liberty, above all others and is therefore surreptitiously

---

1. S Huntington, *The Clash of Civilisations and the Remaking of World Order* (New York: Touchstone, 1997).

committed to a conception of the 'good', and to a whole political outlook and way of life, that is associated with that particular value (liberty). Thus the critics of western liberalism allege that it only appears to be sympathetic to 'value pluralism' and opposed to any state-imposed ranking of human values, but that it is in fact neither. One critic who directs this kind of criticism against liberalism is John Gray.[2] He holds that liberalism, far from implying a commitment to value pluralism, is profoundly at odds with it, and that the ranking implied by liberalism, specifically the manner in which it privileges the goods of personal autonomy, rights and toleration, renders spurious and untenable its claim to uphold (i) state neutrality (who can doubt the commitment of the liberal state to its own prized values?), (ii) objectivity (Is liberalism really even handed towards the values that citizens might choose to privilege?) and even (iii) freedom (Is one really free to reject the 'liberal lifestyle'?). Another critic is John Kekes who holds that in the light of the incommensurability of values (value pluralism) and their particularity (the 'determination' of our values by the concrete circumstances of our lives and the specific traditions and ways of life that we have inherited), liberalism simply has to be regarded

---

2. J Gray, *Post-Liberalism; Studies in Political Thought* (London: Routledge, 1993); J Gray, *Berlin*, (New York: Harper Collins, 1995); J Gray, *Enlightenment's Wake: Politics and Culture at the Close of the Modern Age* (London: Routledge, 1995); J Gray, 'Pluralism and Toleration in Contemporary Political Philosophy', in *Political Studies*, 48 (200): 323–33; J Gray, *Two Faces of Liberalism* (Cambridge: Polity, 2000).

as universally illegitimate and unethical.[3] He holds that the commitment of members of a political community to a particular set of values and their prizing or privileging of that set above others is unintelligible without reference to a background tradition. However, this local and particular ranking of values by a political community, which Kekes regards (rightly, I believe) as perfectly wholesome, healthy and legitimate, as a routine part of the ethical life is disallowed, he believes, (erroneously, as I shall argue) by what he regards as the single, general universal ranking imposed by liberalism. In brief, then, (western) liberals hold that individuals should be maximally free to choose their own way of life, to stand before an array of incommensurable values and make their own authentic, ethical choices, and that the state should be largely neutral, more concerned with protecting the rights of citizens than pursuing its own agenda. However, in developing this liberal position, they fail, the critics allege, to acknowledge the value biases and 'inherent hierachialism' of their convictions.

To what extent are these criticisms of liberalism justified? I shall argue that, by and large, the liberal position is capable of withstanding the force of these criticisms and that it is actually the critics themselves who are at fault in failing to properly take into account the full significance of the crucial distinction in moral and political theory be-

---

3. J Kekes, J 1993, *The Morality of Pluralism*, (Princeton, NJ: Princeton University Press, 1993); J Kekes, J 1997, *Against Liberalism*, (Ithaca: Cornell University Press, 1997); J Kekes, *A Case for Conservatism* (Ithaca: Cornell University Press, 1998).

tween the 'right/just' and the 'good'. This familiar distinction has of course been discussed at great length[4] but for our present purposes it will be sufficient to point out that in the ethical consciousness the 'right/just' ('right' used in the sense of 'just') primarily consists in our *recognition* of the value of persons, whereas the 'good' consists mainly in our endeavours to *realise* values, more precisely, to realise absolute value through the prism of the familiar (and relative) human values.[5] When acting justly or when considering the requirements of justice, our primary concern is to act in conformity with our recognition or acknowledgement of the absolute value of persons or spiritual beings. Now, I would suggest that 'liberty' or the 'right to liberty' is not to be construed as simply 'one good among others' but that the right to liberty is an entitlement of every person *as* a person (child of God) or as a Kantian 'end-in-itself'. Thus, the 'privileging' of liberty/rights/toleration in liberal theory is not, as Gray and Kekes appear to believe, a matter of arbitrary and almost whimsical choice, but rather a matter of *justice*, something that is *required* of us as persons in our dealings with our fellow human beings. Where matters of justice are concerned, it is not a question of realising value in our quest for the good but rather of recognising or acknowledging each person as a free individual, or as a distinctive centre

---

4. B Trainor, *Justice and the State: On Liberal Organicism and the Foundations of Emancipatory Politics* (Quebec: World Heritage Press, 1998), 25–31.
5. This absolute/relative distinction is discussed and explained in chapter three, section (iii) of this book.

of consciousness in the universe. Liberty, tolerance, rights etc simply follow from this acknowledgement, this *justly* required acknowledgement, of the absolute value of the free individual and of the freedom (the unique 'spiritual initiative') of each one of the Father's children. Thus liberalism's allegedly unfair privileging of (the value of) liberty turns out to be no more than a simple acknowledgement of the requirements of justice, and most especially the requirement that we allow each other the maximum feasible degree of liberty to develop or realise our identity—who we really are or who, and what, we are striving to become—in accordance with our own best judgment.

In the light of the kind of criticism to which liberalism was subjected by Gray and Kekes, it is interesting to note that the work of the early Rawls, a stout defender of liberalism, was criticised for similar sorts of reasons—(i) by Charles Taylor for failing to recognise that even the most neutral or 'procedural' liberalism inevitably harbors a substantive liberal conception of the good life as lived by 'atomistic' individuals,[6] (ii) by Alasdair MacIntyre for failing to grasp the historical specificity and 'contingency' of the liberal tradition and its status as just one of a number of alternative, competing conceptions of the (political) good,[7] and (iii) by Michael Sandel, for his (Rawls's) failure

---

6. C Taylor, 'Cross-purposes; the liberal-communitarian debate', in *Liberalism and the Moral Life*, edited by N Rosenblum (Cambridge MA: Harvard University Press, Cambridge, 1989); C Taylor, *Sources of the Self: The Making of the Modern Identity* (Cambridge MA: Harvard University Press, 1989).
7. A MacIntyre, *After Virtue*, second edition (London: Duckworth, 1985); A MacIntyre, *Whose Justice? Which Rationality?* (Notre Dame

to see that his allegedly impartial theory of justice in fact presupposes a Kantian notion of the person who requires us to separate ourselves, as 'absolute ends', from the very goals, identifications and values that constitute our inner life and make us who we are.[8] However, as in the case of liberalism in general, the early Rawls may be defended against these charges by noting that all that is presupposed by his 'proceduralism' and his impartial theory of justice is a Kantian notion of persons as 'ends-in-themselves' who, as a matter of justice, are to be treated as such at all times and in all places; this is a presupposition which is shared by the Christian-religious consciousness.

Against the 'particularist' Case for Liberalism

So far, I have maintained that the maximum feasible degree of liberty ought to be allowed to the members of each state, and that this principle is properly regarded as prescriptive for humanity as such, so that it is universalisable beyond the limits of western liberal cultures or 'secular liberty/rights' oriented societies. However, as well as supporting a 'universalist' case for liberalism, I also wish to assert that, strictly speaking, a *wholly* 'particularist' case for liberalism, either of the 'neutralist' kind offered by the later Rawls or of the 'perfectionist' kind offered by Joseph Raz, not only implicitly denies (theologically) God's ultimacy (the divine criterion) but simply cannot

---

IN: University of Notre dame Press, 1988).
8. M Sandel, *Liberalism and the Limits of Justice* (Cambridge: Cambridge University Press, 1982).

be sustained (theoretically) in any case. Let us look firstly at the work of Rawls.

In the theory of justice developed in his later work, Rawls eschews any claims to universal truth or speculations concerning the essential nature of persons, but focuses instead upon each specific context and 'upon basic intuitive ideas that are embedded in the political institutions of a constitutional democratic regime and the public traditions of their interpretation. Justice as fairness is a political conception that starts from within a certain political tradition'.[9] In his *Political Liberalism*[10] he takes the view that the argument in his *A Theory of Justice*[11] depended on the reader taking for granted a wide set of liberal principles. However, he holds that these principles are still defensible and legitimately deployed, because *within liberal political cultures* (their 'home' or natural habitat, so to speak), they are acceptable not just to 'liberals' but also to those who subscribe to a wide range of comprehensive moral doctrines. In the public political culture that all citizens share in these societies, we find implicit the ideas that ground 'justice as fairness', such as, for example and centrally, the idea of society as 'a fair system of co-operation among free and equal citizens'. Rawls carefully distinguishes between a public sphere governed by 'public reason' based on principles accepted by all citizens, and a

---

9. J Rawls, 'Justice as fairness: political not metaphysical', in *Philosophy and Public Affairs*, 14 (1985): 223–51.
10. Rawls, *Political Liberalism* (New York: Columbia University Press, 1993).
11. J Rawls, *A Theory of Justice* (Oxford: Oxford University Press, 1971).

private realm in which citizens freely adopt and develop their own conceptions of the good life. He is clear that the liberal state must conscientiously engage in the arduous task of 'public justification' and base public policy on principles acceptable to all reasonable citizens.

The main reservation that arises in my mind concerning the above account is whether or not it is a genuinely 'particularist' account, by which I mean one that does not implicitly appeal to universal principles, to our shared ethical humanity and, ultimately, to the divine criterion. The key issue involved here is highlighted if we ask what is meant by 'sound' or 'just' public policy. For Rawls, at least in the case of liberal political cultures, the answer would be 'policy based on principles acceptable to all reasonable citizens of the liberal state' but is Rawls's appeal here not ultimately and implicitly directed to all reasonable citizens *of our universe*? I think that it is, but in any case, I wish to suggest that in order for the public policy of a liberal democratic state to be 'sound' or 'just', it must indeed be acceptable to all reasonable citizens of our common human universe. This is the ultimate criterion of the soundness, in the sense of the ethical propriety, of any public policy. In the words of Jean Paul Sartre, 'in legislating for ourselves, we legislate for all humanity' which, roughly translated into the present context, means that if a public policy is not justifiable before the court of our common humanity or of 'common grace', it is not justifiable at all. The ethical principles implicitly operative in a particular political culture are universal principles, or at least this is so in the case of a *just* political culture, one whose members are able to hold their heads up high before all of humanity. When, as is normally the case, members of a particular culture express pride in their traditions, regarding them as by and large noble and uplifting and as setting commendably high standards (judged universally), it is their standing in the eyes of God (*sub specie aeternatatis*) that they have in mind. It is interesting to note in this regard that the international community generally reserves its severest judgments for those governments which depart from their own noble and just political traditions. Hence when Rawls claims that 'public reasons' ultimately appeal to ideas and principles inherent in a particular tradition or political culture, the ultimate appeal here is ultimately to humanity as a whole, to the divine/human court of common grace, to ethical principles that are universal in scope and application, to an ethical source or criterion that transcends and judges liberal political cultures. In the final analysis, a particular culture is only legitimate and defensible to the extent that it is self-consciously informed by such universal principles or in so far as they lie latent in the heart, so to speak, of its *mores* and practices. What indeed should we expect to find at the ethical centre or core of a *human* society? What indeed is the inner ethical pulse of each human society but the heartbeat of God's Spirit moving through our common humanity?

It should be noted here that Rawls's 'implicit ideas' (or, as I would say, universal ethical principles) are not in the least 'neutral' with regard to the many kinds of comprehensive doctrines (moral, religious, social) found in political communities but strongly condemn any elements of fanaticism in these doctrines or any tendency in them to absolutise a single value in such a way as to render them immune to criticism in terms of universal ethical principles. For example, the principle of maximum liberty or Rawls's principle of 'fair co-operation among free and equal citizens' stand resolutely opposed to the tendency in radical forms of socialism and feminism to absolutise (or deify) the value of equality and to nullify (or demonise) all other significant human values, especially liberty. Likewise, these principles stand opposed to any conservative tendency to absolutise the value of 'order' in *all* human societies. Hence, I believe that Raz is justified in insisting, contrary to 'Rawlsian neutrality', that it is a legitimate task of the state to intervene to promote some ways of life, for example those supporting the maximum feasible right to liberty, and to discourage others, for example those permanently subserving liberty to other ends deemed to be ultimate. However, I believe that Raz is mistaken in insisting that liberty is not an important value in every human society. 'Not everyone', he claims, 'has an interest in personal autonomy. It is a cultural value, that is, of value to people living in certain societies only.'[12] The reason for this, he maintains, is that what is required in different societies for human well-being varies, not in accordance with different *beliefs* (the stance of cultural relativism) but because of different *conditions*. He holds, for example, that personal autonomy is a social and political value only in advanced industrial societies which 'call for an ability to cope with changing technological,

---

12. J Raz, *The Morality of Freedom* (Oxford: Clarendon Press, 1986), 198, fn 1.

economic and social conditions, for an ability to adjust, to acquire new skills, to move from one subculture to another, to come to terms with new scientific and moral views'.[13] However, if as Raz (correctly, in my view) points out, it is differing conditions rather than different beliefs which best explain why a particular value (liberty, loyalty, equality, solidarity etc) is emphasised in one society and not another, then surely the importance of the value of autonomy/personal liberty is a matter of degree—that is, it is always important to some degree but the precise degree is dependent upon prevailing social and economic conditions—rather than a matter of 'either/or', as Raz here claims. The key point to be grasped here is that liberty is a core divine/human value or principle. In light of the obvious difficulties involved when we, reared in our own society and culture, attempt to ascertain the degree and type of personal autonomy exercised in another society, we should be hesitant, to say the least, to claim that this value is wholly absent, irrelevant or unimportant for members of that society, for that comes dangerously close to saying that it (the 'other' society whose degree and type of personal autonomy 'we' are attempting to assess) is scarcely recognisable as a *human* society at all and perhaps betrays a lack of imagination on our part concerning the way in which personal autonomy may be exercised in societies that are vastly different, culturally and technologically, from our own.

Another reason why the kind of 'particularist' case for liberalism advanced by Raz and the later Rawls cannot be

---

13. *Ibid*, 369–70.

sustained is that the 'particular' is after all, only our universal humanity concretised at a particular point in time and space. What this means is that whatever 'we', whether as a society (a 'collective person') or as private individuals, decide to do in the unique situations we find ourselves in, and in the light of our history, background and traditions, it must be recognisably human and justifiable before the court of our common humanity (of common grace). Liberty is a core human value, and like every human value, simply by virtue of being human, it is implicitly universal in its scope, application and appeal, even if its particular mode of expression and realisation at any specific time and place is thoroughly unique, and even if circumstances (the presence or absence of advanced technology, or mobility of labor etc) largely determine the degree of its relevance and appropriateness at any particular point in time. For this reason, John Gray is, I believe, mistaken, or at least misleading, when he says that 'liberal institutions can have no universal authority'[14] and that liberalism is 'best understood as a particular form of life, practiced by people who have a certain self-conception, in which the activity of unfettered choice is central'.[15] Surely, however, the truth of the matter is that a society governed by liberal institutions, in so far as it genuinely enshrines the key value of liberty, *does* have a kind of 'universal authority' and shines forth its universal light, just as a society governed by conservative institutions may embody and express the value of 'order' and a society governed by socialist in-

---

14. J Gray, *Berlin*, 155.
15. *Ibid*, 161

stitutions may likewise serve the world by casting forth the universal light of 'equality'. Each such society, in its own way, deserves the respect of the others for the manner in which it manifests to the world, and institutionalises for the world, so to speak, a core human value. Gray regards liberalism as being in competition, on an equal moral footing, with alternative social and political forms but whilst this would be wholly unexceptionable if Gray merely meant that each political tradition, in its particularity and historicity, has its own cherished value or set of associated values, the problem is that he seems to assume that each distinctive human value ('liberty' in the case of liberalism, 'order' in the case of conservatism, etc) subsists in a kind of separate universe of discourse (a way of life, a political culture, a particular social and political form) that is hermetically sealed off from the influence of each of the other important human values, from the more open and generous divine criterion, and from the 'separate' political universes in which each of the other values is likewise held to subsist. Again, we need to recollect that each society is a *human* society and that, as such, it is accountable before the court of our common humanity for the way in which it lives out and develops the political tradition it has inherited.

Universal Liberalism and Kekes's Conservatism

In general, my argument so far coheres very well with the broad conservative conviction that there is a transcendent moral order, to which the ways of society ought to conform[16] and that a key role of government is to be 'the guardian of the heritage of civilisation and the principles of justice'.[17] It is hardly surprising then to find the conservative, John Kekes, insisting that there are important, universal human values, and goods—the 'goods of self',[18] the 'goods of intimacy' and the 'goods of social order'— which are 'universally good',[19] and that particular cultures or traditions are to be condemned when they are 'vicious, destructive, nay-saying, and thus not conducive to good lives'.[20] Kekes is in no doubt that traditional practices may properly be judged according to 'the *external* standard established by the minimum requirements of all good lives and formulated on the universal level of morality'.[21] Though broadly and strongly supportive of Kekes's position, I think that his use of the phrase 'the external standard' is unfortunate and injudicious. No doubt, Kekes means precisely what Edmund Burke meant when he said that '[e]very body is satisfied that a conservation and secure enjoyment of our natural rights is the great and ultimate purpose of civil societies and that therefore all forms whatsoever of government are only good as they are subservient to that purpose to which they are en-

---

16. R Kirk, *The Portable Conservative Reader* (Harmondsworth: Penguin, 1982), xv.
17. *Ibid*, xiii.
18. J Kekes, *The Morality of Pluralism*, (Princeton NJ: Princeton University Press, 1993), 39.
19. *Ibid*, 41.
20. J Kekes, *A Case for Conservatism* (Ithaca: Cornell University Press, 1998), 40.
21. *Ibid*, 94. Emphasis added.

tirely subordinate'[22] and when he insisted that 'prejudice' must always be 'just prejudice'.[23] However, in the case of the (spiritual) universal/particular relation in Burke's work, but not, I think, in the case of the internal/external relation in Kekes's work, there is a clear sense of the universal (ethical principles) being concretised or operationalised in a particular tradition and of the Spirit moving in and through each human society. The problem with the implied contrast in Kekes's work between 'external standards' and 'internal practices' is that it exudes a sense of permanent separation, of the 'universal' externally subsisting above or apart from the 'particular', and it thus obscures the fact that the 'universal' is routinely present *in* the 'particular' but may, as required, be separated in thought from the particular for critical, evaluative purposes and to serve as universal ethical criteria. It is precisely these distinctly unhelpful connotations of 'externality' that the relativists, whom Kekes opposes in his work[24] wish to evoke and which renders his position vulnerable to criticism. George Crowder, for example, asks the question: 'if Kekes allows that traditions can be criticised on the basis of external, universal standards, and so are not morally authoritative, then what remains of his conservative "traditionalism"?'.[25] In order to properly respond to

---

22. E Burke, *The Works of Edmund Burke* (London: George Bell and Sons), 6:29.
23. *Ibid*, 2:259.
24. J Kekes, A Case for Conservatism, 193.
25. G Crowder, *Liberalism and Value Pluralism* (London: Continuum, 2002), 124.

this criticism, Kekes would, I think, do better to express his position in terms of the 'universal/particular' relation rather than the 'internal/external' relation. He could then highlight the fact that it is precisely because traditions are themselves particular embodiments or 'sedimentations' of universal ethical principles (i) that they are morally authoritative in the first place and (ii) that they may be effectively criticised by reference either to the universal ethical principles they claim to, but perhaps fail to, embody or to other universal ethical principles.

My main point here could perhaps be put more simply and economically by saying, as I did in an earlier work, (i) that we cannot take the value of our families, associations, or societies seriously unless we believe (even in fear and trembling) that they are genuinely valuable and that our "local site" is a particular embodiment of our common humanity[26] or, (ii) with Michael Walzer, that each human society is 'universal because it is human, particular because it is a society'.[27] Certainly, as we saw in chapter two, section (i), the general viewpoint I have espoused in this book has certain affinities, with the position adopted by Walzer in his *Thick and Thin: Moral Argument at Home and Abroad*.[28] In this work, he argues that there is a universal minimal morality but that it is a mistake to imagine that it exists apart from particular societies or that it is *directly*

---

26. BT Trainor, 'Pluralism, Truth and Social Democracy', in *Dissent* (Fall 2002): 70
27. M Walzer, *Thick and Thin: Moral Argument at Home and Abroad* (Notre Dame IN: University of Notre Dame Press, Notre Dame, 1994), 8.
28. *Ibid.*

shared by all human beings. He rejects as misguided any 'foundational' attempt to establish philosophically the basis of such a minimal morality. Rather, he is adamant that this moral minimum 'is not a freestanding morality. It simply designates some reiterated features of particular thick or maximal moralities'.[29] However, I would hold, or additionally contend, that once we understand that the 'universal' (Walzer's universal minimum morality) is present in the contextualised particular (actual, concrete, historical societies) and that the 'universal' is grasped through the medium of its presence in the particular, then we can readily agree with Walzer that the universal minimum morality is not *directly* shared by all human beings but nevertheless insist that it is *indirectly* shared through the medium of the particular political cultures we each inhabit, each of which embodies (or should embody) aspects of this minimum, largely formal, morality in its own unique way. Interestingly, Joseph Carens has recently contended that this minimum morality, or what he refers to as 'the outermost circle or our morality, the one in which we apply our critical standards universally, is a feature of *our* morality. Indeed, what is so striking about this part of our morality, in my [Carens's] view, is that we are prepared to apply it even to people who may not share it . . .'[30] Surely, however, it hardly needs saying that if the outermost circle of our morality is *only* a feature of *our*

---

29. *Ibid*, 10.
30. JH Carens, *Culture, Citizenship and Community: A Contextual Exploration of Justice as Evenhandedness* (Oxford: Oxford University Press, 2000), 47. Emphasis in the original.

morality, then we have absolutely no right to apply it to people or societies that do not share it. If we do nevertheless proceed to make cross-cultural ethical judgments in the teeth of this acknowledgement, then surely we have either been seized by an ethnocentric sense of superiority, fallen prey to a mood of 'decisionism' or else we're simply being disingenuous.

Universal Liberalism and the Clash of Civilisations

The position I have taken in this book opposes and challenges some of the key tenets advocated by Samuel P Huntington in his renowned *The Clash of Civilisations and the Remaking of World Order*.[31] He states for example that in the emerging world of ethnic conflict and civilisational clash, 'Western belief in the universality of Western culture suffers three problems: it is false; it is immoral; and it is dangerous';[32] he holds, indeed, that imperialism is 'the necessary logical consequence of universalism'.[33] However, a great deal depends here on what precisely is meant by 'the universality of western culture'. It is quite possible and entirely legitimate, for example, to believe in liberty, rights, the rule of law, etc., as universal values without subscribing to the view that the manner in which these core human values have become culturally embedded in (secular) western culture sets some kind of world-

---

31. S Huntington, *The Clash of Civilisations and the Remaking of World Order* (New York: Touchstone, 1997).
32. Ibid, 310.
33. Ibid, 310.

wide universal standard or 'blueprint' for the manner in which they should be embedded in other civilisations or cultures, such as Islam for example. I have in mind here not just moderate or secular minded Muslim societies and their apologists, who might be expected to exhibit a degree of sympathy with these political values, but also more extreme, theocratic Muslim societies and their apologists. We find for example that Hasan al-Banna, who formed the Muslim brotherhood in Ismailiya in the 1920s and who urged the authorities to declare a holy war against the British in Egypt, nevertheless felt that the existing (liberal) constitutional framework in Egypt could, with some reformation, satisfy the political requirements of Islam for a 'Muslim state'.[34] Likewise, a strong disapproval of absolute or tyrannical rule and an appreciation of the need for constitutional restraints are more aptly described as attributes, not just of Western civilisation but of *any* sound human culture. Sayyid Abul Ala Maududi captures the Muslim view in broad terms when he states that only Allah is supremely sovereign, that pain and misery result when human rulers demand that they be obeyed, served and worshipped by their subjects in a manner that befits God alone,[35] and that 'tyranny, despotism, intemperance, unlawful exploitation, and inequality reign supreme, whenever man's overlordship and domination (*uluhiyyat*

---

34. B Musk, *Holy War: Why do some Muslims become fundamentalists?* (London: Monarch Books, 2003), 126.
35. SAA Maududi, 'The Political Theory of Islam', in *Modernist and Fundamentalist Debates in Islam: A Reader*, edited by M Moaddel, and K Talattof (New York: Palgrave Macmillan, 2002), 265–267.

and *rabubiyyal*) over man are established' and when the human soul is thus 'deprived of its natural freedom'.[36] My contention, then, in brief, is that a culture or civilisation for whose members the (in my view) universal notions of liberty or rights were *'wholly* alien' or *'absolutely* other' could scarcely be described as 'human' at all. Thus, it may well be true, as Huntington, (here expressing agreement with Arthur M Schlesinger, Jr) asserts, that Europe is the unique source of the ideas of individual liberty, political democracy, the rule of law, human rights, and cultural freedom or at least it is true, I would suggest, in the sense that Europe was the most notable historical site in which these universal values thrived and developed rich and complex cultural and institutional forms, but it certainly does nor follow, as Huntington and Schlesinger apparently believe, that these are 'European ideas, not Asian, nor African, nor Middle Eastern ideas, except by adoption'.[37] Likewise, although it may well be true that westerners are deluded who insist (i) that the 'liberty' and 'rights' they prize, together with the forms of their cultural and institutional embodiment, should be *also* at the heart of other cultures and civilisations (at their centre of cultural gravity) and that the liberal democratic institutions that have evolved culturally and historically in western jurisdictions may be directly (horizontally) transferable to non-western jurisdictions, yet they are not in the least deluded or dangerous in holding (ii) that the values they prize

---

36. *Ibid*, 268.
37. S Huntington, *The Clash of Civilisations and the Remaking of World Order*, 127.

(liberty, the rule of law, individual rights to privacy, etc) are true, universal, human values that assume a variety of particular cultural forms but which for historical reasons the west has been privileged to represent in the 'court' of humanity and to 'sound' in the chorus of humanity. The difference between (i) and (ii) is the difference between 'false universalism' and 'true universalism' respectively.[38]

The Horizontal Exportation of Liberal Democracy and Christian Realism

When no evidence was found for the existence of weapons of mass destruction in Iraq, the U.S. administration increasingly referred, when justifying its invasion of that country, to the benefits accruing from (i) the removal of Saddam Hussein's brutal dictatorship and (ii) the institution of a new liberal-democratic regime designed to give the Iraqi people a voice in their own affairs. A more gen-

---

38. Interestingly, we find in Huntington's own work the kind of distinction I have just made between false and true universalisms, for he contrasts the false, dangerous and immoral universalism of western civilisation with the (presumably true, wholesome and moral) 'commonalities of civilisations', S Huntington, *The Clash of Civilisations and the Remaking of World Order,* 318. Following Walzer's analysis in *Thick and Thin: Moral Argument at Home and Abroad* (1–11), he holds that '[m]inimal moral concepts of truth and justice are found in all thick moralities and cannot be divorced from them' (318). However, if this is so, and especially if we add to the list 'liberty' and 'rights', then it makes his ringing endorsement of Schlesinger's conviction that Europe is the unique source of the ideas of liberty, democracy, the rule of law and human rights look distinctly odd.

eral issue raised by (ii) concerns the wisdom and propriety of attempting to 'horizontally export' western liberal democratic institutions to non-western jurisdictions. As the reader will no doubt gather from the preceding analysis, I hold that such attempts are neither wise nor proper but are wholly misconceived. When evidence emerges that a nation has been acting unjustly towards its own citizens (arbitrary imprisonment, torture, etc), the international community has a responsibility to be forthright and even aggressive in its response. However, the benefits or otherwise of introducing western liberalism, or elements thereof, as a means of realising the value of liberty in an institutional sense or of realising the common good of its people in its historical and cultural context, is for the authorised representatives of each jurisdiction to determine, just as it is their responsibility to ensure that the universal principles of our humanity are properly integrated into (or 'vertically inform') the ever changing historical and cultural circumstances of their society; it is their task to respond to the divine criterion in their own fashion and in their own time. Thus to the extent that the aim of 'democratic globalism' espoused by many American neoconservatives involves a policy of aggressively promoting the export of American democracy,[39] it is to be rejected as

---

39. GA Fossedal, *The Democratic Imperative: Exporting the American Revolution* (New YorK: Basic Books, 1989); C Krauthammer, 'The Unipolar Moment', *Foreign Affairs*, 70 (1991): 22–33; J Muravchik, *Exporting Democracy: Fulfilling America's Destiny*, (Washington: American Enterprise Institute, 1991); BJ Wattenberg, *The First Universal nation: Leading Indicators and Ideas about the Surge of America in the1990s* (New YorK: Free Press, 1991).

theoretically misconceived and theologically inappropriate; it is a misguided idealism and a 'false universalism' which is bound to be destructive in its effects.

In *The Catholic Ethic and the Spirit of Capitalism*[40] Michael Novak is more restrained and circumspect in his approach but still his claim that democratic capitalism sets a universal standard by which the cultures, economies and political systems of the world are to be judged is unacceptable and even risky or dangerous in that it lends itself so easily to the defence of the indefensible, to the imposition of American style democratic institutions on the rest of the world. A more plausible and defensible position for Novak to adopt would be to hold that democratic capitalism provides a challenging model to the world of how the value of liberty may be enshrined in a society and economy, though he himself is well aware that, despite his fulsome praise of American capitalism in *The Spirit of Democratic Capitalism*[41] and *Towards a Theology of the Corporation*[42], it is no longer as 'publicly defensible' as it once was. It can scarcely be denied that, with the rise of an '(individual) rights-based' culture of 'pornography, abortion and divorce', the claims of 'liberty/rights' in American democratic capitalism have taken precedence

---

40. M Novak, *The Catholic Ethic and the Spirit of Capitalism*, (New YorK: Free Press, 1993).
41. M Novak, *The Spirit of Democratic Capitalism* (New York: American Enterprise Institute/Simon & Schuster, 1982).
42. M Novak, *Towards a Theology of the Corporation* (Washington DC: American Enterprise Institute, 1981).

over the claims of the common good, the wellbeing of the family, and community standards of mutual respect. Novak admits as much when he says that he and his wife have long felt that 'the world of the media was a tidal wave, which we could hardly hold back by ourselves. We have long felt under siege, even in our own home . . . Our own public moral culture, formed pre-eminently by television, cinema, and music, is a disgrace to the human race'.[43] Novak is anxious to place the responsibility for America's current cultural woes on leftist intellectuals in the media, the universities and the churches[44] but whatever the reason, it can hardly be seriously suggested that in the closing decades of the twentieth century, America offered to the world a socio-political model showing how a proper respect for liberty could be prevented from degenerating into license, or how true freedom could be prevented from turning into its opposite or mere appearance.

There is also another side to the misguided idealism of 'horizontal exporters of American democracy' that we should briefly pause to consider. Reinhold Niebuhr, as the foremost exponent of Christian realism in America, never tired of warning of the dangers of 'perverse sentimental-

---

43. M Novak, 'The Revolt against our Public Culture', in *National Review* 36 (May 4 1984): 48.
44. M Novak, 'Changing the Paradigms: The Cultural Deficiencies of Capitalism', in *Democracy and Mediating Structures: A Theological Inquiry* (Washington DC: American Enterprise Institute, 1980); M Novak, 'The Left Still Owns American Culture', in *Forbes* 145 (March 5 1990).

ity', of the egoism of both individuals and nations, and of the foolishness of 'the children of light' in failing to acknowledge the extent to which they were driven in their various 'idealisms' by their own self-will.[45] He held that 'the Marxian misunderstanding of man has contributed to the development of a tyranny in Russia which almost, though not quite, rivals fascist tyranny'.[46] Michael Novak saw himself as assuming the mantle of Niebuhr when he employed a hard-headed, realist analysis to unmask the manner in which the radicals of the 1960s generation—and, more specifically, the new class which gave political expression to its idealism—invariably presented itself in morally virtuous terms, indeed 'with an aura of morality so thick it would make the righteous Anglo-Saxons of a century ago envious'.[47] He also objected to the way in which this class concealed its self interest and lust for power behind its cloak of self-righteousness. Novak did not dispute the elementary goodness or propriety of the main causes of the new class—opposition to the Vietnam war and support for civil rights—but he objected to their use of 'conscience', 'principle' and 'morality' to disguise the extent to which their own power-driven ends were involved in the pursuit of these worthy causes. Perhaps

---

45. R Niebuhr, *The Children of Light and the Children of Darkness: A Vindication of Democracy and a Critique of its Traditional Defence* (New York: Scribner, 1944), x.
46. R Niebuhr, quoted in JC Bennett, 'Tillich and the "Fellowship of Socialist Christians"', in *North American Paul Tillich Society Newsletter* 16 (October 1990): 3.
47. M Novak, 'Needing Niebuhr Again', in *Commentary* 54 (September 1972): 60.

Niebuhr's more general point could be simply put by saying that humanity 'is the glory and scum of the universe', that there is seldom if ever a wholly pure motive behind any human or political act and that just as ostensibly noble human and political acts usually carry a trace of ignobility, so too acts that appear to be wholly ignoble often bear the traces of nobility. Niebuhr would remind us that what we need in our personal and political lives is a strong dose of self-critical candor but it is precisely this element of realistic and candid self-appraisal which—ironically, given the normal conservative distaste for unrealistic and dangerously misguided idealisms–seems to be missing in those neoconservatives who aggressively promote the export of American democracy.

Justice, the State and Our Universal Humanity

I earlier acknowledged that it is quite true, as Sandel asserts, that our historically acquired loyalties, identifications and values are fundamental to our 'contingently conditioned' sense of personhood but I added that there is simply no reason why this should in any way obscure, or be regarded as at odds with, our 'Kantian' conviction that human persons, as children of God, are absolute ends. I suggested that our socially and historically acquired identities, and the 'ways of life' associated with our (acquired) sense of who we are, of our 'lived personhood', may be regarded as truly ethical and legitimate only in so far as they cohere with this Kantian conviction. It is important to stress here that I am claiming that this holds true for humanity as such, for every human society, and not solely or specifically for those born and reared within a liberal tradition or in a Christian culture. The following hypothetical example will hopefully make this clear.

Let us imagine that the members of a particular political community have been born and reared in a society characterised by a strong and pervasive religious ethos (Muslim, Hindu, Christian, etc), that their 'being Muslim', 'being Hindu', etc, is deeply integrated into their sense of personhood and identity and that the laws of their state reflect and embody the religious beliefs and values that they hold dear. None of these considerations, I maintain, would excuse them in any way from being bound by the requirements of justice and universal morality. It is true that the state, as agent of the common good and public values, must be 'biased' in favour of 'itself', that is, of the public values (in the present case, public/religious values) that it upholds and of the common good (in this case, a religiously toned common good) which it is of its very essence to pursue, but this 'pro-attitude' or 'non-neutrality' towards its own essence must not obscure the state's complementary role as upholder of justice, as a 'neutral umpire' that allows each of its citizens the maximum feasible right to liberty in their public and private lives. Thus every state, at all times, is required to be 'liberal' in the sense earlier alluded to; that is, as a matter of justice, it must allow the maximum degree of liberty possible. It is a matter of justice, for example, rather than of 'grace' that the state in, let us say, a predominantly Muslim society is required to be tolerant towards its non-Muslim citizens and to acknowledge and respect their entitlement to the maximum feasible degree of freedom. (It is important to note here that the relation between toleration—the acceptance of diversity and difference—and orthodoxy—a devotion to, and proclamation of, universal, shared public values—is not just one of contrastive opposition between two virtues but is also one of mutual implication. Ideally, these two virtues 'balance' and 'address' each other, for *tolerance is a virtue exhibited by the orthodox* towards those who do not share, or do not fully share, the public values they proclaim to be essential to sound public life and their shared social inheritance.)

The state then, by virtue of what it is (that is, always and everywhere) has two key functions; firstly, to uphold justice and, secondly, to pursue the common good, understood in terms of the key public values and beliefs of its citizens. The state's responsibility to ensure that justice prevails and that the right to liberty is respected is largely 'context-independent' and hence, to an important degree, 'universally the same', whereas the state's responsibility to pursue the common good of its citizens is largely 'context-dependent' and hence, to an important degree, 'universally different' and strongly influenced by the predominant ethos (secular, religious, etc) of its members in the case of each particular state. However, at the present time, it is useful to distinguish between what we might call 'secular liberty/rights' oriented societies (most liberal democracies) and 'public-religious values/common good' oriented societies of the type discussed in our hypothetical example. Clearly, the challenge for citizens and governments in the latter kind of society is to meet the ('universally the same') requirement to be just, to allow all citizens the maximum feasible degree of freedom and to exhibit the virtue of tolerance, whereas the challenge for citizens and governments in the former type of society is to maintain unity in the midst of the plurality and diversity generated and legitimated by 'rights' and to exhibit the virtue of empathy, or a heightened sensitivity, to the ('universally different') exigencies of ethico-political unity and to the needs of the political community *as a whole*. In the case of liberal democratic societies, we perhaps need reminding that they are, after all, or at least aspire to be, single unified societies with a collective identity and a common 'way of life', and that sensitivity to the broad requirements of social cohesion and public unity is a vitally important political virtue.

Islam and Our Way of Life

What is, I hope, plain from the preceding analysis is that we need to take the utmost care to ensure that our use of the expression 'our tradition' or 'our way of life' should not be used as an instrument of closure or separation from our universal humanity. As we saw earlier, the great disadvantage of the kind of 'particularist' defences of liberalism presented by Rawls, Raz and Gray is that they do just that, regarding 'our way of life' as somehow self-justifying, as beyond the reach of universal criticism, and as wholly resistant, so to speak, to the 'divine flow of the universe' into our personal and cultural world. What is also clear, I believe, is that if the cultural and socio-legal practices of our way of life (Muslim or non-Muslim) are not justifiable in universal terms before the court of our common humanity (of common grace), then they are not justifiable at all. We have seen that for the defence of 'our way of life' to be adequate or, that is to say, for it to be genuinely universal, it should not be restricted to an appeal to a single value, to liberty/autonomy, for example, in the case of western liberal societies or to religious truth/order in the case of Muslim societies. The reader will here recall my earlier claim that Rawls's 'implicit ideas'—in effect, universal ethical principles so deeply held by members of a political community that they sink for the most part beneath the level of conscious thought—are not in the least 'neutral' with regard to the comprehensive doctrines (moral, religious, social) of (some of) its members. Let me add here that these 'implicit ideas' strongly condemn any elements of fanaticism in these doctrines, and any person or group in society (or even the society as a whole) that endeavours to absolutise a single value in such a way as to render its way of life immune to criticism in terms of (other) universal ethical principles and universally acknowledged values. For example, if the criticism is directed against western liberal culture that it sanctions the death of unborn children through legalised abortion, the break-up of the family and unwarranted disruption of the lives of children through easy divorce laws, and that it sanctions the emergence of a sexually saturated, pornographic culture through the abandonment of community standards, it is insufficient to reply that all of the above are legitimated solely under the rubric of 'freedom' (of women, of lifestyle choice, etc). Likewise if the criticism is directed at Muslim culture that it sanctions harsh and barbaric punishments for acts that should be regarded as perfectly legal free choices (the act of adultery, for example), the subordination of women and the persecution of homosexuals, it is insufficient to reply that these things are legitimated under the rubric of 'order' (religious order, social order). If a political community (Muslim or non-Muslim) can only defend its current cultural practices before the court of our universal humanity by reference to a single value, the suspicion must surely arise in the minds of its more conscientious citizens and in the 'mind' of the international community that it has a fanatical attachment to a single value, that its cultural practices are indefensible in terms of universal ethical principles and universally acknowledged values, and that it wishes its way of life to be immune to criticism and beyond the reach of judgment by the court of our common humanity.

In western liberal cultures at the present time there is, I think, a widespread conviction that in Muslim cultures there is a tendency towards fanaticism, towards a simple justification of cultural practices in terms of 'religious truth/holy order'. At the same time, in Muslim cultures, there is also, I think, an equally widespread conviction that the west has allowed a fanatical obsession with liberty to degenerate into decadence and a low-minded licentiousness. Surely, then, the task of intellectuals at the present time, Muslim and non-Muslim alike, is to critically distance themselves from their respective 'cultural chauvinisms' and to keep the lines of communication between the two cultures as open as possible. Writing as a 'westerner', I wish to encourage my 'fellow westerners' to be as open as possible to the force of the 'universal criticism' directed against us and to eschew the strategy of retreat into the protective, isolating cocoon of 'our way of life'. By the expression 'open to criticism', I mean 'subject to the divine criterion' or 'subject to the full force of public reason'—not quite the 'public reason' that Rawls had in mind, for his reasons were public only in the (perfectly proper) sense that they could in principle be shared by the citizens of a particular culture, but rather 'public reasons' that are public in the (equally proper but wider) sense of being acceptable as legitimate by all the citizens of our world. We must not absolutise a single value in such a way as to turn our particularity and historical concreteness ('our way of life') into a private hermetically sealed zone that is immune to critical appraisal by the court of our common humanity and that operates as an instrument of closure or separation from the wider ethical world that envelops us. Only if the rivers of 'universal criticism' are allowed to run freely can we realise (find and be found by) our common humanity and prevent claustrophobic, self-absorbed, narrow and fanatical thinking from taking root in dark places cut off from its universal light.

Part Three

Christ and State

Chapter Six

The Ethical Theory of the State

Behold, the dwelling of God is with men. He will dwell with them, and they shall be his peoples, and God himself will be with them.
Revelation 21:3

We, who are many, are one body in Christ, and individually we are members one of another.
Romans: 12:5

Introduction

My main purpose in this chapter is to show that the kind of ethical-metaphysical theory of the state that we broadly associate with idealist political philosophy provides us with a theoretical account of the state that is both sound and insightful and that, far from having been consigned to the dustbin of history by the hostile criticisms to which it has been subjected in the twentieth century (from pluralism, behaviouralism and postmodernism), it still remains the most profound and powerful account of the state available to the political science community to-day. Firstly, however, I wish to highlight what I consider to be most distinctive and uniquely valuable about this theory at the present time.

Recently, Elizabeth Van Acker made the comment that the state refers to 'a spectrum of political institutions including government, bureaucracies, health and social security services, judiciaries and public enterprises, as well as the military and police'.[1] She also noted that '[t]he *state* is therefore a broader concept than *government* as it includes a vast, governing set of political institutions'.[2] Early in the last century Bernard Bosanquet made a similar point when he said that the state is 'society as a unit, recognised as rightly exercising control over its members'[3] and John Dewey was obviously thinking along the same lines when he held that 'a public articulated and operating through representative officers is the state'.[4] All three authors would, I think, regard themselves as being utterly uncontentious in pointing out that the 'state', broadly conceived of as 'society organised to act on its own behalf' is wider in scope than what we mean by 'government', that the state 'includes' government or, to put it the other way around, that government

---

1. E Van Acker, 'The Role of Government in a Global World', in *Business, Government and Globalization*, edited by E Van Acker and G Curran (French Forest: Longman, 2002), 1.
2. *Ibid*, 2.
3. B Bosanquet, *The Philosophical Theory of the State* (London: Macmillan, 1965), 172.
4. J Dewey, *The Public and its Problems* (Athens, Ohio: Ohio University Press, 1988), 67.

is 'enveloped' by the state. However, whilst all three authors would agree that we should think of 'government' as nestled at the heart of the institutional matrix known as the state, it is only Bosanquet, the idealist political thinker, who takes the further step of maintaining that the state, as well as being an institutional reality, is *also* an ethical or spiritual reality, and that the term 'state' applies both to an interconnected set of empirical institutions *and* to its ethical substance or guiding spirit. He has in mind here the state as the public interest or general will, as the font of authority (the 'ethical' state) which confers legitimacy on whatever government acts in its name, rather than the state as the empirical set of public institutions (the 'empirical' state) through which a government tries to realise the general will of a political community. Thus what Van Acker takes the state to be is precisely what exponents of the ethical-metaphysical theory of the state take it to be, that is, a broad network of political and judicial institutions, but they are also interested in the state as an ethical community or a 'living ethical reality' in whose name governments act and in whose name emancipatory criticism may be directed against governments that fail to adequately realise or express the public interest or general will. Other names for this 'living ethical reality' are the 'person' of the state, the Holy Spirit or the 'angelic presence' of the Spirit in the socio-political realm.

For Bosanquet, and for exponents of the ethical-metaphysical theory of the state in general, to pose the question, 'Is the state a (common, ethical) will or a set of institutions?' is like posing the question 'Is the human person a will/spirit/mind or an inter-related set of material elements?' From the perspective of the ethical theory, the answer to both questions is the same, namely that the *definiendum* is both, at one and the same time; it is the state as the 'public interest' and 'general will' that informs, enlivens, guides and 'ethically constitutes' the state as an empirical set of institutions or, broadly, as the interconnected 'arms of government'. Admittedly, if we use the term 'government' to refer to the range of civic officials actually charged with executive, judicial, administrative and legislative responsibilities, and if the 'state' is indeed society organised to act on its own behalf through these officials, then it might seem that both concepts (i.e., 'state' and 'government') point to precisely the same reality (that is, society organised to act through its officials) and that it is therefore pointless to distinguish between the two. However, if the state is most appropriately conceived of in the manner of Rousseau as a 'moral person' or as the 'own self' of society as a collective or public person (the 'person' of the state), then our manner of both distinguishing and routinely identifying 'state' and 'government' becomes perfectly understandable; for just as our personal 'own self' is said to operate through our conscious thoughts and actions, so too the 'own self' of society, or the state (the angelic presence of the Spirit), may be said to routinely operate *through* the conscious thoughts and acts of 'its' officials.[5] All of this is extremely important when considering the state as the font of emancipatory

---

5. BT Trainor, *Justice and the State: On Liberal Organicism and the Foundations of Emancipatory Politics* (Quebec: World Heritage Press, 1998), 100–112.

political criticism or as 'the divine criterion in political judgment'.

I will suggest in this chapter that the ethical-metaphysical theory of the state (hereafter generally referred to simply as the 'ethical theory') has the distinct advantage and benefit of providing us with a genuine 'theory of the state', for it alone wholeheartedly subscribes to the view that the state is the inner core or substance of political life or its 'foundational reality', whereas its critics (pluralist, behaviouralist and post-modern) hold that the state thus understood—and the corresponding notion of politics as 'the ongoing quest for unity'—is a dangerous illusion that must be exposed to prevent its inherent totalistic tendency from wreaking havoc in the political universe. It is unfortunate, to say the least, that the ethical unity of the state proclaimed by the ethical theory—and the kind of 'politics as the quest for unity that it endorses—has been generally (and misleadingly) portrayed by hostile critics as, of necessity and by virtue of its essence, unitary rather than unifying, as a noun rather than a verb, a thing rather than a process, in short as a unitary, homogenising entity emanating from a single point rather than as a universal, enveloping, endlessly unifying will, with the result that the ethical theory has been portrayed as a sinister theoretical harbinger of dangerous totalising tendencies. Likewise, it is regrettable that what the ethical theory regards as the true ethical unity of the state, that is, the unifying will that holds the differences of group life in place, is portrayed by its critics as (again, by its very nature) a bare, universal form or will that descends with destructive force on the rich, living diversity of group life. I will suggest in this chapter that the misgivings expressed by critics of the ethical theory draw our attention, not to any grave weakness in the ethical theory itself but to the importance of distinguishing between the 'unitary' and the 'unifying', that is, between the constant unifying will of the state (the unifying movement of the Spirit) and the, at times, unitary and totalising will of governments and political leaders. We normally, and for the most part correctly, think of the latter (a unitary and totalising will) as repressive, as a 'monistic' will that silences the 'voices of difference' and negates the legitimate claims of 'diversity'. However, as I shall show in section (ii), under certain extreme circumstances, such as when the very survival of the body politic is at stake, the unifying will of the state (its true ethical unity) can *only* be expressed politically as a unitary 'monistic' will but this certainly does not provide us with a good reason for holding (in the manner of Carl Schmitt, for example) that the ethical unity of the state, or its unifying will, is unitary, monistic and oppressive (or, in Schmitt's language, 'exceptional') by its very nature.

Pluralism, Behaviorism and Postmodernism

In the case of the pluralist critique of the state, it is important to note that the pluralists did not reject the state as such but a unitary, monolithic state which they mistook for the state as such. Thus, for example, Barker [6] spoke of the state as 'a bare and forced universal, purchased at the cost of many individuals'[7] and Laski spoke of avoiding 'the temptation that bids us make our State a unity. It is to be all-absorptive. All groups within itself are to be but ministrants to its life'.[8] The pluralists were quite right to reject the unitary monolithic state but wrong, in doing so, to reject the state as such, just as they were right to criticise actual governments that acted as 'bare universals' repressing the difference and autonomy of group life, but mistaken in believing that the state in whose name such governments acted was itself, in essence, such a bare universal. Likewise, pluralist critics were right to assert that the idea of 'the state' exudes the assumption of a unified political whole but wrong in holding that intensified conflict between social groups (between, for example, capital and labor) made such a 'whole' practically and theoretically obsolete; far from heralding the demise of the state

---

6. E Barker, 'The Discredited State: Thoughts on Politics before the War', *The Political Quarterly*, 7/5 (1915): 101–121. In conceding that the state (or, as I would prefer to say, those representing the state) *may* act as a 'bare and forced universal', Barker acknowledges that its acting in this way is a matter of empirical possibility rather than of analytical or theoretical necessity and is thus, I think, less hostile to the ethical theory of the state than other pluralist critics and later behaviouralist and post-modern critics.
7. E Baker, 'The Discredited State: Thoughts on Politics before the War', 116.
8. HJ Laski, *Studies in the Problem of Sovereignty* (New Haven CT: Yale University Press, 1917), 1.

and its 'call' to ethical unity, the elimination of intense social conflict is its very *raison d'etre* and poses the ultimate challenge to the ethical unity of the state—one, indeed, to which only the promptings and intimations of the ever watchful Spirit can enable the body of citizens to adequately respond. Also, pluralist critics were right to insist that the state claims for itself a kind of ethical primacy or superiority, but only because its authority stems from (indeed, actually *is*) the eternal font of justice and 'Love universal' flowing into each socio-political world and thus, as the unique 'own self' of society,[9] it is owed the moral allegiance of its citizens, in much the same way as the 'true self' or 'own self' commands the moral allegiance of each person.

When considering the pluralist critique of the ethical theory of the state, it is also important to note that what the ethical theory regards as absolute and sovereign is not the executive, the legislature or the judiciary in a particular jurisdiction, or even these three arms of government acting in unison, but, quite simply, justice and the common good, or the 'Spirit-in-us', understood as an operative, unifying will that is ever oriented to and informed by justice and the common good and which alone legitimises the policies, deeds and decisions of the various arms of government. This unifying common or universal will is, in Bosanquet's words, 'a positive unity throughout

---

9. BT Trainor, *Justice and the State: On Liberal Organicism and the Foundations of Emancipatory Politics*, 100–112.

the selves that compose a society'[10] and, as a constitutive feature of the state as such, it is an integral element of any political entity recognisable as a state—of the liberal state, the democratic socialist state, the modern nation state or the post-modern state. The primacy or sovereignty of the ethical unity of the state (of the unifying Spirit) underlies ordinary political life and its unifying will routinely envelops the diversity of its political world, but this ethical unity or its source is not identifiable with any particular 'point' in the socio-political structure, for all 'points' are, so to speak, enveloped by it. Whether or not it is true that in the case of the kind of sovereignty exercised by the modern nation state there is, in the words of Laski, 'the necessity for its concentration at a single point in the social structure',[11] this telescoping of sovereignty and authority into a single 'point of issue' is not a feature of the state as such and is certainly not a feature of pre-modern and post-modern states.[12] Since the ethical theory acknowledges the sovereignty of the general will or the unifying will of the public spirit as the font of legitimacy in socio-political life but not the sovereignty of any agency in the social structure or constitutional terrain (executive, legislature, judiciary, etc), it has no quarrel with the pluralists' insistence that it is a serious error and 'dangerous to diversity'

---

10. B Bosanquet, *The Philosophical Theory of the State* (London: Macmillan, 1965), 72.
11. HJ Laski, *Authority in the Modern State* (New Haven CT: Yale University Press, 1919), 74.
12. BT Trainor, *Justice and the State: On Liberal Organicism and the Foundations of Emancipatory Politics*, 112–116.

to attempt to trace all authority in a political community to a single point of origin at its apex or elsewhere. Hence, I would argue that Hobhouse is mistaken in suggesting that, for those adhering to the ethical theory, beyond the state 'there is no higher association and states have no duties to one another or to humanity'.[13] On the contrary, when the state is understood in the manner commended by the ethical theory, its governmental institutions (and its unifying will) are seen as the means whereby our universal humanity and God's will for us in the political sphere is expressed and realised in a unique, concrete socio-political form and the common good is likewise understood as the good of humanity as such, expressed and realised in a particular society. Once we recognise that membership of the state and membership of God's human family are internally related and mutually implicative, it ceases to be objectionable (unduly zealous, nationalistic or chauvinistic) to assert that 'the highest duty of the individual is to be a member of the State'[14] for our universal humanity *requires* of us that we develop our distinctive humanity *through* our membership of a particular socio-political community located at a definite point in human history. As Luis Lugo remarks in his discussion of Caesar's coin, the idea of the common good 'cannot be confined to the well-being of particular political communities' for the state's performance of its legitimate functions 'also involves a proper concern for the well-being of the interna-

---

13. LT Hobhouse, *The Metaphysical Theory of the State* (London: Allen and Unwin, 1918), 33.
14. *Ibid.*

tional community'.[15] The same point is forcefully made in the Catechism of the Catholic Church[16] which holds that the unity of the human family 'implies a *universal common good*' which 'calls for an organisation of the community of nations' that can meet the different needs of humanity.

Hobhouse's fear is of the state becoming its own end[17] but for adherents of the ethical theory, the great fear is that a government may attempt to become an end-in-itself by telescoping the authority of the state into itself, so that, cut off from the state as its originary authority, it may attempt to become the self-sufficient source of its 'own' authority, thereby denying, in effect, that it is enveloped by God's Spirit and subject to God's authority. The real fear and danger is that a government may fail completely to represent the state, to acknowledge its 'ethical sovereignty' and to convey its 'ethical intimations' into public life.[18] The state, then, when properly understood, is not to be feared; it is 'always itself' in the midst of its many empirical appearances, always the same pure idea with a multiplicity of practical approximations and concrete historical realisations, always the one Spirit in many different 'angelic presences', always the one identical thread of

---

15. LE Lugo, 'Man, Society and the State: A Catholic Perspective', comments, in *Caesar's Coin Revisited: Christians and the Limits of Government*, edited by M Cromarties (Grand Rapids: Eerdmans, 1996), 21.
16. *Catechism of the Catholic Church* (Missouri: Ligouri Publications, 1995), no 1911.
17. LT Hobhouse, *The Metaphysical Theory of the State*, 33.
18. BT Trainor, *Justice and the State: On Liberal Organicism and the Foundations of Emancipatory Politics*, 100–112.

universal humanity as it weaves through the social fabric of a multiplicity of human societies.

The great weakness of pluralism is not its fondness for the particular, for living, concrete, empirical 'matter', but its hostility to the 'containing' universal, to the 'form' of the state as such, not its celebration of the rich diversity of group life but its blindness to the ethical unity of the state (its unifying general will) that strives to hold the various elements of that diversity in place and that both reveals and, in part, constitutes their character as parts of a single, living political whole. However, in the case of the behaviouralist and post-modern critiques of the state, precisely the same weakness appears, for behaviouralists and postmodernists likewise attribute a peculiar 'life of its own' (a kind of incomprehensible subsistence) to the realm of the empirical (behaviouralism) and to the endless succession of technologies of power (postmodernism) at the expense of the inner, constitutive ethical-divine dimension of political life, the universal (unifying and constituting) forms which breathe life into empirical political 'matter' and legitimacy into governments (technologies of power). Thus, we find David Easton insisting that in political science the state is empirically unknowable and therefore dispensable[19] and Lasswell and Kaplan holding that '[e]very proposition about the abstraction 'state' can be replaced by a set of propositions referring only to the concrete acts of certain persons and groups'.[20] As several

---

19. D Easton, *The Political System: An Inquiry into the State of Political Science* (New York: Kropf, 1953), 108.
20. HD Lasswell, and A Kaplan, *Power and Society: a Framework for Po-*

critics pointed out at the time,[21] this scientific approach to the state (and its ethical unity) led not only to the dismissal of the state on the grounds of its irrelevance in empirical, scientific terms, but also to an uncritical acceptance of the *status quo*. More recently, Jens Bartelson has called behaviouralism the 'politics of depolitisation' and has described its emergence as 'the coming of a new political technology based on the denial of the political contestability of state authority'.[22] However, from the point of view of those sympathetic to the ethical of the state, it is the denial of the political contestability of *governmental* authority (of the acts and policies of the executive, the laws of the legislative and the rulings and interpretations of the judiciary) by means of an appeal *to* the state (that is, to the justice and general will which these arms of government are supposed to give practical expression to in their distinctive spheres) that leads to the behaviouralist 'depolitisation of the political'—and, as we shall see shortly, to its post-modern 'de-statisation' as well.

Springing from the eternal font of authority, and as eternity drawing time to its fullness in itself, the state flows into ordinary, everyday (legitimate) political exis-

---

litical Inquiry (New Haven, CT: Yale University Press, 1950), 184.
21. G Duncan, and S Lukes, 1970, 'Democracy Restated', in HS Kariel, *Frontiers of Democratic Theory*, edited by HS Kariel (New York: Random House, 1970), 188–213 and JL Walker, 'Normative Consequences of Democratic Theory', in *Frontiers of Democratic Theory*, edited by HS Kariel (New York: Random House, 1970), 227–247.
22. J Bartelson, *The Critique of the State* (Cambridge: Cambridge University Press, 2001), 103.

tence and helps to explain its systematic character, but it is also the font of the critical spirit of emancipatory politics that, when necessary, takes everyday political existence to task. Hence, it is to the state that we must appeal if we wish to either *prescriptively* condemn or condone the *status quo* (the empirical) but it is *also* to the state, and especially to its unifying will, (and not just to the behaviouralist notion of 'political system') that we must look in order to *descriptively* explain the 'empirical' coherence of everyday, *legitimate* political existence. The latter is simply the state concretised or routinely expressed, whereas, in the case of a corrupt or illegitimate government, the divine 'ought' of the state (the Spirit) is in clear opposition to the 'is' of current political existence, no matter how systematic or coherent in character such a corrupt 'political system' may be. The ethical theory of the state enables us to clarify the distinction between these two opposing types of coherence or 'systemacity', one of which is legitimate and routine, a 'natural' expression of the state or 'eternity in time', so to speak, whereas the other is no more than a debased copy of the ideal order of the state or 'time against eternity'.

In the case of postmodernists, we find an endeavour to temporalise and immanentise the 'containing universality' of the state, not by attributing an exaggerated autonomy to group life (pluralism), nor by means of a descriptive science of bare, brute empirical fact (behaviouralism), but by means of the notions of 'power/knowledge' and the 'discourse of sovereignty'; these have the deliberately contrived effect of endowing the state with a wholly contingent and historical form of existence. For

Foucault, for example, there is no transhistorical dimension of the state, no 'pure idea' that actual states approximate in varying degrees, no Spirit as origin and end of the political, and he would be even more dismissive of the idea of the state as our common, universal humanity (common grace) weaving itself through and legitimising a succession of different social formations; his 'flat and empirical' method transforms the state into no more than a historically contingent mode of government that makes a brief appearance on the stage of history, and he thereby deprives it of its essential character as eternity ever drawing time into itself, as the universal informing the particular, as the universal will to justice and the common good being concretely realised in many different ways in a vast array of different social settings, as the source of the legitimacy of governments and technologies of power, as the vivifying Spirit in our midst and, finally, as the authoritative 'movement' of our social humanity in and through our social institutions. As in the case of pluralism and behaviouralism, we again find a tendency to over-inflate the temporal, ongoing 'horizontal' dimension of political life—construed by Foucault as the discursively constituted patterns and events of daily political life and the ongoing 'flat and empirical' succession of technologies of power—and to entirely disregard its universal or 'vertical' dimension—the transcendent God and the immanent, enveloping Spirit that impart legitimacy to the events and processes of the 'horizontal' political dimension. It is significant that Foucault is entirely oblivious—theoretically, that is, though not in his own practical forms of political engagement—to the ethical sovereignty of justice and the common good. He holds that 'what characterises the end of sovereignty, this common and general good, is in sum nothing other than submission to sovereignty' and that '[g]overnment is defined as a right manner of disposing things so as to lead not to the form of the common good . . . but to an end which is convenient for each of the things that are to be governed'.[23]

Many postmodern authors would wholeheartedly endorse Foucault's view that the ethical unity of the state proclaimed by the ethical theory–and the kind of 'politics as the quest for unity that it endorses–is a dangerous illusion that must be exposed to prevent its inherent totalistic tendency from wreaking havoc in the political universe. Anna Yeatman, for example, insists that postmodern perspectivism exposes as false and illegitimate the quest for rational consensus, for unity and the common good, and that since there is 'an irresolvably complex polyphony of voices and irresolvable differences between them, all that is possible is pragmatically oriented and provisional, negotiated agreements'.[24] Likewise, Chantal Mouffe criticises proponents of deliberative democracy for envisaging 'the political as a space of freedom and public deliberation[25] and for seeking 'rational consensus through free discussion'.[26] She holds that the bond that unites mem-

---

23. M Foucault, 'Governmentality', in *The Foucault Effect: Studies in Governmentality*, edited by G Burchell, C Gordon and P Miller (London: Harvester, 1991), 95.
24. A Yeatman, *Postmodern Revisionings of the Political* (New York: Routledge, 1994), 2.
25. C Mouffe, *On the Political* (London: Routledge, 2005), 9.
26. *Ibid*, 13.

bers of a radical democratic community is 'not that of an engagement in an enterprise to pursue a common substantive purpose or to promote a common interest, but that of loyalty to one another'[27] and she actually insists that as such a community *must* violate the principle of pluralism, diversity and difference if it seeks to pursue a substantive common good.[28] She goes so far as to say that the quest for unity and consensus is not a true or essential feature of democratic politics and that when, empirically, we encounter what seems to be 'consensus' on the political landscape, it is only because a temporary, provisional hegemonic arrangement has been reached.[29] The key task then is *not* to find a common purpose but to 'create a common political identity among persons otherwise engaged in many different enterprises'[30] and to institute a 'demos' of such a kind that it will be compatible with religious, moral and cultural pluralism.[31] In a similar vein, in his 'aesthetic' theory of representative democracy, Frank Ankersmit[32] holds that politics is 'perspectivist', that it is a matter of perspective rather than truth and that representation has nothing to do with achieving unity or identification between rulers and ruled; too many theories of

---

27. C Mouffe, *The Return of the Political* (London: Verso, 1993), 66.
28. Ibid, 66–67.
29. C Mouffe, *The Democratic Paradox* (London: Verso, 2000), 104.
30. C Mouffe, *The Return of the Political*, 67.
31. C Mouffe, (ed) *The Challenge of Carl Schmitt* (London: Verso, 1999), 50.
32. F Ankersmit, *Aesthetic Politics: Political Philosophy beyond Fact and Value* (Standford: Stanford University Press, 1996).

representation, he is convinced, have mistakenly focused on the unity or one-ness shared by representatives and represented, and have tended to erroneously assume that the relationship between rulers and ruled is based upon, or is enveloped within, something more fundamental, such as God, reason or truth. Reason, Ankersmit believes, is an inappropriate means or medium for resolving political conflicts. This is also what Bernard Manin has in mind when he says that because of a lack of common identity and a sense of collective moral purpose, 'representative democracy is not a system in which the community governs itself, but a system in which public policies and decisions are made subject to the verdict of the people'.[33]

These authors, then, are quintessentially postmodern in holding that politics is about perspective rather than the quest for truth and unity (the common good, God's will for us). I wish to suggest, on the contrary, that politics is a representation of the truth of who and what we are, of our identity and mission as a political community. It is the quest to discover how *my* good and my interests fit into, serve, and play their role in, the common (political) good and how *our* common good fits into, serves, and plays its role in, the universal good of humanity. Politics is perspectivist, I wish to suggest, only in the sense that there are many lenses through which the common good is apprehended, just as there are many perspectives or locations from which the individual members of an orchestra view or experience what is in one sense the 'same' melody but

---

33. B Manin, *The Principles of Representative Government* (Cambridge: Cambridge University Press, 1997), 192.

yet is also a melody apprehended from a host of unique perspectives or positions—that of the violin player, the flute player, etc, each of whom experiences, in a sense, an identical (universal) melody but one that is 'differenced' by their unique relation to it, their unique experience of it, and their unique contribution to it. We should not forget that there is one orchestra and one melody, just as there is one society (polity) and one unifying theme (its common good) and, continuing the musical analogy, whenever we encounter 'an irresolvably complex polyphony of voices',[34] we should do our utmost, through what surely is, after all, *the unifying medium of deliberative public discussion*, to transform the 'perspectival knowledges' of these diverse voices into a single harmony and to incorporate their differences within a single universal public good— to raise them to the level of the universal. Yeatman is convinced that 'there is no Reason, only reasons' and she wants to try 'to work reason and differences together'.[35] However, unless it is conceded that 'Reason operates as reasons' as eternity operates in and through time or as the Spirit prompts, sustains and informs our best endeavours, it is by no means clear how this 'working together' can be achieved, for, strictly speaking, it is only when 'reasons' are the instruments or 'face' of Reason itself (of the 'mind' of God) and only when they serve as the means whereby the universal embraces its differences, that practical political reasoning is legitimately employed. In their everyday political lives, public representatives generally

---

34. A Yeatman, *Postmodern Revisionings of the Political*, 2.
35. *Ibid*, viii.

(and rightly) take for granted that the values and ends of
the policies they pursue really are—or at least may really
be—good and true, that is, that the values they seek to realise may be aspects or instances of (universal)Value itself,
that the 'rationalities' they employ to defend those policies are—or at least can be—aspects of (universal) Reason
itself and that the truths of political discourse uttered by
politicians in free and open discussion are—or at least
may really be—vehicles or voices of 'emerging' Truth.
The same holds true, I would like to note in passing, in
the case of public deliberative discussion more generally,
and especially in the case of public theological encounters.
Ratzinger takes issue with a 'pure reason' approach and
holds that we should never pretend that reason is ever
theologically neutral, but he does so in such a way that
he finds himself on (or at least dangerously close to) the
same ground as Yeatman and the postmoderns. We must
indeed recognise, as Yeatman and Ratzinger would insist,
that reason (or, as I would say, Reason) is 'always already'
distilled and concretised within the terms and categories
of a particular theological system, but this should not lead
us to say, as Ratzinger in effect invites us to do, that 'there
is no Reason, only theologically non-neutral reasons', for
the whole point of theological discussion is to try to ensure that, as far as possible, every theological outlook is
a particular distinctive distillation of a 'would-be all-inclusive' Reason or the unique 'face of Reason' expressed
in theological terms under a particular and unique set of
circumstances. Unless 'Reason operates as reasons', then

in Ratzinger's own words 'there are lights, but no Light: words, but no Word'.³⁶

Taking into account (the reality of) the shared orientation of all citizens *qua* citizens (rulers and ruled) to their (single) common good and their shared membership of one society or polity (body politic), it is surely misleading to speak, as Sophia Nasstrom does, of the democratic election of public representatives as giving rise 'to a standing division between governors and governed'³⁷ for both representatives and represented share a common identity and are equally, though differently, informed and guided by the same unifying public/common will. Thus to the question raised by Nasstrom 'In what sense does consenting to power, by election of representatives, mean that I am self-governing?', surely the best and truest response is to say that in voting as a citizen I self-consciously participate in the life of the collective or public self and in its quest for the common good. If this is not the case, then the answer to the next question raised by Nasstrom, namely, 'Am I not simply following the decrees of *others*?', can only be answered by a resounding 'Yes'. *All* legitimate government is, in a very important sense, 'self-government' or government of the empirical communal self by the true or ideal communal self (the state, the Spirit).

---

36. J Ratzinger, *On the Way to Jesus Christ* (San Francisco: Ignatius Press, 2005), 64–65.
37. S Nasstrom, 'Representative Democracy as Tautology; Ankersmitt and Lefort on Representation', in *European Journal of Political Theory*, 5/3 2006: 321–342.

For Foucault himself, the state and the 'discourse of sovereignty' that fuels its life are repressive in their effects and he therefore makes his famous suggestion that it is now time to 'cut off the King's head' and to finally dispense with the paralyzing fiction of sovereignty. Foucault is convinced that absolute sovereignty is integral to the state as such—which is true if we have in mind the ethical sovereignty of the state, of the unifying Spirit in our midst—and hence that they stand or fall together. However, understood in terms of the ethical theory, the kind of relationship which obtains between sovereignty and the state is contingent, rather than essential, a matter for empirical inquiry or historical study rather than conceptual analysis or *a priori* reasoning. My own view is that we (or we in the West) are currently in the midst of a transition from a modern, sovereign nation state to a post-modern, semi-sovereign state, and that it is a mistake to characterise the state, *as such*, as sovereign, semi-sovereign, unitary or federal, for the state may find legitimate existential expression, under varying historical circumstances, in any combination of these political forms. As a matter of historical fact, it would certainly seem that the sovereignty claimed by nation states in Europe from the Enlightenment until fairly recently was anything but 'fictional' and was certainly real in the lives of their subjects, whereas at the present time it would not, I think, be unfair to say that those who regard the state as, in essence, sovereign and autonomous (a unitary, self-contained political 'individual' on the world stage) are caught in the grip of an outdated, anachronistic theory (Foucault's 'paralyzing fiction of sovereignty') that undermines their capacity to understand the developments currently taking place in the western world and, most especially of course, in the European union. Hence if the proposal to 'cut off the King's head' merely means cutting the link—believed by some to be essential and timeless—between sovereignty and the institutions of state, it is entirely congenial to adherents of the ethical theory, or at least to the present author. However, if such a severing is understood as a proposal to abolish the state as the font of authority, as God's vertically descending presence (the Father) and uplifting, ascending presence (the Spirit), as the source of emancipatory criticism, as the ethical/spiritual (noumenal) reality that both ideally and routinely infuses the empirical (phenomenal) order of legitimate government, such a destruction of the vertical dimension of political life (the state) would kill the body politic and make of it an empirical dead husk, a mere appearance or a mere technology of power entirely devoid of public spirit and political legitimacy.

In broad terms, the post-modern 'temporalising gesture' is really a de-divinising, immanentising gesture (immanentising, not in a benign sense that contrasts with and complements the transcendent, but in an invidious sense that denies it) and it exercises the same deleterious effect as the pluralist suspicion towards the state and the behaviouralist 'scientisation' of politics, that is, it prevents us from elaborating ethico-political criteria for the legitimacy of current political practices. We are deprived of any effective way of criticising the current ways in which technologies of power or knowledge/power regimes operate, just as pluralism earlier inhibited any attempts to grasp the ways in which the political universal informs, fails to inform, or represses group life, and just as behaviouralism earlier discouraged consideration of the manner in which the 'political system' meets, or fails to meet, the requirements of justice and the common good. Thus what the ethical theory of the state is designed to provide (ethico-political criteria of current political practices) is precisely what postmodernist, behaviouralist and pluralist critics conspicuously fail to offer and in the absence of which, I submit, we are simply unable to speak intelligibly of human liberation and social reform. How, for example, can we 'theorise'—understand, truly represent, or even speak intelligibly concerning—the struggle of Dr Martin Luther King if not by saying that, despite being arrested thirty times by 'state/government' agencies, he nevertheless represented and expressed the state by his stand for the true meaning of justice and the common good or, alternatively expressed, by his faithful and dedicated attunement to God's ever in-breaking presence in his socio-political world? Despite his own theoretical objections, how else indeed—in what other terms?—can we characterise the practical works of the real, active Foucault who consistently took his stand on the side of the oppressed? Far then from attempting to move beyond the state, as Bartelson has recently suggested, by disentangling 'our notions of authority and identity from the state concept once and for all',[38] we should, rather, embed our notions of identity and authority firmly in the state, for

---

38. J Bartelson, *The Critique of the State* (Cambridge: Cambridge University Press, 2001), 181.

what, after all, was the real appeal of Martin Luther King, if not to America's true communal self, to the real identity of America as a land where his dream of equality could be shared by all, and to the state as the *true* font of authority and justice. As seen through the eyes of faith and in truth, the state in the final analysis is God's mediated presence through us in public and political life.

Geographical versus Geometrical Political Unity

In general, I think it would be true to say that the various critiques of the ethical theory we have so far considered (most especially the pluralist and post-modern critiques) identify the state with a type of political whole, and with a conception of political life, that is unitary, 'geometrical', mechanical and 'Hobbesian', rather than unifying, 'geographical' organic 'anti-Hobbesian'.[39] The kind of distinction I have in mind here is well illustrated by the dispute between Bishop Bramhall and Thomas Hobbes in the seventeenth century. Bramhall complained that Hobbes took a pride 'in removing all ancient landmarks, between prince and subject, father and child, husband and wife, master and servant, man and man'.[40] Phrased in the idiom of this distinction, Bramhall's claim was that Hobbes held in disdain the 'geography' of English political life,

---

39. This distinction is further explored in Brian T Trainor, *The Origin and End of Modernity: Reflections on the meaning of Post-modernism* (Quebec: World Heritage Press, 1998), 95–98; its importance in the emergence of England as the 'first nation' is also briefly discussed.

40. J Bramhall, *The Catching of Leviathan* (London: J Crook, 1658), 542.

the organic rootedness of that life in ancient traditions and its embeddedness in a common law that grew into its present shape over the course of the centuries. Instead, he preferred to regard England's ancient landmarks (ecclesiastical rights, the common law, the time-honored rights of English men) with the eye of a political geometer and to thereby transform them into the artificial, mechanical contrivances of an absolute, unitary sovereign power. It is certainly true that for Hobbes the political whole, being one and indivisible, must be governed by a single undifferentiated public will—equated by Hobbes with the will of the sovereign—and that it must be conceived of geometrically as a kind of structure in which all forms of authority are ultimately deducible from, and exist only by virtue of their derivation from (by the grace of), the superior will of the absolute sovereign power. For Bramhall, the political geographer, the traditional rights of English men were to some extent independent of, whereas for Hobbes, the political geometer, they were wholly dependent upon, the sovereign's *fiat*. Hobbes thus provides us with a geometrical, absolutist and unitary version of the ethical unity of the state, for he equates justice and the common good with the will of the sovereign, whereas Bramhall responds with a geographical, federal and unifying version of the ethical unity of the state. Now, even though there is no one type of political whole required by the state as such or its ethical unity, yet it is as if, in the minds of pluralist and post-modern critics of the ethical theory, the notion of the 'state' and 'unitary political wholeness' have become inextricably intertwined, so that, whilst they may well be convinced that they are rejecting the state, it is in fact a unitary, geometrical, absolutist conception of the state that they are rejecting.

It would be tempting at this point to make the suggestion that the geographical type of political wholeness alone provides the kind of federal, institutional vehicle for the 'true passage' of the state into public life, a safe and secure passage for God's in-breaking into socio-political life. Certainly, at this point one could call upon the insights of many Christian commentators on politics (or more broadly, on church-civil society-state relations) to support this suggestion. For example, as well as the many references to the principle of 'subsidiarity' in Catholic social thought,[41] we could note here Paul Marshall's insistence that the task of the state as a public legal entity 'is to *justly interrelate* the authorities, the areas of responsibility, of others within the creation',[42] Bernard Zylstra's conviction that the state 'must prevent the violation of the internal sphere of one societal structure by another',[43] and John Milbank's distinction between the ('subsidiary' upholding) 'integralism' of the second Vatican Council and the earlier ('subsidiary' denying)

---

41. *Catechism of the Catholic Church* (Missouri: Ligouri Publications, 1995), numbers 1883, 1884 and 1885.
42. P Marshall, *Thine is the Kingdom: A Biblical Perspective on the Nature of Government and Politics Today* (Grand Rapids: Eerdmans, 1984), 58.
43. B Zylstra, 'The Bible, Politics, and the State', in *Confessing Christ and Doing Politics*, edited by JW Skillen (Washington DC: Association for Public Justice Education Fund, 1982), 51–52.

'integrist' politics rejected by the Council.[44] Pope Pius XI provides us with the following summary of the social and political implications of the 'subsidiary' (or 'geographical') principle:

> Just as it is gravely wrong to take from individuals what they can accomplish by their own initiative and industry and give it to the community, so also it is an injustice and at the same time a grave evil and disturbance of right order to assign to a greater and higher association what lesser and subordinate organisations can do. For every social activity ought of its very nature to furnish help to the members of the social body, and never to destroy and absorb them.[45]

However, I wish to suggest that the geographical type of political wholeness provides the kind of federal, institutional vehicle for the 'true passage' of the state into public life *only* when a civil society is not experiencing a crisis that threatens its very existence, autonomy and identity. Under such dire circumstances, and to ensure its survival, the unifying will of the state must also operate as a single unitary will that issues authoritatively—indeed with ab-

---

44. J Milbank, *Theology and Social Theory: Beyond Secular Reason* (Oxford: Blackwell, 1995), 206.
45. Pope Pius XI, Pope 1931, *Quadragesimo Anno* (Reconstruction of the Social Order) May 15 1931, section 79.

solute sovereign authority—from a single, definite point in the socio-political structure; it may even be necessary for the whole general or public will of a nation to momentarily find its only possible avenue of expression and realisation in and through the will of just one person. I have in mind here the will of Sir John Kerr who, as Governor-General of Australia, dismissed a popularly elected government from office in 1975 in order to resolve a crippling constitutional deadlock. Under normal circumstances in Australia, the different arms of government are subject to what I have called the ethical sovereignty of justice and the general will, and this common subjection, so to speak, ensures that the 'separation of powers' (or, at least, in Australia, the differentiation thereof) is also a 'confluence of powers'. This ethical sovereignty is symbolised and represented by the 'crown', for ministers are appointed by the Crown, are ultimately responsible to the crown and are expected to faithfully represent the crown. However, in 1975, when the power of the Senate came into a direct conflict with the power of the House of Representatives, the ideal of a 'confluence of powers' was not even approximated in practice, as political life in fact degenerated into a sordid and acrimonious 'separation of powers'. Faced then not with a confluence of powers but with a hopeless and divisive conflict between them, the governor-general, as the supreme representative of the crown, had no option but to momentarily return those powers to their source in the crown itself. It is interesting to note that, although the way in which the governor-general resolved the constitutional crisis engendered massive anger and resentment at the time, he alone as the supreme representative of the crown *could* properly act to resolve the crisis, could in a sense momentarily *be* the crown by virtue of his position, could indeed act just like a Hobbesian absolute sovereign or a war prime minister, was not be seriously questioned.

The main point I wish to establish through this discussion is that the ethical unity of the state, though normally and properly expressed 'geographically', that is, through its relatively autonomous spheres of government and through the freedom of its social groups and citizens, may at times be realised 'geometrically', that is, by a temporary focusing of all forms of authority at a single, unitary point. Whether expressed 'geographically' or 'geometrically', or indeed whether expressed through a government or a governor-general, it is the *same* ethical sovereignty of the state (or of the 'crown') that is operative and confers legitimacy in both cases. However, what this means, I believe, is that the authority of the state must be acknowledged as, in a qualified sense, absolute. It is, in truth, an awesome, God-like authority that is exercised by a war prime minister (or an Australian governor-general), though we –and especially Christian commentators–should hardly find this surprising, for God's ethical or *de jure* sovereignty is absolute, and the sole font of political legitimacy. Thus whilst Lugo is right to note that the Christian faith introduced a sovereignty credo ('Jesus is Lord') that 'placed it in radical opposition to the claims of absolute state sovereignty ('Augustus the Divine'), the core principle of Caesarism',[46] at the same time we need to note that God's *de jure* sovereignty is not in any way limited by Caesar's prerogatives, for the whole point and purpose of the latter is to enforce God's will (natural law) for the good of all; nor is there a 'secular realm' beyond the reach of God's authority. Certainly, the core principle of Caesarism must be rejected, for there is indeed a radical opposition between the true, original divinity claimed by Jesus as the only begotten Son of the Father (and acknowledged by his disciples) and the divinity claimed by Augustus (and denied by Christ's followers). However, this does not mean, as Kuyper asserts, that the 'total sovereignty of the sinless Messiah implies at the same time the forthright denial and contradiction of all absolute sovereignty among sinful men on earth'[47] or, at least, we need to be guarded and circumspect in the terms that we use to depict the kind of sovereignty rightly exercised by Caesar and its relationship to God's *de jure* sovereignty. As the *medium* of God's absolute authority, Caesar is, in a sense, absolute as well but we must note here that to recognise the 'divine' or the quality of 'absoluteness' in the state is not to divinise the state, any more than to recognise the presence of the Holy Spirit in a person is to

---

46. LE Lugo, 'Caesar's Coin and the Politics of the Kingdom: A Pluralist Perspective', in *Caesar's Coin Revisited: Christians and the Limits of Government*, edited by M Cromartie (Grand Rapids: Eerdmans, 1996), 5.
47. Kuyper, A, 1991 "The Anti Revolutionary Program" edited by James W Skillen and Rockne M McCarthy. *Political Order and the Plural Structure of Society*, Scholars Press, Atlanta.

divinise that person. One could say that a state operating through its government as ordained by God and nature is 'phenomenal divinity' manifesting (making present) 'noumenal divinity' or, as Barth might say, the divinity of the earthly state is in reality the divinity of the heavenly Jerusalem.[48] We may say, then, that Caesar is the medium or visible representation of God's absolute sovereignty, that he is 'absolute within his realm', that he exercises a kind of 'borrowed or derived sovereignty' or, again, that he is absolute within the limits of natural law. Caesar's authority, as derived from God, is not absolute but, as the bearer and medium of God's authority, it is indeed absolute, legitimate and the bearer of good order into public life. As we shall see in more detail in chapter ten when we consider Hobbes's account of God, natural law and the 'person' of the state, a government representing its state is, in a sense, the face of God before its citizens, especially when considered in their unredeemed state.

The state, then, is the face of God and constantly seeks to mirror and represent the eternal unity-in-diversity of the triune God in the temporal unity-in-diversity of social and political life; as a collective 'moral' person, it can only live, move and have its being in and through its citizens and its political institutions. In this respect, the 'person' of the state is (i) like the Trinity and (ii) like the way in which the Trinity operates in human affairs. It is like the Trinity in this way; whilst there are three 'persons' in the Godhead who are, to use Pannenberg's expression, 'separate cen-

---

48. K Barth, *Community, State and Church: Three Essays* (Gloucester Mass: Peter Smith, Gloucester, 1968), 124–125.

tres of action',[49] yet this does nor preclude us from speaking of a *single divine will* that is differently entertained by the three divine persons, and from thinking of the divine unity in terms of *one* will expressed differentially in the three divine persons, or in terms of the will of one subject, or macro-subject. God as 'macro-subject', as the unity of God, as ever the same divine will, lives differentially in the three divine persons. In a similar way, whilst the natural persons, groups and institutions that make up a political society are from one point of view 'separate centres of action', yet this does not preclude us (i) from speaking of a *single* 'person' of the state as a kind of 'macro-subject' that lives in and through these separate centres of action, but that lives differently in (and is experienced differently by) each of them, and (ii) from thinking of the unity of the state in terms of *one* will ideally, though differentially, entertained in the persons (individual and collective) comprising it, or in terms of the true or ideal will of one subject, or macro-subject. Just as God as 'macro Subject' lives in and through the members of the Trinity, so too the 'person' of the state as 'macro-subject', as the unity of the people, as ever the same common (general) will, lives differentially in the lives of its citizens and has no life apart from them. Likewise, the way in which the Trinity operates in human affairs, moving in and through all, and drawing all unto itself (the holy source and summit of all human life), is like the way in which the 'person' of the state (or the 'angelic' presence of the Spirit) operates as a

---

49. W Pannenberg, *Systematic Theology*, volume 1 (Edinburgh: T&T Clark, 1997), 319.

unity or universal presence that permeates, elevates, enables and enlivens the diversity of social and political life and draws each element of particularity (diversity) into its fullness in the unity of the social. Just as the fact that there are three 'persons' in the Godhead who are 'separate centres of action' does not preclude us from speaking of a single divine will (i) that is differently entertained by the three divine persons, (ii) that is directed towards and operative in humanity and (iii) that enables us to think of the divine unity, so too the fact that there is a multiplicity of persons in a state does nor preclude us from speaking of a single collective or general will (i) that is differently entertained by the citizens ('separate centres of action') of a jurisdiction, (ii) that lives in and draws each member of the citizen body to itself and (iii) that enables us to think of the unity of the state. Thus, when Pannenberg speaks of three 'persons' in the Godhead who are 'separate centres of action',[50] and staunchly challenges 'Rahner's rejection of the idea of three subjectivities in God in favour of a single divine Subject within the Trinity',[51] I would suggest that whilst there are indeed three 'persons' in the Godhead who are 'separate centres of action' (and, in terms of our present analogy, a multiplicity of citizens in a state), this does nor preclude us from speaking of a *single* divine will (or, again analogously, of a single collective or general will) that is differently entertained by the three divine persons and that enables us to think of the divine unity (and, correspondingly, of the unity of the state) in a way

---

50. *Ibid*, 319.
51. *Ibid*, 308.

that is closer to Rahner's single divine subject. The latter (Rahner's single divine subject) better represents the unity of God and is to be preferred to the loose kind of connectivity (unity) implied in Pannenberg's notion of a 'field' or 'field of force', just as it is preferable to regard the diverse elements of social and political life as ordered to the 'unity of a subject', rather than as being held together externally in a loose federation.

Marxism, the Return of the State and 'Relative Autonomy'

When, early in the twentieth century, Bosanquet said that the state is 'society as a unit, recognised as rightly exercising control over its members'[52] and when John Dewey remarked that 'a public articulated and operating through representative officers is the State',[53] it is unlikely that they regarded themselves as having said anything remarkable, profound or deeply insightful, and yet it was only by the most tortuous intellectual pathway that political science, later in the century, gradually worked its way towards, or back to, the simple truth of what they had to say. This could be theoretically expressed in terms of the ethical theory by saying that the state is analytically but not ontologically distinct from society or, more strictly speaking, that the state, considered apart from society, is analytically distinct from society, considered apart from

---

52. B Bosanquet, *The Philosophical Theory of the State*, 172.
53. J Dewey, *The Public and its Problems* (Athens, Ohio: Ohio University Press, 1988), 67.

the (its) state, but that this is a distinction within a single, differentiated reality; the distinction is analytical rather than ontological. It was only as a result of considerable intellectual pain and suffering (and unprecedented intellectual gyrations) that neo-Marxist theorising on the state in the 1960s and 1970s finally returned to this original, simple insight of the ethical theory when it arrived at, or eventually stumbled upon, the notion of the state's 'relative autonomy'. It will help us to understand this tortuous intellectual journey pursued by neo-Marxists and to see the clear advantages of the ethical theory, if at this point we raise the question: Is the state autonomous or determined, an acting subject or a passive instrument, independent of or dependent upon societal forces?

If by the state we mean 'a government acting in the name of the state' or 'the state operating through its government', then exponents of the ethical theory, bearing in mind that it is permissible to distinguish between, but not to ontologically separate, state and society, would insist that the state is the instrument of society, in that it is the 'objective' means whereby its collective purposes are realised, but that it is also an acting subject in so far as it has the task, as an autonomous agent, of realising these purposes. However, neo-Marxist theorising vacillated for quite some time between the 'state as instrument'—that is, of the will of the dominant classes, as in the work of Miliband,[54] and Domhoff[55]—and the 'state as acting sub-

---

54. R Miliband, *The State in Capitalist Society: the Analysis of the Western System of Power* (London: Quartet Books, 1973), 51–61.
55. GW Domhoff, *Who Rules America?* (Englewood Cliffs, NJ: Prentice

ject'—though conditioned in its actions by the structure of capitalist society, as in the reaction of Poulantzas[56] and Offe[57]—before arriving at the point at which the ethical theory begins, that is, with a clear acknowledgment of the profound 'inner'-relatedness between state and society. In adopting the expression 'the relative autonomy of the state', the neo-Marxists, or at least the Marxist structuralists, arrived at a resolution of their 'state as agent/state as instrument' dilemma by holding that the state is assuredly a subject but one whose actions are determined 'objectively' by the requirements of the social structure. Now, to say that structural dependence conditions state autonomy is surely not noticeably different from what Bosanquet and Dewey said more simply and economically earlier in the century. Thus, despite their different slants, exponents of the ethical theory and exponents of structural Marxism actually agree on the central point that the relationship of the state, as acting subject, to society's needs is one of (Hegelian) 'willed necessity' and hence both would take exception to Bartelson's claim that 'we have to face the *prima facie* insoluble dilemma between the attempt to make sense of the state as a unity in its own right, vested with the capacity to act autonomously, and the imperative to regard its existence as derivative of

---

Hall, 1967), 5.
56. N Poulantzas, 'The Problems of the Capitalist State', in *New Left Review*, 58 (1969): 67–78.
57. C Offe, 'Structural Problems of the Capitalist State, Class Rule and the Political System', in *German Political Studies*, volume 1, edited by Klaus von Beyme (London: Sage, London, 1974), 31–57.

and dependent on something other than itself.'[58] For exponents of the ethical theory and of structural Marxism, there is no such insoluble dilemma, because we are dealing here with aspects of, or distinctions within, a single, differentiated reality. Bartelson draws a useful distinction between what he calls 'state autonomy in relation to the societal inside'[59] and the international 'outside' but in doing so, he gives the reader the misleading impression that, for the state to be autonomous, it must enjoy some sort of separate and independent existence 'between' the societal inside and the international outside. Hence, we need to recall, yet again, that the state is analytically, but not ontologically, distinct from both its inside—it is, after all, *its* inside, *its* society; hence the appropriateness of the expressions 'relative autonomy' and 'willed necessity'—and its outside—it is, after all, *its* outside, a universal community extending beyond it 'spatially' but of which it is 'spiritually' a member. Thus when Bartelson holds that 'in its structuralist or systems theory versions, the relatively autonomous state is no longer object or subject, but is turned into a relation, either between the mode of production and the rest of society, or between social classes, themselves defined in relational terms',[60] it would, I think, be truer to say that the relatively autonomous state, in its structuralist and ethical theory versions, never ceases to be a subject that (i) mediates social relations, (ii) is inter-

---

58. J Bartelson, *The Critique of the State* (Cambridge: Cambridge University Press, 2001), 144.
59. *Ibid*, 115.
60. *Ibid*, 144.

nally, not externally, related to the social relations it mediates, and (iii) is best understood as the subject *of its* objects; the state *of its* society.

The notion of the 'relative autonomy' of the state is helpful, as we have seen, when considering the relation of the state to society and its socio-economic institutions, but it is also useful when considering what kind of relation (autonomous or heteronomous) obtains between the state and God. Were we to regard the state as wholly autonomous *vis-à-vis* God, we would thereby deprive it of its legitimating origin and end, an error to which modernity seems to have increasingly succumbed since the demise of Christendom, and of which it is now becoming more painfully aware;[61] but O'Donovan[62] reminds us that we face an 'opposite danger' when those claiming divine authority threaten to overwhelm the (in my terms, 'relatively autonomous') authority of political structures. He mentions John Wycliffe as a major figure in the high period of political theology who believed in 'dominion by grace' and in the sole right of God's sanctified righteous (excluding sinners) to the legitimate exercise of dominion (meaning property and jurisdiction). O'Donovan points out that, for Wyclif, '[t]he law of love validates and invalidates in detail decisions made under the authority of secular law' so that, for example, 'the right of a mon-

---

61. J Habermas, and J Ratzinger, *Dialectics of Secularization: On Reason and Religion* (San Francisco: Ignatius Press, 2006).
62. O O'Donovan, *The Desire of the Nations: Rediscovering the Roots of Political Theology* (Cambridge: Cambridge University Press, 2003), 8.

arch's son to inherit the throne is determined at the time by a judgement as to whether God has in fact rewarded the deceased king with a *godly* son!'.[63] As well, then, as challenging the false idea of the wholly autonomous state on the one hand, the idea of the 'relatively autonomous state' serves also, on the other, as a counter to the idea of the 'heterenomous rule of God's elect' and to the corresponding reduction of the role of the state/government to a mere (mechanical and inert) instrument of the divine.

Finally, the ethical (or ethical/divine) theory of the state is quite capable of dealing with the criticism that, precisely because of its emphasis on the ethical centrality of the state, it is unable to illuminate a globalising world or to address transnational issues. Simply stated, this criticism holds that the state can only be 'the inner core or substance of political life' in a world in which social, economic and environmental concerns fall within the jurisdiction of the territorial boundaries of the state, but since this is not the case, one should not ascribe to the state this kind of ethical centrality. When considering this criticism, it is important to bear in mind that the state is 'spiritually' related to its divine origin and end, and is 'spiritually' a member of the universal human community that extends 'spatially' beyond it. Whilst this criticism raises the hotly disputed issue of the degree of autonomy enjoyed by the nation-state at the present time, yet more important by far than this 'question of degree' is the effect (what is it?) of what we might call 'universal consciousness', 'spiritual globalisation' or 'emerging global consciousness' on the

---

63. *Ibid*, 26.

nation-state. No-one doubts that the nation state continues to wield significant institutional power and authority within its jurisdictional boundaries but what we are not sure about is how we should characterise and understand the way in which 'global consciousness' affects the manner and spirit in which that power and authority (whether increasing or declining) is exercised. The fact that members of states have a more and more pronounced 'world' consciousness obviously has a bearing on how the state functions and how it should be understood. There are, of course, those who would say that 'nothing has changed'. Eurosceptics in the British Conservative partly would no doubt insist that the 'world' is no more than a system of fully sovereign states and that international relations should be governed by contractual (treaty) obligations which promote the interests of all nations whilst in no way affecting or diminishing their national sovereignty. The current trend, however, seems to be towards a less contractual/atomistic and more organic/'substantive' view of the international community, one which raises complex questions about the (post) modern state, its role as a medium of the international community and the source of its authority when it acts in the latter capacity. In one way, the authority exercised by the state (or by a government acting in the name of the state) is always fully its own, deriving from the will and consent of its 'own' people, but given the 'world consciousness' *of* its own people and the fact that they increasingly see themselves as *members* of a world community, state authority almost becomes a kind of delegated authority. It is as if the 'own self' of a people, whilst substantive and real, must nevertheless be viewed as an aspect of and as being symbiotically linked to, the will of the world community (a world 'soul', 'spirit' or 'substance'), so that the state's actions concerning matters of world significance (the environment, the war on terror, etc) possess authority and legitimacy to the extent that they are genuine 'particularisations' of the 'universal will' of the international community.

State-government-citizen/subject: God-Pilate-Jesus/ Son of God

In this section I wish to suggest that there is an important analogy or correspondence between the state-government-citizen/subject relationship and the God-Pilate-Jesus/Son of God relationship. I hold that we will be in a better position to understand the latter if we approach it from the perspective on the state-government-citizen/subject relationship outlined in this section and first presented in my *Justice and the State; On Liberal Organicism and the Foundations of Emancipatory Politics*.[64] Because the state, I have argued, is most appropriately conceived of as the 'own self' of society as a collective or public person, our manner of both distinguishing and routinely identifying 'state' and 'government' becomes perfectly understandable, for just as the 'own self' of a man is said to operate *through* or *by means of* 'his' conscious thoughts and actions, so too the 'own self' of society, or the state,

---

64. BT Trainor, *Justice and the State: On Liberal Organicism and the Foundations of Emancipatory Politics* (Quebec: World Heritage Press, 1998), 84–117.

may be said to routinely operate *through* or *by means of* the conscious thoughts and acts of 'its' officials. What I have in mind here is the same as, or at least analogous to, what St Paul had in mind in saying that 'if by the Spirit *you* put to death your sinful actions, *you* will live' (Romans 8:13, emphasis added). This 'you' refers with equal force and validity to 'you' as a person, as a family, as a community or as a nation. In each case it is true to say that it is *through* or *by means of* the Spirit that we can put to death our sinful actions and live. It is *we* (as individuals, as families, as nations, etc) who must act in order to put to death our sin but we are to do so 'by the Spirit'. We, as human agents of action, and the Holy Spirit, as divine agent of action, are not mutually repellent entities. On the contrary; it is by the agency of the Spirit that our agency in the struggle against sin is operative and effective, as we shall see in greater detail in chapter ten. We and the Spirit are co-present as agents. The kind of agency exercised by the Spirit through the individual self, and which may be expressed by saying that in the 'own self' of each of us the Spirit and our spirit are co-present, is the same as that exercised by the Spirit through our families, communities and nations, and which, in the case of a nation or society, may be expressed by saying that in the 'own self' of each society or nation, the Spirit and our spirit are co-present. As Paul said, 'God's Spirit joins himself to our spirits to declare that we are God's children' (Romans 8:16). The state, then, is 'the own self of society as a collective or public person' (sometimes referred to as the moral person of the state) and this 'own self' may be more precisely described, following St Paul, as 'the Holy Spirit joining itself to our collective or public spirit'. Just as 'we' and the Spirit are somehow (and 'somewhere') co-present in our everyday lives as individuals and family members as we put to death our sinful actions and grow together in holiness, so too 'we' or our government (our political, judicial and administrative personnel) and the Spirit (the state in action through us and our representative institutions) are somehow (and 'somewhere') co-present in our everyday political lives as subjects and citizens as we put to death our selfish attitudes and collectively seek the common good of our society. I will now proceed (i) to justify and further elaborate this conception of the state as the own self of society and (ii), in the process, to illuminate the God-Pilate-Jesus/Son of God relationship. I will show that Rousseau's expression 'the moral person of the state' is susceptible to (at least) two quite different interpretations, for I maintain that, after rejecting the first interpretation (the 'nowhere' view) as initially attractive but ultimately implausible, and having suitably amended the second (the 'everywhere' view) to retain its formidable strengths whilst eliminating its more damaging defects, what we are left with is precisely the 'somewhere' view of the state (that is, as society's own self) which I wish to commend and which shows the God-Pilate-Jesus/Son of God relationship in its proper light and context.

The first view or interpretation of the state as a moral person that I wish to consider holds that state and government are radically distinct. According to this view, what is meant by the 'moral personhood' of the state is that it is a mysterious, pure, untainted presence above and beyond the political realm but in the name of which and in reference to which political (governmental and judicial) actions take place and acquire their aura of legitimacy. Perhaps this 'moral person' has the aura of the Spirit but, if so, it is a Spirit that hovers idly above the political realm, that is untainted by significant contact with the affairs of sinful humanity, that is in no intelligible sense an 'agent' and that cannot therefore be conceived of as, in Paul's words, a 'Spirit that joins himself to our spirits' to fight evil and do good in the world. With regard to the relationship that obtains between state and government, this view of the 'moral person' (of the state) holds that the latter represents or, alternatively, acts with the authority of (and in the name of), the former. At first glance, this view seems to be superbly equipped to deal with the theoretical difficulties which arise when a state is 'represented' by a corrupt government or a corrupt judge, as in the case of Pilate. The simple solution is to say that such a government or judge conspicuously fails to act in the name of the state as moral person or simply abuses the authority conferred by the Spirit. This advantage, however, is secured at an unacceptably high price. If we ask, for example, what kind of presence does this 'moral person' or aloof Spirit have in, or how does its influence bear upon, the political realm, we seem to be forced to the embarrassing conclusion that it is entirely non-active and nowhere actually present in a practical, operative and effective sense.

According to this 'nowhere' view, the state has a kind of abstract, idle and aloof essence. It is, so to speak, 'purity itself' but not a purity *in* anything or anyone. It is an 'unjoined purity' subsisting apart in an eternal realm as an aloof Spirit untainted by any contact with the actualities of the temporal. So conceived, the state has no existence or agency (it is in no sense operative in the real world), which provides us with a striking contrast to the second interpretation of the 'state as moral person', which holds that the essence of the state coincides with and thoroughly pervades its existence and its very real activity in the world. Far from being 'nowhere' with respect to the goings-on of government, the state is in fact 'everywhere'; for, with respect to 'its' government, a state is the 'what' or essence thereof, and with respect to 'its' state, a government is its 'that', its existential counterpart or the mode of existence which the state, as its essence, assumes. If we wish to know how this close identification of state and government, this essence—existence relationship, can be defended or explained in the case of a blatantly corrupt government, the answer is that the latter, at least to the extent that it is corrupt, simply falls outside the range of existence of which the state as moral person is the essence, and sets itself apart from the 'flow' of essence into existence. Thus, for example, according to this (everywhere) view, the corrupt judge Pilate who condemns an innocent man to death, simply sets himself apart from the 'flow' of essence into existence. Thus the moral person of the state, or alternatively expressed, 'the Spirit acting through us and our political institutions' is not present at all where, and in so far as, corruption prevails, but is fully and everywhere present through the range of a government's legitimate activities—including not just the overt acts of its officials but also their thoughts related thereto, and the whole system of psychic dispositions associated with and underlying these acts.

The great advantage of what we might call this 'everywhere' view of the state is that it corresponds so neatly to, and offers us an appropriate terminology with which to articulate, both the familiar facts of our social and political experience and the encounter between Pilate and Jesus. For example, we generally regard a break-and-enter thief as standing, in this criminal role at least, outside the mind of society and as having adopted an attitude of outright hostility towards it. If we take society as an interconnected system of legitimate social roles, and if we regard the social mind as its corresponding system of physical dispositions (that is, as the inner or spiritual side in each citizen and civic official of the established system of legitimate social roles), then the thief, as a thief, is a 'singular being' or 'isolated atom' who forms no part of the mind of society; or, if we take the case of Pilate as the judge who knowingly condemns to death an innocent person, it seems considerably more appropriate to adopt the kind of terminology that emanates naturally from the 'everywhere' view and to say that the judicial mind, as an operative organ of the mind of society, is not present in Pilate's judgment. He does not properly enact the role of a judge but merely performs or 'behaves' this role for non-judicial purposes. Of course, Pilate is nonetheless a judge, at least outwardly, but with regard to the subjective, inner side of his judgment in this case, he clearly does not qualify for entry into the 'mind of the state as moral person'. He is 'outside' it; since the mind of the state is everywhere present in the proper and legitimate exercise of its various organs, Pilate is 'nowhere' with respect to it.

According to the 'everywhere' view, there is an important difference to be noted between the iniquity of Pilate and that of the thief. As natural, or ordinary moral persons, their iniquity sets each of them apart from the social mind but the difference is that the thief has at least the redeeming decency of standing outside the social mind both in thought and in his overt acts (the humble confession of which, in the case of the good thief, ultimately won him eternal salvation) whereas Pilate, the corrupt judge, pretends to stand within it. Inwardly, in condemning Jesus to death, Pilate is just as much a 'singular being' as the thief, but he endeavours to secure his non-judicial ends (appeasing the mob) by 'behaving' and distorting his judicial role. His act of judgment, as empirically existent, subverts the essence of the judicial role. Thus the expression 'a corrupt judge' is in a sense contradictory, or at least reveals a kind of inner incompatibility or lack of self-consistency, for as a judge, Pilate is a part of the social mind but as corrupt, he is not. The 'everywhere' view resolves the contradiction by saying that as a man, he is iniquitous but that as a judge, he has only a kind of bastardised existence and certainly cannot be regarded as part of the judicial mind in action or as an operative organ of the moral person of the state. Also, it is both interesting and significant to note that, in the case of the thief, it may be said that, whilst engaged in the act of thieving, he is either doing his job well or badly but not that he is not doing his job at all. However, in the case of Pilate, who knowingly delivers an unjust verdict, it is idle to speculate upon whether he is doing his job well or badly for, with regard to the essence of his role, he is simply not doing his job at all.

The great merit of the 'everywhere' view is that it allows us to routinely identify state and government whilst insisting that where corruption prevails, the government responsible is distinct from, indeed 'exists' wholly apart from, the moral person of the state. Just as we routinely expect judges to dispense justice, so too we routinely expect governments to endeavour to realise the common good, and thus to give concrete embodiment and 'living substance' to the moral person of the state or to the 'public spirit' (the Holy Spirit's co-presence with our spirits). However, this merit of the 'everywhere' view is also its greatest disadvantage because it means that the state as moral person is either *wholly* present in the organs of government when properly functioning, so that essence and existence coincide perfectly or, where corruption prevails, it is *wholly* absent and exists apart from the realm of corruption in its own separate realm. In the latter case, the two realms do not meet; they run, so to speak, along parallel lines. As the Holy Spirit living in us (and joined to our spirits as we seek the political good), the moral person of the state lives, moves and has its being in a realm of truth and reality, of 'real' existence, and has no relationship at all with the sub-realm of falsehood and unreality, inhabited by the mind of Pilate. This sub-realm 'exists' empirically but it is a false mode of existence, a kind of limbo of unreality. Since the two realms are so totally disconnected, an unworkable dualism looms before us once more; the person of the state (the Spirit co-present in us) warmly and wholly envelops, and is wholly present in, the legitimate affairs of everyday government activity (broadly, legitimate political existence) but it is wholly absent from, unconnected to and has no significant relation to (or contact with, or bearing upon) the corrupt attitudes and activities of a government in so far as it is corrupt (illegitimate political existence), or of Pilate as he condemns to death an innocent man. Christ 'became sin' for our sake but the best that the state, conceived of according to this view can achieve, is to subsist alongside and apart from the sub-realm of corruption. The result is that the dramatic encounter between Jesus and Pilate with which we are familiar ceases to be dramatic or even an 'encounter', for they each live in separate worlds (Jesus in a 'world of reality, Pilate in a sub-world of unreality or of 'bastardised existence') between which there can be no significant contact. Moreover, in my view, the damage cannot be averted by engaging in minor modifications of this conception of the state, for if once the point is conceded that the moral person of the state and the realm of corruption can have any kind of significant relationship to each other, then the 'everywhere' view collapses into incoherence: either the moral person of the state (the Spirit operative through us) is affected by this contact, in which case its 'purity' is tainted by its contact with falsehood and it is therefore no longer 'pure', in the sense of having no significant relationship to 'impurity', or the realm of corruption is slightly ennobled, in which case it is not entirely corrupt (it refuses to forfeit the possibility of being ennobled) and becomes a realm penetrable by the 'light' of the state, so that the Spirit in us (the state) must be deemed to be present there in some sense as well.

I now wish to propose that to understand the 'moral person' of the state as the 'own self' of society and as comparable to the own or true self of a natural person, avoids the defects whilst retaining the strengths of the everywhere view. Admittedly, in my view, the term 'person' in the expression 'moral person' is somewhat misleading, for what I am suggesting is that the state is the 'own self' *of* society regarded as a public or collective person, and that the state or 'own self' of society is precisely analogous to the own self *of* a natural person. At the heart of this own self is the single common purpose entertained by all subjects to secure justice and the common good. Empirically, or in the actual minds of citizens, this 'universal' purpose is differentially willed or entertained by the citizens of a state; it may, for example, enter into their lives in the form of a conscious will directed thereto (constantly or falteringly) or in the form of a recognition (spontaneous or begrudged) of the authoritative nature of the demands made upon them which derive from this single collective purpose. Still, however this purpose enters their lives, as a 'lord that is certainly expected' or as an unexpected intrusion, as the self-evidently right thing to do or as the unwelcome command of a civic official, it is always the *same* purpose, though operating in a different manner in each individual case. The authority of this common purpose is, in the end, recognisable by us all, evoking our free response, and in this respect it resembles the authority of Yhwh's kingship as portrayed by O'Donovan:

> Yhwh's kingship is not a creation *ex nihilo* but an act of providence, keeping faith with cre-

ation once made. It is, therefore, true to say that the goodness of his authority lies in the fact that it demands what is recognizable—but not recognisable as a reflection of the worshippers' *wills*, rather as a calling to their *fulfilment*. They are summoned to fulfilment from beyond themselves, a fulfilment that is recognisable and yet unknown. Hence the alien-familiar character of Yhwh's command: the purpose it expressed was not their purpose, but it was a purpose that corresponded to the *telos* of their own beings. That purpose was that they should live together as a people, that they should be 'Israel'.[65]

Like the everywhere view, this view of the state as the 'own self' of society enables us to routinely identify state and government in the same way that we hold together in our minds the 'own self' of an ordinary natural man and his acting or operative self. The state is precisely analogous to the own self of a natural person in that it is not radically distinguishable from the conscious medium through which it operates in the world (its government) but is rather the own self *of* this conscious medium. Furthermore, just as the 'own self' of a natural person does not directly induce 'movement' in the world but can only act, or at least exercise an influence, through the co-operative medium of a conscious ego, so too the state (the Spirit in us)

---

65. O O'Donovan, *The Desire of the Nations: Rediscovering the Roots of Political Theology*, 32.

does not directly 'move' in the social and political world but can only operate through the co-operative medium of its officials' deliberations. At any event, it is normally the case that where one 'acts', the other 'acts' also, so that the routine or 'for the most part' identification of state (own self) and government (the actual, operative 'self' of society as a public person) is certainly justifiable. With regard to those occasions in which the state (own self) cannot be associated with the deeds of 'its' corrupt government, we may characterise this situation—in a manner forbidden to us by the everywhere view—by saying that existence, though of a false or distorted kind, is in open revolt against essence and that, in the specific case of Pilate, his existence as a corrupt judge is in open revolt against the very essence of his judicial role. Although there ceases to be an ideal, in-forming, essence-existence relationship between state and government, between justice and judge/judgment (between 'what' and 'that'), yet the two remain in a dynamic, meaningful and 'inner' relationship to each other. If the state is other than its government under such circumstances, still it is, as Hegel would say, *its* other and not a separate entity to which it is externally related. The person of the state, our deepest own self, the Spirit co-present in us, is deeply affected and offended by Pilate's verdict, for no matter how corrupt government or civic officials may be, they are never wholly beyond the reach of the state; it's as if the light ever emanating from the 'Spirit ever in us' must be constantly rejected by the darkness of corruption. It is worth noting at this point that if the authoritative voice of the public spirit was ever to be *totally* silenced, then at the precise moment of its silencing, partisanship and corruption would automatically forfeit their immoral character, which derives ultimately from their antagonistic relation to the public spirit, and simply become amoral qualities. A corrupt government, then, is one in which the public spirit has been reduced to virtual impotence, but in which it continues to attempt to make its presence felt as a vital, re-unifying factor in the life of what passes for a 'state'. The Holy Spirit in us is, above all else, a unifying spirit and, as such, can never be contained on one side of a dualistic divide. To allow this Spirit room to breathe and to exercise its vivifying influence within the *whole* social realm, no part of the latter can be marked 'out of bounds', especially not the mind of the Pilate who condemns Christ. It is, then, I think, an important merit of this 'own self' theory of the state that, unlike the everywhere view, it takes due account of the fact that there is no element in the life of the whole which is *totally* immune from the pervasive influence of the Spirit.

It will be clear from the preceding analysis that the 'own self' theory of the state is similar to the everywhere view in holding that the state can no more be 'besmirched' than can the own self of a natural person. We generally concede that no matter how far a man like Pilate descends into the depths of degradation, he is still a man 'for all that'. Since consciousness and volition stand, so to speak, between our inner essence and our outer existence, it is our task—ever accompanied by the risk of failure—to in-'form' the 'matter' of our assorted desires, hopes, fears, etc, in accordance with the requirements of our nature as a whole. We naturally hope that our outer existence will be an expression or realisation of our inner essence but when this fails to happen and things go disastrously wrong, it would be a mistake to conclude that our own self, our enduring, inner humanity or the Spirit within us, has disappeared altogether or been damaged beyond repair. Rather than being *itself* altered, damaged, and besmirched by the surrounding conditions of degradation, it would be truer to say that it is affronted by, and struggles unceasingly against, these very conditions. But then precisely the same kind of relation holds between the state as the own self of society and the surrounding conditions of corruption by which it is confronted and which it attempts to oppose and transform; no matter how corrupt a government may be, 'its' state is still a state 'for all that'. The state, as own self of society, can never be wholly silenced, even if its inner essence appears to be largely deprived of any expression in outer existence. In a sense, the state is present in the turmoil and confusion of Pilate and especially in the futile gesture of washing guilt from his hands, for this was after all no more than a vain symbolic attempt to protect 'government' (his claim to rightfully govern and justly judge) from the inevitable consequences (his personal spiritual guilt and the de-legitimising and 'de-authorising' of his political rule) of abusing the state; it was, in effect, an admission that 'government' needed re-legitimising and 're-authorising' by the state.

Jesus proclaimed that his kingdom is not of this world. His kingdom is providential/pastoral rather than political/power-centred and it is the true origin and end of every earthly political authority/kingdom. We need to view the Pilate-Jesus encounter in this light and to see Jesus as the proclaimer and presence of the former (God's kingdom) and Pilate as a representative of the latter (earthly kingdoms). In this encounter, the 'created' passes judgment on the creator, 'government' comes face to face with 'the origin and end of government' and 'political existence' condemns to death its own 'essence'. In this encounter, too, it is important to note, God's rule (more properly designated as 'reign') is exercised, not through Christ, but through Pilate, as God's official representative and as the bearer of God's authority into the earthly realm through his political rule and judicial office. Hence, rather than seeing Christ, in the manner recommended by O'Donovan, as 'the mediator of God's rule'[66] and as announcing as 'the coming of God's kingdom to sweep away existing orders of government',[67] we should, rather, see earthly rulers, including Pilate, as the divinely ordained political mediators of God's reign and see Christ as the (immediate) presence of God and of God's reign in the midst of earthly political rule, and as the transcendent origin and end of all earthly kingdoms standing immanently but powerlessly before the earthly power of Pilate. Judgment is proper to kingship and to Pilate's rule but Pilate is to be *God's* judge. He is to be the presence and instrument of God's reign (and judgment) but he is also subject to divine judgment whilst being God's judge. Properly, divine judgment is *upon* the political, and yet in the Pilate-Jesus encounter the human/political kingship that is properly subject to divine judgment finds itself passing judgment *upon* its own divine source. Just as the

---

66. *Ibid*, 123.
67. *Ibid*, 137.

Old Testament prophets fearlessly presented the judgement of God upon earthly political authorities and upon their betrayal of their true role (that is, to represent Yhwh, to judge on Yhwh's behalf, to *be* Yhwh's judgement, and to *be* the political bearer of God's reign), so too the words of Jesus proclaim that the true role of Pilate is to be God's righteous judge on earth ("You would have no power if you did not receive it from above") and the innocence of Jesus exposes the false and distorting way in which Pilate executes, or fails to execute, his divinely ordained role as 'mediator of God's rule' or, as I would prefer to say, as 'political mediator of God's reign on earth'.

We are not God; God is not us, and yet God is also Emmanuel, God-with-us, and we are temples of the Holy Spirit who dwells immanently in our midst. All of this is, I believe, expressed in the Jewish religious refrain 'Yhwh is king' and in the kind of kingship claimed and 'lived out' by Jesus as he confronted Pilate, that is, a kingship not of this world but operating in and through this world, and a kingship exercised on behalf of the Father and through the Spirit. The 'objective otherness' of God (we are not God) is reflected in the 'objective otherness' of political authority as its will descends upon us, or at least in what confronts us in our sinful experience as the 'external' and 'alien' will of an all powerful, inscrutable Father-God ('the descending objective'), just as 'God-with-us' is reflected in our personal and social identification with *our* political authorities, with the Spirit rising within us ('the ascending subjective'). Both the 'objective otherness' and the 'for-us-ness' of God and his laws are, I suggest, reflected in the Jewish religious refrain 'Yhwh is king'. Commenting on this refrain, O'Donovan makes the following incisive point:

> The kingship of Yhwh was not an expression of the *potentia absoluta* which philosophical theology ascribes to the divine creator on the brink, as it were, of creating, able to bring about this world of meaning that he has brought about but equally able to bring about alternatives. It is divine authority, not divine power, that is communicated by the idea. This authority evokes free action because it holds out to the worshippers a fulfilment of their agency within the created order in which their agency has a place and a meaning. Yhwh's kingship is not a creation *ex nihilo* but an act of providence, keeping faith with creation once made.[68]

However, I think it would be more precise to say here that a forceful divine presence suffused with righteousness—divine force/power *and* authority, though not, to be sure, the *potentia absoluta* of creation but the righteousness of God's power and the power of God's righteousness—are included in the 'descending objective' and that *both* divine power and authority are communicated by the idea of Yhwh's kingship, so that it is with both power and authority in mind that we can say with O'Donovan that Yhwh's kingship is, first and foremost, 'an act of provi-

---

68. *Ibid*, 32.

dence, keeping faith with creation once made'.[69] God's kingdom (God's authority/power) is providential rather than political, for it is not 'political' in any of the senses with which we are familiar. In commenting upon Marc Brettler's study *God is King*,[70] O'Donovan emphasises that Yhwh's kingship is not 'secondary to the experience of human kingship' and rightly insists that Saul and David were kings 'by virtue of some relation to Yhwh rather than vice versa'[71] but I would suggest that the relation involved here is that between earthly political rule and Yhwh's reign, between 'government' and 'the origin and end of government', between immanent earthly kingship and its divine transcendent point and purpose—in short, between Pilate and Jesus. The creation is an expression of God's love and power, in equal measure so to speak, but God's kingdom is more properly identified with the love of God (though made real in our experience through the *power* of the Spirit), and the earthly political kingdoms of this world are more properly associated with power and force (though these are only properly exercisable in our world under the *sovereignty* of the descending Father and the ascending Spirit). It is significant, I think, that we normally find it both more proper and more 'natural' to speak of the 'reign of [God's] grace', rather than of the 'rule of [God's] grace', or of God's reign, rather than of God's rule, over the human world (individuals and na-

---

69. *Ibid.*
70. MZ Brettler, *God is King* (Sheffield: JSOT Press, 1989).
71. O O'Donovan, *The Desire of the Nations: Rediscovering the Roots of Political Theology*, 35.

tions). God's reign operates in this world *through* our rule (personal and political); we are to be the ruling instruments of God's reign; we are to rule *under* God's reign which means that our divinely ordained task (as much 'political' as 'personal') is to make God's kingdom, God's love and God's presence real in the world. It is legitimate to think and speak of earthly political authorities as 'mediators of God's rule' so long as we have this 'reign/rule' ('state/government') sense of 'rule' in mind.

Conclusion: Marxism and Bartelson's 'Unicorn State'

One of the great achievements of the theoretically sophisticated Marxism that appeared in the 1960s and 1970s,[72] was that it paved the way for the mainly empirically oriented movement to 'bring the state back in'[73] later in the twentieth century. However, it did so, I believe, by surreptitiously appealing to and implicitly endorsing the ethical theory of the state, for the real appeal of Marxism is surely to the state as such or as an ideal counterpoint to the debased, false, capitalist state. The Marxist denunciation of the capitalist state invites a contrast between the state as such, or in its essence as a 'true universal' and the bour-

---

72. R Miliband, *The State in Capitalist Society: the Analysis of the Western System of Power* (London: Quartet Books, 1973); GW Domhoff, *Who Rules America?* (Englewood Cliffs, NJ: Prentice Hall, 1967) and N Poulantzas, 'The Problems of the Capitalist State', in *New Left Review*, 58 (1969): 67–78.
73. *Bringing the State Back In* edited by B Evans, D Rueschemeyer, and T Skocpol (Cambridge: Cambridge University Press, 1987).

geois state as a 'false universal', as indeed 'particularity' dressing itself up as 'universality'. Thus whilst Marxism explicitly rejects the ethical theory as bourgeois ideology, the true ethical unity of the state insisted upon by the ethical theory is the real, ultimate source of the ethical force of the Marxist critique of capitalist governments as endemically partisan. There is, surely, a pervasive sense in Marx's critical writings of 'an awesome authority mightily abused' that provides the motivation for his theoretical analysis. Curiously, and in contrast to the theoretically sophisticated Marxism that preceded it and paved its pathway, the movement to bring the state back in that gained momentum in the 1980s was largely uncritical, untheorised and could indeed be said to provide a theoretically impoverished version of the ethical theory of the state or a kind of 'pure' empirical 'practice' wholly devoid of any theoretical illumination.[74] Clearly, what is needed at the present time, or so I would suggest, is a reconsideration of the ethical theory of the state by the political science community as a whole, leading (its adherents may hope) to a more widespread acknowledgement of its theoretical benefits. However, according to Bartelson, this is precise-

---

74. Thus we find John Dearlove in 'Bringing the Constitution back In', in *Political Studies*, 37/4, 1989: 529 holding that 'instead of seeking to develop a general theory of the state, state-centred theorists should turn their backs on this myth-making objective and emphasise the need for solid empirical research . . .' See also Theda Skocpol 'Bringing the State Back In: Strategies of Analysis in Current Research', in *Bringing the State Back In*, edited by B Evans, D Ruuschemeyer and T Skocpol (Cambridge, Cambridge University Press, 1987), 8.

ly what is not needed. Rather, he believes, the time has come to dispense with the state altogether.

In his recent work on the state, Bartelson holds that during the twentieth century, 'theorists dealing with the state concept have gone about their critical project as if the state were "out there", yet representing something opaque to be unmasked in order to find its underlying truth'[75] and that, in doing so, they have had as the ultimate target of their criticism the 'objective reality and self-identity of the state'. Bartelson, however, is convinced that the efforts of these critical theorists have been largely futile because of the constantly presupposed presence, in their criticism, of the very object (the state) they wish to dispense with. He then adds that 'if no-one could be suspected of believing the state to be self-identical and somehow real, the criticism would not only lose its bite but also is rationale. A critical theory of the state would then look as relevant and useful to us as a critical theory of unicorns'.[76]

What Bartelson is here recommending, I wish to suggest, is that we simply ignore the state altogether and pretend that it simply isn't there. Again, I would suggest that the failure of twentieth century theorists to undermine the objective reality and self-identity of the state is perfectly understandable; the conviction that the state is indeed somehow real, that it is really 'out there' and that it is an enduring and significant ethico-political identity, is too deep-seated and soundly based to be easily dis-

---

75. J Bartelson, *The Critique of the State*, 184.
76. Ibid.

lodged. As exponents of the ethical theory will insist, the state, as well as being 'in here', in the sense that the public spirit (or the Holy Spirit in our particular patch) lives in each of us, is also, assuredly, 'out there' in the sense that it is a unifying ethical force that descends upon our inner, subjective world with the descending authority of the Father, in the sense that the reality of the common good both transcends and yet also includes each of us—it is, so to speak, a common and shared ethical reality—and, finally, in the sense that it is sedimented in sound and just social institutions and mores (Godly customs). There may, perhaps, be some merit in Bartelson's proposal to abandon the quest for a sound 'critical theory of the state', but only because the expression is highly misleading; the state itself is the font of social and political criticism, the very condition of its possibility, and so it is critical theories of government and politics, not of the 'state', that we require and for which the ethical theory of the state provides a sound justification.

The ethical theory of the state presented and defended in this chapter is idealist in the sense that it holds that the political realm is a medium in and through which significant, life-giving ideas and values find expression and realisation, and it is metaphysical in the sense that it holds (i) that the state is an unseen reality that yet pervades and constitutes empirical political institutions and practices and (ii) that each state, through its government, represents locally, and culturally embodies, universal right. However, whilst the theory is undoubtedly metaphysical with respect to the state, to its reality or 'that-ness' (its 'existential there-ness'), so that it may be fairly called an 'existential/

metaphysical theory', nevertheless it may, I think, be fairly described as metaphysically neutral or agnostic with regard to the 'whatness' or the true ultimate nature (the 'final essence') of the state. To say that the state, in the elementary sense of 'the constant, ideal, social will to justice and the common good', is the ethical 'reality' that informs political practice, scarcely goes beyond the simple claim that the state exists, but this 'existential claim' becomes also a more substantive, 'deeply' metaphysical and religious/theological claim if it is held that the 'person' of the state is none other than the Holy Spirit or an angelic presence that bears the Spirit into political life. Having put the matter thus, at this point (i) we may say that the state is a form requiring a further form, or needing an explanation in terms of something (or Someone) more ultimate, that it is an essence that exists but which yet requires reference to something deeper, truer or more essential still in order to be intelligible, or (ii) we may rather be content to say that the state is an essence or form whose 'simple' existence we can easily, as we have seen, infer from the ordinary dynamics of political life and which requires no 'deeper' explanation or no further form. I would suggest that, *as political philosophers*, we should choose (i) (the former) which involves pressing on towards a more general and ultimate understanding and explanation of the state, and entering into a discussion of the what-ness or whoness of the ultimate reality (the Absolute, God, Platonic ideas, Husserlian meanings-in-themselves, thing-in-itself, the agathon, etc) that constitutes the source and summit of political life, but that *as citizens*—and especially as citizens living in liberal pluralist democracy—we should choose (ii) (the latter), and thereby, in our discussions of practical political issues, avoid needless disputes over the deeper metaphysical and theological issues concerning the state. It is of the utmost importance that we do what we can to reach agreement in the 'operative sphere'. Habermas and Ratzinger[77] lead us in the right direction by highlighting the fact that they reach very similar conclusions in the 'operative sphere', even though they differ dramatically in the justifications they each propose for their practical recommendations.

At the same time, we are all aware that everyday political life raises issues for discussion and resolution that are deeply metaphysical and religious/theological, and whilst these issues need to be confronted and dealt with, even at the risk of exacerbating divisions within the body politic, still they need to be approached in a manner that minimises as far as possible their undoubtedly explosive and divisive potential. In the case of the issues of abortion and euthanasia, for example, if Christian *believers* respect human life *because* it has been assigned an absolute or priceless value by the Author of all life, they will see these things as wholly unacceptable but as Christian *citizens*, they must be prepared to offer sound public reasons as to why *all* citizens should find these things offensive. A true unity of purpose in their collective life is only achievable if all citizens, whatever their metaphysical or religious convictions, endeavour to employ public rather than partial reasons but this involves expressing their views in

---

77. J Habermas, and J Ratzinger, *Dialectics of Secularization: On Reason and Religion*.

a manner which is as metaphysically neutral and 'non-metaphysically driven' as possible and which establishes as many contact points as possible with values and beliefs that are widespread in the culture and especially in the beliefs of one's political opponents. Indeed, precisely because an ethical/metaphysical account of the state insists so strongly on the importance of a true unity of purpose and of a genuinely general will as the summit and source of the life of a political community, as what 'draws and drives' its life, the deep religious and metaphysical convictions of citizens should generally not enter openly and directly into political discussions but should be filtered, as far as possible, through the medium of 'public reason'. In my view, there is no problem with Christians being motivated politically by their deeply held metaphysical convictions and religious beliefs ('each human person has an absolute value and dignity as a child of God and as eternally loved by God.') but in the civil or political sphere, where they live as citizens among citizens, they should (i) make common cause with all those who, for whatever metaphysical reason or without any clearly held metaphysical reasons at all, are prepared to uphold the dignity of human life and (ii) refrain from metaphysical or religious assertions not strictly germane to the political issue at hand. In Barth's words, 'the Christian community shares common interests with the world and its task is to give resolute practical expression to this community of interest';[78] 'the civil cause (and not merely the

---

78. K Barth, *Community, State and Church: Three Essays*, 159,

Christian cause) is also the cause of the one God',[79] so that Christians must 'apply themselves to the same task with non-Christians and submit themselves to the same rule',[80] and thereby contribute to 'the fulfilment of the State's own righteous purposes'.[81] This is good sound advice for us all as citizens but when, as political philosophers—and especially if as political philosophers we also happen to be Christian–we press forward to seek an understanding of the state in terms of something (or Someone) more ultimate, we will also find that the reflections of Karl Barth on political theology and the state can provide us with invaluable assistance.

---

79. *Ibid*, 160.
80. *Ibid*, 159.
81. *Ibid*, 171.

Chapter Seven

Barth and the State

And we win the victory over the world by means of our faith
I John 5:4.

When it says 'he ascended', what can it mean if not that he descended right down to the lower regions of the earth?
Ephesians 4:9

Introduction

In this chapter, I present a modified Barthian view of the state and respond to a variety of criticisms that have been directed against Barth's 'political theology'. I will focus almost exclusively on the later work of Barth, for in his early work his theological (Kierkegaardian) conviction that 'there is an infinite, qualitative difference between time and eternity, between God and man' leads directly to his early (Foucauldian) political conviction that politics is a power-obsessed, evil game that is enthusiastically engaged in by conservative and radical alike. The holy, transcendent God, he holds, comes to us 'straight down from above' and confronts the immanent political realm here below as hostile enemy territory.[1] Since the 'existing order as such is the evil',[2] the false world of human hopes and possibilities it contains needs to be shattered, rather than enveloped or elevated, by God's 'perpendicular descent'. Understandably, in this early period, he sees politics as 'fundamentally uninteresting'[3] and world history as characterised by a pervasive 'monotony'.[4] Fortunately, however, in his later work his theological conviction that the God who comes to us in judgment (the divine 'No') also comes to us in redeeming grace (the divine 'Yes') has equally important epistemological and political repercussions. This 'triumph of grace' endows us with a certain confidence in our knowledge, even in our knowledge of God[5] and enables us to think of a 'righteous state' here on earth that (i) is approved of by God, (ii) is not just a point of contact for God's perpendicular descent but a locus of his gracious presence, and (iii)can offer resistance to oppression. (In the case of Barth, of course, this meant that he had the theoretical and theological wherewithal to resist the National-Socialist state and society.)

For the later Barth upon whom we shall now concentrate, Christ is Lord and all earthly power and authority already belong to him. In answering the question 'What

---

1. K Barth, *The Epistle to the Romans* (Oxford: Oxford University Press, 1933) 479.
2. *Ibid.*
3. K Barth, *Church Dogmatics*, volume 4 (Edinburgh: T&T Clark, 1975), 307.
4. *Ibid.*
5. *Ibid*, volume 2, 225.

is the State?' he directs our attention to the execution of Jesus Christ by Pontius Pilate in the name of the state. He tells us that the state is an 'angelic power'[6] and that if Pontius Pilate, having declared the innocence of Jesus, had then proceeded to pronounce the sentence of acquittal, 'the State would have shown its *true* face':[7]

> If only Pilate had taken himself absolutely seriously as a representative of the State he would have made a different use of his power. Yet the fact that he used it as he did could not alter the fact that this power was really given him "from above". But he could not use it as he did without contradicting his true function; under the cloak of legality he trampled on the law which he should have upheld; in doing so, however, it became evident that if he had been true to his commission he would have had to decide otherwise. Certainly, in deflecting the course of justice he became the involuntary agent and herald of divine justification; yet at the same time he makes it clear that real human justice, a real exposure of the true face of the State, would inevitably have meant the recognition of the right to proclaim divine justification, the Kingdom of Christ

---

6. K Barth, *Community, State and Church: Three Essays* (Gloucester, Mass: Peter Smith, 1968), 107.
7. *Ibid*, 113.

which is not of this world, freely and deliberately.[8]

He holds that the state 'belongs originally and ultimately to Jesus Christ; that in its comparatively independent substance, in its dignity, in its function, and its purpose, it should serve the Person and Work of Jesus Christ and therefore the justification of the sinner'.[9] The state's authority is 'included in the authority' of the Lord.[10] He holds that a legitimate and 'true order of human affairs'[11] is not beyond our reach, even on this side of eternity, and is achievable 'in this present age, in this world of sin and sinners'.[12] Such a true state will be '[no] eternal Solomon, free from temptation and without sin, but nonetheless a Solomon, an image of Him whose Kingdom will be a Kingdom of peace without frontiers and without end'.[13]

What Barth has to say here is, in my view, unexceptionable. Although Barth simply restates Colossians 1:20, Ephesians 1:10 and Colossians 2:15 (and, as far as I can see, does not engage in any controversial interpretive moves or leaps in so doing), yet he has been extensively criticised (by, for example, Jurgen Moltmann and Will Herberg) for presenting an untenable, implausible and overly Christological theory of the state. Later in this chapter, I defend Barth against these criticisms, although I also point to a

---

8. *Ibid*, 113–114.
9. *Ibid*, 118.
10. *Ibid*, 140.
11. *Ibid*, 148.
12. *Ibid*.
13. *Ibid*.

weakness in Barth's account and show the way in which it can be easily corrected and modified without, I hope, pressing too hard against the grain or spirit of his reflections on the state. I argue that Barth rightly insists that the rebellious powers and principalities have been created in and for God, that they do not belong to themselves, and that from the first 'they stand at the disposal of Jesus Christ'[14] but he wrongly assumes that Schlier takes a contrary view. In actual fact, they are both making an identical point, namely that governing political authorities, to the extent that they fall under the influence of 'the hosts of spiritual darkness' and attempt to exist in their own right and apart from God, will be destroyed in their 'separateness', their bastardised form of existence, and reintegrated into God's creation (or restored to their true point and purpose in Christ). I then suggest that when reflecting upon this 'fading away' of the principalities and powers (in the sense of the spiritual forces of darkness), it is helpful to think in terms of the 'twin flows of salvation' from God to humanity (creation) and from humanity (creation) to God.

The State, Angels and Demons

Barth tells us that, at the time when he was formulating his own views on 'the essence of the state',[15] fresh emphasis had been laid on the fact the terms translated as 'governing authorities' referred to in Romans 13:1–7, Titus 3:1,

---

14. *Ibid*, 117
15. *Ibid*, 114

1Corinthians 15:24, Colossians 1:16; 2:10, 15, Ephesians 1:21; 3:10, 6:12 and 1Peter 3:22 were used to refer not just to (political) authority but also, especially when used in the plural, 'to indicate a group of those angelic powers which are so characteristic of the biblical conception of the world and of man'[16] and which 'constitute created, but invisible, spiritual and heavenly powers'.[17] He also expresses the view, arising, he believes, from the language of the New Testament and confirmed by the research of G Dehn, that 'when the Church of the New testament spoke of the state, the emperor or king, and of his representatives and their activities, it had in mind the picture of an "angelic power" of this kind, represented by this state and active within it'.[18] Barth here opens up an incredibly wide vista of theoretical possibilities and questions. Is this 'angelic' power or presence the true essence of the state, the ultimate font of its legitimacy? Is the invisible angelic power, which the visible state/government represents, a kind of public person or one of those spiritual, intelligent, heavenly agencies that, to use Barth's words,[19] 'exercise, in and above the rest of creation, a certain independence, and in this independence have a certain superior dignity, task and function, and exert a certain real influence?' Is it proper to regard the state as a 'created but invisible, spiritual and heavenly power',[20] both 'in and above the rest of

---

16. *Ibid.*
17. *Ibid*, 115
18. *Ibid.*
19. *Ibid.*
20. *Ibid.*

creation'? Could it be that each particular state is a real will to justice and the common good, or a real public spirit that lives both 'in and above' the members of 'its' society? Is the state the living breath of the (universal) Holy Spirit, transcending and yet immanent ('co-present' with us) within the collective life of the members of a human society, indwelling universally in each society but doing so through a unique 'angelic presence', sent 'from above' and yet at home 'below'?

My answer would be 'yes' to all of the above but Barth, though his theology of the state presses in this direction, doesn't go quite this far. In general, Barth thinks in terms of an 'angelic power' represented by a particular state and active within it,[21] whereas I regard the state itself as an 'angelic power' represented by its government and active within it. I hold that the state, conceived of as an angelic presence of the Spirit, bearing and mediating the 'will to justice' and goodness of the Father into our minds as members of a commonwealth, is beyond corruption, but this is not Barth's view. He has no reservations in contemplating

> how it came to pass that the State, from being the defender of the law, established by God's will and ordinance, could become 'the beast out of the abyss of Revelation 13 . . . ' An angelic power may indeed become wild, degenerate, perverted, and so become a 'demonic' power. That, clearly, had happened with the

---

21. *Ibid.*

State, as represented by Pilate, which crucified Jesus.[22]

Though puzzled by the passage, Barth is convinced that in 1 Corinthians 15:24 ('Then the end will come, when he hands over the kingdom to God the Father, after he has annihilated all dominion, authority and power') the term 'annihilate' is here misleading, for immediately afterwards, in verse 25 the passage continues to say that Jesus must reign until he has sovereign power over his enemies. In a similar vein 1 Peter 3:22 speaks of 'angels and authorities and powers being made subject unto Him' (See also Ephesians 1:20, 21 and Colossians 2:15), all of which leads Barth to believe that the various (angelic) powers and authorities will not be destroyed, 'but that they will be pressed into the service and glorification of Christ, and, through Him, of God'.[23] Consequently, he takes exception to Schlier's view that these powers and authorities represent the world which lives on itself and by itself, that cuts itself off from God, and as such, in its isolation, is the antipodes and exact opposite of creation'.[24]

The key task that confronts us here is of really understanding, and grasping the manifold implications of, Barth's crucial claim that the state, ultimately and originally belongs to Jesus Christ. In particular, we need to ask if what 'ultimately belongs to Christ', in this case the state, can degenerate and become demonic. This is a pos-

---

22. *Ibid*.
23. *Ibid*, 116.
24. *Ibid*, 117.

sibility (the 'corruptibility' of the state) which Barth accepts but which I reject. My view is that Pilate, in allowing an innocent man to be legally executed, failed to represent the state or to be an agent (a governing instrument) of its will to justice and this surely is what Barth too seems to have in mind when he says that had Pilate pronounced a sentence of acquittal, 'the State would have shown its *true* face'.[25] I maintain that a government can, whereas the state as such cannot, become degenerate or demonic, although it is only by claiming to represent the state–by taking on the deceitful appearance of the state's angelic presence, by becoming a Lucifer, an apparent bearer of heavenly light–that it can become demonic. Thus whilst I would say that Hitler's regime must be regarded as not really a state at all but as an 'un-state', as 'matter' in revolt against its own 'form' or an 'existent' denying its own 'essence', Barth generally takes the view that Hitler's regime should be seen as a corrupt or demonic state. However, if the State as such belongs originally and ultimately to Jesus Christ, if that is its true essence, reality and substance, and if that is what the state is (ontologically rather than empirically), then how can the state become demonic? Barth speaks of the state losing its legitimacy and its true substance[26] but how can the state 'lose' its very essence? Is not the will to justice, to use Barth's own expression, the *true* (eternal, incorruptible) face of the state? Clearly Barth has in mind those critical situations where 'existence' is in revolt against 'essence', where a government

---

25. *Ibid*, 113.
26. *Ibid*, 118.

acts against its own true being or essence, namely *its* state, where it empirically subverts its own reason for existence (the common good) and thereby assumes a bastardised (actual but 'ought not to be') form of existence, but strictly speaking, it is the government of a state (the empirical civil authority) which becomes demonic. Barth of course is delighted when a state shows 'its true face as a just State'[27] but surely a government acting justly *is* the true face of the state, indeed of *its* state, and an 'unjust State'[28] is simply an ontological impossibility. What is all too possible is that a government as the empirical arm of the state (an actual state in its 'empiricity') may falsely represent the state and fail to be the real presence or true face of the state in every day life.

We normally expect 'government' to be the phenomenal appearance or empirical epiphany of the state but when this is not the case, when a government behaves reprehensibly, this is because the angelic presence of the state is not represented, because an 'existential' government is in revolt against its own essence (its own reality or noumenon) and not because the angelic presence of the state has degenerated into a demonic presence. No doubt, as Barth points out, an angelic power (Satan, for example) may 'become wild, degenerate, perverted, and so become a 'demonic' power'[29] but if as I propose (and as Barth at times seems to propose as well), we understand the state as 'the Holy Spirit co-present in us', as the 'particularised

---

27. *Ibid*, 119.
28. *Ibid*.
29.

presence' of the universal Spirit in us and for us, and as an angelic power or public/moral person (our collective 'own true self' as a society), then it is clearly incapable of such degeneration. Thus, governments and civil authorities (principalities and powers) in which the State dwells need to be radically distinguished from the principalities and powers and the 'spiritual hosts of wickedness in the heavenly places' referred to in Ephesians 6:12. ('For we are not contending against flesh and blood but against the principalities, against the powers, against the world rulers of this present darkness, against the spiritual hosts of wickedness in the heavenly places.') In broad exegetical terms, it is, I submit, entirely proper, as the occasion requires and as the Scriptural context makes plain, to think of the principalities and powers in three ways or senses, that is, (i) as, truly and ultimately, agents of the Holy Spirit, (ii) as instruments of Satan in the sense of being temporarily being held captive by Satan and his minions or, finally, (iii) as purely spiritual powers that 'properly' belong to Satan in a manner and sense that is, admittedly, difficult to understand. Thus, when Paul speaks in Ephesians 6:12 of 'powers and principalities', he could conceivably have in mind (i) visible ('earthly') powers and principalities *as distinct from* the spiritual hosts of darkness, (ii) visible ('earthly') powers and principalities *as corrupted by* the spiritual hosts of darkness, or (iii) invisible ('in the heavenly places') powers and principalities *of* the spiritual hosts of darkness. Surely, however, it is most unlikely that Paul was thinking of 'powers and principalities' in the first sense—that is, as media of God's will or as the earthly voice of angels (angelic powers) that stand in God's presence—in the context of Ephesians 6:12, for his mind in this passage was focused on what Christians must be against, what they need to resolutely oppose. The general drift of what Paul has to say here strongly suggests that he had either the second or third sense of 'principalities and powers' in mind and that he was not thinking of the latter in this context in the first sense as 'real and created', as subject to evil and yet also as capable of restoration and redemption, as liable to corruption and yet also as destined to 'return home' to be enfolded by Christ.

In my view, when Paul refers in the specific case of Ephesians 6:12 to rulers and authorities (principalities and powers) etc, he has in mind in this instance and context the spiritual kingdom of darkness as a whole. These spiritual forces or demons can possess at best a bastardised form of existence, both in themselves and in their presence in the empirical spatio-temporal civil authorities (governments) that they infect. Indeed, the sense in which they 'exist' at all is difficult to articulate, for they inhabit a kind of realm of 'unreality', a zone (or vacuum) of anti-Being and anti-Life that attempts to swerve God's world away from its predestined course towards the new creation, towards its divinely ordained fullness of being; they have no ultimate being, to true ontic reality or ontological status. While time lasts, these spiritual hosts of wickedness 'are' in some sense but the dubious status as 'existents' that they enjoy in time will vanish when the God of eternity establishes the fullness of the new creation, wholly 'invading' creation with His presence. The very memory of them will be erased as the 'Is' of eternity wholly infuses the 'is' of time and Christ becomes 'All-in-all'. Everything that truly is will be in its proper place under Christ. Barth, referring to Colossians 1:15 and Colossians 2:10, rightly insists that the rebellious powers and principalities have been created in and for God, that they do not belong to themselves, and that from the first 'they stand at the disposal of Jesus Christ',[30] but he wrongly assumes that Schlier takes a contrary view. In actual fact, they are both making an identical point, namely that governing political authorities, to the extent that they fall under the influence of 'the hosts of spiritual darkness' and attempt to exist in their own right and apart from God, will be destroyed in their 'separateness', their bastardised form of existence, and re-integrated into God's creation (or restored to their true point and purpose in Christ). This was precisely the point made by Augustine when he insisted that Jonah's prophecy *was* fulfilled and Nineveh *was* overthrown when the imperial city repented and believed (*Serm* 361.2; *Enarrationes in Psalmos*, 50.11). However, unlike Barth, Schlier, I believe, is thinking, as I do, (i) of the (one) Spirit constantly renewing and elevating creation in general and the principalities and powers of this earth (governments and civil authorities) in particular and (ii) of states as angelic powers (or 'persons') that convey the socio-political presence of the Spirit, that possess untarnished the beauty and truth of their original being and that mediate socially and politically God's will and intent for humanity through the principalities and powers of this earth (governments and civil authorities),

---

30. K Barth, *Community, State and Church: Three Essays*, 117.

in contrast to the spiritual powers of darkness that draw (tempt) the powers and principalities (good in themselves as originally created and ordained by God) into the murky realm of evil, violence and non-being. These dark spiritual forces can at best claim to have a bastardised 'ought-not-to-be' form of existence that one day will disappear altogether.

Principalities and Powers; the 'Single Flow of Authority' and the 'Twin Flows of Salvation'

When pondering this 'fading away' of the principalities and powers (in the sense of the spiritual forces of darkness), it is helpful to think in terms of the 'single flow of authority' and the 'twin flows of salvation' from God to humanity (creation) and from humanity (creation) to God. The Father has what Tom Smail refers to as 'initiating sovereignty';[31] He is the original Author in the sense that He creates the world of time through the Son, who may be said to 'author' the will of the Father into existence. The Father is Author; the Son Authors; the Son is the 'verb' of the Father's 'noun'. The Son is the Word of God and very God. Wayne Grudem holds that '[s]upreme authority always belongs to the Father'[32] and that the expression 'seated at the right hand of the Father' indicates that Jesus is second to God the Father in authority but I

---

31. T Smail, *Like Father, Like Son: The Trinity Imaged in our Humanity* (Milton Keynes: Paternoster, 2005), 103.
32. W Grudem, *Evangelical Feminism and Biblical Truth* (Sisters, Ore: Multnomah, 2004), 412.

would suggest that we should think, on the contrary, in terms of the Son having all authority and the Father having none. Jesus is not second to the Father in authority, for Jesus *is* the Word of the Father, *is* the authority of the Father as original Author, *is* the One who conveys, 'authors', makes present, bears, crystallises and expresses in his Person, the Father as original Author. The Father is the original, eternally begetting Author of all, the font whence His initiating sovereignty flows through Christ into the universe, the 'Author-as-such' whose authorial presence is eternally borne or expressed by the Son; it is his authorial presence, eternally begetting the Son, that lives in and is expressed in the Son. As Athanasius remarks, for 'as the Father is first, so also is he [the Son] as the image of the first'.[33] Athanasius regards as wholly unscriptural the suggestion that the Son came into being by the Father's 'will and pleasure', for He 'is himself the Father's living counsel (*patros agathon boulema*) and power'.[34] As Alvyn Pettersen remarks, for Athanasius 'The Logos *is* the Father's will, and is not the consequence of the Father's will'.[35] (When Paul noted that, in the exercise of authority in the church, it needs to be borne in mind that 'Adam was formed first, then Eve' (1 Tim 2:13), perhaps what he had uppermost in mind was precisely this flow of author-

---

33. Athanasius, 1971, 'Discourses', in *The Nicene Creed and Post Nicene Fathers of the Christian Church*, abbreviated in main text as NPNF, 4:2.57, edited by Philip Schaff and Henry Wace (Grand Rapids: Eerdmans, 1971), 399.
34. *Ibid*, 429
35. A Pettersen, *Athanasius* (New York: Morehouse, 1996), 172.

ity—this series of successive crystallisations of the same authority—from the Father through Jesus/Adam/Eve. As the Father loves us with the same love that He has for His Son—'that the love with which You have loved me may be in them' (John 17:26)—so too He bestows upon us through His Son the very authority of the Christ and His own Authorial presence.)

Corresponding to the eternal flow of the initiating sovereignty of the Father through the Word to the world, there is an eternal reverse flow, empowered by the Spirit, from the world, through the Son back to the Father. In this scheme, Christ's death and burial ends the 'incarnational flow' from the Father to the world through the Son, and Christ's resurrection begins the reverse flow from the world through the Son to the Father, culminating in 1 Corinthians 15:24–28 where Paul speaks of Christ returning all rulership and authority to the Father, the original 'initiating' Author. Paradoxically, in the incarnational flow, the emphasis is on Christ as God (on Barth's electing God or Rahner's descending God), though reduced and 'telescoped' into our humanity, whereas in the reverse flow towards the Father, the emphasis is on Christ as man (on Barth's elect human or Rahner's ascending man), though expanded and glorified into His divinity. Due to this twin flow (God humanised/flesh deified) and because, as Rahner says, the Son is the 'absolute bringer of salvation' and in the Son 'the Father, his will, his salvation, his pardon, his kingdom "are there" in absolute and final proximity',[36] humanity as a whole may be taken up

---

36. K Rahner, *The Trinity* (New York: Herder and Herder, 1997), 63.

into the circle of God's life and love, into God's own family as adopted sons and daughters. The culmination and fulfilment of this whole salvation process (the twin flows) is the return of all kingdoms, all powers and principalities to the Father. To bring all nations, all peoples, and all believers before the throne of grace in the fullness of revelation, crying in heart-felt recognition 'Abba/Father' is the whole point and purpose of the authority exercised by Christ and through Christ's veiled presence in the authoritative rule of the heads of nations, regions, communities and families. This elimination, on the one hand, of all rule and power not of God and this complete suffusion, on the other hand, of all rule and power with the full, unmediated presence of God, ensures the *fulfilment* of the authority of Christ (as it is also the fulfilment of 'the desire of the nations') and allows God to be truly and undisguisedly 'All-in-all', dispelling finally and forever the power of sin and transforming the veiled presence of God in the disguised form of authority (political, social, familial, etc) into the unmediated, unveiled, undisguised full presence of God in all and through all. The ultimate point and purpose of Christ's authority, its consummation and fruition in the 'project' of salvation, is, as St Augustine says, to hand over 'at the end' the kingdom to the Father and to bring 'believers to a direct contemplation of God the Father'.[37] Far from the Son being in any sense deprived or diminished, this deliverance of all to the Father is the fruition and goal of Christ's role as mediator.

---

37. Augustine, *The Trinity*, 1:16 (Brooklyn: New City Press, Brooklyn, 1991), 76.

As Calvin remarks, Christ at that point 'returns the lordship to his Father so that—far from diminishing his own majesty—it may shine all the more brightly'.[38] The reverse side, so to speak, of the handing over of all kingship and power to the Father is that the glory enjoyed by the Son for all eternity with the Father is now fully revealed to all; the 'desire of the nations' is fully realised. In all of this we can hear distant echoes from the inner life of the Trinity itself or the very 'heartbeat' of God. Through the economy of salvation (God *ad extra*) or through our sense of the 'twin flows' we have just considered, perhaps we can catch a glimpse of this inner divine life (God *ad intra*), that is, of the never beginning/never ending flow of the love of the eternally begetting Father to the Son in the Spirit and of the eternal reverse flow of the love of the eternally begotten Son to the Father through the Spirit.

As I mentioned earlier, Barth generally thinks in terms of an 'angelic power' represented by a particular state and active within it, whereas I regard the state itself as an angelic power or presence represented by its government and active within it. An advantage of the interpretation of the state I am espousing is that it enables us, especially when pondering the passage of Scripture that Barth found so puzzling (that is, I Corinthians 15:24 and its use of the term 'annihilate'), to acknowledge the creative/redemptive side of every act of (apparent) divine destruction, for the 'annihilation' of every regime/authority that claims to exist in and by its own right or authority is si-

---

38. J Calvin, *Institutes of the Christian Religion*, 2.14.3 edited by JT Neill (London: SCM, 1961), 485.

multaneously a restoration of that regime/authority to its true form in Christ and under God's authority. Concerning the 'spiritual hosts of wickedness in the heavenly places' referred to in Ephesians 6:12, their 'destruction' is at the same time their 're-creation' or redemption, for a 'fall from Being', a retreat into separate existence apart from God, or a posture of 'anti-Being' (a rejection of God and of all authority as divinely instituted) is replaced by the full restoration of, and re-integration into, their original (and originally intended) 'fullness of Being' or 'life in God'. Concerning such powers understood as a 'world', as an unholy league of powers and principalities allowed a form of bastardised existence by God (Colossians 1:15, Colossians 2:10) but existing apart from God and in defiance of his authority, we may say, with Schlier, that they represent the world which lives on itself and by itself and which atrophies into evil in isolation from God.[39] Whatever has true being is from God and in God; whatever, through pride, falls away from Being into a false sense of independence, is of the 'world' in a negative sense and is under the reign of spiritual darkness to some degree. The state represents on earth the being or reality of justice and goodness and opposes the anti-being or 'fall from being' of sin and pride, in the sense here of false independence or mere 'bastardised existence'. A government may either truly represent the state, in which case it plays a significant role in 'the order of redemption' in restraining the destructive effects of pride and promoting the common good, or it may fall (wholly or in part) under the illusion

---

39. K Barth, *Community, State and Church: Three Essays*, 117.

that it is itself the source of its own authority, in which case it becomes (wholly or in part) a 'power or principality' in the invidious sense. Because Barth holds that the 'State, as State knows nothing of the Spirit',[40] he is unable, I think, to fully grasp it as the mediated presence of the Father's will to justice and goodness and as the Spirit elevating and restoring the created world.

My distinction between (i) a state as the will to justice and the common good, as an 'angelic' will or purpose that indwells a particular political community and (ii) a corrupt government that opposes and fails to represent its state, corresponds to (and, I think, even overlaps and partly coincides with) the distinction between (i) spiritual or angelic powers that serve God, that stand in God's presence and mediate the presence of the Holy Spirit into us and our political world and (ii) principalities and powers, in the sense of the spiritual kingdom of darkness (of anti-Being or of the 'world' in the insidious sense) that opposes God's kingdom on this earth from its fortress 'in the heavenly places' (Ephesians 6:12). The actual principalities and powers that we are familiar with (that is, governments and civil or political authorities) exist in their own domain in our space-time world and yet their spiritual character, so to speak, depends on the position they take in the spiritual battle between these two kingdoms (kingdoms that are both in and out of time, both on earth and 'in the heavenly places'). Their ideal task is to represent their state and thereby mediate God's presence into the political world, but they may fail in varying degrees

---

40. *Ibid*, 132.

to do so and they may even outrightly reject the will to justice emanating from the Father's heart. We may summarise, then, by saying that God is real, that the state is real as an emanation from God (as His will to justice alive in men through the Spirit) or as an angelic presence mediating that will, that governments are real (legitimate and true) as genuine representatives of the state but unreal or 'merely actual' in failing to represent, or in opposing, the state, and that the spiritual forces of darkness are 'actual but unreal' and have a bastardised 'ought-not-to-be' form of existence that will one day vanish altogether.

Moltmann's criticism of Barth

We now turn to some important criticisms that have been directed against Barth's political theology. We will begin with Moltmann's criticism, the main gist of which is presented in a summary form in the following paragraph:

> The doctrine of the lordship of Christ over the Christian community and the civil community is based on Christological eschatology: *Christ is the Pantocrator* who already rules over heaven and earth. This Christology was first powerfully proclaimed in early Christian hymns and then in Ephesians and Colossians. These hymns actually proclaim the already initiated *lordship of Christ over the world* and the already accomplished subjugation of cosmic and political powers. Therefore in doxological jubilation Christians already partici-

pate in the universal lordship of Christ. They
are themselves already raised with Christ.
They share in his *resurrected* lordship. They
already *rule* with him. But this, according to
Ernst Kasemann, is an enthusiastic congregational piety that forgets the crucified one and
retreats from earthly reality.[41]

As this criticism by Moltmann makes clear, the main difficulty posed by Barth lies in arriving at a proper understanding of the political implications of his conviction that
the whole world is already objectively in Christ. Is this
a prescriptive statement of the way in which the world
ought to be rather than a descriptive statement of the way
it actually is? Does he mean that earthly states, powers
and principalities, etc, henceforth (that is, after Christ's
victorious resurrection) exist only *de facto* but have no
de jure existence apart from Christ or does he mean that
Christ's lordship over these powers is already established,
that he is ruler in every sense (as a matter of *fact* as well
as of *right*) so that, for example we would have to regard
Christ's second coming as 'the public unveiling of this already accomplished victory of Christ'?[42] Does Barth in-
tend us to distinguish between Christ's objective and his
subjective lordship? Finally, is this statement 'ontological'
in a sense that contrasts with 'empirical'? Of the series of
distinctions just mentioned in these questions (prescrip-

---

41. J Moltmann, *On Human Dignity; Political Theology and Ethics* (London: SCM Press, 1984), 93.
42. *Ibid*, 85.

tive/descriptive, *de jure/de facto*, objective/subjective, ontological/empirical) my suggestion is that Barth's political thought (in particular, the political implications of his statement that the whole world is already objectively in Christ) is best approached through the last distinction and is best understood by asking the last question first.

In effect, Moltmann accuses Barth of taking too seriously and literally the adage 'Jesus is Lord of all or not lord at all'. He interprets Barth as saying that the Lordship of Christ means that every power in heaven and earth has already been given to Christ and that these powers belong to Christ not just *de jure* (that is, legitimately, ethically, and as a matter of right) but also *de facto* (that is, actually, immediately and as a matter of fact). He believes then that, for Barth, Christ's lordship of all, including the political, is a real, actually operative, sovereign rulership over all, that it is the 'truth' or 'reality' behind all (political) appearances to the contrary. In summary, Christ is the Pantocrator who already, and in every sense, rules over all, over every power and principality in heaven and earth. However, if we focus on Barth's (in my view, more fundamental and central) distinction and contrast between the 'ontological' and the 'empirical', an altogether different, more nuanced and complex picture of Barth's political thought emerges. To say that the whole world is already objectively in Christ, as an ontological statement, is to claim to offer a description (non-empirical or at least not necessarily empirical) of the way things really are, truly and objectively, in an ultimate sense. One is speaking descriptively of their true being, so to speak, and yet what one says when speaking in this 'descriptive' ontological vein may well have 'prescriptive' implications for the way things are empirically. Thus it may be said of the powers and principalities that, as they are, in their truth, they belong to Christ and are what they are in and through Him, whilst acknowledging that this ontological truth may or may not coincide with the empirical truth, in much the same way that persons are in truth (ontologically) children of God, and are what they are in and through Him, even when they empirically behave as children of Satan and even if they are wholly unaware that God is their Father. Generally, however, it is important to note, these two different kinds of truth ('ontological' and 'empirical') routinely coincide; most actual (empirical) governments are not corrupt but simply administer law and order and pursue worthwhile public policies as best they can and in so doing are an image of the 'eternal Solomon'. Even the empirical truth of Pilate 'I have power to execute you' (John 19:10) coincides with or is the 'empirical side' of Christ's ultimate, 'ontological' truth that 'All power is from above'. (John 19:11) The 'empirical' diverged from the 'ontological' when Pilate used his rightful power to wrongly condemn to death a man that he judged to be innocent, for justice truly and essentially belongs to the state and the empirical (Pilate's actual verdict) in this case was unjust.

Interestingly, the routine identification of the 'ontological' and the 'empirical' is not duplicated in the case of the 'objective' and 'subjective'. We find that when we interpret Christ's lordship in terms of this distinction that the contrast is much sharper and it is painfully felt as such in our experience. Subjectively, our experience is as Luther describes it; an almost constant inner battle is being waged between good and evil, between the call to virtue and the temptation to vice, and yet objectively, Christ has broken the power of Satan and assured us of final victory in our ongoing struggle. What this (objective) assurance renders groundless is any fear we might have in our battles with evil that Satan might be victorious in any final sense. However many battles we may lose on the battle ground of our inner selves, the war is already won. Moltmann is quite right to say that, for Barth, 'Christian faith lives in the certainty of Christ's victory'[43] but fails to realise that what this means for Barth (and for us) is Christ's victory in the war and not in each individual battle that takes place in each human heart. We should note at this point the deep inner connection between the objective truth (Christ's lordship and our final victory in Christ) and our subjective grasp of it, for this truth inspires confidence in the most trying times. In the light of this truth and the hope it justifies, to say that we 'rule with Christ' or that we participate in his lordship is not merely, to use Moltmann's phrase, 'an enthusiastic congregational piety' but the simple truth. It is a truth that faith, bearing the 'objective' into the 'subjective', brings into the inner world of our experience and lays a sure foundation for hope in our final (in a sense, 'already won') victory in Christ. In this case our hope is based on faith in what is objectively, truly and ontologically the case. ('And we win the victory over the world by means of our faith'. I John 5:4.) We can rest assured that sin ('the ontological impossibility') can never

---

43. *Ibid*, 84.

achieve 'true being' in the human soul, which is eternally destined to find itself in the Being of God; Satan's victories are the evanescent victories of an imposter, for in the end he is Prince of Darkness, of 'anti-being' and can never achieve more than an 'actual but ought not to be' kind of 'bastardised' presence in the human soul. (Precisely the same holds true, we may note here in passing, of the 'collective soul' of society.)

Moltmann's misunderstanding of Barth (more precisely, of what we might call Barth's 'political ontology') has an unfortunate effect on his own political thought, for in insisting, against what he takes to be Barth's position, that only 'when the lordship of the crucified one becomes the lordship of God, will all earthly lordships, authorities, and powers, together with death, *then* be destroyed', he ignores altogether the enormous significance of the *de jure*, already won, objective and ontological lordship of Christ between now and then. What Moltmann fails to grasp is Barth's 'ontological/ethical' point that apart from Christ, after his victorious resurrection, earthly powers no longer have any legitimate existence; apart from Him, these powers can have only a bastardised (actual but 'ought not to be') form of existence. Even if an earthly power proceeds diligently about its business in the pursuit of justice and the common good, though without any acknowledgement of the ultimate lordship of Christ, it is nevertheless 'objectively' in and under Christ; its rule is *de jure* as well as *de facto*, unlike the merely *de facto* rule of every earthly power outside of or in contravention of God's law. The revelation of Christ in God has radically and permanently exposed and condemned the false autonomy and illegitimacy of the latter. In 1 Colossians 2:8–15, we find a dramatic account of the way in which the humble lamb that was slain disarms the powers and principalities, for the revelation of the lamb as the one in whom the fullness of deity dwells and who is the head of all rule and authority is at the same time the exposure and disarming of the false autonomy and arrogance of earthly rulership apart from Christ. 'He disarmed the principalities and powers and made a public example of them, triumphing over them in the cross' (1 Colossians 2:15). Thus Christ triumphs over Pilate; because he is 'the head of all rule and authority' (1 Colossians 3:10), there is no *true* headship apart from him. In brief, this triumphal procession of Christ should, I believe, be understood 'ontologically' rather than 'empirically'. It may be said of the powers and principalities that to serve the lord is their true origin and end. This is the final, ultimate truth of their being and apart from this truth, they can possess only a bastardised form of existence.

Herberg's Criticism of Barth

Barth holds that there is a correspondence between what is 'above' and what is 'below', between the heavenly *polis* and the earthly *polis*,[44] that 'the original and final pattern of [the earthly order of the state] is the eternal Kingdom of God and the eternal righteousness of His grace',[45] and that the state should be seen 'as an allegory, as a corre-

---

44. K Barth, *Community, State and Church: Three Essays*, 135.
45. *Ibid*, 154.

spondence and analogue to the Kingdom of God which the church preaches and believes in'.[46] He speaks in a Platonic-Origenistic fashion of the 'true state' as '[no] eternal Solomon, free from temptation and without sin, but nonetheless a Solomon, an image of Him whose Kingdom will be a Kingdom of peace without frontiers and without end';[47] in the state, he holds, God's kingdom 'has an external, relative and provisional embodiment'.[48] Consequently, the church has this responsibility: 'Among the political possibilities open at any particular time, it [the church] will choose those which most suggest a correspondence to, an analogy and a reflection of, the content of its own faith and gospel'.[49] In Barth's judgment, this meant a constant interest by the church 'in human beings, and not in some abstract cause or other',[50] the equal protection of all before the law,[51] the right to live one's life within the law without interference from the state,[52] the separation of powers,[53] the rejection 'of all secret policies and secret diplomacy',[54] freedom of speech (free use of the 'word'),[55] an understanding of 'ruling' as primarily

---

46. *Ibid*, 169.
47. *Ibid*, 148.
48. *Ibid*, 154.
49. *Ibid*, 170.
50. *Ibid*, 171.
51. *Ibid*, 173.
52. *Ibid*, 173–174.
53. *Ibid*, 175.
54. *Ibid*, 176.
55. *Ibid*, 176–177.

a form of service,[56] reconciling the interests of the nation (legitimate though at times indefensibly parochial) with the wider needs of humanity as a whole, and, finally, the rejection of violence except when it is employed as a last resort in dire circumstances.[57]

All of this is, I would suggest, perfectly unexceptionable and scriptural but Will Herberg is not at all impressed; he regards Barth's view that there is a correspondence between what is 'above' and what is 'below', between the heavenly *polis* and the earthly *polis* as simply too vague and indeterminate and, moreover, as too easily adjusted to, and manipulated by, one's own personal predilections. He holds that following Barth's method of analogy is very arbitrary, more so even than the natural law approach to politics which Barth decisively rejects as 'Janus-faced'. He finds Barth's conclusions entirely commendable but insists that it is clear that 'very different conclusions could just as easily have been drawn from the same premises by the same method'.[58] He is in full agreement with the criticism directed by Emil Brunner against Barth, namely that 'anything and everything can be derived from the same principle of analogy: a monarchy just as well as a republic (Christ the King), a totalitarian state just as much as a state with civil liberties (Christ the Lord of all, man a servant, indeed a slave, of Jesus Christ).'[59] One can hardly

---

56. *Ibid*, 177.
57. *Ibid*, 178–179.
58. W Herberg, 'Introduction' to K Barth, *Community, State and Church: Three Essays*, 35.
59. E Brunner, *The Christian Doctrine of Creation and Redemption* (Westminster: Lutterworth Press, 1952), 319.

doubt then, Herberg believes, that Barth simply adjusted his 'Christological' arguments to suit conclusions which he had already reached on other grounds.

The first point to be noted here is that Barth does not attempt to deduce anything from his principle of analogy. When he says that '[a]mong the political possibilities open at any particular time, it [the Church] will choose those which most suggest a correspondence to, an analogy and a reflection of, the content of its own faith and gospel',[60] the relationship involved here is one of intimation, of reflective elaboration, or of spiritual discernment, rather than of 'deduction' in a simple, mechanical, syllogistic sense. Barth, for example talks of the democratic conception of the state as 'a justifiable expansion of the thought of the New Testament' which suggests that, far from crowning his own 'privately arrived at' judgment with the 'aura' of Scripture in the manner suggested by Herberg and Brunner, Barth was interpreting the Scriptures into the political circumstances of his time, and in doing so, found himself drawn in spirit, and sympathetically inclined, towards constitutional democracy.

Barth's insistence upon the necessity and importance of making discriminate judgments in politics which are 'time-and-place' specific is actually acknowledged by Herberg[61] and yet he agrees with Brunner that 'Barth takes the values of a pluralistic constitutional democracy as given, ingeniously discovers more or less plausible counterparts for them in the realm of the Church and the

---

60. K Barth, *Community, State and Church: Three Essays*, 145.
61. *In Ibid*, 45.

Gospel, and then proceeds to "derive" the former from the latter'.[62] Barth, however, was not under the illusion that one could easily work out, 'derive' or 'deduce' a (let alone 'the') 'Christian position' on political or constitutional issues: rather, each generation of Christians will confront a unique set of political circumstances and must do its best, in the light of the Gospel, to discern God's will therein. How the gospel is to be interpreted into everyday (political) life, what are the key and vital correspondences, etc, is for each successive generation of Christians to determine. It is a question, Barth says, 'of continual decisions, and therefore of distinctions between one state and another, between the state of yesterday and the state of today'.[63] The establishment of a monarchy was not widely considered as a live option at the time but that is not to say that in other circumstances another country, with a different history and culture, might well find a monarchy to be a real possibility or one of a number of 'live option' possibilities to be considered. At the time of writing, the 'cutting edge' question for Barth was whether the Scriptures endorsed and 'authorised' Nazi totalitarianism or liberal constitutionalism. Both were very real possibilities, truly 'live options', so to speak at the time, but which 'political possibility' should the Christian endeavour to realise? His judgment, no doubt arrived at after his own process of discernment, is that *in Germany in the 1930s*, the values of constitutional democracy did, whereas the values of totalitarianism did not, correspond to the content and faith

---

62. *Ibid*, 36.
63. *Ibid*, 45.

of the Gospel. There is not, it should be noted, any way in which the process of spiritual discernment (or what I have called 'interpreting the scriptures into our lives') that Barth regarded as so important, can be dispensed with.[64] Interestingly, the misplaced criticism directed by Herberg against Barth is echoed in the adverse (and, in my view, equally misplaced) criticisms more recently made against Reinhold Niebuhr. When the latter insists that liberty, order and equality are important regulative principles of justice to be referred to when governments and citizens are attempting to achieve the highest attainable social good (or to negotiate the gap between the actual and the

---

64. Herberg notes the Augustinian/Reformation view of the centrality of the state in the 'order of preservation', that is, in preserving society and social order against the threat of disruption posed by human arrogance and sinfulness, and the centrality of the Church in the 'order of redemption', which mediates the saving word of God to sinful humanity, and then states that if Barth had focused on the role played by human sinfulness in generating the need for the order of preservation, he 'might have derived all of his conclusions in a much more secure and Biblically true manner' ('Introduction', in K Barth, *Community, State and Church: Three Essays*, 37). Herberg has in mind here Barth's endorsement of (or his 'conclusion' in favour of) democracy and constitutionalism. It is quite true, as Herberg points out, that Calvin, the Puritans and the framers of the United States constitution all argued, in their own way, from human sinfulness to the need to place institutional curbs on the exercise of power and thence to the 'separation of powers and constitutionalism. However, we should note here that Thomas Hobbes used precisely the same Biblical premise (human sinfulness) to arrive at precisely the opposite conclusion, that is, to justify an 'absolutist' state.

ideal), he is accused by Dorrien[65] of being 'vague' and 'inherently slippery' in his treatment of justice and its universal norms (Niebuhr's mediating principles of justice) and by Dennis McCann[66] and Karen Lebacqz[67] for failing to provide adequate criteria for distinguishing between just and unjust uses of power.[2]

Secondly, I doubt if we will ever know whether what Herberg claims is true. He betrays his own uncertainty by rhetorically asking 'is it possible to doubt that what Barth is really doing is adjusting his "Christological" arguments to conclusions *already* reached *on other grounds?*'.[68] It is abundantly clear, Herberg believes, that Barth was totally opposed to totalitarianism and that he simply looked for and found appropriate passages in scripture which justified his position. Perhaps Barth did indeed use Holy Scripture in this way, as a seal and confirmation of his own views, but perhaps he didn't; perhaps the true direction of causation was the other way around. Perhaps Barth was challenged by what be believed the scriptures were saying to him to wholeheartedly oppose, rather than to seek a *modus vivendi* with, Hitler's totalitarian regime. We will never know; perhaps, even Barth never knew. I

---

65. G Dorrien, *Soul in Society: The Making and Renewal of Social Christianity* (Minneapolis: Fortress Press), 152.
66. D McCann, *Christian Realism and Liberation Theology: Practical Theologies in Creative Conflict* (Maryknoll, NY: Orbis Books, 1980), 80–93, 103.
67. K Lebacqz, K 1986, *Six Theories of Justice* (Minneapolis: Augsburg Press, 1986), 83–99.
68. 'Introduction', in K Barth, *Community, State and Church: Three Essays*, 35.

suspect that at no stage in his intellectual career did he feel sufficiently motivated to try to uncover the 'true' order of causality (his own personal antipathy to totalitarianism, generating an interest in certain passages of scripture or the other way around).

The move from biblical premises to political conclusions, I would suggest, is less a matter of deductive logic than of spiritual discernment or judgment under circumstances unique to each individual. The element of personal responsibility for one's 'exegetical decision' (and of existential anguish) is inescapable. The fact that a number of quite different, even incompatible, conclusions can be drawn from the same biblical premises may be taken (i), in the manner of Herberg, as indicating that whatever conclusion is reached is in effect arrived at, or already entertained, independently of scripture—which presumably means that when we think that 'Scripture speaks to us', we are in effect speaking to ourselves—or (ii), in the manner of Barth, as evidence that the bible is a living document for all ages and needs to be interpreted into the lives of people in different historical periods—which presumably means that the Holy Spirit can, after all, speak to us through the Scriptures and guide our spiritual reflections on God's will for our times.

Conclusion

The account presented in this chapter of the 'twin flows of salvation' fully coheres, I maintain, with my account of the state outlined in chapter seven but both accounts are distinctly at odds with the analysis and interpretation of the state and of the proper role of government offered recently by O'Donovan in his *The Desire of the Nations*.[69] In this concluding segment, I will present a brief summary of my views and the way in which they contrast with those of O'Donovan. The latter, like Moltmann, holds that Christ's victorious return to the Father means that 'the authorities are subdued, reformed and given a limited authorisation',[70] that 'the whole rationale of government is [now] seen to rest on its capacity to effect the judicial task'[71] and that we are left with 'the rump of political authority',[72] whereas I see secular authority (political, judicial and administrative), and indeed authority in general, as confirmed and strengthened by it. He holds that 'secular authorities are no longer in the fullest sense mediators of the rule of God',[73] whereas I maintain that they remain in the fullest sense mediators of the rule of God. He locates Romans 13:1–7 in the context of St Paul's 'claim for the continued significance of Israel as a social entity in God's plan for final redemption',[74] whereas I see it as part of his exposition on what it means to offer ourselves 'as a living sacrifice to God' (Rom 12:1) and to be inwardly transformed by God (Rom 12:2). Interestingly, O'Donovan notes the suggestion that 'Paul's choice of the term "prevailing authorities" alludes directly to the angel-

---

69. O O'Donovan, *The Desire of the Nations; Rediscovering the Roots of Political Theology* (Cambridge: Cambridge University Press, 2003).
70. *Ibid*, 146.
71. *Ibid*, 148.
72. *Ibid*, 151.
73. *Ibid*.
74. *Ibid*, 147.

ic character assigned to national governments in ancient Hebrew culture'[75] but then, with regard to these 'angelic governments', he proceeds to ask, almost in defiance of their 'angelic' character, 'Given that Christ has overcome the principalities and powers by his death and resurrection, what rights can they still claim?'.[76] My response, as we have seen, is that Christ 'overcomes' the principalities and powers in precisely the same way that Yhwh 'overcomes' the wayward Israel for the sake of the true Israel, and that their God-ordained rights and responsibilities are more securely grounded than ever. (Christ confirms Pilate's right to rule, its authorisation 'from above' and does not diminish it in any way.) Finally, O'Donovan holds that in light of our membership in Christ, the true representative of the human race, we can no longer respect the role of government 'as a focus of collective identity, either in Israel or in any other community',[77] whereas I would hold that our membership in Christ simultaneously brings fulfillment and proper ordering to all our other identities and that it is impossible to even think of 'government' (or the 'state') except as the institutional expression and 'formal bearer' of the collective identity of a people or nation. On this last point especially, Barth, I think, would wholly agree; a key aim of his ethical and righteous theory of the state was to show his fellow Germans that their true identity in Christ embraces, and does not exclude, their other identities, and that their 'membership in Christ' (i)

---

75. *Ibid*, 147.
76. *Ibid*.
77. *Ibid*, 148.

brings into proper alignment these other identities and (ii) prevents them from becoming subordinated to, and 'swallowed up' in, the totalistic 'true identity' offered by membership of the Third Reich. In the following chapter, I will show that the ethical-metaphysical theory of the state does not exhibit any unfortunate 'totalistic' tendencies and that it stands against the kind of 'statism' that Barth encountered and resisted.

Chapter Eight

Statism and Totalitarianism

Our hearts are restless until they rest in Thee
St Augustine

In the last chapter we saw that it was as a response to the emerging totalitarian regime in Germany that Barth developed his ethical or righteous theory of the state; the latter was intended to be a critique, not a justification, of the former. It is impossible to exaggerate the importance of this point, for too often the ethical theory of the state associated with Green and Bosanquet is seen as a sinister harbinger of totalitarian tendencies, whereas the truth is the very opposite; it was actually Barth's righteous theory of the state that enabled him to challenge the legitimacy of the Nazi regime. In this chapter, I wish to show that the kind of ethical-metaphysical theory of the state that we associate with Green and Bosanquet is both sound and insightful and that it does not exhibit a form of 'statism' and anti-juristic moralism. As in the case of Barth's ethical/ righteous theory of the state, the ethical theory of the state does not lead to, but stands firmly against and roundly condemns, totalitarian political ideologies. Contrary to the prevalent 'inherited' view of Bosanquet as an unrepentant moralist whose forceful endorsement of the ethical theory led him to engage enthusiastically in a form of state worship, he does not disregard or de-emphasise the rights of individuals *vis-à-vis* the state and the freedom-protecting aspects of law. Unfortunately, so strong and widely held is this view that David Runciman can state in an almost matter-of-fact fashion that he [Bosanquet]:

> regards technical jurisprudence as something a philosophical theory of the state must get beyond, as it 'move[s] toward a point of view which deals more completely with life and culture'. . . . He [Bosanquet] does not provide a secure juristic foundation for the part he wishes groups to play in the life of the state. He does not in fact provide what is an overtly moral conception of order with any juristic basis at all.[1]

He contrasts Bosanquet with theorists such as Hobbes and Rousseau 'who sought to formulate the unity of the state in juristic terms'[2] and states that 'Bosanquet did not address any of those problems which are commonly understood in legal terms—the problems of representation, or of obedience, or of ownership'.[3] Runciman holds, in-

---

1. D Runciman, *Pluralism and the Personality of the State* (Cambridge: Cambridge University Press, 1997), 77.
2. *Ibid.*
3. *Ibid*, 77–78.

deed, that 'it was precisely the purpose of Bosanquet's political philosophy to transcend such legalistic notions altogether'.[4] This line of criticism is a serious one because it resurrects the ghost of 'statism'. Put simply, if the juristic concern for justice and the rights of individuals as Kantian ends-in-themselves suffers annihilation, and justice is forced to vacate its legitimate place in the moral sphere, justice can no longer operate in that sphere as a complement or counterpoint to the 'common good' and the vacuum is liable to be filled by a triumphalist state.

Elsewhere,[5] I have argued that the concern for justice and individual rights suffered no such annihilation in the mind and work of Bosanquet and that since he was not an anti-juristic moralist, he was not, for that very reason, a 'statist' either. However, it has to be acknowledged that Bosanquet does make himself vulnerable to the charges of statism and anti-juristic moralism by his outright and, in my view, ill-considered rejection of the tradition of civil association which we now generally associate with the work of Michael Oakeshott. It is certainly a weakness in the case for Bosanquet as a genuinely juristic (and hence non-totalitarian) thinker that he condemns, instead of taking advantage of, this tradition, for it lends powerful practical and theoretical support to the juristic concern for justice and for solidly grounded individual rights. Thus, despite the fact that there is considerable textual evidence in support of Bosanquet as a genuinely juristic thinker, I

---

4. *Ibid*, 78.
5. BT Trainor, 'Statism and Anti-juristic Moralism in Bosanquet's Political Philosophy', in *Animus*, 7 (2002)

will be obliged in what follows to concentrate on the way in which he lays himself open to the charge of being an anti-juristic 'statist', for, in so doing, it becomes clear what the ethical theory must do to avoid the charges of statism and totalitarianism directed against it. In brief, the ethical theory must do what Bosanquet failed to do; it must unreservedly embrace the tradition of civil association as its true counterpart and completion.

Bosanquet and 'Statism'

Bosanquet notes, correctly in my view, that the point and purpose of what he calls 'negative or juristic' liberty is to facilitate 'positive or political' liberty, but is it its *only* point? When considering the contrast between the two conceptions of liberty, Bosanquet is right to point out that 'the apparently negative has its roots and its meaning in the positive'[6] but is the positive to be construed *only* in terms of the common good or general will? My own view is that (i) the 'positive' in which the 'negative' has its roots is not only the positive realisation of the common good but *also* the positive affirmation in the law of the value, integrity and inherent dignity of each person and (ii) this positive affirmation is an important aspect of every law, so that if the law's point and purpose (its essence) is to promote the common good, this aspect (that is, its 'jurisprudential' aspect of positively affirming the

---

6. B Bosanquet, *The Philosophical Theory of the State* (London: Macmillan, 1965), 127.

value of persons as ends-in-themselves) is nevertheless 'co-integral' to that essence or purpose.

Laws generally have as their aim the common good or public interest but it is important to recognise that laws also implicitly (and at times, when necessary, explicitly) acknowledge the value of each person as an absolute end. If we isolate and consider separately the role of law in positively affirming and reinforcing the supreme dignity and value of each person, we can readily see that this 'positive' element of law has a 'negative' dimension that corresponds to it, that is, the positive 'Thou shalt respect others as absolute ends or as Kantian ends-in-themselves' complements and corresponds to the negative 'Thou shalt not interfere with the life and freedom of another person, as absolute end, without due warrant.' Now, it is of course true that in the case of Bosanquet's 'negative freedom/positive common good' relationship, the negative aspect of law has its roots in the positive dimension of law but there lurks the suspicion in many minds that for Bosanquet the positive dimension of law is exhausted by its intent to realise the common good, and that he ignores the kind of positivity which pertains to law independently of the common good and which recognises and reinforces the absolute value of each individual as such. What he is suspected of ignoring, in brief, is the positivity of justice, not only in the ordinary sense of being fair to all but in the fundamental sense of 'positive acknowledgment of individuals as centres of absolute value' that the ordinary sense implies. It is Bosanquet's commitment to justice in this sense, and to the autonomy of justice in this sense *vis-à-vis* the common good, that appears tenuous at times in

The Philosophical Theory of the State, whereas his commitment to justice in the equally legitimate (Platonic) sense of 'each person being obliged to make their distinctive contribution to the common good' is beyond question.

It would be helpful at this point to refer once again to the distinction between the right and the good that I discussed in chapter three section (iii) and which I have presented at greater length elsewhere.[7] In the moral consciousness the 'good', including the 'common good', consists of our endeavours (individual or collective) to realise values or to realise 'absolute value' through the prism of the distinctive human values, whereas the 'just' primarily consists in the requirement to recognise the absolute value of persons or persons as Kantian ends-in-themselves. The former is concerned with (absolute) value as the ultimate goal or end of human endeavour, whereas the latter is concerned with absolute value in the form of a person and as present in, and inherent in, a person or spiritual being. Now it could be argued that Bosanquet certainly treats with complete seriousness absolute value in the former sense (that is, as the goal of human endeavour) but not in the latter sense (that, as inherent in persons) and that a consequence of his doing so is that he tends to see the person or human subject merely as a locus in which the drama of absolute value is enacted (which, in a certain, though non-exclusive sense, it certainly is) and to see true individuality as consisting only of an inner response

---

7. Trainor, BT 1998, *Justice and the State: On Liberal Organicism and the Foundations of Emancipatory Politics*, World Heritage Press, Quebec, 19-32.

to the call of absolute value (which, again, in a non-exclusive sense, I would agree that it is). The danger is that the inherence of absolute value in persons may be lost sight of and that the insight or truth that 'persons are for values' may override or suppress the insight or truth that 'values are for persons'. Thus the case made by his critics against Bosanquet as a genuinely juristic (and non-totalitarian) thinker turns, in the end, on whether or not we can find in his political writings the kind of individuals that we would expect to find in a truly juristic world, that is, rights/bearing autonomous individuals. Law, justice and right (jurisprudence) focus deontologically on persons or individuals as centres rather than seekers of absolute value, as Kantian ends-in-themselves or as 'sacred sites' in which absolute value inheres, rather than as agents in quest of the (personal or collective) good. Certainly, some such juristic conception of the individual, or one not too far removed from it in spirit, is presupposed by justice and jurisprudence.

The 'juristic' conception of the individual finds its 'natural' juristic/political expression in the state conceived of as a (civil) association but this is a conception that Bosanquet decisively rejects. No doubt, the state is much more than a 'mere' association. It is, after all, concerned to realise the association's point and purpose, but if it is more than an association, yet it is not less than one, and the fact of its being an association should not be seen as only a springboard to higher or nobler purposes. The state, as a civil association, is a system of mutual recognition which is important in itself in so far as it is a constant affirmation of the absolute value of each person. Now Bosanquet of course is positively hostile in his attitude to this conception of the state and to the conception of the individual of which it is both a kind of expression and justification at the same time, as the following quote makes clear.

> If you call the state an association, you speak the language of individualism, and still more so, if you speak of individual rights which can be asserted against it, and of the individual judgment as ultimate. To call it an 'association' is contrary, I think, both to usage and truth.[8]

Hegel once remarked that 'though marriage begins in contract, it is precisely a contract to transcend the standpoint of contract, the standpoint from which persons are regarded in their individuality as self—subsistent units'.[9] His key point is that a marriage may well be more than, but is not less than, its contractual/legal frame and a broadly similar kind of relationship surely obtains between the legal contractual obligations of the individual to the state (the state's juristic frame) and the purposes pursued by the state. In brief, the state, too, is more than but yet is not less than, its juristic frame (or its aspect as a civil association). However, Bosanquet insists that the state is

---

8. B Bosanquet, *Social and International Ideals: Being Studies in Patriotism* (London: Macmillan, 1917), 282–283.
9. GWF Hegel, *The Philosophy of Right* in Great Books of the Western World (Chicago: William Benton, 1989), 58.

not a civil association at all, whereas Michael Oakeshott[10] strenuously insists that, properly understood, it is only an association. Thus, Bosanquet, in rightly denying that the state as a whole can properly be characterised as a civil association, forgets—or seems here to forget—the state's juristic aspect or frame. He also seems to challenge the existence of the individual as an independent complement and counterpoint to the state, the kind of 'individual' presupposed, as we have seen, by the juristic world. He insists that individuals have rights, not by the virtue of being individuals or in acknowledgment of their status as absolute ends, but because they have been conferred on them by society. He says that the state's role is to protect rights but he defines rights as 'the claims recognised by the will of the community as the *sine qua non* of the highest obtainable fulfillment of the capacities for the best life possessed by its members'.[11]

If, as it seems reasonable to suggest, the political world of liberal society is marked by an ongoing tension between the (private) rights of individuals and the (public) pursuit of the common good, and if this tension is more like the tension of 'sexual opposition', promising the emergence of a deeper harmony (of a recognition and embrace of the other as its other) than it is like the tension of combatants facing each other in mortal combat, then both the tension and the deeper harmony have to be acknowledged. However, this is precisely what Bosanquet fails to do. The

---

10. M Oakeshott, *On Human Conduct* (Oxford: Clarendon Press, 1975).
11. B Bosanquet, *Social and International Ideals: Being Studies in Patriotism*, 271.

key task of a liberal government is to try to ensure that (i) liberal societies, as societies or organised states, are fully aware of the risk that, in their endeavours to be more than a mere association of individuals and to pursue the common good, they may become less than such an association, that is, they may fail to respect the rights and liberties of subjects; and (ii) liberal societies, concerned in their liberal character with the maintenance of individual rights, are constantly alert to the risk of lapsing into a mere association of individuals, like a loveless marriage. However, a political philosopher may be tempted to try to overcome the tension by destroying the pole considered to be offensive, that is, by conceiving the state, for example, as only a civil association, thereby confirming the status of individuals as absolute ends but making it very difficult for the government to pursue any common purposes, or by absolutising the state and its common or general will in such a way as to make individuals solely its media or instruments, thereby effectively eliminating individuals as rival centres of real (independent) value.

When we call ourselves 'individual members' of a community, we wish to be acknowledged both as 'individuals' and as 'members', with perhaps a special emphasis or one term or the other as the occasion requires but normally with an equal emphasis on each term. However, it could be argued that Bosanquet seems to merge the 'individual' into the 'member' and that he provides us with no stopping rule which could prevent his disappearance. His 'individuals' are assuredly at the service of the state as its loyal members but we lack any assurance that the state is equally at the service of individuals. For this reason, the ethical theory of the state, with its orientation to the 'good' (and to society's wellbeing) needs the tradition of civil association, with its orientation to justice (and to the rights of individuals) as its true counterpart and completion. This will ensure that the 'individual' is properly apprehended as the 'end' of society, for in so far as an aspect of justice/law is the constant recognition and affirmation of the dignity of each person/citizen as a child of God, the law may be truly said to be the 'end' of society/politics, just as, in so far as the individual is fulfilled in realising and participating in the social good, society/politics (the social good) is the 'end' of each individual, of each child of God living in communion with the family of God. Interestingly, as we shall now see, it is in Bosanquet's work, taken as a whole, that we find what is perhaps the finest appreciation of this mutuality and complementarity, this 'for-each-otherness', of the individual and society.

The Mutuality of Self and Society

Bosanquet recognises clearly and incisively that the 'self' (the individual) and 'society as the state' are inseparable. They each have a real, though mutually implicative and interdependent, existence. They are intimate aspects and expressions of each other, and they 'contain' each other, so we that need to remember that the distinction between the two may well be analytically useful but becomes disastrous if we come to think of the two as distinct or separate in any absolute sense. As he says, 'the fact is that the decisive issue is not whether we call the "individual" or "society" the "end" but what we take to be the nature at once of individuals and of society'.[12] The root of error in this matter, he insists, 'lies, on both sides, in an insufficient appreciation of what is involved in man's social being',[13] for this leads to the adoption of the following two extreme and erroneous positions.

> The one party credits the individual—the supposed self-existent isolable being—with all that does not emanate from the formal procedure of the political group as such; and thus, setting down, for example, art and religion as 'individual' activities and concerns, has a certain justification for alleging that the individual is the end to which society ... is the means. The other, rightly aware that the deepest and loftiest achievements of man do not belong to the particular human being in his repellent isolation, and, like his antagonist, recognising only two opposites, society as the state and man at his minimum as the individual, naturally claims for the state the glamour which belongs to the highest self-expression by which man transcends his isolation.[14]

Being mesmerised and misled by these two parties, we miss the profounder meaning of the term 'social', for our

---

12. B Bosanquet, *The Philosophical Theory of the State* (London: Macmillan, 1965), 76.
13. *Ibid*, xxxii.
14. *Ibid*, xxxiii.

minds are captivated by this confrontation between society as the state and the atomic individual, 'the private person who hugs his privateness',[15] and we thereby 'forfeit all possibility of understanding the nature of an activity which is neither semi-political on the one hand, nor "individualistic" on the other'.[16] We fail to properly understand the vast areas of social life, including for example art, religion and philosophy, that are 'at once ultra-social as being above all compulsory social arrangements, and ultra-individual as being beyond the aspect of exclusiveness, which, however falsely, clings to the current conception of individuality'.[17]

The 'for-each-otherness'of (i) the individual and (ii) society that Bosanquet draws our attention to is reflected in the relationship between (i) law (thought of as *made* by individuals) and (ii) the wider life of society (thought of as a living organism guided by *its* general will). Bosanquet holds that 'facts of law' are what he terms 'ideal facts' that constitute the frame or 'formal mind' of society. It is important, he notes, 'to comprehend that the social phenomena which are among the most solid and unyielding of our experiences, are nevertheless ideal in their nature, and consist of conscious recognitions, by intelligent beings, of the relations in which they stand'.[18] The system of law, understood in this way (that is, 'ideally') as formal

---

15. *Ibid*, xxxiv.
16. *Ibid*.
17. *Ibid*.
18. *Ibid*, 33.

acts 'of mind and will',[19] is often seen as being 'in opposition to the idea of a social growth'[20] or to the idea of society as a living, moving, breathing and growing totality, but there is, he holds, no need to choose between (i) 'society as artifact' and (ii) 'society as growth' or as a living organism; for Bosanquet, the former is but one aspect of the latter. A society may be more than, but is not less than, a formal or artificial system of law. As he says,'it remains true that the social whole has an artificial aspect'.[21]

Thus the system of law, or the formal artificial juristic aspect of society, is entirely necessary and also natural in a sense which he then proceeds to explain.[22] There is thus no question of Bosanquet transcending justice and the law in the manner in which Runciman suggests. The latter is, in a sense, quite correct to say that Bosanquet fails to provide his 'overtly moral conception of order with any juristic basis at all',[23] but this is only because, for Bosanquet, the juristic dimension is so thoroughly integrated into the social whole that whilst it can be separated and treated separately for analytical purposes, it cannot be treated as a 'basis', as that which 'comes first' and 'founds' society. (There is surely an element of internality or integrality associated with the terms 'dimension' or 'aspect' which contrasts with the externality or non-integrality associated with the terms 'basis' or 'foundation'.)

---

19. *Ibid*, 32.
20. *Ibid*, 33.
21. *Ibid* 33.
22. *Ibid* 33.
23. D Runciman, *Pluralism and the Personality of the State*, 77

If we turn our attention from the relationship obtaining between (i) 'society as artifice' (society as *made* by individuals through law) and (ii) 'society as living whole' to the close (indeed parallel) relationship obtaining between (i) procedures for making law (the process whereby individuals seek the general will) and (ii) the law itself (society's attempted embodiment of *its* general will), it will be agreed on all sides that there is no question of deriving the latter from the former or, to here use Runciman's expression, of 'deriving a general will from mere legal procedures'.[24] As he rightly says, for Bosanquet (and, I would add, for the ethical theory of the state more broadly) 'the general will was an expression of the "moral" personality of the state; the will of all, in contrast, was an expression only of its "legal" personality, since it was arrived at by legalistic conventions (that is, contracts and shows of hands)'.[25] Certainly, Bosanquet would regard such merely legalistic procedures and conventions as an inadequate means of realising the general will. Whilst necessary and important, they are nevertheless insufficient, for such procedures, Bosanquet would insist, are unable to guarantee that the wisdom and experience stored in the rich institutional life of a modern complex society will be brought to bear on a particular issue or proposed law. What Bosanquet objects to in Rousseau's account is not the procedures he employs to arrive at the general will but the fact that Rousseau so strenuously insists that individuals who hope to realise this will are to be completely

---

24. *Ibid*, footnote.
25. *Ibid*, footnote.

unassisted in their task. They are forbidden access to an invaluable resource that comes from their membership of (and deeply belonging to) a 'society of inheritance', that is, the treasure stored in society's institutional life and traditions. He holds that Rousseau ensures 'the exact reverse of what the professes to aim at' by 'appealing from the organised life, institutions, and selected capacity of a nation regarded as an aggregate of isolated individuals.[26]

In summary, I would suggest that, for exponents of the ethical/metaphysical theory of the state, mere legal or formal procedures, in so far as they enable, through free flowing discussion, the wisdom of the past to be brought to bear on the problems of the present, cease, in a sense, to be 'mere' legal procedures and become the living instruments of the 'ongoing birth' of a more truly general will. It is important to note that (i) the quest for the general will of society as a living organism (really, society's quest for its own true or authentic will) by means of these procedures *is* the moral life of the state but that (ii) in pursuing this quest, we must take care never to succumb to the 'totalitarian temptation' to concentrate absoluteness (or absolute value) in the state at the expense of the absoluteness (or absolute value) inhering in each individual.

Conclusion: Each Restless Human Heart

It is unfortunate and injudicious to depict individuals or 'individuality', as Bosanquet does, as 'adjectival'[27] for

---

26. B Bosanquet,*The Philosophical Theory of the State*, 109.
27. Concerning the criticism that the brand of idealism espoused by

this seems, in true totalitarian fashion, to reduce the individual to a mere aspect of the socio-political. However if, as I believe, his reason for describing 'the mode of being of finite individuals' in this way (as adjectival) is that he wished to challenge the view that persons are self-existent, self-subsistent, complete in themselves, solid self-standing subjects, conceivable as unchangeable soul-substances or metaphysical atoms, and to thus decisively undermine 'the pre-eminence claimed for singular beings

---

Bosanquet (and especially his depiction of the mode of being of persons as 'adjectival') is in clear opposition to that espoused by the 'personalists', and that the latter offer precisely the kind of philosophical account of the 'person' needed to underwrite the juristic world which Bosanquet's Absolute Idealism undermines, it is important to note that in a recent article William Sweet has marshaled a considerable body of textual evidence which indicates that Absolute Idealism does not take a uniform view of the human person and that Bosanquet's style of Absolute Idealism, as contrasted with Bradley's, was more in tune with, or at least more compatible with, 'personalism'. Sweet holds that Bosanquet departs from Bradley in regarding the finite individual self as 'the climax and sum and substance of evolution' as having a central role in the realisation of the whole, as the conscious medium through which nature acquires its significance and value (the individual is conceived of as a 'copula' between nature and the Absolute) and, finally as a unique and distinctive 'world' enveloped by a 'world of worlds' (the Absolute). Sweet is entirely persuasive in his account of Bosanquet but not of Bradley, who was, I think, more of a 'personalist' than Sweet is prepared to concede. Though he holds that the relation of the self to the Absolute is inexplicable, Bradley is confident that the self is in some sense 'in' the Absolute, which certainly suggests that he assigned the greatest possible dignity and importance to the human person.

in the pluralistic sense',[28] then what he has to say in this regard is not only unexceptionable but anthropologically beneficial and important. He is against 'the substantiation of provisional subjects'[29] and holds that the 'mere individual' as a definite substance or solid, unvarying subject nowhere exists[30] and is a misleading abstraction. However, Bosanquet is in no doubt that spiritual finite individuals do possess substantive reality as moral beings in quest of unity and coherence within themselves and the universe as a whole. We carry within us, he asserts, 'a pretension to be ourself, which includes less and more than we find in our existence'[31] and which seeks a 'truer' self beyond our actual or empirical self. We can either attempt to escape this quest for unity determined from within by descending to the status of an inert thing that coincides with itself (Browning's 'finite clod untroubled by a spark' or Sartre's 'bad faith') or pursue the 'ascending' quest for unity in the full (and terrifying) recognition that we will become utterly transformed and 'no longer be what we experience our existence as being'.[32] This 'ascending unity' (my expression) or the unifying 'pretension to be ourself' (Bosanquet's expression) is what he calls our 'substantive reality', our true mode of being as 'substantival solidly

---

28. B Bosanquet, 'Do Finite Individuals Possess a Substantive or an Adjectival Mode of Being?', *Proceedings of the Aristotelian Society*, volume 18: 1917–1918: 484.
29. *Ibid*, 485.
30. *Ibid*, 489.
31. *Ibid*, 496.
32. *Ibid*, 497

founded entities, possessed of an indefeasible unity'.[33] Bosanquet's reflections on this 'substantive reality' of the finite individual are instructive:

> Yet, what is the nature and structure of this reality? Is it the self as we experience it in detail? Surely not; or it is that self, but in an illumination more intense than the customary, and revealing a further structure. It *is* a substance and an ultimate subject, but not in its own right. Its existence, as an existence, bears the unmistakable stamp of the fragmentary and the provisional. Can there be anyone who does not feel it so in every act and in every thought? But through all this, and operative in it, there shines the intentional unity. It is not my monad or my star. It is the life which lives in me, but it is more of that life than I succeed in living. I *am* substantive and subject, then, but only so far as I recognise myself to be adjective and predicate. If . . . I set up to be in myself a self-centred real, I become *ipso facto* in the main a false appearance and all but worthless. This is when I come nearest to being a substantive in my own right, in error and in sin.[34]

---

33. *Ibid*, 497.
34. *Ibid*.

In insisting in this crucial passage that we are not the source and centre of our own being, Bosanquet here shows that his intention is not to absorb the individual into the social whole in a totalitarian manner but to illuminate the relationship between our human form of individuality and the ultimate and absolute Individual, between restless individuals in time and the eternal divine Thee. He thus expresses in clear philosophical terms what Augustine expressed in religious terms in saying that 'our hearts are restless until they rest in Thee'.

Part Four

The Holy Spirit, Law and the State

Chapter Nine

Hobbes, the Holy Spirit and the Holy Spirit

It has been decided by the Holy Spirit and by ourselves . . .
Acts 15: 28

The creation of each individual creature is itself already an expression of the divine love that grants existence to each creature, enabling it during the time of its existence to share in the vital power of the divine Spirit.
Wolfhart Pannenberg, Systematic Theology, volume 3, 644-45

Introduction; uplifting law and the Holy Spirit

If we take seriously Barth's point that the law itself is a grace, then we shall have to modify and refine the Augustinian/Reformation view that the role of the state is exclusively, or even mainly, restricted to the 'order of preservation', that is, to preserving society and social order against the threat of disruption posed by human arrogance and sinfulness, and that the Church is the sole player in the 'order of redemption'; that is, in mediating the saving word of God to sinful humanity. Likewise, if we accept with Reinhold Niebuhr that universal principles of justice are embodied in civil laws and social policy, that they are 'the servants and instruments of the spirit of brotherhood in so far as they extend the sense of obligation towards the other, (i) from an immediately felt obligation, prompted by obvious need, to a continued obligation expressed in fixed principles of support; (ii) from a simple relation between a self and one "other" to the complex relations of the self and the "others"; and (iii) finally from the obligations, discerned by the individual self, to the wider obligations which the community defines from its more impartial perspective',[1] then we will accept that in these three ways 'rules and laws of justice stand in a positive relation to the law of love'[2]. In both cases, the redeeming or uplifting role of the law is affirmed; Niebuhr in particular holds that the justice immanent in the civil law is designed for our betterment and draws us deeper into the orbit of love and O'Donovan makes a similar point when, reflecting on 1 Peter 2:13–17, he holds that the institution of secular government 'belongs to humankind as such, so that the common grace of God, rather than his saving purposes, forms the foundation of secular authority'.[3] Niebuhr warns us against 'the error of excluding rules of justice from the domain of love' and rightly takes Emil

---
1. R Niebuhr, The *Nature and Destiny of Man; A Christian Interpretation*, Volume 2 (London: Nisbet & Co Ltd, 1944), 257.
2. *Ibid.*
3. O O'Donovan, *The Desire of the Nations; Rediscovering the Roots of Political Theology* (Cambridge University Press, 2003), 149.

Brunner to task for holding that the role of politics and law is of secondary importance and that 'what is decisive always takes place in the realm of personal relations and not in the political sphere'.[4] Niebuhr certainly saw empirical systems of justice as uplifting, as training the ethical self and extending its vision, as further developing and elaborating our moral capacities and as thus, in a sense, 'redeeming' the citizen body.

As far as I am aware, (Reinhold) Niebuhr nowhere links the 'law as grace' to a particular person in the divine Trinity but Barth of course wished to link 'law as grace' to Christ. However, as one sympathetic to the natural law tradition, I see in the law's condemnation of pride, arrogance and unrighteousness and in the way it instigates consciousness of sin and sets in train the processes of redemption and salvation, the operative presence in our

---

4. E Brunner, *The Divine Imperative: A Study in Christian Ethics* (Philadelphia: Westminster Press, 1957), 233. The fact that Niebuhr holds that 'rules and laws of justice stand in a positive relation to the law of love' and that he takes Emile Brunner to task for holding that the role of politics and law is of secondary importance means that he actually envisaged a limited role for the law in socially uplifting, and even redeeming, individual citizens and that he may not , after all, have been wholly out of sympathy (or at an unfathomable intellectual and theological distance from) Rauschenbusch's belief that regenerated social institutions could have redeeming effects on individuals. Thus I would say that we should not accept without qualification Gary Dorrien's claim that 'for Niebuhr, society was inevitably immoral' and that we should be circumspect about his claim that Niebuhr outrightly rejected Rauschenbusch's belief 'that democratized collectivities could have redeeming effects on individuals' (Dorrien, G 1995, *Soul in Society: The Making and Renewal of Social Christianity*, Fortress press, Minneapolis, 149)

lives of the Spirit. It is the Holy Spirit that unites *individual* believers *in common* to the Son—Pannenberg speaks of the fellowship of believers being engendered by the elevation through the Spirit of our particularity[5]—and 'law as grace' may likewise be seen, as it is by Thomas Hobbes for example in the political realm, as the respect for the law *commonly* felt by *individual* citizens who are aware of its foundational role in social life. The link between 'grace as law' and the Holy Spirit, or rather, 'law as the gracious presence of the Spirit' can, indeed, be illustrated by using the work of Thomas Hobbes who, perhaps more than any other political philosopher, exhibits a very fine and subtle understanding of the ennobling and constructive role of law. Those familiar with the latter's work need not be concerned that I am about to engage in the implausible (indeed hopeless) task of presenting Hobbes as a 'philosopher of the Holy Spirit'. He was certainly no such thing and yet the manner in which he outlines the dynamic progression of the nascent will to peace (or spirit of peace) into what he terms the 'person' of the state has all the hallmarks of (i) what believers will instantly recognise as the vivifying, unifying movement of the Holy Spirit in the collective affairs of humanity and (ii) what Yves Congar and Karl Rahner would recognise as the intrinsic *spiritual* significance of the dynamics of the 'social' or secular sphere. Hobbes can also help us in another way. Through the Scriptures, we have some idea of what it is like for God (the Father) to be 'directly' present (or to be re-presented

---

5. W Pannenberg, *Systematic Theology*, Volume 3 (Edinburgh: T&T Clark, 1997), 135–136.

or to have a 'face' or appearance/epiphany) in the world through Jesus Christ. ('Whoever sees me sees the Father'. The Father is present or re-presented through His Son). Also, we have some idea through the Scriptures what it might be like for God, through Christ and the Holy Spirit, to be present in the Church (as Christ's body) or in the individual believer (as a temple of the Holy Spirit). However, we have very little idea—and an insignificant armoury of concepts to help us reflect upon and ascertain—what it might be like, or what is involved, in God being 'indirectly' present (again, being re-presented or having a 'face') in the world through the state. The political theory of Thomas Hobbes can help us here, for he speaks in a very illuminating way of the 'person' of the state, of this 'person' being present in and through the collective will of those seeking peace with each other in good conscience in a state of nature and guiding them to the formation of a political community. Now all of this sounds suspiciously like God's 'indirect presence' or 'immanent spiritual presence' in the political realm and appears indeed to be the political counterpart or analogue of the presence of the Holy Spirit in the gathered community of believers.

Finally, Hobbes can help us because he was both an exponent of (Catholic) natural law and yet also associated with the Reformation tradition and with its Occamite, nominalist tendencies and his work may serve in certain respects as a bridge between the two. With Luther, he regarded our fallen human reason as limited but nevertheless adequate to the task of forming a state, to grasping the state as a necessary form whereby our relations with each other are regulated. By the reason which governs human affairs, both Luther and Hobbes have in mind not any kind of immanent reason in the social or political order that is immediately accessible to, or within the grasp of, ordinary sinful mortals but the all too fallible reason or judgment of the specific person of the prince or magistrate. (For Hobbes, God's reason is not immanent in the political order but in the state or, rather, it is only truly present in the political order to the degree that the 'person' of the state is present and reflected in it, even though the subjects of a Commonwealth are required to regard the sovereign's political order as God's 'operative reason' in civil affairs.) Thielicke is right to point out that because Luther does not believe in such an order (reason immanent in the socio-political order and discernible by us as rational creatures) and because he 'uses a personalistically determined concept of reason, he has no explicit doctrine of the state'[6] and yet Hobbes does have such a doctrine. The reason is that, unlike Luther who thought in terms of the person *rather than* the institution (marriage, family, the state, etc),[7] Hobbes thought in terms of the individual person *in relation to* the institution. Hobbes would say that, however precarious and unstable the presence of reason in each proud and sinful individual person and in the judgment of rulers, reason is present in the institutions of the state; the latter are ordained by God's reason, for these institutions are set up at the behest of God's natural law operating in humanity. Hobbes's deficiently rational

---

6. H Thielicke, *Theological Ethics, Volume 2: Politics* (Grand Rapids: Eerdmans, 1979), 18.
7. Ibid.

man is slowly led to see or acknowledge—we may even say that he eventually 'bumps into'—the 'reason' of the state and the reason immanent in it. Thus, whereas the 'natural man' of Aristotle and Aquinas 'discerns' with his reason the tenets of natural law and the necessity, based thereon, of organised political life, the 'natural man' of Hobbes 'discovers' these same laws through hard experience. The discerning reason of the former participates and shares, from the beginning, in the life of immanent reason or reason-in-general (or the ever integrating, ever unifying movement of the Holy Spirit in life in all its forms), whereas Hobbes's passionate and proud denizens of the state of nature get pushed into the life of reason or become incorporated, half willingly, half reluctantly, into it. However, whether seen by nature's clear light of reason shining through us (Aquinas) or encountered in the heart of darkness and grasped as lifelines (Hobbes), the actual content of God's natural law is precisely the same and the state to which it is intrinsically connected—the state in effect is the spirit of natural law, a spirit of peace and cooperation—is precisely the same. What Hobbes, I think, helps us to see is that these very different ways of 'coming to know' God's laws of nature and what they ordain simply highlight different operations of the Holy Spirit in our human experience. How we each come to know 'what the state is all about' is similar to how we each come to know 'what marriage is all about'. Marriage, like the state, is an institution ordained by the divine laws of nature and individuals may contractually enter into it with a clear acknowledgement of the importance of intertwining their separate identities into a single person (a plurality becoming one), with an appreciation of its beauty and the good it intends for life together in a greater whole, or they may be merely following, willingly but unthinkingly, the custom of their time and place, or, again, they may be half forced or even fully forced into it. Still, however it is entered into and experienced (or subjectively 'known'), marriage ever remains what it is, a divinely ordained institution, a blessed work of 'God's reason for us' and precisely the same holds true for the state.

We noted in part three of this book that exponents of the ethical theory of the state see a common moral purpose or unifying will informing our lives as citizens. It was precisely this 'ethical unity of the state', as we may call it, that Hobbes believed in so ardently and which, through his notion of the 'person' of the state, received perhaps its strongest, most intellectually daring and articulate expression. For Hobbes, the spirit of natural law, and of civil law as its expression, *is* the state; the 'person' of the state *is* the will or intent behind the law; the Spirit in this sense is very near to us. In the seventeenth century, Hobbes theorised this notion in a very insightful manner and made it the climactic point of his account of how men emerged from the chaos of the state of nature (a 'natural condition' without organised government and law enforcement) and made the transition to organised civil society with enforceable civil laws. His account of the emergence of a 'person' of the state or of a unifying 'public will' is extremely valuable and helpful, if a little surprising to a reader who innocently approaches the Leviathan without any preconceptions concerning Hobbes's goals and objectives. Indeed, if one were to progress as far as the sixteenth chapter of *Leviathan* and no further, one could very possibly have gained the impression that the general thrust of Hobbes's argument is to show how essentially separate individuals in a state of nature are motivated by fear and self-interest to make a political covenant, that the latter is essentially the product of a utilitarian calculus, and that while it certainly brings about a new equilibrium of forces (the commonwealth), yet in other respects it leaves the individuals concerned as separate as they were before. Having finished the seventeenth chapter, one may be just as convinced (perhaps even more so) that this initial impression was correct. However, in that chapter, at a critical stage in his argument, Hobbes makes a brief comment which is bound to cause at least a modicum of discomfort. He sounds a single note of dissonance which is perplexing, to say the least. Having pointed out that all of those who leave the chaos of the state of nature and enter into the political covenant that establishes the state and civilised order must submit their wills to the will of the newly established sovereign, Hobbes then insists that 'this is more than consent, or concord; it is a real unity of them all, in one and the same person, made by covenant of every man with every man'.[8] A problem naturally arises as to what this brief remark actually means.

Apparently, we are witnessing the strange spectacle of essentially separate individuals somehow merging their identity with the 'person' of the state. It would certainly seem that the political covenant, by engendering or

---

8. T Hobbes, *Leviathan* in *The English Works of Thomas Hobbes*, Volume 3, edited by W Molesworth (London: J. Bohn, 1839), 158; .

at least facilitating a 'real unity', brings about a radical transformation of the isolated will of the individual. But how? Harald Hoffding once remarked that 'what we miss in Hobbes is any indication as to how the isolated will, when it is thus interwoven into a greater totality, can suffer a metamorphosis'.[9] We need to ask then, 'Does the political covenant, by some means or another, serve to facilitate the emergence of a *real unity* that is more than consent or concord, or should we regard this brief remark as a single note of dissonance in an otherwise coherent progression of thought?' I wish to argue for the former view, while holding that its acceptance does not entail any adverse repercussions for the coherence of Hobbes's argument as a whole. What may initially appear as a note of dissonance in the *Leviathan* is in fact the climactic point of Hobbes's entire political argument, so that the earlier chapters largely serve as a grounding or preparation for, and the later chapters as a systematic application of, the insights gained from the perspective achieved at this climactic point.

In section two of this chapter, I will argue that it is possible for Hobbes's essentially separate individual to merge their identity with the 'person' of the state (as represented by the sovereign) because he holds that they all share a rational desire for peace. By experiencing the discord of the state of nature and recognising that it is evil, 'all men easily acknowledge' that 'peace is good'. Reason's constant

---

9. H Hoffding, *A History of Modern Philosophy*, translated by BE Meyer (New York: Dover Publications, 1955), 287.

end is 'peace and defence' and 'he who tends to this with his whole might ... is a just man'.[10] While holding that the rational desire for peace is universal, Hobbes concedes that it is nevertheless frail, for it is 'contrary to our natural passions'; it is largely ineffectual in practical terms until, through the device of a political covenant, it acquires the institutional support of the sovereign power. For Hobbes, God (the Father) is the ultimate font of political authority. God is the Author of the laws of nature prescribing peace and concord, and the political sovereign has the divinely ordained task of representing and enforcing His will. However, the movement that takes place in the minds and hearts of men that induces them to set up a political sovereign who enforces peace is, in effect, a 'movement of the Spirit' in our collective human affairs. In saying 'in effect', I mean 'in truth'. Hobbes certainly regards this movement or progression from the state of nature to civil society as being in accord with the will of God (the Father) but while he does not portray it as the operative presence in human affairs of God (the Spirit) as such, that is nevertheless precisely what it is, and Hobbes actually describes it (this prompting or movement of the Spirit in our collective affairs) in very vivid and precise terms. In section three, I look at how Hobbes deals with the problem of a political sovereign who not only fails to secure peace but actually acts in such a way as to undermine the goal of peace and I argue that Hobbes deals with this problem by distinguishing between the idea of sovereignty (its es-

---

10. T Hobbes, *Leviathan* in *The English Works of Thomas Hobbes*, Volume 2, edited by W Molesworth (London: J. Bohn, 1839), 47.

sence) and the actual sovereign power (its existence) or between the 'person' of the state and the concrete spatio-temporal representative thereof. In section four, I examine the nature and extent of the transformation effected by the political covenant. Obviously, the sovereign gains sufficient countervailing power to wield against the force of our natural passions, but the real importance of this countervailing power is that it helps individual subjects themselves to control their own passionate nature. The sovereign's 'fearsome' punitive power, though a form of coercion that guarantees the practical, actual unity of the commonwealth, is also a form of assistance to individual subjects struggling against their 'pride and passions' to be true to the laws of nature prescribing peace, and as such, it is an instrument of the 'real unity' of the state; we may say that it is elevating, as well as curtailing and controlling. In this section, I also focus upon Hobbes's employment of the philosophical device of a 'state of nature' to elucidate the permanent tension between the natural desire for power and the fear of death, as a result of which it becomes clear that the primary function of the political covenant is to hold this imperious power drive in check. This enables us to see how, once again through the medium of the political covenant, the desire for power-fear of death antithesis of man's 'original' nature ultimately becomes the pride-law antithesis of political experience in civil society. In section five, I then focus more specifically on Hobbes's account of the 'person' of the state and on his attempt (successful in my view) to show that it is neither implausible and counter-intuitive for him to both (i) describe the 'person' of the state as 'artificial', as a creature of the political covenant and as being created or ushered into existence at the 'time' of the political covenant and, at the same time, (ii) to claim that this 'person' is the origin and font of political authority and legitimacy in the commonwealth. I suggest that (i) and (ii) above are in fact quite consistent and that they may be shown to be consistent by demonstrating that Hobbes's 'person' of the state has a respectable lineage in the state of nature in the form of a definite, if embryonic, collective will to peace and concord. However, in this section, I also suggest that as Christians, we are perfectly at liberty to call this 'person' of the state (this 'spirit of natural law' moving in and through a people) the Holy Spirit; when so regarded, as we shall see, this helps us (i) to see the Holy Spirit as 'artificial' in a sense, as a 'creature' of the political covenant and, at the same time, (ii) to claim that the Holy Spirit is the origin and font of political authority and legitimacy in the commonwealth.

The Political Covenant and the Human Predicament

If we are to grasp the nature of the problem to which the political covenant provides a solution, we must begin with Hobbes's conception of human nature and the human predicament. In the *Leviathan* we find individuals who are centres of volition and who act in such a manner as to realise their private ends. Indeed, they not only act, but in principle, they only can act in order to pursue such ends. Hobbes insists that we all act with our own welfare in view, for 'of all voluntary acts, the object is to every man his own good'. Now this clearly is not the human raw material out of which a 'real unity' can be created. An unredeemed, essentially separate, self-focused individual (as yet 'unelevated' by the grace of the law) can only possibly regard the collectivity which the state embodies in an instrumental fashion, to be set up, manipulated, feared, obeyed, or even disobeyed, with his own private ends in view. Motivated by rational fear of a violent death at the hands of his 'fellow' men, this separate individual comes to realise that it is in his best interests to follow the laws of nature prescribing peace but the sheer force of his passions constantly stretches his rational will to breaking point. Hobbes neatly summarises the situation by saying that the laws of nature, which express the rational will to peace, 'are contrary to our natural passions, that carry us to partiality, pride, revenge and the like.[11] Our human passions are so powerful and the light of reason so dim, that we generally succumb to the stronger force of the former.[12]

Each 'natural man', Hobbes maintains, acts to secure his own good, as he perceives it. On the one hand, this is an elementary datum of Hobbes's political theory; yet, on the other, it is the very problem to be overcome, for our ability to discern and judge is unsound. The forceful movement of passion overpowers his rational will and its accompanying 'heat' distorts his judgment with regard to his own best interests. Inevitably, then, the actual will that

---

11. T Hobbes, *Leviathan* in *The English Works of Thomas Hobbes*, Volume 3, edited by W Molesworth (London: J Bohn, 1839), 117.
12. T Hobbes, *De Cive* in *The English Works of Thomas Hobbes*, Volume 2, edited by W Molesworth (London: J. Bohn, 1839), 75.

flows into action, though designed to procure his 'good', must tend to be self-destructive. Both the problem and the task are clear. Hobbes must show how the human will can be so formed as to willingly pursue the path of peace. Obviously, this is a tall order. At first glance, the situation seems somewhat forlorn. The will to peace is genuine, yet frail. It is universal and yet, in its particular manifestations, its clear rationality is obscured by fiery passions. It is the political covenant that makes all the difference. Through its mediation, the precarious will to peace crystallises into a living force in a collectivity with real power and strength to counterbalance the force of our natural passions. There is strength in unity, so that the will to peace at last acquires a real existence, with effective force, in human affairs.

In Hobbes's view it is pride and vainglory which, above all else, distort natural man's understanding of his position in the human universe and leads him to deviate from the 'precepts of nature'; it is the greatest, single obstacle along the pathway of peace. Hobbes's natural man is at once deemed to be vainglorious and proud; the *Leviathan* is 'king of the proud;' and yet pride is adjudged to be 'unnatural' or alien to man's essence. When Hobbes says that reason 'teaches every man to fly a contra-natural dissolution, as the greatest mischief that can arrive to nature', he has pride and vainglory in mind as the root cause of this 'contra-natural dissolution'.[13] (Pride, then, is a universal, yet 'unnatural' characteristic of our humanity, a plague or

---

13. T Hobbes, *De Cive* in *The English Works of Thomas Hobbes*, Volume 2, edited by W Molesworth (London: J Bohn, 1839), vii.

temptation that haunts all of us and which is yet deemed to be 'contra-natural' in so far as 'nature' is associated with the 'fullness' and proper ordering of 'life' in all its forms; vainglory is that which distorts and opposes 'natural existence'. That is the way things are, and the way we each are, by nature. If death is 'that terrible enemy of nature',[14] then assuredly pride is no less of an adversary. In one sense, to accuse natural man of being proud is ridiculous, for one is in fact saying no more than that he is human. An ability to properly appreciate one's strength, position and power *vis-à-vis* others is a virtue *only* in those who are prone to pride. Even the 'fairest conditioned' are not immune to pride, since they too, at times, are more concerned about their honor and less concerned about the precepts of peace than they ought to be. However, what the charge of pride generally contends is that the sinister attraction away from what is really the 'fullness' of nature or the 'truth' of one's natural existence has actually taken firm root in a person's mind or, alternatively, that the enemy, death, has passed through the gateway of a human life and become almost an integral part thereof. In castigating pride, Hobbes was particularly alarmed by those 'fiery spirits' described in *De Cive* who succumbed to its sinister attraction to the greatest degree. He makes it clear that they are not informed by natural law (the precepts of the Father) but wish rather to form and forge a world

---

14. T Hobbes, *Elements of Law* in *The English Works of Thomas Hobbes*, Volume 4, edited by W Molesworth (London: J Bohn, 1839), 83.

which accords with their every wish.[15] The tragic irony is that they have a craving for what they see as the 'fullness of life', but they (mis-)understand this as a 'free' and unrestrained existence. Moreover, their longing for the kind of sovereignty that properly belongs to God and to the political sovereign hopelessly distorts their judgment and gives them an exaggerated view of their ability to arrange the human world in accordance with their own designs.

Hobbes's sovereign power is established primarily to curtail pride and its destructive effects but precisely because he so often lets us know what the sovereign power is directed *against*, it is all too easy to dwell upon its negative import and to overlook the fact that to be against pride and death is to be *for* the law and life that is for a harmonious, natural existence. Hobbes, in fact, construes pride, in an almost Augustinian fashion, as the worm at the core of an originally uncontaminated human nature. To the degree that we are proud and eschew natural equality, 'natural existence' eludes us, the fullness of life intended by the Artificer of Nature lies beyond our grasp, and our passionate nature, which in itself tends to foster human health and happiness, is distorted. Similarly, however, to the degree that the sovereign is successful in curtailing the 'contra-natural' force of pride and in implementing laws which operate as 'hedges', not impeding our journey but enabling us to follow our own path,[16] our

---

15. T Hobbes, *De Cive* in *The English Works of Thomas Hobbes*, Volume 2, edited by W Molesworth (London: J Bohn, 1839),7 .
16. T Hobbes, *Leviathan* in *The English Works of Thomas Hobbes*, Volume 3, edited by W Molesworth (London: J Bohn, 1839), 239–240 .

true, God-ordained nature is allowed to resurface in civil society in a manner that at least resembles its original innocence and its intended wholesomeness.

Natural law is a kind of unchanging redemptive, God-given grace. It is through the laws of nature prescribing the way to peace that 'natural men' find political salvation from their vainglorious ways. They know and accept, and do not make, the laws of nature. Hobbes tells us that they universally acknowledge their general validity and independence of human volition, at least in their cooler moments of deliberation.[17] In contrast, the civil law of the sovereign power is clearly an artificial construct but for Hobbes there is a very intimate link, even a kind of identity, between nature and artifice; indeed, 'art/artifice' is almost a kind of necessary, assuaging expression of 'nature':

> The law of nature, and the civil law, contain each other, and are of equal extent. For the laws of nature . . . in the condition of mere nature . . . are not properly laws, but qualities that dispose men to peace and obedience. When a commonwealth is once settled, then are they actually laws, and not before; as being then the commands of the commonwealth; and therefore also civil laws: for it is the sovereign power that obliges men to obey them . . . Civil, and natural law are not differ-

---

17. T Hobbes, *De Cive* in *The English Works of Thomas Hobbes*, Volume 2, edited by W Moles worth, (London: J. Bohn, 1839), 44.

ent kinds, but different parts of law; whereof one part being written is called civil, the other unwritten, natural.[18]

If we ask then 'What is the role of human art/artifice/civil law in relation to natural law/justice?' Hobbes offers a series of interlocking responses which together constitute a God-ordained movement in and towards the realisation of our humanity in and through the state ('person' of the state/Spirit). Firstly, the universal yet frail desire for peace (embryonic grace) acquires a high degree of efficacy when the war-weary warriors of the state of nature come together and collectively express their will to peace (public/collective grace) and when it is bolstered by the sovereign's law and power of punishment (law as facilitating/enabling grace). Secondly, the unwritten, privately interpreted laws of nature (the 'articles of peace') now acquire a publicly recognisable form and are clearly written and promulgated (public grace). Thirdly, whilst it is perfectly correct to regard the artifice of civil law, made possible by the political covenant, as a 'crystallisation' of natural law (dynamic grace), in the sense that the desire for peace crystallises into a definitive, institutional form, yet at the same time, 'art' or the civil law, serves thereafter as the criterion of natural justice. This is Hobbes's public and artificial solution to the problem posed by the variety of conflicting interpretations of the laws of nature made by individual men in the natural condition.

---

18. T Hobbes, *Leviathan* in *The English Works of Thomas Hobbes*, Volume 3, edited by W Molesworth (London: J Bohn, 1839), 185.

In the circumstances of civil society, it is human art that now determines and precisely defines what is, and is not, in accord with natural law/justice; and yet, at the same time, it is natural law that legitimises the whole artificial system of rules governing civil society, for it is the third law of nature forbidding violation of faith which obliges men to obey the civil laws of the sovereign, and, indeed, to regard them as the public expression of the laws of nature to which they are each privately bound. Thus, as Hobbes says, natural and civil law 'contain each other and are of equal extent'. Those equipped with the power and authority to legislate are simultaneously 'declarers' and 'also makers of the justice and injustice of actions'.[19] In assessing the implications (or, perhaps 'intimations') of the eternal laws of nature for the subjects of his kingdom in time, and in exercising his human powers of discretion to make enactments which take into account particular circumstances, the sovereign both declares what is in accord with natural law and, at the same time, makes the civil law. Hobbes concedes that the *laws* of nature were scarcely recognisable as such in the state of nature (the natural condition or the war of all against all) and that their status as laws is only finally recognised by a 'retrospective' judgment made from the vantage point of civil society; that is, natural law only comes clearly into focus for those who have experienced, and are already familiar with, natural law as publicly interpreted and enforced. Prior to the establishment of the commonwealth, the laws

---

19. T Hobbes, *Leviathan* in *The English Works of Thomas Hobbes*, Volume 3, edited by W Molesworth (London: J Bohn, 1839), 386.

of nature are mainly 'known' as dispositions to peace. It is only when natural law is expressed in a civil form and equipped with the power of the sword that individuals feel the full weight of its moral and 'physical' presence in a way that would be impossible outside of civil society. For Hobbes, 'nature' is most transparent through 'the law as grace', but this grace also exposes, in true Pauline fashion, the full force of the 'contra-natural', anti-life, force of sin and pride (the ferocity of opposition).

The political covenant is a collectivisation and unification of a vast number of frail rational wills (as the frontispiece of the *Leviathan* aptly illustrates); unless they so unite into a single will, they cannot become a living force. The covenant is a promise to engage in a collective endeavour to undermine the power of human pride and partisanship and it is only for those who have reached a just and proper estimate of the limits of their own powers; or, to put the matter differently, it is for those who acknowledge their need to be redeemed from themselves, from their own captivity to sin. The 'graced' initiates who voluntarily enter political society through the medium of common grace (the political covenant) commit themselves to an ongoing process of collective self-control and 'mutual edification' (ascending grace). They then experience in an ongoing way the benign, uplifting influence of the collectivised rational will enforced through the firm decrees of the sovereign power (descending grace). 'Ascending grace' thus opens the channels for sinful men seeking peace and concord (*justus et peccator*) to receive 'descending grace'. Hobbes's citizens look upward, for stretching downward into their souls they find the golden cord of divinely ordained sovereignty and justice that guarantees peace, rather than sideways, where they still experience the ferocious force of their own sin, pride and partisanship.

According to Hobbes, 'the final cause, end, or design of men who naturally love liberty, and dominion over others, in the introduction of that restraint upon themselves, in which we see them live in commonwealths, is the foresight of their own preservation, and of a more contented life thereby'.[20] This overarching end or design is constantly present but, as we saw earlier, it assumes different forms and appears under different guises (as the rational desire for preservation, as the maxims of peace, as God's voice speaking through natural law, as the civil law of a duly constituted sovereign). It is, then, reasonable to speak of the 'spirit' of the law (or the Spirit that breathes though the law, natural or civil) as *at all times* requiring peace or at least the maintenance and cultivation of a favourable disposition towards peace under the unfavourable conditions prevalent in the state of nature. However, in view of the precarious nature of the rational will to peace and its struggle for dominion over 'pride and the other passions', Hobbes points out that the precepts of nature are also *commanded* by God and that when thus endowed with a formal character (as God's commands), they are obligatory in the full sense. In this way, the promptings of God (the Spirit) in each human heart correspond to and

---

20. T Hobbes, Leviathan in *The English Works of Thomas Hobbes*, Volume 3, edited by W Molesworth (London: J Bohn, 1839), 117.

complement the expressed will of God (the Father) for all of humanity.

Essence and Existence: Sovereignty and the Sovereign Power

In this section, I look at how Hobbes deals with the problem of a political sovereign who not only fails to secure peace but actually acts in such a way as to undermine the goal of peace, for in such a case the political sovereign representing God (the Father and ultimate author of natural law) is in direct conflict with God (the Spirit of natural law) and with the state (the 'person' of the state) that he is supposed to personify. Hobbes deals with this problem by distinguishing between the idea of sovereignty (its essence) and the actual sovereign power (its existence), between the 'person' of the state and the concrete temporal representative thereof, and between the ethical unity of the state and its visible presence or public face in the commonwealth. We will see that Hobbes regards the political sovereign as a 'mortal god', as a kind of link or mid-way point between eternity and time, between God and ordinary mortals, between the 'person' of the state whom he represents and the subjects of the commonwealth whose ordinary (fallen) humanity he shares.

Hobbes describes the power and dignity of the sovereign in awesome, almost mystical terms. (The imagery he employs sounds faintly ridiculous when we try to envisage the sovereign as an assembly of representatives and this was probably quite intentional on Hobbes's part.) He is seated on a throne of majesty, well above even those of his subjects who might claim to shine in their own right.

> For in the sovereignty is the fountain of honor. The dignities of lord, earl, duke and prince are his creatures. As in the presence of the master, the servants are equal, and without any honor at all; so are the subjects, in the presence of the sovereign. And though they shine some more, some less, when they are out of his sights; yet in his presence, they shine no more than the stars in the presence of the sun.[21]

It would not then be an exaggeration to say that the majesty of the bearer of sovereign power almost fades into transcendence. The sovereign is the 'word made flesh' who dwells among us as a mortal god and as a visible sign of the immortal God. He is also the subjects' own collective moral will to peace and concord objectified and embodied in a visible political form. His power not only rests upon but, in a sense, actually *is* the subjects' collectivised conscience, their sense of obligation under the laws of nature prescribing peace. However, what an individual experiences in the loneliness of the state of nature as a general desire for peace (the voice of God, the Spirit speaking privately, albeit obscurely and indirectly) is now experienced directly and unambiguously as the command of the sovereign (the voice of God, the Father,

---

21. T Hobbes, *Leviathan* in *The English Works of Thomas Hobbes*, Volume 3, edited by W Molesworth (London: J Bohn, 1839), 128.

speaking publicly and authoritatively through the civil law of his mortal God). It is as if God was miraculously made visible and certainly the imagery Hobbes employs, as we have just seen, suggests nothing less. Then quite suddenly, this real unity seems to vanish. At one point in the *Leviathan* we find sovereign and subject in conversation with each other, just like a man discussing a point with a friend, each putting his case to the other in reasonable and persuasive terms. Somehow, a cloud passes over the sun; the individual stars are seen again and a sort of dialogue takes place. It seems that the legitimate claims of 'diversity' may pose a challenge to the sovereignty of 'unity'. The subject forcefully reminds the sovereign that, whatever the precise terms of the political covenant, its end is peace and protection, and Hobbes even talks of a liberty to refuse to obey the sovereign's command, if the latter should exceed his brief.

> No man is bound by the words themselves, either to kill himself, or any other man; and consequently, that the obligation a man may sometimes have, upon the command of the sovereign to execute any dangerous, or dishonorable office, dependeth not on the words of our submission; but on the intention; which is to be understood by the end thereof. When therefore our refusal to obey, frustrates the end for which the sovereignty was ordained,

then there is no liberty to refuse; otherwise there is.[22]

However, this is not a let-out clause for any truculent readers of the *Leviathan* with a puritan caste of mind. It is not the old Adam who speaks here but the new, and he speaks not against but for the real ethical unity of the state.

In the *Leviathan*, the essence of the commonwealth, the font of its unity, is the *intencio populi*, their unity of intent. The common desire for peace is what the sovereign power represents, while in turn being restricted by it, for it sets the boundaries within which legitimate authority may be exercised. The sovereign both embodies the desire for peace and has the practical task of securing it. His subjects play their part by promising not to interfere with his natural liberty, a promise which is almost, but not quite, unconditional. As the representative of the collective desire for peace, as the visible presence of the invisible essence of the commonwealth and as the sign and seal of its real unity, the sovereign power is *always* beyond criticism because it politically expresses and represents the spirit of God's natural law. It is *this* aspect of the sovereign power that shines like the sun. His reputation, or lack of it, in practical affairs does not impinge at all upon his majesty. Unlike Machiavelli's Prince, the dignity of Hobbes's sovereign does not depend on what he does or fails to do. His majesty would remain without blemish even after we had

---

22. T Hobbes, *Leviathan* in *The English Works of Thomas Hobbes*, Volume 3, edited by W Molesworth (London: J Bohn, 1839), 204–205.

drawn up a lengthy catalogue of his misdeeds and this is so simply by virtue of what he *represents*, namely the soul of the commonwealth. Yet what he *does* as a natural person may threaten to tarnish the soul of the subject. As a natural person, the sovereign has a job to do and he may do it either well or badly. He may even be thoroughly corrupt and irresponsible. However, Hobbes insists that the terms of the political covenant are such that the sovereign cannot be accused of injustice by his subjects. Moreover, if the sovereign behaves iniquitously, breaching the laws of nature in all sorts of ways, this must be borne in silence by his subjects and treated as a private affair between the mortal and immortal God. The silence may only be broken when the sovereign (the mortal God) acts in such a way as to directly frustrate the end of the covenant (the purpose of the immortal God) and in this eventuality a subject may refuse to obey without injustice. The essence of sovereignty then—the *intencio populi* , the collective will to peace and concord, the 'person' of the state—is one thing, but its existence, in the form of a natural person or persons (broadly, in the form of a 'government'), is quite another. In the case of a mortal God, the two do not necessarily coincide; indeed Hobbes squarely acknowledges the possibility that 'existence' (government) may be in open revolt against 'essence' (the state).

When confronted by a political sovereign who issues a reprehensible command, the only possible response of a 'civilised' citizen is the Socratic one of perfect respect combined with perfect contempt, namely passive disobedience. The element of passivity accords to the sovereign the perfect respect which is his due as God's representative (the 'person' of the state), while disobedience is the only course of action which accords with his own self-respect. One of the most fascinating episodes of the *Leviathan* is the encounter between the individual, who has been civilised by the grace of the law and in whom the desire for peace and concord is a real and living force, and the natural person of the sovereign who is untouched by the grace of the law and who, whilst representing that force, may nevertheless be a perfect scoundrel. Ideally, however, the sovereign power that is immediately operative in the political world (broadly speaking, the 'government') will be the mediating instrument of what is truly and finally sovereign, that is, the *intencio populi*, the ethical unity of the state, the spirit of natural law, the 'person' of the state, the will of the Author of nature or, in a word, God. Hobbes does his best to ensure that this is the case by insisting, in the manner of Reinhold Niebuhr, that the sovereign, as well as instilling fear in his subjects, must also instill in them a deeper appreciation of the point and purpose of the law; in this way, their 'naked' fear will become a 'reverent' fear. The sovereign's task, on the one hand, is to erect 'hedges of fear' that will help his subjects to restrain their wayward ways and avoid civil strife'; that is their immediate point but, on the other hand, he will also speak more gently to them when they are 'in a quiet mind' and teach them that the ultimate point of these 'hedges of fear' is to achieve peace, not just in the sense of 'absence of strife' but in the sense of 'peace and concord', of a 'real unity' between them,. The way in which the law of God (the Father) facilitates, enables and elicits the emergence of what Reinhold Niebuhr calls the 'spirit of brotherhood' (a movement of the Spirit) or the way in which, in more specifically Christian terms, the 'descending' common grace of the Father (the Author of the law in our hearts that ultimately becomes the civil law) meets and greets the 'ascending' common grace of the Spirit of Life in us (the movement of 'real unity' engendered in us), is vividly and precisely expressed when Hobbes asks the question 'What happens to the pravity of mankind in civil society?'

Before and After (the Political Covenant)

To this question Hobbes does not provide us with a straightforward response but points instead to the complexity of the issue as seen from different perspectives. In effect, the answer depends on who is asking the question and with what end in view. We find, for example, that Hobbes speaks most disrespectfully about the masses of humanity on those occasions when he is considering the problem of order from the point of view of a sovereign concerned with law enforcement. As he sets about his task, the sovereign should treat the well known 'pravity of mankind' as an elementary datum,[23] with the result that 'the passion to be reckoned upon is fear.[24] From this perspective, and given the sovereign's primarily practical concerns, the unity of the state (in the sense of the 'absence

---

23. T Hobbes, *De Cive* in *The English Work of Thomas Hobbes*, Volume 2, edited by W Molesworth (London: J Bohn, 1839), 75.
24. T Hobbes, *Leviathan* in *The English Works of Thomas Hobbes*, Volume 3, edited by W Molesworth (London: J Bohn, 1839), 99.

of discord') will persist only so long as the sovereign can wield sufficient countervailing power against the force of those natural passions which lead men to partiality, pride and revenge. Man's 'well-known pravity' is not abolished, but is simply contained in civil society. The unity achieved, in so far as it is simply engineered by superior force, is hardly what we would call a 'real unity'. However, Hobbes's famous 'the passion to be reckoned upon is fear' is, as we have seen, a positional judgment; it is an operational principle that works well in the day-to-day business of sovereignty but it is not Hobbes's final word on the matter, nor even the most important principle that the sovereign should take into account. From the perspective of the individual subject (which a wise sovereign will take into account), rational will—or a heartfelt desire for peace and concord rather than a fear-inspired desire to avoid civil strife and a violent death—emerges into view in civil society as a force that can at least attempt a proper ordering of natural impulse. The citizens do not simply regard their sovereign as an object of fear and awe. They know and understand, or at least they are beginning to know and understand, the laws of nature.

> It is true, that hope, fear, anger, ambition, covetousness, vainglory, and other perturbations of the mind, do hinder a man, so as he cannot attain to the knowledge of these laws whilst those passions prevail in him; but there is no man who is not sometimes in a quiet mind.[25]

---

25. T Hobbes, *De Cive* in *The English Works of Thomas Hobbes*, Volume 2,

Moreover, they understand the rationale of sovereignty, for they can appreciate, at least in their cooler moments of deliberation, that the sovereign, in forcing them to obey his commands, is doing something for them which they are incapable of doing for themselves. He is keeping the peace, and in doing so, he is promoting the true, long-term interests of everyone. Hobbes also urges the sovereign to teach his subjects the basis of his power lest they be misinformed but this would quite evidently be a superfluous exercise if the sovereign's power depended entirely on the fear and awe of his subjects. In his enumeration of the duties of the 'Sovereign Representative' in the *Leviathan*, Hobbes says that it is against his duty 'to let the people be misinformed of the grounds and reasons of those his essential Rights' and in *Behemoth* we are told that 'the power of the mighty hath no foundation but in the opinion and belief of the people'.[26] However important as a motive for the sovereign's subjects, fear is in itself insufficient to explain their allegiance to the state. Hobbes tells us that this fear must be mingled with a kind of reverential respect, a recognition that the power of the sovereign is legitimately exercised because it rests on the authority of the divinely ordained laws of nature and because it is drawing them into the fuller life of the Spirit, into the real unity of the commonwealth.

What unites subjects to their sovereign is their com-

---

edited by W Molesworth (London: J Bohn, 1839), 44.
26. T Hobbes, *Behemot* in *The English Works of Thomas Hobbes*, Volume 6, edited by W Molesworth (London: J Bohn, 1839), 184.

mon desire to secure peace and this unity will persist so long as the rationale of sovereignty is alive and well in the minds of individual subjects. It is important that the sovereign's subjects continue to acknowledge that the sovereign power is doing for them what they cannot do for themselves and that the public sword, even when it is wielded against them, is nevertheless the instrument of their own earlier resolve. Only if that resolve had entirely melted away would an individual experience law and punishment (ultimately, we need to remember God's law and punishment as well) as a *wholly* external or alien force, as an outright act of hostility. Such a person would in effect be in the state of nature *vis-à-vis* the sovereign power, and willfully beyond the reach of the Father's 'descending' grace, whereas an individual who breaches the civil law in a moment of passion would not. The sovereign power therefore does not simply exist as an external force which effectively counteracts the powerful thrust of our passionate and wayward nature; it actually participates in and bolsters our inner, moral life and elicits within us a movement of the Spirit, a desire within us for 'real unity'. As Hobbes pointedly asks, 'if men know not their duty, what is there that can force them to obey the laws?'[27]

As commentators generally agree, Hobbes employs the 'state of nature' as a useful philosophical fiction. However, there is also a sense in which the 'time' dimension of Hobbes's natural condition is real rather than fictional, an account of actual events and not just a tool of analysis, and this is the sense in which it reflects Hobbes's own experi-

---

27. *Ibid*, 237.

ence. In this sense, it is an invitation to participate in the 'inner' time of Hobbes's private universe. When Hobbes asks us to consider men as if newly sprung from the earth in a pre-political 'natural condition, he stipulates that this can only be done by each of us reading ourselves introspectively; each of us must embark on our own individual 'journey of grace'. Hobbes takes the first step himself and then asks the reader 'only to consider, if he also finds not the same in himself'. Just as our knowledge of the world begins with our sensations, which beget movements in the brain, called ideas, so too political science, in Hobbes's experience at least, begins with the direct apprehension of brute, natural facts upon which degrees of control are then successively imposed. The first imposition is the law of nature, as the expression of the desire for peace; the second is the more effective imposition of the sovereign's civil law. The second imposition brings us right out of the realm of the natural condition but then the end point of the inner time of Hobbes's experience is the present under a sovereign under God. This order of causes or series of 'begettings' is both sequential and hierarchical. The universal desire for power and precedence that plagues us all engenders conflict among us and begets fear of each other, which begets the desire for order, but the power drive in us does not then cease to be relevant. It is not like one billiard ball that stops once it has imparted movement to another. What the desire for power begets is an ascending spiral of ordering forces with higher degrees of effectiveness at each stage. Anarchic power-seeking by free individuals in the state of nature begets the fearful quest for its own restraint but order, once established, then descends upon its maker as a restraining force, like soldiers returning with greater strength to besiege a city from which they have been evicted. Each stage of the ascent from this elementary impulse has as its goal a descent upon it with real effectiveness and this is finally achieved by the collectivisation of fear under a sovereign. Only then have individuals the strength to return to besiege their own city where the anarchic power drive reigns; only then can the power of sin be effectively restrained. (We may think here of the prodigal son wanting to fashion a world in which he has the power to indulge his wishes and whims, realising the futility of it all as he faces near-starvation and fears becoming the mere instrument of others, and then beginning to be sorry and seeking the love and forgiveness—and, I suspect too, the benign, strong restraint, now welcome and appreciated—of the Father.) Thus, the end point of this spiraling hierarchy is the 'full reality' of the ethical unity of the state, for this unity is the 'still point' of the entire process, its origin as an incipient desire for peace in the state of nature and its end as the full-blown collective will to peace institutionally reinforced by the sovereign power. However, its end point (or 'still point') is also God, in so far as fallen human nature requires the full force of the authoritative commands of the divine author of the laws of nature in order to emerge from the private, desire-driven mire of the state of nature into redemptive socio-political life, and in so far as these laws of nature, or precepts of peace, and the 'fullness of being' they promise, are a kind of point at which the divine and human spirit converge.

In essence, Hobbes's account of the natural condition is his experience of self and others laid bare and as such, it is absolute and immune to criticism. What the account claims is not so much propositional truth as a clear representation of his experience. In short, he claims to be authentic; he is being true to his own self and he believes that he cannot then be false to any man, but he invites his readers to verify or 'authenticate' his account by a ruthlessly honest probing of their own inner world. There, he claims, we find an everlasting tension between the power drive and fear, but in his natural condition, he lets this drive run amok as a way of expressing what he felt in his own experience as its awesome anarchic potential. This drive, and the passions generally, are constantly in opposition to the laws of nature,[28] and Hobbes uses the term *pride* to refer to this general oppositional character. Thus, when employed in this sense, all men are proud; *Leviathan* is 'king of the proud',[29] and it is man's 'pride and other passions' which government subdues.[30] Pride, in this sense, is a general straining against the ethical leash; it refers to the force that ethics encounters in its efforts to order wayward impulses. Hobbes's pride is, in effect, very close in meaning to the Pauline 'flesh'. It also encompasses the general human desire for non-interference, for the non-interrupted use of our power, the enduring and rebellious wish of men who 'naturally love liberty' to be

---

28. T Hobbes, *Leviathan* in *The English Works of Thomas Hobbes*, Volume 3, edited by W Molesworth (London: J. Bohn, 1839), 117.
29. *Ibid*, 221.
30. *Ibid*.

left alone and to tell both the mortal God and the immortal God to mind their own business. In short, it is a lack of 'humility, and patience, to suffer the rude and cumbersome points of their present greatness to be taken off'.[31] Thus, the desire for power-fear of death antithesis of original nature, which generates ethics, then becomes the pride-law antithesis of political experience in civil society but in the case of the latter, there has been a very definite shift in the balance of power in favour of law. This may be mainly due to the terror of the sovereign's punishments but it is also due to the 'grace of law', to our enhanced ability to order our actions in accordance with the laws of nature that lead us to the kingdom and that draw us away from the separate paths along which passion drives us and into the 'real unity' of the state and of the Spirit.

Hobbes and the 'Person' of the State

Hobbes, as we have seen, theorized on the 'person' of the state in a very insightful manner and regarded it as a notion that was indispensable to a true science of politics, and yet this notion, to which Hobbes assigned such crucial importance, has all but disappeared from the conceptual armoury of contemporary political science. Does the disappearance of this notion represent an analytic loss or gain for political philosophy? This is a question that Quentin Skinner posed in a stark, direct and challenging fashion during the course of a public lecture on Hobbes

---

31. *Ibid.*

delivered in Adelaide in 1988. My own response then was, and still remains, that our political language (and our ethico-theological language) has indeed been impoverished by the 'loss' of this notion in current speculations on the nature and meaning of the 'political'. Indeed, I would go as far as to suggest that Hobbes's conception of a 'person' of the state or of a unifying 'public will' is actually implicit in, and is a crucial presupposition of, political experience *per se* and that the manner in which Hobbes tackles the problems associated with this notion helps us to gain a deeper appreciation of what is meant by, and what is involved in, our common membership of a political community or state. My main concern in this section is to clarify this notion as it appears in Hobbes's work and to show that what may appear to be the key problem with Hobbes's theorising on this notion (and, by implication, with theorising on this notion in general) is not a problem at all. This 'problem' or difficulty may be briefly stated as follows.

It seems implausible and counter-intuitive for Hobbes to both (i) describe the 'person' of the state as 'artificial', as a creature of the political covenant and as being created or ushered into existence at the 'time' of the political covenant and, at the same time, (ii) to claim that this 'person' is the origin and font of political authority and legitimacy in the commonwealth. We may further highlight the extent of the problem facing Hobbes by posing the following question. Is the 'person' of the state *our* creation or is it rather the 'collectivised civility' of our life as citizens living together in a commonwealth, a 'collective will to peace' that can be characterised as a kind of 'God-like person' that acts on the core of our being or perhaps even *is* the core of our being? I will suggest that (i) and (ii) above are in fact quite consistent and that they may be shown to be consistent by demonstrating that Hobbes's 'person' of the state has a respectable lineage in the state of nature in the form of a definite, if embryonic, collective will to peace and concord.

In the earlier sections we noted that men's common desire for peace and concord, which finds expression in the laws of nature or 'maxims of peace', undergoes successive transformations whilst remaining in essence the same. At the 'mystical' moment of the political covenant, their desire becomes transformed by a lightning flash of universal consent into the 'person' of the state, that is, into 'a real unity of them all in *one and the same person* made by covenant of every man with every man'.[32] There is, then, a sense of the 'person' of the state being ushered into existence by the political covenant and a sense of the 'always already' existence of the state, and, likewise, a sense of the 'newness' (a fresh and definite temporality) of civil law and the 'oldness' (eternity) of natural law. The natural law prescribing peace is to civil law as the universal, ethically significant desire for peace is to the 'person' of the state, for just as the civil law is eminently natural, that is, 'nature fulfilled' or 'nature in another guise', so too the 'person' of the state is the perfect expression of the desire for peace, its fulfilment and its presence in a civil guise.

---

32. T Hobbes, *Leviathan* in *The English Works of Thomas Hobbes*, Volume 3, edited by W Molesworth (London: J Bohn, 1839), 158.

An analysis of the 'common desire for peace'/'person' of the state' relation in Hobbes's work shows that it is neither implausible nor counter-intuitive (i) to describe the 'person' of the state as 'artificial', as a creature of the political covenant and as being created or ushered into existence at the 'time' of the political covenant and, at the same time, (ii) to claim that this 'person' is the origin and font of political authority and legitimacy in the commonwealth. There is a useful and elucidating sense in which the 'person' of the state is the creation of free individuals, which complements its sense as the 'collectivised civility' of citizens living together in a commonwealth, their 'collective will to peace', for just as the civil law has a respectable and intelligible lineage in a pre-civil natural condition governed only by natural law, so too the 'person' of the state has an intelligible origin and a kind of embryonic existence in the state of nature in the form of the collective will to peace. Likewise, however, when we as Christians identify this 'person' of the state by its proper name (simply, the Holy Spirit, or the Holy Spirit in our political world, or the angelic presence of the Spirit in our 'political' midst), Hobbes helps us (i) to understand how the Holy Spirit is a 'creature' of the political covenant in the sense that this covenant 'ushers' the Spirit into a fuller existence in us and, at the same time, helps us (ii) to see more clearly that the Holy Spirit is the origin and font of political authority and legitimacy in the commonwealth. All of this needs to be borne in mind as we now proceed to analyze a number of important points raised by Skinner in his recent work on Hobbes and the 'person' of the state.

Skinner points out that Hobbes's entire line of thought on persons, representatives and authority is vulnerable—or has at least been thought to be vulnerable—to a knockdown argument raised by Joel Feinberg.[33] The latter, when considering Hobbes's example of a master who commands his servant to give money to a stranger, quite correctly observes that for Hobbes the act of payment, though performed by the servant, must nevertheless be attributed to the master. However, Feinberg takes the view that it is misleading to overlook the plain fact that the master did not act at all and that we should rather say that his servant acted for him. There is no doubt that (i) the plain facts of the case in question are indeed as Feinberg states and that (ii) these can be legitimately (or not incorrectly) described by saying 'The servant acted on his master's behalf'. However, to claim, as Feinberg appears to do, that this is the *only* way of articulating, and fully conveying the truth of, these plain facts, is by no means justified; indeed, it leads to a restrictive and quite unnecessary impoverishment of our language, for there are other concepts and categories available to us—those for example provided by Hobbes—which enable us to depict other more nuanced and subtle, but very real and important, features of the case in question.

What is misleading in Feinberg's account is his assumption that there is a single, unambiguous and discrete actor/agent of every action and that given that this is so, we can make a clear distinction between the question of

---

33. J Feinberg, *Doing and Deserving: Essays in the Theory of Responsibility* (Princeteon: Princeton University Press), 227.

agency (who did the action?) and the question of authority (who authorised the action?). He seems to suggest that only what we might call 'material' agency is real agency, that is, that the servant is to be considered the exclusive agent of action in this case because the payment was carried out by the movements of his arms and legs and whatever other material processes were involved in the payment. Following this line of thought, it is (or would be deemed to be) proper to attribute actions only to (human) servants or representatives, and to assign authority only to masters, 'authorisers' or God. What we are forbidden to say—and this seems to be a pointless, unnecessary and impoverishing restriction—is that the master acted *through* or by means of the servant or that while the acts of payment may be initially, materially or actually attributed to the servant, there is nevertheless a legitimate and true sense in which these acts are ultimately, genuinely or really attributable to the master; nor are we allowed to say, in the case of a good and dutiful master acting in accordance with God's will, that there is a legitimate and true sense in which this master's acts are ultimately, genuinely or really attributable to God as well. What we are also, of course, forbidden to say on Feinberg's account—which is precisely what we want, with Hobbes, to say—is that there is a legitimate and true sense in which the acts of Hobbes's sovereign representative are ultimately, genuinely or really attributable to the 'person' of the state, the final source of their authority.

Skinner is obviously concerned by Feinberg's objection and considers various possible retorts but his final word on the matter is that whilst Hobbes undeniably 'likes to speak of attributed actions as if they are genuine instances of action', nevertheless it is sufficient for his purposes to make the relatively non-controversial claim that:

> when someone acts as an accredited representative, the person being represented must 'own' the consequences of the action as if they had performed it themselves. The action counts as theirs, and is called their action, not because they actually perform it, but because they are under an obligation to take responsibility for its occurrence.[34]

Thus whilst Hobbes might *like* to speak of attributed actions as genuine instances of action, yet to be safe from Feinberg's objection, it would be safer and more prudent not to do so and to restrict himself instead to the language of ownership and authorisation. Surely at this point Skinner concedes far too much ground to cope with Feinberg's objection and underestimates the damage done to the coherence of Hobbes's theory by such a concession. It is quite true, as Skinner asserts, that Hobbes's claim about 'ownership' is sufficient for the purpose of guaranteeing that the subjects of a commonwealth must acknowledge as their own the acts of their sovereign representative since they have formally conferred legitimacy and authority on the sovereign and his public deeds *via* the terms of the political covenant, but it is not, I wish to suggest, sufficient

---

34. Q Skinner, 'Hobbes and the Purely Artificial 'person' of the state', in *The Journal of Political Philosophy*, VII/1 (1999): 10.

to guarantee the *full* legitimacy and authority of the sovereign's acts, for the sovereign *also* exercises legitimate authority as the medium or 'bearer' of the divine laws of nature prescribing peace and as (though this comes close to saying the same thing) the representative medium of the 'person' of the state.

It is important to recollect that the whole point and purpose of the political covenant is to 'materialise' the collective will to peace, that the sovereign/subject relation comes into being to realise this will and that there is an important sense in which this collective will (that is, the 'real unity' of the commonwealth or the 'person' of the state) authorises and legitimates the deeds of the sovereign. Indeed one could even say, I believe, that the largely 'formal' process of authorisation entailed by the political covenant (ultimately initiated by the Father as the Author of natural law) takes place in order to breathe life into a more 'substantive' sense of authorisation, that is, of the sovereign representative by the 'person' of the state/ collective will to peace/real unity of the commonwealth/ Holy Spirit. If the sovereign's 'substantive' authority derives from the latter and from his role as its representative medium, then it is important (i) that the acts of the sovereign be attributed to this 'person' of the state—who, as a non-natural person cannot 'own' them in the way that a natural person can, so that Hobbes cannot employ 'ownership' in this regard simply and unguardedly, that is, without important qualifications—and (ii) that they be regarded as genuine instances of action by the 'person' of the state when they serve the ends of peace. The whole point and purpose of the device of representation is to provide a means of expressing (representing) in the significant world of human interaction a real/true interest (most importantly in the present context, the interest of God and humanity in peace and concord) that can gain expression in no other way. A real or true interest that is communicated, and *only* can be communicated, by means of an authorised actor is said by Hobbes to be 'represented by fiction' (fictitious representation) but the manner of its communication or conveyance does not detract in the least either from the truth, reality or genuineness of the interest being conveyed or from the effectiveness of its actions and consequences in the real world.

If Hobbes is to be properly defended against Feinberg's objection, I would suggest that it can only be by justifying Hobbes's endorsement of a 'shared agency' or 'multiple agency' view of human acts, for Hobbes insists that in every political act of the sovereign there are at least four agents or 'subjects' involved, that is, (i) the sovereign who acts representatively, (ii) his subjects who authorise his actions, (iii) the 'person' of the state as a collective person who acts through the sovereign in his pursuit of peace, and (iv) God (the Father), who authorises the laws of nature implanted in men's hearts and whose Spirit 'moves' them towards peace. It would surely be a mistake to regard one type of agency or subjectivity, even God's, as 'alone real' and to thereby assign a merely derivative ('not really real') status to the other types. If God is a 'macro-Subject who absorbs into Himself every form of subjectivity, He presumably cannot be the God of the Bible who addresses human subjects with serious intent as in *some* sense 'other' and asks them to 'Stand up man so that I might speak with you' (Ezekiel 2:1). The Bible is a real form of communication between God and persons, that is, between real, if distinct, kinds of subjectivity.

Skinner holds[35] that the terminology Hobbes employed in speaking about representation was taken from the theatre rather than covenanting theology[36] and quotes the following passage from Hobbes's *De Homine*:

> For it was understood in the theatre that not the player himself but someone else was speaking, for example Agamemnon, namely when the player, putting on the fictitious mask of Agamemnon, was for the time being Agamemnon. At a later stage, however, this was understood to be so even in the absence of the fictitious mask, namely when the actor declared publicly which person he was going to play.[37]

Hobbes clearly felt that theatrical representation was in many respects analogous to other kinds of representation such as the fictitious representation of children, madmen or churches.[38] The strength of the analogy is that it high-

---

35. *Ibid*, 6.
36. Skinner is no doubt correct in his assertion, although Pauline expressions such as 'putting on Christ' (Romans 13:14) and 'no longer I but Christ who lives in me' (Galatians 2;20) clearly have a strong 'theatrical' ring about them.
37. *Ibid*, 15.
38. T Hobbes, *Leviathan* in *The English Works of Thomas Hobbes*, Volume 3, edited by W Molesworth (London: J Bohn, 1839), 146.

lights the manner in which this representative stratagem achieves representation for the otherwise unrepresentable, the manner in which for example a rector represents his church by (re-) presenting himself as the public and visible mask or 'face' of its otherwise invisible and unrepresentable interests or, for that matter, the way in which Jesus represents or is the visible face of, the 'interest in humanity' of the invisible God. However, whilst the theatrical metaphor captures very well the way in which the Spirit 'takes shape' in the specific, peace-directed acts of the political sovereign, (the Spirit's 'substantive' authorisation of the political realm through representation by fiction), it misses entirely the more formal aspect of Hobbes's theory (the 'formal' authorisation of the political realm that ultimately stems from the law of the Father). Still, the metaphor on the whole is extremely valuable and illuminating, and Skinner, I believe, is entirely right to defend Hobbes against Pitkin's charge that it is inappropriate and distinctly unhelpful. Pitkin points out, quite correctly, that for Hobbes it is a strict (formal) requirement of a valid act of representation that there must be some collectivity or natural person in possession of the right to authorise it and that this requirement simply makes no sense in the case of actors in a play.[39] But this, surely, is simply to point out that the theatrical analogy elucidates only substantive, and not formal, authorisation of the political realm, and to highlight a respect in which Hobbes's account of fictitious representation for legal and political purposes

---

39. HF Pitkin, *The Concept of Representation* (Berkeley: University of California Press, 1967), 25.

(the formal conditions of its operation) is *not* analogous to theatrical representation. Thus Pitkin simply highlights what the theatrical model 'fails' to illuminate—I say 'fails' since Hobbes, surely, never intended the analogy to illuminate the formal requirements of representation by fiction—and neglects to acknowledge what it illuminates very well, namely the *point* of this representative strategy, which is to represent otherwise unrepresentable interests and, in particular and most importantly, our collective interest in peace and security.

As a concluding remark, I would like to briefly point out the contemporary relevance of Hobbes's theorising on the 'person' of the state. In the last three decades or so, we have clearly traveled far and fast from what we might call the 'substantive state', that is, from a legal and political world in which the state as a kind of party or person (our 'best selves' personified) had a direct interest in the wellbeing of marriage, the family and society[40] to a legal and political world in which the current 'procedural state'[41] has almost ceased to be regarded as the authoritative 'bearer' of the life and common purpose of organised society. We have largely abandoned, or at least we are presently in danger of abandoning, a substantive state which, whilst exhibiting a strict impartiality in its role as enforcer of justice (that is, in its dealings with individuals as distinct legal persons), does not eschew its crucial

---

40. BT Trainor, *Gender, the Marriage Contract and the State: The Role of Promise Keeping in the Conjugal Body Politic* (Quebec: World Heritage Press, 1998), 57–81.
41. J Sacks, The *Politics of Hope* (London: Johnathon Cape, 1997), 192.

role as the representative or 'bearer' of the public interest and as the forceful and very 'partial' voice of those least capable of representing their own interests (children, the poor, etc). However, the 'substantive state' that we are in danger of losing, Hobbes's 'person' of the state can help us to retrieve. It is important to note at this point that Hobbes's collectivisation and personalisation of the universal desire for peace and concord, and of civility in general, is not an arbitrary or whimsical 'move' on his part but a way of recognising that a common moral purpose or unifying will informs our lives as citizens. Whilst we participate as citizens/subjects in the formation of this shared moral purpose or collective will, we are also, as subjects/citizens, governed by it in the form of law. Behind every 'law' Hobbes, rightly I believe, discerns 'will' and he is also right, I believe, in suggesting that the will of the 'person' of the state both 'ascends' from the wills of the individuals who collectively constitute the commonwealth (the ascent of the immanent Spirit) and also 'descends' upon them in the form of a collective or general will embodied in law (the descent of the transcendent Father God); for, surely, to speak of a common moral purpose entertained by a citizen body as such—and to assign, in so doing, to 'common' and 'purpose' a real meaning and real existence both in, and yet also beyond, each individual citizen—is to concede that the 'entertainer' of that purpose is a 'person' in some sense or at least a person-like entity, even if this person-like entity or (non-natural) 'collective persona' can only live, move and have its being in and through citizens as natural persons. This 'in us but more than us' aspect of political life is what Hobbes's 'person' of the state illuminates so well and what the religious consciousness recognises as the operative presence of the Spirit. Certainly he articulates and theorises this notion in a manner which is not only still relevant today but is perhaps more necessary now to sound reflection on political life than ever.

Chapter Ten

Barth, Reformation Theology and Natural Law

Stand up man so that I might speak with you
Ezekiel 2:1

Hobbes, as we have seen, is illuminating and 'ecumenically valuable' because he is associated both with the (Catholic) natural law tradition and yet also with the (Protestant) Occamite, nominalist tendencies of the Reformation tradition, so that his work still serves, even today, as a bridge between the two. In contrast, Barth, of course, is well known for the antagonism he expressed towards the Catholic natural law tradition associated with Thomas Aquinas and towards the view that all persons, having been created in the image of God and with God's law written on their hearts, have at least a natural foundation or divine compass that points to God, or a kind of 'pathway to God' in their souls. Broadly, this tradition holds that the fundamental principles of social and political life are given in human nature, that the common nature shared by all human persons is rational and contains an inner law that directs the various aspects of our humanity towards their unified and harmonious fulfilment, and that our humanity fully alive, or human nature developed in the direction of its true perfection, is the glory God seeks. The various principles which lead our human nature universally (in all times and places) towards this perfection are the 'laws of nature'; they are both moral and political for our very nature as human persons finds expression and fulfilment in organised political life. Created nature is revelatory of the trinitarian God's reason and purpose, of the original creative will of the Father, through the Word ('reason-in-action') of the Son and sustained by the immanent power and presence of the Spirit, and the created human person is made in the image of the Trinitarian God. When we consider our nature with the reason God has gifted us with, Aquinas is convinced that we will appreciate that our purpose as intelligent, willing beings, is the proper development of our potentialities, of our minds as alert to and guided by universal truth and of our wills as alert to and guided by universal goodness. Dante Germino explains well the interweaving of the central themes of universal natural order, truth-oriented *telos* and 'goodness-drawn' purpose in this tradition:

> The natural order is the organisation of the human community in a manner conducive to the fulfilment of the ends proper to man's distinctively human nature. Such an ordering of human nature is an embodiment of the natural law . . . Natural law demands that the rational element in the human constitu-

tion be cultivated, and that it serve as master of the passions. There is thus a hierarchy of the psyche's impulses and faculties, which, if disturbed, results in profound disorder of the soul. There is similarly a hierarchy of goals for the political community, which grows out of and reflects the ranking of ends in man's own being, for the end of the state is not qualitatively different from the end of its members.[1]

Christian natural law thinkers, then, hold that there is a natural foundation or divine compass that points to God in each human soul. Barth, however, is out of sympathy with the broad outlook of natural law, at least ostensibly and 'publicly'. (I introduce this note of caution because in section (iii) I shall suggest that whilst Barth, in his earlier work, is clearly out of sympathy with these views both rhetorically and substantively, yet in his later work, it appears that he is out of sympathy rhetorically *rather than* substantively.) Certainly in his earlier work he insists upon the Kierkegaardian 'infinite qualitative difference between time and eternity, between God and man', between God's grace and our human hatred of grace, and he is convinced that, since there is no natural launching pad (not even a heart that is restless until it finds its peace in Thee) from which humanity might actively ascend or passively be drawn to the divine, God must create his own point of contact with us by coming to us *senkrecht*

---

1. DL Germino, 1959, 'Two Types of Recent Christian Thought', in *The Journal of Politics*, volume 21 (1959): 455–486.

von oben, that is, 'straight down (perpendicularly) from above.' Barth regards our faith in Jesus descending from above as a kind of sharing in Jesus's faith in God; we are justified by God because Jesus Christ, in his humanity, believed.[2] Thus Barth's christological emphasis, his rigid separation between time (humanity) and eternity (God) and his antagonism to natural law are all of a piece. In this chapter we will firstly look at what I call 'the three prepositions of faith' namely faith 'in', 'with', and 'of' Jesus. I hope, as a result of this analysis, to show (i) that we cannot accept Barth's claim that 'the meaning of the first commandment and thus of all the commandments, and thus of our obedience to God's law, can and must be that we believe *in* Jesus Christ'[3] and (ii) that whilst his antipathy to faith 'with' Jesus is in line with his opposition to natural law, it puts him at odds with his own Reformed tradition.

Faith in, with, and of Jesus

Barth believes that Paul's statement in Galatians 2:20 ('And the life I now live in the flesh, I live in the faith of the Son of God, who loved me and gave himself up for me) should be 'understood quite literally: I live—not, for instance, somehow in my belief in the Son of God, but in the fact that the Son of God believed'.[4] He tells us that 'in

---

2. K Barth, *Community, State and Church: Three Essays* (Gloucester, Mass: Peter Smith, 1968), 74.
3. *Ibid*, 82–83
4. *Ibid*, 76.

this faith, he bore our punishment', not so much as an example but 'first of all and above all representatively'.⁵ Barth draws out the following consequence:

> Being certain Jesus Christ is God but we are men, we will do well not to try to imitate Jesus in this faith and thus to believe *as* Jesus believed. However, the meaning of the first commandment and thus of all the commandments, and thus of our obedience to God's law, can and must be that we believe *in* Jesus Christ, that we—since the Word became flesh, remained obedient in the flesh, and was exalted in the flesh—acknowledge his representative faith, which we will never realise, and allow it to count as our life, which we do not have here in our hand and at our disposal but have above, hidden with him in God (Colossians 3:1f).⁶

Because of the God-humanity divide and our certainty that 'Jesus Christ is God but we are men', Barth is convinced that 'we will do well not to try to imitate Jesus in this faith and thus to believe *as* Jesus believed', and yet he also believes that Jesus crossed and conquered the great divide, for he became 'like one of us' and 'without ceasing to be God, he added our humanity to and assimilated it in

---

5. *Ibid*, 74.
6. *Ibid*, 82–83

his deity'.[7] However Barth fails, I think, to grasp the full significance and unfathomable graciousness of Jesus, the second person of the Trinity, sharing our human subjectivity and becoming 'one like us'. This seems a strange thing to say of Barth, of all people, but what I have in mind is this; Barth is right to say that Jesus became 'one like us' without ceasing to be God. In Paul's words, Jesus 'though he was by nature God, did not consider being equal to God a thing to be clung to, but emptied himself, taking the nature of a slave and being made like unto men' (Philippians 2:6–7). My suggestion here is that objectively, ontologically and in 'the order of truth', Jesus is ever God, always the second Person of the Trinity, even when he assumes the condition of a man, but that subjectively, or in the order of human experience, he emptied himself or 'backgrounded' his divinity in order to fully (and with a condescension and graciousness beyond words) enter into the order of our bodily, spatio-temporal humanity. I agree with those who hold that Jesus, as a child in the womb and in his infancy, was (subjectively) like any other human child but that, through the Spirit, he grew in consciousness of his divinity and his equality with God as he matured in years. I believe that Jesus saved us from our sins, from the punishment our sins justly deserve, by ever remaining fully God in the order of truth, even whilst assuming our humanity, by allowing his divinity to fade into the background and remain hidden from view in order to enter into the 'corrupt' order of human experience and

---

7. *Ibid*, 73.

human subjectivity.[8] Barth is, I think, right when he says that our belief is a kind of participation in the 'representative' faith of Christ but then for there to be a possibility of Jesus having faith *as we humans have faith*, it was necessary that Jesus should 'empty himself', should 'background' his divinity on our behalf that he might take it up again at the appointed time and draw us with him into the fullness of his divine life, should discover through his human subjectivity (or 'recover' or restore to the foreground the unchanging truth) that he is the beloved Son in whom the Father is well pleased, in order that we might discover through our human subjectivity that we are beloved children of the Father. However, what this means (or would mean if correct) is that Barth then is surely wrong to suggest that we should not imitate the faith of Jesus or try to believe as he believed; that is precisely what we *should* do. Being certain that Jesus, unlike us, is God but acknowledging that he emptied himself to become like one of us, we must try to imitate the 'human' faith of the Jesus who prayed the '*Our* Father'. (It is interesting to note here in passing that at the beginning of the paragraph from which the verses from Philippians were quoted above, it states 'Have this mind in you which was also in Christ Jesus' (Philippians 2:5); if the Scriptures encourage us to 'put on the mind of Christ', why should we hesitate to 'put on the faith of Christ'?)

As well as believing *in* Jesus, we must also believe *with* Jesus, just as Christians who believe in the community

---

8. Barth reminds us that Jesus assumed 'our humanity in the shape resulting from sin's darkening and destruction'. *Ibid*, 73.

of saints pray to the Jesus *in* whom they believe as their Lord and Savior but *with* (not to) the saints who are asked to join them in prayers of petition for themselves ('Pray for us') and the church. We believe *in* Jesus as God; we believe *with* Jesus as human. When we pray *to* Jesus, we implicitly express our faith in Him but when we say the Our Father, we pray *with* Jesus as our brother, as one who shared our humanity, who with us—He said '*Our* Father'—prayed on earth to the Father in heaven. However, if this is so, and Barth himself with his notion of sharing in Christ's representative faith gives us good reasons for believing it is so, then we cannot accept Barth's claim that 'the meaning of the first commandment and thus of all the commandments, and thus of our obedience to God's law, can and must be that we believe *in* Jesus Christ'.[9] If the archetypal faith of Jesus lives in us, if in our human faith in the Father, we actually share in Christ's faith in the Father, if in our human believing *with* Jesus as our human brother, we experience the love and forgiveness of God—and this 'we', potentially in our collective consciousness and ontologically in truth, includes the whole of humanity— then an important meaning of the first commandment (not the only one) is that, *with* Jesus, we must love God as our heavenly Father. Though obviously related, our faith in Jesus as divine savior is distinct from our faith with our 'human' brother Jesus in our heavenly Father. What Barth I think fails to realise or to fully grasp is that whilst our faith *in* Jesus identifies us as specifically Christian, our faith *with* Jesus in the Father identifies us with all those

---

9. *Ibid*, 82–83.

(Jews, Muslims, believers in the love of God, etc) whose hands are raised in prayer to God and whose heads are bowed before His law, as revealed in the Word of God or as written on the 'tablets' of each human heart; ideally and in truth, our faith with Jesus in the Father identifies us with the whole of humanity.

Barth's predilection for 'in' and his antipathy to 'with' is in line with his antagonism to natural law but strangely enough, it puts him at odds with his own reformed tradition. He poses the question: 'is there a connection between justification of the sinner through faith alone, completed once for all by God through Jesus Christ, and the problem of justice, the problem of human law?'[10] Is there, he asks, 'an inward and vital connection' between divine justification (which concerns the Church) and human justice (the concern of the state)? He holds that there is but that it is not found in his own reformed tradition. Certainly, as he says, 'the reformation confessional writers and reformation theology as a whole' affirmed the existence of both realities, of divine justification and human justice, taking 'great pains to make it clear that the two are not in conflict, but that they can very well exist side by side, each being competent in its own sphere'.[11] However, Barth expresses a sense of disappointment with the Reformation tradition for, he insists, 'we need to know not only that the two are not in conflict, but, first and foremost, to what extent they are connected'.[12] The Reformation writ-

---

10. *Ibid*, 101.
11. *Ibid*, 102.
12. *Ibid*.

ers, he believes, are culpably silent on this crucial point. Interestingly, however, Barth says very little to justify this criticism. Indeed, he actually acknowledges that Zwingli seems to take for granted the existence of a vital connection between the two by speaking in the same breath of 'divine and human justice'[13] and by insisting that the secular power has 'strength and assurance from the teaching and action of Christ'.[14] However, he expresses disappointment with Zwingli's position because it is based only on Christ's injunction to render unto Caesar the things that are Caesar's and unto God the things that are God's (Matthew 22:21) and because 'it is based not on the Gospel but on the Law'.[15] However, what this means, I wish to suggest, is that Zwingli *does* assert that there is a real and vital connection between justification and justice but that Barth *disagrees* with his view of the way in which they are connected, that is, by means of the law rather than the gospel. In this dispute, I am on Zwingli's side, although by the 'law' Zwingli would presumably have in mind 'as found in Scripture', whereas I would also have in mind 'as written on the tablets of the human heart' (natural law). Certainly, Zwingli's position is much closer to the natural law viewpoint than Barth's.

Hopefully the following analysis of the (divine) justification/(human) justice relationship in terms of the 'order of truth/order of human experience' distinction will add a little support to Zwingli's case and show that what

---

13. *Ibid.*
14. *Ibid*, 104
15. *Ibid*, 104.

Barth refers to as a 'gap in the teaching that we have received from the fathers of our church'[16] may be, in effect, no more than a gap engendered by his own disagreement with the 'Reformation fathers' and, in particular, with their conviction that God and his law can be understood, apart form the person and work of Christ 'in a general way as Creator and Ruler'.[17]

Divine Justification and Human Justice

Objectively, ontologically and in truth, God alone has justified us through his Son Jesus Christ and this is ever so, whether we know it or not and whether we appreciate it or not. It is not faith—which is, after all, a human act or work—that justifies, but God alone through Christ. Christians do not believe in faith; they believe in God, in the Father, Son and Holy Spirit. However, faith occupies a vital, pivotal position between the objective and the subjective, between the order of truth and the order of human experience, between the truth about God and our consciousness of it (Hebrews 11:1); for it is through faith that the order of truth (God's truth) enters into and begins to transform the order of our human experience into its image and that God's justification—its reality and truth *for us,* its ordained role *within us* to subjectively constitute us and form our true identity in Christ—sets in train our sanctification. It's as if we are freely given the grace of salvation and justification but we receive and act on

---

16. *Ibid.*
17. *Ibid,* 120.

it through faith. 'By grace you have been saved through faith' (Ephesians 2:8). It is by faith that we receive God's power (Hebrews 11:11) and yet, though itself God's gift and grace, faith has to be received, to be accepted and enacted by us. Our faith 'yes' allows God to more effectively reconstitute our inner life, our subjective existence and the same could be said for God's law which is likewise a gift that should be received (as graciously as possible) enacted and obeyed. It is faith that vitally connects the objective and the subjective, that allows the objectively ever present divine to become subjectively present for us and to flood our receiving, humble grateful souls with its grace and light, which is why it occupies such a pivotal role in our spiritual lives as Christians and why the 'active' receiving of it and the 'cultivated' retaining of it is considered a Christian virtue.[18] An important part of the whole faith experience is our response or consent, given 'from the inside,' from the thirsty heart of our deepest self that awaits God's call through the mists of our subjective sinfulness. There is then no escaping the fact that faith, especially when considered 'from our (human) side', in terms of our response to God's call, is in some measure and in some respects a human work. It is simultaneously God's gift and our receiving and retaining thereof. Likewise, however, our receiving of the Law, our endeavours to be just are simultaneously God's gift to us—divinely inspired initiatives, however small the actions concerned—

---

18. CS Lewis explains this point particularly well in his *Mere Christianity*, 119–124.

as well as our own actions, done by us and for which we accept responsibility.

The manner in which faith opens a doorway for God's truth to enter into us (from the 'objective outside' to the 'subjective inside') and the manner in which the embracing dynamism of the Spirit links God's action (initiative) and our actions (reactions in faith) is elegantly and economically conveyed by Paul as follows; 'Work out your own salvation in fear and trembling, for God is at work within you.' (Philippians 2:12, See also Hebrews 13:21) On the one hand, we are to take the initiative ('Work out . . .') but, on the other hand this genuine initiative on our part is simultaneously God's initiative working through us ('for God is at work . . . ') What Paul is surely emphasising here is the importance of 'shared agency', of human response as well as of divine initiative, in effecting our salvation. Perhaps we should say that God, in his plan of salvation, made provision for a degree of 'relative autonomy' on our (human) part. Hence, I would suggest that Helmut Thielicke[19] is not justified in positing an opposition (invidious rather than contrastive), between 'true' and 'derived' subjectivity, that is, the true subjectivity of God as opposed to the derived subjectivity of humanity. It is true, as Thielicke implies, that subjectivity-in-itself or original subjectivity belongs to God and that our human subjectivity ultimately stems therefrom and is modeled thereon, but this does not mean that 'God is always the

---

19. H Thielicke, *Theological Ethics, Volume 2: Politics* (Grand Rapids: Eerdmans, 1979), 223.

subject';[20] nor does it mean that God does not create in humanity a genuine form of subjectivity apart from Himself, a type that is true and real as deriving from or 'drawing from', as I would prefer to say, the font of subjectivity itself. If this were not so, Yahweh's address to us in 'Stand up man so that I might speak with you' (Ezekiel 2:1) would have to be viewed as a nonsensical impossibility, as (ultimately) a form of self-address on God's part. For me, the lesson to be taken from what Paul has to say ('Work out your own salvation in fear and trembling, for God is at work within you.') is (i) that we should not focus too exclusively on the order of human experience (which makes it seem that we solely effect our own salvation through our own works) at the expense of the order of truth (the importance of the divine initiative and divine justification) and (ii) that we should not focus on the order of truth (the importance of the divine justification) so exclusively that we treat as naught the degree of relative autonomy and freedom that God in his mercy and trust has assigned to us, and thereby downplay, de-emphasise or ignore altogether the order of human experience, that is, the *felt* importance and *real* importance in our subjective experience of our *human* response to God, our good works, our just endeavours to live by the (natural) law implanted in our hearts

---

20. *Ibid*, 224.

Barth and Natural Law

In this section, I wish to look at where precisely Barth stands in relation to the natural law tradition. Perhaps its most important and elementary claim (at least for our present purposes) is that, by virtue of their common human nature, all human beings share certain universal moral and social norms but this is actually a claim that Barth readily accepts; nor has he any reservations in referring to these universal norms as 'natural law'. He even says that the civil community 'has no other choice but to think, speak and act on the basis of this allegedly natural law'.[21] His objection to natural law seems to be mainly based on its aloofness or abstract generality; addressing his Christian brethren in Britain who relied on natural law as a really sure foundation in their resistance to Hitler, he insisted that '[a]ll arguments based on natural law are Janus-headed. They do not lead to the light of clear decisions, but to the misty twilight in which all cats become gray';[22] his British colleagues should rather, he believed, speak solely and exclusively out of the word of God. He also speaks of natural law in a dismissive fashion as merely human law (to be contrasted with the clear divine laws revealed in scriptures) and, as such, inevitably tainted by the 'human illusions and confusions'[23] that characterise 'the ignorant, neutral, pagan civil community'.[24] Finally, his existentialism and theological actualism (his convic-

---

21. K Barth, *Community, State and Church: Three Essays*, 164.
22. *Ibid*, 49.
23. *Ibid*, 165.
24. *Ibid*, 164.

tion that every act and event is a free act of a free sovereign God and that there is no immanent continuity in the world and in humanity, engendered by an immanent reason) led Barth to treat with suspicion what he saw as natural law's metaphysical claim that there is a universal human 'essence' that requires realisation through 'act'. However, the strong antipathy that Barth exhibits to the natural law tradition is, I would suggest, more a feature of his early than of his later work. At the end of this section I will suggest that whilst Barth, in his earlier work, is clearly out of sympathy with natural law both rhetorically and substantively, yet in his later work, it appears that he is out of sympathy rhetorically (and explicitly) *rather than* substantively (and implicitly) with the natural law tradition.

Barth's criticism of natural law on account of its vagueness and abstract generality is, I think, weak and unsustainable. It is clear what he means; given that universal natural laws require individual judgment concerning the proper mode of their practical application in specific situations, he is concerned that an acknowledgment of the universal validity of these principles does not of itself lead to 'the light of clear decisions'. This is of course true. Imagine the case of a young German in 1940 who is a Christian and who accepts the basic principles of natural law, summed up in the maxim 'Do unto others as you would be done by' or 'Love one another'. He is told by some that natural law condemns, and by others that it condones fascism; he is told by some that Hitler is demonic, and by others that God has sent Hitler to the German people to help them in their hour of need, that Hitler's devotion to the good of the German people is beyond dispute and that he will save Germany from the threat of world communism and the machinations of International Jewry. There is no easy answer to this young German's dilemma. Unlike us, he is *in* the situation, and his vision is unilluminated by the 'retrospective light' available to us. He must make his decision in good conscience, as indeed must Barth who acted on his belief during the war that (in his own words at the time) '*this* group of nations (the United Nations today) has on the whole remained more righteous than *that* one (the Axis Coalition)'.[25]

We can then clearly see what Barth has in mind when he says that natural law provides no sure means of adjudicating between opposing ethical positions (the gist of his 'all cats are gray' comment) but what he fails to realise is that all difficult ethical decisions have to be made in this 'murky grayness'. There is simply no escape from the necessity of ethical judgment in the often difficult (gray) circumstances of the present moment. We will always, in a sense, be 'looking through the glass darkly', always praying and hoping that we are acting in the light of God's love and grace but wondering if the path we did not choose (the other horn of the ethical dilemma) would have been more in accord with God's will. We can also see what Barth means when he says that the state or civil community can do no more than 'grope around and experiment with the convictions which it derives from 'natural law', never certain whether it may not in the end be an illusion to rely on it as the final authority and there-

---

25. *Ibid*, 50–51.

fore always making vigorous use, openly or secretly, of a more or less refined positivism'[26] but this is surely a rather truculent and ill-tempered way of referring to the fact that the state, in fulfilling its obligation to interpret the broad principles of natural law into the current political circumstances of a political community, must not underestimate the difficulty and complexity of the practical decisions involved. It must not, for example, try to pass off its decisions as simply the self-evident dictates of natural law but be prepared (i) to give publicly defensible reasons as to why in its (all too fallible) political judgment, its decisions are deemed to be the best possible under the prevailing circumstances and (ii) to attempt to reduce the margin of error by being as comprehensive and detailed as it can be in taking empirical circumstances into account, which is presumably what Barth means by the vigorous use of 'a more or less refined positivism'. Against the prescriptive vagueness of natural law, Barth urges Christians to rely upon the Word of God to provide a sound christological basis for an anti-Hitler strategy but the manner in which the Bible is less vague or somehow more definite in its 'anti-Hitler credentials' is not immediately obvious. Is it not perfectly possible, and indeed thoroughly understandable, for our young German to wholeheartedly believe the Word of God and yet to be convinced that God in His providential care sent Hitler to save Germany from its ills and woes? The terrible tragedy and paradox in all this is that the young German who believes that right (and God) is on Hitler's side can say, with his 'opponent' Barth:

---

26. *Ibid*, 164.

The more readily we realise and admit that we all stand equally under God's judgment in this war . . . which, while bringing unavoidable suffering to all, may be a defence of the 'righteous' state . . . the more cold-bloodedly and energetically will the war be waged, for then, and only then, will we have a good conscience in this hard and terrible business.[27]

We saw earlier, when reflecting on Barth and the State, that Will Herberg was not at all impressed by Barth's method of analogy; the view that there is a correspondence between what is 'above' and what is 'below', between the heavenly *polis* and the earthly *polis*. Herberg dismisses this view as simply too vague and indeterminate and, moreover, as too easily adjusted to, and manipulated by, one's own personal predilections. In brief, he holds that Barth's method of analogy is unacceptably arbitrary. This criticism, I earlier suggested, is well wide of the mark but ironically Barth's criticism of natural law is also misdirected for precisely the same reasons. He advises the Christian community not 'to seek the criterion of its political decisions in some form of the so-called natural law'[28] but exponents of the natural law viewpoint have consistently acknowledged the necessity of political judgment and of taking local and particular circumstances into account, and certainly they would never have suggested that natural law always provides (though in relatively

---

27. *Ibid*, 51.
28. *Ibid*, 165.

straightforward cases it certainly does provide) clear or definite criteria for political decision-making. Just as the divine laws contained in scripture need to be interpreted into the life of the believer, so too the (prescriptively indeterminate) laws of nature need to be interpreted (with ease or with difficulty) into the political circumstances encountered by the body of citizens at any particular time. Again, as we saw earlier, the fact that a number of quite different, even incompatible, conclusions can be drawn from the same biblical premises (or the same general laws of nature) may be taken (i), in the manner of Herberg, as indicating that whatever conclusion is reached is in effect arrived at, or already entertained, independently of scripture (or of natural law) or (ii) as evidence that the bible (or the natural law of our humanity) is relevant for all ages and needs to be interpreted into the lives of people in different historical periods.

In many ways Barth's opposition to natural law is surprising because later in his career, most notably in *Church Dogmatics*, his anti-essentialism was modified by his adoption of what Herberg calls 'a kind of objectivism with its own theological continuity'[29] and Barth's famous 'no' of divine judgment on a humanity rightly condemned for its sinfulness was thereafter accompanied by the 'yes' of universal grace; the 'no' is as shattering as ever but universal grace now gathers up the shattered pieces of a fallen world into a new creation. Now, at first glance, there doesn't appear to be a wide gap between (i) the (Christian natural law) view that all human beings share a com-

---

29. *Ibid*, 19.

mon God-given nature, that humanity fully alive is the glory God seeks, that grace fulfils or perfects nature and (ii) the (Barthian) view that grace is universally operative in human beings to bring about a new creation by 'disintegrating' our fallen, sinful nature and 're-integrating' into a harmonious whole the redeemed pieces of our humanity, and, hence, between the Christian exponents of natural law and Barth. Can we then find any sign of such a hoped for development or reconciliation in Barth's later work? In his *Church Dogmatics*, the God whom he earlier designated as 'wholly other' becomes a God who is within reach of human knowledge but is what we might call this 'epistemological outworking' of the 'triumph of grace' matched by a parallel 'ethical outworking', by an acknowledgement that the law of God (in the form of natural law or universal ethical principles) is indelibly written on each human heart and that the Holy Spirit is present in the everyday *bona fides* workings of the human conscience? My answer would be superficially and rhetorically 'No', for rhetorically Barth's antipathy to natural law continues unabated, but in fact or substantively my reply would be 'Yes', for Barth does in fact move much closer to a natural law position.

As early as 1926 in a lecture delivered in Amsterdam after his appointment as professor at the University of Munster[30], Barth speaks of 'redeemed society',[31] of culture as 'the promise originally given to man of what he is

---

30. K Barth, *Theology and Church*, translated by Louise Pettibone Smith (London: SCM Press, 1962), 334–354.
31. *Ibid*, 334–354.

to become',[32] of the separation between God and human culture being overcome by the incarnation of the Word into our sinful human world, and of Christ's incarnation renewing 'the status of the creation with its great 'Yes' to man, with its reasonableness of reason'[33] in a manner that is strongly reminiscent of Thomas Aquinas. Barth warns us that by a 'redeemed society' he does not have in mind a Schleiermacherian or a Hegelian idealised Prussian culture but the reader could be forgiven for having in mind here the kind of relationship between God and culture envisaged by Aquinas; for Barth here exhibits the same anxiety as Aquinas to see societal and cultural structures and achievements as partially embodying and anticipating the fullness of the promise and fact of reconciliation. RE Hood points out that 'for Barth reconciled or redeemed culture has primarily an eschatological significance which does not allow the Christian to underestimate or undervalue cultural and political phenomena, but rather liberates him to see these phenomena in light of the *telos* for which all cultural and political activity is striving'.[34] However, in this important respect, Barth and Aquinas speak with one voice. Consider in this regard Niebuhr's summary of Aquinas's position on the relationship between Christ and culture:

---

32. *Ibid*, 341.
33. *Ibid*, 343.
34. RE Hood, 1980, 'Karl Barth's Christological Basis for the State and Political Praxis', in *Scottish Journal of Theology*, Volume 33 (1980): 235.

... he is the fulfilment of cultural aspirations and the restorer of the institutions of true society. Yet there is in him something that neither arises out of culture nor contributes directly to it. He is discontinuous as well as continuous with social life and its culture. The latter, indeed, leads men to Christ, yet only in so preliminary a fashion that a great leap is necessary if men are to reach him or, better, true culture is not possible unless beyond all human achievement, all human search for values, all human society, Christ enters into life from above with gifts which human aspiration has not envisioned and which human effort cannot attain unless he relates men to a supernatural society and a new value-centre.[35]

With this broad characterisation of Aquinas's understanding of the relationship between Christ and culture, Barth could hardly disagree and he would no doubt positively applaud any acknowledgement of the necessity of Christ's (perpendicular) descent from above to make up the deficiencies of the fumbling, inadequate efforts of our natural 'ascent' from below. Likewise Aquinas would have wholeheartedly agreed with Barth's insistence in *Church Dogmatics*[36] that Christ's reconciliation of culture to God is

---

35. HR Niebuhr, *Christ and Culture* (New York: Harper Collins, 2001), 42.
36. K Barth, *Church Dogmatics*, IV/1 (Edinburgh: T&T Clark, 1997), 188.

effected not only by God *to* culture but by God *in* culture as an act of grace by One who has poured himself into our culture and world; both agree that there is reconciliation from within culture, so to speak, as well as from without and that God's summons is both beyond culture and yet operative within human culture. The natural law tradition is then, I maintain, not only consistent with Barth's later theology but may indeed be used to broadly support Barth's 'theological politics' and more specifically, his theological account of the state (See chapter eight on 'Barth and the State'). In the following section, I will (i) look at the strained relationship between the 'Catholic' natural law tradition and 'Protestant' Reformation theology in general, (ii) indicate whilst doing so that precisely the same strain has arisen more recently within Catholic theology itself and then (iii) suggest that, in a similar vein, there is actually a basic compatibility between apparently contending positions held (over the centuries) between Catholic and Protestant thinkers and held (more recently) within Catholic theological circles.

The 'Catholic' Natural Law Tradition and 'Protestant' Reformation Theology

In general, Catholic natural law exponents maintain or assume, whereas reformation theologians query or deny, that there are certain ontic elements or qualities that together, in their inter-relatedness, constitute the *imago Dei*. This is a broad and difficult topic but it is helpful in approaching it to note that 'qualities in relation' or 'differences/diversities in a unifying relation,' as totalities or unities, may be of different types. In the case of higher spiritual unities, we usually, and I believe entirely appropriately, speak of 'unity-*in*-diversity' since the type of unity involved is clearly and definitively inner or internal, permeating *its* diverse elements, whereas in the case of mechanical or physical unities, we usually, and again entirely appropriately, speak of 'unity-*of*-diversity' since the qualities or parts of unities of this kind are linked together externally or spatially. We may think for example of the 'person' as a 'unity in diversity' combining the qualities 'human' and 'animal'. In this case, the quality 'human' cannot be abstracted from the quality 'animal' or regarded as a kind of super added or external characteristic which is joined to, or added 'from the outside' to, our animality. The predicate 'human' qualifies the noun 'animal' through and through, so to speak; we may say that the element or quality 'animal' qualifies, is present throughout, applies to and is integrally related to, the person as a whole; it is an aspect, or constitutive dimension, *of* the person. As Helmut Thielicke remarks, 'the anthropology of the New Testament is so structured that, when the terms 'body', 'soul', 'flesh' and 'reason' are used of man, they do not imply that man is divided into different spheres in the sense of strata of the ego. On the contrary, each of these terms denotes the whole man but from a different angle or standpoint'.[37] Now what Thielicke has to say here has, I hope to show, important implications for our understanding of the effects of the fall on our human nature and what kind of role natural law might, or might

---

37. H Thielicke, *Theological Ethics, Volume 2: Politics*, 435.

not have, in helping us to retrieve our lost innocence and to restore to good health our fallen humanity

If, as a result of the fall, we lost our original righteousness and if, as I personally believe and prefer to say, what once were divine gifts in the sense of steadfast dispositions of character became instead, after the fall, obligations and duties imposed on us, then this loss must qualify and radically affect our entire being. The group of Catholic scholars that formed the *Ressourcement* school (de Lubac, von Balthasar, Ratzinger) before the second Vatican Council, and that, in broad terms, used the work of Augustine as a counter weight to Aquinas, has, I think, largely conceded this point. Ratzinger has been particularly sensitive to the Protestant criticism that Thomist Catholicism is too intellectual and abstract and insufficiently scriptural and Christocentric, and he warmly commends Augustine's recognition that God can only be seen and known through a purified and redeemed reason and that this 'necessary purification of sight takes place through faith (Acts 15:9) and through love, at all events not as a result of reflection alone and not at all by man's own power'.[38] With other members of this school, he is steadfast in his opposition to an 'autonomous' philosophical account of our humanity or to an 'anthropology' which is not at the same time a 'theology'. The Reformation is surely justified, then, in regarding the effect of the fall as 'total' (in a sense to be shortly explained more fully); every part of human nature or all of the key ontic elements (reason, sensuality, voli-

---

38. T Rowland, *Ratzinger's Faith: The Theology of Pope Benedict XVI* (Oxford: Oxford University Press, 2008), 4.

tion, etc) must be drastically affected by it and there is no neutral area or remnant of nature that is unaffected by it. God needs to dramatically intervene on our behalf. What this means is that the Catholic scholastics (more specifically, the post-Tridentine scholastics or Neo-Scholastics) were surely mistaken if, as Thielicke believes,[39] (i) they held that there were two ontic spheres in our humanity (nature and super nature or grace) that could be marked off from each other, the first constant and invariable and the second an extra contingently added by God that in no way affects the ontic qualities of the original *imago Dei* in humanity, and if (ii) they held that the order [*ordo*] which ordained the relations between the ontic elements of the *imago Dei* merely added order, from the outside to ontic qualities deemed to each have a constant form of existence, like unchanging and unchangeable atoms, but requiring only to be externally ordered in the right way.

Whilst the Reformation was then indeed justified in regarding the effect of the fall as 'total', at the same time the Catholic scholastics were surely right to remind us that the key point and purpose of natural law is to counteract and redress this 'total' disorder of our human nature. When considering the effects of the fall, we need to distinguish between two uses or senses of the term 'total', the one relative and intelligible, the other absolute and unintelligible. If the entry of sin into the world through the fall is held to involve the total (in an absolute sense) destruction or corruption of the *imago Dei* in us and the complete loss of our original righteousness, our account

---

39. H Thielicke, *Theological Ethics, Volume 2: Politics*, 203.

and understanding of the fall and its effects becomes unintelligible; sin presupposes some kind of knowledge, even if only implicit, of the law but if the fall destroys the *imago Dei* totally (in an absolute sense) and therewith the human capacity to somehow know the law and grasp (even in the most rudimentary and distorted fashion) its righteousness, it thereby also destroys sin itself, for as Paul makes all too clear, it is the law which designates or 'uncovers' certain acts and dispositions as 'sin', as negatively related to the righteousness of the law. However, by using the term 'total' in the sense of 'totality of intent' or 'would-be totality' to describe the effects of the fall, we may avoid veering close to or stumbling into the extreme (and ultimately unintelligible) conviction of Flacius that original sin is the substance of our humanity.

To understand what I mean by a 'totality of intent', we need here to bear in mind Thielike's point that 'the anthropology of the New Testament is so structured that, when the terms "body", "soul", "flesh" and "reason" are used of man, they do not imply that man is divided into different spheres in the sense of strata of the ego. On the contrary, each of these terms denotes the whole man but from a different angle or standpoint'.[40] His key point, I take it, is that when viewed from a particular perspective, our humanity may be seen as essentially characterised (that is, capable of being modified in a manner which affects or permeates his whole being) by any one of a number of determinative qualities (body, reason, etc). This is perfectly true and Thielicke's point is well made but we

---

40. *Ibid*, 435.

need to note here that our humanity so considered and (descriptively) portrayed (as body, soul, reason, emotion, etc) is, in a sense, illusory, perhaps indeed no more than a mere possibility and only a very dubious *description* (a misleading statistical average) of fallen man; for the latter is a battlefield, or rather a host of battlefields (as many as there are individuals) on which 'what humanity is to be or to become' is fought out to the death, so that the human qualities we referred to earlier (body, soul, feeling, reason) are 'universals of hope' that each ideally (though not necessarily actually) qualifies the human person as a whole and that collectively (again ideally but by no means necessarily) complement and reinforce each other in bringing about the fullness of our humanity. The 'to and fro' of each battle will determine whether the individual ascends towards heaven (towards the ideal complementarity and mutual reinforcing of aspects or qualities—the fullness of being—that God intends) or degenerates towards hell (to a state of anti-being in which the ideal universals are a perversion or pale deathly shadow of themselves).

Thus, what are generally referred to by scholastics as ontic elements of the *imago Dei* could perhaps be more appropriately referred to as ideal universals (universals of hope), whose *actual* role in each human life is largely determined by what I would call antagonistically related 'totalities of intent' ('spirit and flesh', 'righteousness and sin' 'good and evil' 'grace and despair'). What I have in mind here is that it is of the nature of righteousness, goodness and the spirit to *totally* permeate and bring the 'body', 'soul', 'desire' and 'reason' of humanity to their God—destined fullness, just as it is of the nature of evil, flesh and sin to *totally* permeate these noble qualities in man and bring about their complete annihilation or, rather, to absorb them totally into a vacuum of nothingness or 'anti-being'. Totalities of intent *aspire towards* totality or absoluteness in the fallen world of each person, whereas for Flacius sin was a kind of substance, an ontic element or an 'already achieved absolute totality' in each person's fallen world. Likewise, for Pelagius 'free will' was a determinate self-identical faculty (again, an 'already achieved absolute totality'), an unchanging ontic element to be used by each person for either good or ill, whereas Augustine correctly discerned that such a free will was in a sense illusory, that what we call free will (as if it was always there with us, never changing and unmodifiable) is in fact always 'in process', always becoming what it truly is (Augustine's 'liberated free will') or else falling ever deeper into self-destruction (Augustine's 'captive free will'). Reformation theology is, I would suggest, at its best when it portrays the fallen state of our humanity in terms of the former (conflictual totalities of intent) and eschews the latter (ontic, self-identical, absolute totalities).

Pannenberg is, I believe, right to suggest that 'Christian theology must read the Old Testament [OT] saying about our divine likeness in the light of the Pauline statements that call Jesus Christ the image of God . . . and that speak of the transforming of believers into this image'[41] but this must not be done in a way that nullifies the original meaning and intended effect of the Old Testament *imago Dei*

---

41. W Pannenberg, *Systematic Theology*, Volume 2 (Edinburgh: T&T Clark, 1997), 208.

sayings. The latter need to be approached on their own account and in their own light *as well as* in reference to the New Testament. It is because we are images of God in one sense (the OT sense) that we may be transformed into the image of God in another sense (the NT sense). The factual, descriptive ('this is empirically so') OT sense of the *imago Dei* emphasised by Latin scholarship is in no way at odds with the more deeply ideal and ontological sense ('this is our ideal state and ultimate destiny') of the NT Pauline statements emphasised by the Reformation. Our being the image of God is in one sense a fact and in another sense a task; it is a description and a work currently in progress, a pale reflection of God in us and the Spirit within us drawing us towards the perfection of the Son, our present empirical state and our ultimate ontological condition. In the *imago Dei/Deus* relation, we are like a 'subject' in quest of its true 'object', like a seed in relation to sun and earth, discovering that its true being lies not within itself but in its ec-static relation (Pannenberg's expression) to what lies beyond it, like a husband in relation to his wife as the desired object and 'reality' of his life and affections, and in ec-static relation to whom he is fully himself. In many ways, we are 'unfulfilled images of God' or 'unfulfilled temporal images of the eternal God', ever experiencing the tension of becoming, as the 'Spirit drawing us forth into Truth' ever encounters the resistance experienced as the 'flesh'. In O'Donovan's view, the tension between 'the Spirit' and 'the flesh' is 'not an anthropological contrast but an eschatological one'[42] but it is, rather, I believe, an-

---

42. O O'Donovan, *The Desire of the Nations: Rediscovering the Roots of*

thropological *as well as* eschatological; this tension, at least on this side of eternity, is the constant resistance of the 'actual' to the 'real', of the 'empirical' to the 'ontological', of 'sin' to Christ's victory.

Broadly, we can say that our being the *imago Dei* means that as God is, so in some limited and lesser sense are we, even in our creatureliness, but this descriptive piece of OT anthropology is not the last word, but is rather the ground or precondition for the NT transformation of sinners into the likeness of the Son through the gift of the Spirit. This fact/task, ground/fulfilment, seed/development relationship between the OT and NT senses of the *imago Dei* is captured very well in Pannenberg's observation that 'our creation in the image of God stands implicitly related to full similarity'[43] and that, by being changed by the Spirit into the likeness of Christ, St Paul had in mind 'not merely restoration of the image, but a closeness to God that goes beyond the divine likeness grounded in creation'.[44] As *imago Dei*, we are also *imago trinitatis*; the trinitarian possibility present in humanity from the time of creation is finally actualised. The developmental trajectory is completed in and through Christ and his victory over sin and death; the *imago Dei* is adopted into and participates in the very *vita Dei*.

Political Theology (Cambridge: Cambridge University Press, 2003), 129.
43. W Pannenberg, *Systematic Theology*, Volume 2, 217.
44. *Ibid*, 215.

The Reformation Rift; Ontological versus Personalistic Thinking

One advantage which I would claim for the preceding analysis is that it casts a helpful light on the supposed rift between the 'personalistic' emphasis of Reformation theology (and of the Catholic *Ressourcement* scholars) and the 'ontological' emphasis of Catholic Thomistic theology and helps us to realise that there is ultimately a complementarity or even reciprocity (a relationship of mutual implication) between the two. Thielicke summarises the differences between the two styles of thinking as follows:

> Roman Catholic thinking is profoundly ontological, Reformation thinking profoundly personalistic. To think ontologically is to see being and its forms . . . as elementary constituents to be demonstrated in their qualitative particularity, eg, reason, conscience, sensuality, body, and spirit . . . [and to] postulate certain constant factors which are simply given facts; these are thought to be quite independent of the question 'Christian or non-Christian, faith or unbelief' . . . To think personalistically, on the other hand, is to see all the realities of human life exclusively in terms of the personal relatedness of God and man, or more precisely, in terms of the fellowship between God and man given in Christ. Since this fellowship is given only in faith, personalistic thinking also means to see all these realities exclusively from the standpoint

of faith. It means to see them under the sway of the alternative that they are characterised either by the believer's existence in faith and are therefore 'justified', or by unbelief and are therefore 'sin' (Romans 14:23). But in this case there would be no constant factor, no continuum, no neutral base of the ego, and consequently no common ground (how could there be?) between Christians and non-Christians.[45]

Now I wish to suggest that Thielicke's ontological and personalistic approaches or modes of thinking actually presuppose each other; there is a relation of mutual implication, or at least of 'mutual reinforcement' (each enlightening and completing the other) between the two. When we regard the realities of human life (or, in more technical philosophical terms, the 'ontic elements of the *imago Dei*) from the standpoint of the all-or-nothing struggle for the human soul between good and evil, God and Satan, our thinking is inevitably 'personalistic' or an inner 'matter of the heart', as Augustine or Ratzinger might say. Crucially, who and what I am as a person is at stake. (The 'who' here is personalistic, referring to my identity, whereas the 'what' is ontological, referring to what kind of person I am, to the ontic elements of my being.) Is who and what I am as a person to be determined by 'good'—by the goodness of God, by the personal relationship to God that 'expands' my whole being and reality into Him—or is it to be determined by evil–by the designs of the evil one, by

---

45. H Thielicke, *Theological Ethics, Volume 2: Politics*, 197–198.

a personal relationship to Satan that diminishes my being and reality and turns it into a mere shadow or negative image of its self? In the case of the realities of human life ('mind', 'reason', 'will', 'thought', 'desire' 'feeling' etc, in human experience), their destiny, their sound development or their corruption, their descent into death is ultimately determined by whose side we take in the ongoing battle for our souls. This is a fight to the death. God and Satan will settle for nothing less than *total* (absolute) victory—either fullness of being for each human person or corruption to the point of death. This tension is, I think, expressed in the 'ongoing' birth pangs of the new creation (2 Corinthians: 5:17), the unceasing challenge of the old, (of sinful Adam) to the full-blown emergence of the new (of Christ, the new Adam).

Now when we regard the realities (the ontic elements) of human life from the standpoint of this all-or-nothing struggle between good and evil, it is possible to do so without distinguishing between Christians and non-Christians, or even between religious believers and non-believers, for what is at stake is whether individual persons realise their human essence (and thereby 'grow' knowingly, unknowingly or semi-knowingly into the fullness of humanity God intends) or fall deeper into death (in which case sin and Satan prevail in them, also knowingly, unknowingly or semi-knowingly). Our universal human destiny is here at stake. However, this universal struggle between good and evil for the soul and final destiny of each human soul takes on an intensified form and has a special significance in the case of the Christian believer. As Pannenberg remarks:

In Paul's sayings about Christ as the image of God into which all others must be transformed, the Christian doctrine of the divine likeness must see an elucidation of our general destiny of divine likeness. But in so doing it may not expunge the differences between the fulfilling of our divine likeness in and by Jesus Christ on the one hand, and the OT statements about Adam's divine likeness on the other. To do this is to miss the point that our destiny as creatures is brought to fulfilment by Jesus Christ.[46]

When the ontic elements or realities of human life are then seen from the standpoint of faith (and from the standpoint of our ultimate human destiny in Christ) as they truly are, that is, as gifts from God whose innermost nature is to serve and glorify God, as qualities to be totally enveloped by God's spirit and lifted up in the fullness of praise but at the same time as also being gifts that are subject to the perversions of sin. (Flacius may have been mistaken in regarding original sin as a permanent ontic fact or as the very 'substance' of our humanity but this certainly does not mean that we should treat lightly the fact–maybe, after all, this was Flacius's real intent–that original sin contains within itself the dreadful permanent threat or possibility of *totally* devouring *every* quality that makes us human.) Considered apart from this cosmic struggle, we may regard human realities ('mind', 'reason', 'will',

---

46. W Pannenberg, *Systematic Theology*, Volume 2, 210.

'thought', 'desire' 'feeling' etc) as 'neutral', permanent, ontic features, as Catholic theologians might say, but so considered, these qualities are mere abstract possibilities, as Protestant theologians might rightly respond: for once we re-introduce the context of the cosmic struggle between good and evil, they are seen in their true light as anything but neutral; they are the prizes for which God and Satan contend in contending for our souls. They are 'always already' affected by this struggle; they are constantly 'on their way' to life or death; in the course of the struggle, their true nature is revealed or lost, thrives in God or dies through Satan. It is only from the standpoint of faith (and not by means of our debased reason) that our humanity can be seen, understood and grasped in its full truth; it is only in the light of faith that what Catholic theologians call the ontic elements or realities of our nature are first seen for what they truly are.

Christians then should, I believe, exhibit a healthy skepticism towards any view, theological or philosophical, which draws a wedge between nature, essence, the ontic, on the one hand and the realm of the personal and relational on the other, for it is only through (personal) faith that our true nature (our God-intended nature) can be seen. Thielicke, as we have seen, exhibits this tendency[47] but the same tendency appears in the distinction

---

47. We should note here, however, that Thielicke acknowledges that 'the bible is not lacking in ontological references' and that '[o]ntological statements concerning the *imago Dei* are to be found already in the early church fathers, who consistently regard reason and freedom as ontically distinctive features of man' (H Thielicke, *Theological Ethics, Volume 2: Politics*, 199.)

often drawn in Catholic thought between nature or essence on the one hand and the (merely) contingent individual on the other. Consider, for example, MJ Scheeben's Catholic understanding of nature and individuality. He regards nature in its broadest sense as 'that which is in general the essence of things so far as their activity is concerned. Here nature is regarded as an abstract, as essence itself, which as such does not include that which after all determines what it will be in any given being, namely, individuality'.[48] In a sense, individuality and contingency are scarcely 'natural' at all, at least while the tendency to contrast 'essence and nature' (unchanging) with 'individuality and contingency' (changing) prevails. Now, if we consider nature in the abstract, it is of course 'abstract', but 'real nature' or our divinely ordained and divinely revealed human essence, in so far as it constantly challenges the sinful existence of each individual, is ever active and dynamic in a unique way in each person and is indeed, properly understood, the dynamism of the Holy Spirit and God's love operating in all aspects of our being, bringing the ontic elements of our being to their fullness and truth. Catholic theologians are right to say that nature or essence 'forms' or 'informs' our individual (sinful) existence, but we must insist that it does so in an active, dynamic challenging way; indeed, in the light of the radical extent of our sin and our fallen-ness (which Reformation theologians rightly emphasise), perhaps we should also say that by forming or informing, nature or essence simultaneously *transforms* our sinful nature or, follow-

---

48. H Thielicke, *Theological Ethics, Volume 2: Politics*, 200–201.

ing James Gustafson, that grace redirects or transforms nature and addresses our fallen condition (the 'human fault') through 'a governing and reordering of our natural desires, loves, natural instincts, and aspirations'.[49] Law, as Barth would remind us, is 'grace against sin', so that 'what is sin' is transformed into its opposite, or at least the law has a key role to play in this transformation that the spirit of God intends in us.

Essence as 'for Us' and against Sin; the 'Prescriptive Ontic'

The sense of essence being 'for us' as persons and individuals, in the midst of our uniqueness and the contingencies of our lives, may, I believe, be more easily recognised and strengthened by noting and duly emphasising the prescriptivity or 'ideality' of (human) nature *for fallen sinful creatures*. Scheeben helps us here by insisting that '[t]o the natural . . . the antithesis strictly speaking is not the supernatural but the non-natural, ie, that which does not belong to nature or proceed from it or correspond to it'.[50] What this means is that the antithesis of 'nature', in the sense of 'life as God intended it to be', is the 'non-natural' in the sense of a 'fall from being', or a Luciferic descent into the depths of death. 'Essence' or 'nature' is certainly characterisable descriptively or ontologically as 'form'

---

49. SJ Grenz, *The Moral Quest: Foundations of Christian Ethics* (Downers Grove Illinois: InterVarsity Press, 1997), 174.
50. MJ Scheeben, quoted in Thielicke, H, *Theological Ethics, Volume 2: Politics*, 200.

as opposed to matter, but it is also the prescriptive claim exercised by the eternal and unfallen upon the temporal and fallen, the voice of essence/form addressed to existential (sinful and rebellious) human matter. No doubt, nature conceived of 'in its broadest sense as that which is in general the essence of things so far as their activity is concerned'[51] or as 'being-in-itself' is unalterable and simply 'is what it is' in a descriptive, ontological sense but in its reference to and significance for rebellious and recalcitrant fallen human beings, it is prescriptive and obligatory and designates for us what ought to be.

Bonhoeffer rightly tells us that the orders of creation are to be regarded as ethical mandates or commands to live in a certain way.[52] In the case of those sinfully inclined to unnatural acts and called upon to act upon their true nature, 'what is' objectively and ontologically is 'what ought to be' subjectively, empirically and existentially. This, I believe, is what Rahner has in mind when he speaks of a 'pure nature' that operates in a regulative fashion upon real human beings who actually exist; it is 'pure', not in the neo-scholastic sense of 'merely and only natural' as opposed to 'supernatural', but in what I take to be a prescriptive, ideal, ontological sense that makes it scarcely distinguishable from supernatural grace itself. It is also, I believe—more controversially, for John Milbank is convinced that Blondel and Rahner are mostly at odds[53]—

---

51. *Ibid*, 201.
52. D Bonhoeffer, *Ethics* (New York: Macmillan, 1955), 207.
53. J Milbank, *Theology and Social Theory: Beyond Secular Reason* (Oxford: Blackwell, 1995), 210–223.

what Blondel has in mind when he holds that the ontological question is only seriously posed and answered in practice, for in our acts we discover the very (ontological) presence of God 'and that is why the thought that follows the act is richer by an infinity than that which precedes it'.[54] His logic of action demands the supernatural, for in every act, Blondel insists, we have an implicit faith that a new and 'true' synthesis is emerging, that God is present in the unfolding of each act, that Love itself draws us unknowingly or semi-knowingly into its orbit. He holds that the ground holding together the meaning of our actions is an intuited harmony and not 'substance'[55] but surely we can bring the two together and say that the (ontological) reality of Love itself, of 'spiritual substance' or the Holy Spirit, is empirically present at all times in our groping efforts. However, although the logic of action demands the supernatural, the 'empirical' does not always respond as it should to the ever extended 'ontological invitation'. This spiritual substance, drawing our actions in faith towards an intuited harmony, this 'inviting ontological' or 'eliciting ontological', is the dynamic driving force of Blondel's logic of action. The latter, despite Milbank's claim to the contrary, can and does decipher the true meaning of action as Love or, viewed in terms of our ontological-empirical distinction, it reveals the routine ontological presence of Love itself in our everyday empirical acts.

---

54. M Blondel, *Action: Essay on a Critique of Life and a Science of Practice*, translated Olivia Blanchette (Notre dame: University of Notre Dame Press, 1984), 371.
55. J Milbank, *Theology and Social Theory: Beyond Secular Reason*, 217.

By recognising the prescriptivity (for us) of nature and essence, we are able, I believe, to move towards a reconciliation of Catholic and Reformation views on the extent of the consequences of the fall. When Scheeben, here representing the Catholic scholastics (and the 'anthropocentric' approach to ethics), says that our human nature constitutes a substance which is not variable and that it is indestructible even by the powerful attack of the sin and evil that entered the world with the fall,[56] this is often seen by Protestant critics (and those sympathetic to a 'theocentric' approach to ethics) as severely underestimating the fall and its consequences. However, if nature/essence is understood in the prescriptive manner I have here commended, then it is clearly seen as complete, perfect and unchangeable only in idea (objectively and ontologically) but not in fact (existentially and empirically), or 'in itself' but not in us. Scheeben tries to capture the impact of the 'ontological objective' upon the 'empirical/experiential subjective' by referring to nature in this encounter as a 'disposition' [Anlage] or as a potentiality which points beyond itself to a 'called-for' fulfilment and Aquinas speaks of the 'gift of rectitude' [donum rectitudinis] as bringing nature to itself (or the parts thereof to their intended destiny in the hierarchy of rectitude) but I believe myself that it is necessary, to do justice to our experience of this encounter, to use more explicitly prescriptive terminology. Also, to understand nature as 'prescriptive essence for our sin-ridden existence' enables us

---

56. MJ Scheeben, quoted in Thielicke, H, *Theological Ethics, Volume 2: Politics*, 202.

to see that when Thielicke, here representing Reformation theology, says that for Roman Catholic anthropology and its doctrine of the divine likeness, the 'sphere of the *imago* includes nature' and that in terms of its substance, 'this nature is static and self-contained' and 'cannot be augmented or diminished, improved or destroyed,'[57] what he says is, in a sense, unexceptionable; once it is understood that nature as essence (or as an ideally ordered connection of permanent ontic factors, to use Thielicke's way of portraying the Catholic scholastics), *in being descriptive of our true nature is prescriptive for our fallen nature*, then clearly 'nature', so understood, cannot be improved or destroyed. However, if nature is understood in this way (as prescriptive essence), this in turn problematises the conviction of Catholic scholastics that nature 'cannot be destroyed because it consists of an accumulation of ontic parts, each of which is in itself unalterable',[58] for it is only 'nature as prescriptive or ideal', or the very idea of nature (nature 'in itself') that cannot be destroyed or diminished, not the 'ontic parts' which as a result of the fall may grow towards heaven or degenerate towards hell.

This point has been well made by Reformation Theology. Thielicke, as we noted earlier, rightly insists that for humanity after the fall sin is total (pervasive) in its effect, corrupting our entire nature, and that only Christ can save us from our iniquity. However, Thielicke is, I believe, mistaken in making the inference that we must 'therefore' draw a hard and fast distinction between those who are

---

57. H Thielicke, *Theological Ethics, Volume 2: Politics*, 206.
58. *Ibid*, 206–207.

saved by Christ from their iniquity (Christians) and those who are not (non-Christians). He holds that because of the pervasiveness of the effects of the power of sin and the fact that only Christians are rescued from this power through Christ, there can be 'no constant factor, no continuum, no neutral base of the ego, and consequently no common ground (how could there be?) between Christians and non-Christians'.[59] What I would suggest, however, is that whilst there may indeed be no constant factor or neutral basis of the ego (all having been tainted by sin), yet there is assuredly a constant ethical factor (nature as prescriptive essence for all humanity) and hence a continuum and common ground between Christians and non-Christians. We also need to take into account what I earlier referred to as 'universals of hope' and what Pannenberg might call 'our general human destiny' (seeds of destiny, of hope for the future). Through the Holy Spirit, the Law first induces in us (that is, in *all* of us) a 'worldly grief' a regretful or despairing acknowledgement of the extent of our sinfulness before transforming it into the 'holy grief' of the repentant believer (2 Corinthians 7:10); we may say that the 'universal implicit' (the silent workings of the Spirit in us through the universality of the law) becomes the 'particular (non-universal) explicit' (the Godly grief of the repentant Christian). If, then, we must acknowledge that Satan's intent is to 'pervade all' (and especially all of our humanity), we must also acknowledge that the Spirit too 'pervades all' (and especially all of our humanity), for through goodness and love the Spirit intends to bring full-

---

59. *Ibid*, 198.

ness of life to all, just as Satan intends the total destruction of our humanity. If the universal ethical/ontological presence of 'nature as prescriptive essence' is a form of God's grace ever drawing humanity from fallen-ness to fullness of life, then it is a 'universal grace' that operates in all without distinction. We should not then attempt to divide or separate the 'human' and the 'divine', the 'anthropological' and the 'theological', an 'anthropological/ anthropocentric' approach to ethics and a 'theological/ theocentric' approach. Rather, we should see the anthropocentric approach as (rightly) serving to draw attention to our nature as a divinely implanted unchanging human essence or ideal, and the theocentric approach as (rightly) emphasising the prescriptivity or 'oughtness-for-our-fallen-humanity' of this same ideal. Thus, Oliver O'Donovan is right to insist that a 'natural ethic' is not at all at odds with a 'resurrection ethic', since what is noteworthy about the 'history of divine action' (paradigmatically, the divine/historical saving act of the resurrection of Jesus) is, in his terms, its vindication of 'creation order as a basis for rational action'[60] and, in my terms, its vindication of 'nature as prescriptive essence issuing imperatives of reason to our fallen humanity'. In contrast, Stanley Grenz is, I think, too harsh and dichotomous in his judgment that general ethics (including natural law ethics) is 'flawed by an all-pervasive defect, namely its "anthropocentricity" or fundamental human-centredness'[61] and that 'whereas

---

60. O O'Donovan, *The Desire of the Nations; Rediscovering the Roots of Political Theology*, 19.
61. SJ Grenz, *The Moral Quest; Foundations of Christian Ethics*, 216.

general ethics is necessarily anthropocentric, Christian ethics must be thoroughly theocentric'.[62]

We should also note here that nature as prescriptive essence operates as a necessary counterpoint and corrective to our fallen sinful nature and that when this is lost sight of, the stage is set for a Flacius to regard 'sin' as the substance of our humanity (that is, as having some form of positive being, rather than as being negatively related to man's true nature/prescriptive essence, as a fall from being, a flight into non-being etc) or for a Gerhard to cling to 'certain tiny remnants of the divine image' unaffected by the fall[63] and we then lose sight of God's 'prescriptive presence' in the form of a call to a return to our true nature. No doubt there is a contrast to be drawn between the original (undistorted) divine likeness enjoyed by Adam before the Fall and the 'negative mode' of the divine likeness that characterised the fallen Adam (his sense of loss and lack) but we should note here that what is missing in post-paradisal Adam—and this is what opens the way for Flacius and Gerhard—is not just the relation of fel-

---

62. *Ibid*, 218.
63. J Gerhard, quoted in Thielicke, H, *Theological Ethics, Volume 2: Politics* (Grand Rapids: Eerdmans, 1979), 215. Recognising that 'outside of faith' good and dutiful deeds are performed and acknowledged as such by the Lord, Thielicke actually comes very close to Gerhard's position, for he explains the commendable ethical endeavours of the pre-or non-Christian, and his reasons for believing that it really matters 'whether I am a criminal or a virtuous idealist' (Thielicke, 1979, 256.) in the following terms. 'Thinking in terms of gradations cannot be done away so long as out there beyond the pale of faith the divine likeness itself is not done away with and completely destroyed' (Thielicke, 1979, 261).

lowship with God (a loss properly emphasised by Reformation theology) but also the ideality, spontaneity and 'virtual automaticity' of Adam's 'subjection' to God's 'order for humanity'. Before the Fall, Adam, I suspect, wore the yoke of this order so lightly—almost unconsciously or semi-consciously—that he would scarcely have been aware of it at all but would rather have merely 'felt' his God-given essence flowing into his idealised existence. However, along with the fellowship of God, Adam also loses the spontaneity of the essence/existence relationship. We could perhaps say that law replaces grace, for after the fall the free and easy flow of essence into existence ('spontaneous essence') is replaced by the law, duty and obligation ('prescriptive essence'), but it would I think be more precise to say that since grace is 'God's presence', then grace in the form of God's immediate presence for Adam in the Garden of Eden is replaced by grace in the form of God's mediated presence in and through the law and the prescriptive call of our true, original nature on our fallen nature.

What we have said so far concerning the advantages of 'nature as prescriptive essence' as an analytical tool in a Catholic-Protestant dialogue could also be said of 'the ontic as prescriptive essence'. Consider the following quote from Thielicke:

> The Reformers must of course concede to Roman Catholicism that the image of God, indeed the humanity of man in general, has an ontic 'side', just as faith has its psychology and believing thus involves real psychical

and even physiological processes. There can be no doubt on this score. However, there is on the other hand every reason to doubt, indeed to reject, the idea that man or his faith is in some way characterised by these ontic factors. On the contrary, he is characterised solely by what he receives from the alien factor of divine grace.[64]

Now what, it must be asked, does Thielicke have in mind by the ontic 'side' of the image of God and by (what certainly appears to be) his simultaneous acceptance/rejection of the ontological structure of the *imago Dei*? 'Ontic/ontological' normally connotes the (truly) real or essential, in contrast to the appearing or empirical (the merely 'given') and in this respect it (or, more precisely, the ontic/empirical contrast) would seem to be a member of a family of paired contrasting terms: reality/appearance, essence/accident, noumenon/phenomenon, necessary/contingent, (determining) form/(determined) matter, familiar/alien . . .; unless we are Derridean poststructuralists, we normally acknowledge the closer proximity to truth, the higher degree of reality and the logical, epistemological and metaphysical preponderance or priority of the first of each of these opposing terms in comparison to the second. Thielicke, however, seems to reverse this conventional expectation in a manner which Derridean poststructuralists might well approve of but which makes intelligible communication well-nigh impossible, for he

---

64. H Thielicke, *Theological Ethics, Volume 2: Politics*, 217–218.

clearly regards the ontic elements of our humanity as non-essential or as not really characterising our humanity. At this point, it might seem that Thielicke simply follows Reformation theology into an abyss of inconsistency and unintelligibility but in actual fact Reformation theology is perfectly sound and acceptable in so far as its main thrust is (simply and primarily) to insist that the human person is 'ontically vacant' in the sense that each human soul is a battlefield of opposing forces and that what we are to be or to become depends on the side we take in the great spiritual struggle taking place in us and in the world. This insight of Reformation theology must not be lost sight of but it is perfectly compatible with an acknowledgement on our part that the ontic *is* the divine or the divinely ordained, our true nature or the truth of who we really are, which means that the 'victory of the ontic' is God's victory, a blow successfully delivered by God (the divine 'call' of the goodness of our original nature) against Satan (the self-destructive recalcitrance of pride lodged in our fallen humanity). Considered in the light of the ongoing struggle between God and Satan for each human soul, the human person is indeed 'ontically vacant' in the sense that our true nature and destiny is precisely what is being fought over, but considered in the light of God's everlasting faithfulness and final victory, each person, by the grace of God, is 'ontically saturated' or 'ever ontically oriented and determined'—oriented in the sense that the 'ontic compass' of our humanity ever points towards God and that 'our hearts are restless until they rest in Thee', and 'determined' in the sense that God, the font of Being and of our being, ever descends upon our fallen nature with the imperative, life-giving demands of the law.

In a similar vein, Thielicke may well be true to the spirit of Reformation theology in insisting that the Decalogue was primarily intended for the physical preservation of the Jewish people as the bearers of salvation history,[65] rather than for the good of humanity as a whole, but this does not exclude the possibility that the Law (the Decalogue) has an important prescriptive and preservative role in the 'orders of creation'. Certainly, when considered from the perspective of the Jewish people in the light of their experience as the bearers of salvation history, the Law was assuredly (specifically) 'for us' (here meaning 'for us as Jews') whether or not it was also intended for all of humanity and certainly too, when what was made 'available to us Jews' (the experience of the Jews) is then made 'available to all' (Romans 11:11–12), we may say with Thielicke that 'the divine commandments take on a new significance. That is, their significance is no longer confined to the covenant people alone, for the covenant is now available to the "nations"'.[66] Could it be, however, that the law not only takes on a *new* significance but that it also takes on *its true* significance, (that is, the universal or 'for all' meaning and role God intended 'from the beginning'), that its true 'for us/for all' character is now fully and finally revealed, that God's ultimate purpose was to school the Jewish people of the Old Testament in the ways of the Law in order that they (or the 'new' Israel) might be

---

65. H Thielicke, *Theological Ethics, Volume 2: Politics*, 273.
66. H Thielicke, *Theological Ethics, Volume 2: Politics*, 277.

to all the nations a light revealing the true nature of God's Law as 'for us/for all'? If, as I am suggesting, the true, universal significance of God's Law is finally and definitively revealed in the New Testament, then we may say that 'Nature' has from the beginning carried in its womb the precepts which Yahweh taught the Jewish people to appreciate and love, in which case there is certainly a place (contrary to Thielicke's suggestion) for 'the idea that there are certain basic laws which are immanent in the cosmos since creation, and which must be maintained if the world is not to perish'.[67]

Finally, the idea of essence being 'for us' (or the notion of the 'prescriptive ontic') is useful, I would suggest, in helping us to more confidently approach the vexed question of 'universals', at least with regard to the 'universal form' of our common (but fallen) humanity, which is our present and main concern (though a similar analysis may, I believe, be usefully, if guardedly applied to all the forms present in the whole of creation as adversely affected or infected by the fall). In his dialogue *Parmenides* Plato outlined the difficulty as follows. If one and the same Form (human) is said to be *in* many different particulars (Fred, Sheila, Socrates...) as one thing may be said to be in many different things, then how can the Form be single and undivided and still be *in* many distinct individuals. Either the Form will be broken up into the number of individuals, in which case the unity and common (single) identity of the Form is lost, or the identical, universal presence of the Form in each of its particulars destroys their distinc-

---

67. H Thielicke, *Theological Ethics, Volume 2: Politics*, 274.

tiveness and individuality. However, if the Form of our common humanity or the universal 'human' is, as I have suggested, a 'prescriptive ontic', then it may subsist separately (*universale ante rem*) and apart from its 'members' as an ideal which exercises a constant gravitational pull upon them—in this sense, our humanity transcends each of us and draws us towards a fullness beyond time—and yet it may also be said to be *in* each of its members (*universale in re*) precisely as just such a universal empirical orientation *in* each of them—in this sense humanity is an immanent orientation in each of us towards a personal and common fulfilment in this life and beyond. The same universal (humanity), by virtue of being present *to*, is also at the same time (though in varying degrees) present *in* each of its distinct particulars. There is then only one ideal form of our humanity but in so far as we are each oriented, in our own specific and unique way to its enveloping light, it may be truly said to be present in us without destroying our distinctiveness. Thus, we may say with Aquinas and moderate realists that the intellect is able to *abstract from* sensible particulars their common nature (*universale post rem*) but, on the view I am here commending, it would be more precise and appropriate to say that the intellect is able to *detect in* sensible particulars their common orientation to their Form or 'true' ideal nature. Certainly, 'universals' exist in our minds as concepts but not only in our minds, for each universal exists in our minds as the subjective imprint of its objective correlative; what we grasp intellectually in many empirical instances is their common striving or *nisus* towards a single Form. When Aquinas makes use of the modified

Platonism passed on to him though Augustine by speaking of divine thoughts or exemplars that are *imitable* by many creatures,[68] he comes closest to what I have in mind by the 'prescriptive essence/ontic'.

Like the kind of fusion of a 'creation ethic' with a 'kingdom ethic' that we find in Oliver O'Donovan's *Resurrection and Moral Order: An Outline for Evangelical Ethics*,[69] the position I have been advocating in this chapter likewise involves a synthesis of the universally operative dynamism of the Spirit with the 'ethical empowerment' unleashed by the resurrection of Jesus in the lives of those being saved. O'Donovan's 'redeemed creation' that 'does not merely confront us moral agents but includes us and enables us to participate in it'[70] could surely be spoken of and understood as (i) the original and restored fullness of our nature/essence, our 'ontological truth' forcefully and universally speaking to the whole of fallen humanity on behalf of the God of creation and drawing all of humanity through the Spirit to the fullness of truth and existence intended by the Father of all, but also as (ii) the intimately and personally operative presence of the Spirit in those (only those) being saved, being empowered by resurrection grace and entering thereby into the new life of redeemed creation. However, in this chapter, because of its political relevance and importance, I have focused mainly

---

68. T Aquinas, *Summa Theologica* (London: Eyre and Spotiswoode, 1974), 1.15, I, ad 1.
69. O O'Donovan, *Resurrection and Moral Order: An Outline for Evangelical Ethics* (Grand Rapids: Eerdmans, 1986), 14–15.
70. *Ibid*, 101.

on the *universal*, unceasing dynamism of the Spirit, rather than on the new world (redeemed creation) being entered *only* by those powerfully touched in blessed moments by resurrection grace, for even though the former (the universal dynamism of the Spirit) intends the *universal* victory of resurrection grace, the resistance of sin leaves the Spirit with continuing work to do and delays the realisation of the Spirit's universal purpose. With this politically significant '*universal*, unceasing dynamism of the Spirit' in mind, I have suggested in this chapter that the 'prescriptive essence', considered as prescriptive, is the voice of God as the mystical font of law entering our lives with authority but that considered as essence or 'holy essence' present in us, it is the uplifting Spirit constantly flowing through us and bringing our humanity to its proper fulfilment. With a holy indifference to 'Hume's fork', the universal Spirit is eternity flowing through time, (ontological) reality challenging our 'empiricity', necessity and truth informing our contingency and freedom, the divine *a priori* incorporating our synthetic humanity into its life, His will becoming our peace. Hobbes treats it as such, as we saw in the last chapter, whereas Derrida regards it as emanating, not from its source in God, but from an originary or 'foundational' act of violence, as we shall see in the following chapter.

Chapter Eleven

Derrida, Foundational Violence and the Mystical Foundation of Authority

He looked for justice but found bloodshed
Isaiah 5:7

Power as structured by law, and at the service of law, is the antithesis of violence
Joseph Ratzinger, *The Dialectics of Secularization*, 2006, 58.

In a dramatic outburst, Gregory VII once described kingship as an artifact of violent men who were ignorant of God's ways and he even, referring to Matthew 4:9, suggested that Satan is the final source of all political authority. Perhaps he had in mind Augustine's comparison of the mighty who wield power to large-scale criminal gangs. More recently, in his book *A Generous Orthodoxy* Brian McLaren makes the following comments:

> I am an American. My nation was founded on land theft and countless broken treaties, on the suppression, exclusion, ethnic cleansing,

and near eradication of the people who inhabited this land (Native Peoples) . . . Everything I know of God tells me that God was outraged by the atrocities of my European ancestors and brokenhearted for the victims . . . But what is God to do? Forever curse Americans, refusing to assist them, refusing to respond when we sing 'God bless America'? Should God forsake American children and grandchildren to a hundred generations because of the original American holocaust? Wouldn't God's blessing of a nation so conceived imply an endorsement of the atrocities that were and are committed? . . . If God blesses anyone, he must bless the violent and the children of the violent because there is no-one else to bless. This is not an excuse but it is a reality. We can't remove ourselves from this equation. There is no other material for God to work with but this ugly, violent, primitive raw material.[1]

McLaren here captures very well the sheer pervasiveness of political violence, its insidious persistence, its empirical diffusion into the interstices of political life, the continuing pain (the despair of indigenous peoples) it inflicts on its victims, its grotesque inevitability (or so it seems at times) in a fallen world, and yet God's absolute abhorrence of it. McLaren here reminds us of the fundamentals

---

1. B McLaren, *A Generous Orthodoxy* (Grand Rapids: Zondervan, 2004), 168–169.

of the Christian faith, of God's hatred of sin and love of the sinner, of God's anguish at our evil acts and redeeming love for us, of God's hatred of the violence (sin) in each of us and love of the violent (sinner). True or legitimate political authority can have no truck with political violence, with the kind of murderous acts of foundational violence that established 'European America' and its laws ('European Australia' and its laws, etc). What then is the status of governments instituted and laws enacted by violent conquerors? Do these governments have, or can they acquire, legitimacy and do the laws of these political regimes have authority? In this chapter I wish to suggest that when Jacques Derrida contends that the ultimate font or origin (what he calls the 'mystical foundation of authority') of law is an originary or 'foundational' act of violence, this is tantamount to saying that God's blessing of a violent people implies God's 'endorsement of the atrocities that were and are committed'.[2] I argue that Derrida is correct in holding that the law is always an authorised force but that he is mistaken in suggesting that the ultimate font of (legitimate) political authority is a 'foundational' act of violence.

In considering this 'mystical foundation of authority', Derrida briefly discusses the work of Montaigne, who first used this expression, and of Pascal, who later borrowed and used the same expression. I too will briefly discuss these two prominent thinkers and then refer to a comment by Kant which is particularly important in this regard. I will suggest that Derrida and, more recently, Jens Bartel-

---

2. *Ibid*, 168.

son fall prey to a curious, one-sided narrow view of 'foundationalism' and contrast their overly 'architecturalised' image of the 'foundation' of authority with the foundationalism of Thomas Hobbes which is, I shall argue, architectural only as and when appropriate. Also, I argue that Derrida's account of the relationship between justice, law and force/violence is profoundly mistaken, that his attempt to put 'prohibition' and violence at the heart of law fails, that he is mistaken in refusing to acknowledge that routine rules of obedience to the law may be in some sense just, and that he is blind to the presence of the universal (of universal justice) in those difficult cases where we face what he calls 'the order of the undecidable'.[3] I then discuss whether or not these cases illustrate the 'absence of universality', as Derrida suggests, or a 'surplus of universality', as I suggest. However, I also argue that Derrida is extremely helpful in drawing our attention to the violent foundations of political regimes and that we should employ his insights to draw a distinction between the empirical, historical *de facto* origins (causes) of political regimes and the (universal) ethical grounds or reasons for regarding them as legitimate (*de jure*) or illegitimate, just or unjust. I also suggest that, despite his rejection of metaphysics, Derrida is implicitly metaphysical in his treatment of justice, that the key reason for his apparent blindness to the presence of universal justice is that he calls it by another name and that, as a consequence, Derrida is able to successfully address the various criticisms

---

3. J Derrida, 'Force of Law: The Mystical Foundation of Authority', in *Cardozo Law Review*, 11:5–6 (1990): 921–1045.

directed against him by such commentators as Thomas McCarthy, Richard Wolin and Mark Lilla.

Montaigne, Pascal and Kant

Derrida takes up the expression 'the mystical foundation of authority' from Montaigne and Pascal in order, as he says, 'to reinterpret and consider [it] apart from its most conventional meaning'.[4] I now wish to briefly investigate what this expression meant—or at least could possibly and plausibly have meant—in the minds of these two prominent French figures, before considering, in the following section, Derrida's positing of an originating violence as the foundation of law and authority.

At first glance, the accounts of the mystical foundation of authority provided by these two thinkers present us with a strange mixture of the banal and the bizarre or, rather, they are bizarre because they are banal when banality is the last thing we would expect. Surely, it is odd to say, as Montaigne does, that 'laws keep up their good standing, not because they are just, but because they are laws; that are the mystical foundation of their authority'.[5] Thus the authority of the law and the respect it evokes has, it would appear, no deeper source than the law itself and seemingly rests upon the simplistic statement (or tautological claim) that 'the law is what the law is' or 'the law evokes what the law evokes in us'. Now surely a sim-

---
4. *Ibid*, 937.
5. ME de Montaigne, in J Derrida, J 'Force of Law. The Mystical Foundation of Authority', *ibid*, 939.

plistic tautology seems like an unworthy and bizarre candidate for the elevated status of 'ultimate font of legitimacy.' Moreover, we are just as surprised, and for the same reason, to find Pascal making the following contention:

> [O]ne man says that the essence of justice is the authority of the legislator, another that it is the convenience of the King, another that it is current custom; and the latter is closest to the truth; simple reason tells us that nothing is just in itself; everything crumbles with time. Custom is the sole basis for equity, for the simple reason that it is received; it is the mystical foundation of its authority.[6]

Once again we sense a marked discrepancy between the expectation of 'depth' conjured up by the expression 'the mystical foundation' and the mundane entity or actuality to which the expression actually refers. Perhaps, however, we only experience a disorienting sense of dissonance because—and this is, perhaps, a deliberate ploy on the part of Montaigne and Pascal—we are *only* regarding the 'mystical' through or, in terms of, the 'mundane', which is legitimate as far as it goes but which, as our only viewpoint, makes it appear as if the 'mundane' is the underlying reality (or truth) of the 'mystical' and explains it away. What we need to do then is to *also* regard the 'mundane' in terms of the 'mystical', that is, as expressive of the mys-

---

6. B Pascall, in J Derrida, 'Force of Law. The Mystical Foundation of Authority', 939.

tical by which it is thoroughly permeated, and if we do so, it naturally casts in an altogether different light the claim that law constitutes (is thoroughly permeated by?) its own mystical foundation (Montaigne) and the claim that the mystical foundation of authority is the same as (expresses itself through?) what is received through custom (Pascal).[7] The key point and central claim being made by Pascal and Montaigne is that the law is, first and foremost, *our* law or that, in the words of Oliver O'Donovan, acknowledgement—these authorities are *there* and they are *ours*—'is the fundamental relation that obtains between a society and its own political authorities'.[8] Perhaps the real insight of Pascal is that in receiving the law as custom and custom as law, we (in one sense) speak to ourselves (in another sense), that is, our living past as 'form' speaks to our living present as its 'matter' and the collective self expressed through our ongoing traditions envelops us as its living members and carries its authoritative presence into our lives. Perhaps, too, it was this authoritative presence of the law, or our own collective self finding expression through our government and laws and reaching us as a voice that echoes our own intimations, that Montaigne

---

7. Derrida reminds us that Montaigne speaks of the legitimate fictions on which our law 'founds the truth of its justice' (*Ibid*, 939), the meaning of which is, admittedly, not crystal clear. However, it is at least clear enough to indicate that when Montaigne says that it is not because they are just that 'laws keep up their good standing', he accepts that laws should be as just as possible.
8. O O'Donovan, *The Desire of the Nations; Rediscovering the Roots of Political Theology* (Cambridge: Cambridge University Press, 203), 47.

had in mind when he insisted that anyone who obeys the laws 'because they are just is not obeying them the way he ought to'.[9] The more general point here is that what we might call the current practices of authority or the routine execution of the law (or of law/custom) should not be regarded as, or at least *only* as, an external force that descends upon us from on high but rather, or at least *also*, as our very own voice in another guise or as the sociopolitical 'form of life' in and through which our social being is collectively expressed, realised and constituted. Hence any investigation into the authority of the laws and government to which we are currently subject should *not* be undertaken in order to ascertain whether or not we should be subject to that authority. In Pascal's words, anyone who traces the mystical foundation of the authority of custom/law 'to its source, annihilates it'[10] but this is not, I think, a ban on theoretical speculation as such (which is precisely what Pascal is engaged in after all) but rather an insistence that a theoretical inquiry into the foundations of authority should in the main be undertaken with a view to clarifying and explicating what it is to be obliged. Kant makes the same point in the following way:

> [The] origin of supreme power . . . is *not discoverable* by the people who are subject to it. In other words, the subject *ought not* to indulge in *speculations* about its origin with a view

---

9. ME de Montaigne, in J Derrida, J 'Force of Law. The Mystical Foundation of Authority', *ibid*, 939.
10. *Ibid*, 939.

to acting upon them . . . Whether in fact an actual contract originally preceded their submission to the State's authority, whether the power came first and the law only appeared after it, or whether they ought to have followed this order—these are completely futile arguments for a people which is already subject to civil law, and they constitute a menace to the state.[11]

In my view, these prominent figures are *not* saying that it is simply wrong to investigate the origins of authority with a view to drawing important practical conclusions or as a form of practical critique; nor are they objecting to the obviously wholesome practice of judging the merits and demerits of current legislation and making appropriate practical suggestions. Are they, however, saying that it *is* simply wrong to investigate the origins of authority in the radical or potentially revolutionary sense of challenging or undermining the law itself and its foundations? Are they saying that to even raise the question 'Why obey the law?' is like raising the question 'Why be moral?' since it betrays and violates the deeper structure or very essence of who and what we are as citizens and as moral and social beings who have a share and a place in the life of a political community? I think that their answer would be to say that the decision to question the foundations of authority with a view to formulating a radical or subversive

---

11. I Kant, 'The Metaphysics of Morals', *Kant's Political Writings* edited by H Reiss(Cambridge: Cambridge University Press, 1991), 143.

critique thereof, should itself be questioned and itself requires justification. The normal presumption, they might say, is that the laws currently in force are *our* laws, the laws of *our* Commonwealth (God's ongoing, 'sedimented presence' with us) and that as such, our obedience requires no special justification but is simply routinely required. This means that it would only be legitimate for us to raise the question 'Why obey the law?' without violating our identity as moral beings and members of a community when we, the citizens of a Commonwealth, genuinely feel that the current laws and policies are no longer *ours* but are, rather, experienced as the constraining, silencing voice of a wholly alien 'other' or as an external force or 'presence' with which we have lost all affinity and can no longer identify. Rebellion then, they might say in summary, is only justifiable when the government of the day, as a result of its policies and laws, no longer bears the authoritative presence of the state (the 'general will') into our life in common.

Derrida; Justice, Law and Force/Violence

Jacques Derrida holds the law (of the state) is always an authorised force and that its ultimate font or origin (what he calls the 'mystical foundation of authority') is an originary or 'foundational' act of violence. Before discussing his account, it will be helpful to first make a preliminary, broad statement on the relationship between justice, law and force ('enforceability', 'authorised force'). The difference between law and justice, and the manner in which they each relate to 'force' and 'enforceability' may, I think, be more clearly seen if we consider the kind of universality they each exhibit. When we think of justice as a universal idea in the Platonic sense, that is, as a universal that is differentially approximated and instantiated in diverse times and places, our thoughts are primarily focused on its 'universality-as-such' (or apart from specific contexts and circumstances), its perfection, its allure and its constant call upon us in *all* circumstances. We do not know the kinds of contexts, or 'discursive specificities' we will find ourselves in as the future unfolds but we do know that, whatever they may be, we are required to be just. At this point, it would be tempting to simply state that this 'universality' of justice contrasts with the 'specificity' of law but it is important to acknowledge that, at least ideally and in normal intent, the specific laws of a society that are geared to its particular circumstances are, routinely, 'universal' justice concretely embodied in a particular time and place. Ultimately, it is (universal) justice, not (specific, jurisdictional) law, that authorises force or, alternatively expressed, jurisdictional law properly authorises force only in as far as it expresses, and is the legislative instrument of, universal justice. What is fascinating—though, I think, counter intuitive and profoundly mistaken—is Derrida's suggestion in the 'Force of Law' that force or violence 'authorises' law and justice. It is to Derrida's account that we now turn our attention.

In the 'Force of Law' Derrida seems to almost perversely subvert what I would regard as the proper or 'intuitive' relation between justice, law and force/violence. He holds, I think correctly, that 'the essence of law is not prohibitive but affirmative'[12] and that—or should we say 'but that': that is the point we are about to investigate— 'there is no such thing as law (*droit*) that doesn't imply *in itself, a priori, in the analytic structure of its concept*, the possibility of being "enforced", applied by force'.[13] Now this allegedly analytical link between law and force/ enforceability suggested by Derrida certainly seems to imply that the essence of the law is prohibitory (enforcing its will against opposition) as well as affirmative. How then are we to conceive of the prohibitory aspect of law? Is it essential or accidental? The issue is anything but clearcut. I think it would be true to say that whilst the essence of law is indeed affirmative (Barth's divine 'Yes'), yet at the same time, in the light of our human weakness and proneness to self indulgence, it is invariably prohibitive as well (the divine 'No'); its prohibitive character could, I think, be best characterised as a 'necessary accident'. Thus justice/law is affirmative by essence and prohibitory by empirical human necessity or by virtue of the waywardness of humanity. It is as if the ideal of justice is an affirmation and celebration of life and value in all its aspects, a spontaneous or authentically willed harmony of the good in all things (including humanity) but the 'pragmatism of law' is obliged to acknowledge our human waywardness and thus the regrettable empirical necessity

---

12. J Derrida, 'Force of Law: The Mystical Foundation of Authority', 929.
13. *Ibid*, 925.

of enforcement and compulsion. Thus it is entirely proper, I believe, for Derrida to emphasise the importance, and even the necessity, of the link between law and force/enforceability but the problem with Derrida's manner of speaking here is that it suggests that, at the heart of law, we find not only an affirmative essence of life in its fullness (the fullness of being God intends for each person and society) but also a 'prohibitory' essence or even a 'force/violence' essence. To lodge 'prohibition' at the heart of law paves the way for 'enforcement' and then 'force/violence' as its co-inhabitants. It is no small matter, but of fundamental importance, to grasp the empirical necessity of the prohibitory aspect of law, rather than seeing it as, in essence, lodged in 'the analytic structure of the concept' of law. By claiming that there is an intrinsic link between law and prohibition/force, rather than, as I've suggested, a necessary but external link, Derrida is able to also insist that force/violence is at the very heart (at the core or essence) of justice itself and thus also, in so far as the law is 'God for us', at the very heart of the 'God who is for us'. Thus, for Derrida, enforceability is not 'an exterior or secondary possibility that may or may not be added as a supplement to law; it is the force *essentially implied* (emphasis added) in the very concept of *justice as law* (*droit*).[14] Speaking in the same vein, he regards justice as 'appealing to force from its first moment, from its first word' and holds that '[i]n the beginning there will

---

14. *Ibid*, 925

have been force'.[15] Surely, however, all of this in effect—Derrida's actual intent is unclear—puts the 'merely accidental' at the heart of the 'truly essential', violence and death at the heart of the God of love, and transforms justice as the 'essence that authorises', that confers legitimacy and an ordered fullness of life through law, that descends as God's life-giving form on recalcitrant human matter, into a mere effect or creation of its very opposite, force/violence.

Only as it is intrinsically linked to universal justice, to its origin and end, is law truly itself, and yet, as Derrida forcefully reminds us, there is scarcely a jurisdiction in existence that does not have feet of clay, that was not 'born' in violence or the violently asserted 'right' of the stronger. This is what Derrida/Benjamin insist upon and, no doubt, they are historically and empirically in the right. However, at this point, the critical question arises; is it possible for a new political regime to be 'conceived', or empirically generated, in the darkness of power seeking and violence, and yet to be 'born' (or perhaps 'born again' or redeemed), through the light of justice and a growing sense of civility? I believe that it can, that a political regime founded in an act of violence may become genuinely legitimate through its just and civil treatment of the vanquished. The task or process of 'legitimisation' involves transforming (i) those involuntarily subjugated into voluntary citizens, (ii) *de facto* control into *de jure* rule and (iii) mere 'government' or the empirical exercise of

---

15. *Ibid*, 935.

power into a newly born state. Derrida himself does not directly address this question[16] but we shall see later, when discussing the 'ordeal of the undecidable', that his deep respect for the spirit of (incalculable) justice brings him very close indeed to just this position. Certainly, he holds, as we shall see, that all persons (and hence both victors and vanquished) are at all times subject to the requirements—unique and incalculable, yet pressing and 'real'—of universal justice.

Bartelson, Derrida and Hobbes: Architecturalism

No doubt, the foundation of the authority of law and government is 'mystical' in the sense that the term definitely connotes a 'deep' quest into the true meaning or essence

---

16. In 'Asylum Seekers, Colonialism and the de-legitimization of the Australian State' (*Australian Quarterly*, 2003: 18–24), I note ethe simple but uncontested fact that the continent of Australia was secured by means of the superior force exercised by the first British settlers against its indigenous inhabitants. In Michael Walzer's words, the 'right of white Australians to the great empty spaces of the subcontinent rested on nothing more than the claim they had staked, and enforced against the aboriginal people, before anyone else' ('The Distribution of Membership' *Boundaries: National Autonomy and its Limits* edited by P Brown and H Shu [Totowa, NJ: Rowman and Littlefield, 1981], 17.). In this article, however, I argue that it is possible for any state, even if illegitimate in its origins, to later acquire legitimacy by dint of the just, wise and compassionate policies that its government pursues and that in Australia this process of acquiring legitimacy was well under way until it was suddenly stopped, and indeed reversed, by the arrival of John Howard's anti-asylum seeker rhetoric ('Tampa populism') on the political scene.

of our subjectivity (as individuals and as participants in the general will or in the life of civil society as a collective subject) and of our own self (again, personal or collective). Our reflections on the 'own self' may lead us to consider it as the eternal subject or subjectivity-in-itself at the core of our empirical subjectivity[17], as eternity entering time, as the sacred centre of our lives together, as the still point of our turning world, as the conscious site or 'sensorium' of divine intimations or, finally, as the Absolute (Holy) Spirit enveloping our spirits, but wherever our reflections lead us, we certainly feel that we are pursuing some kind of mystical quest. However, the foundation of the authority of law and government is also 'mundane' in the sense that the state is always near at hand or ever present in the form of our customary political practices and living traditions, as Pascal, Hegel (*Sittlichkeit*) and Bradley ('My station and its duties') would rightly insist. Here we come across a very real difficulty for, whether we think of the 'foundation' of authority mystically or mundanely, its normal architectural meaning of 'the base of' or 'that on which something else is erected' is clearly misleading. It strongly suggests a separation and external relationship between substructure and superstructure, whereas what we need is a term that evokes the sense of an intimate, organic, living relationship between an inner, noumenal 'heart' of political life (the Spirit) that flows into its phenomenal appearances and is expressed through the em-

---

17. Trainor, BT 1998a, *Justice and the State: On Liberal Organicism and the Foundations of Emancipatory Politics*, World Heritage Press, Quebec.

pirical 'outer' of public life. In this regard the term 'foundation' is not wholly inadequate but neither is it, as we have seen, entirely adequate either. If we continue to use the term in legal and political theory (I personally have no objections), we must attempt to ensure that it is not saturated with architectural imagery to the point where it ceases to be serviceable and becomes seriously misleading. Such a narrow and one-sided understanding of foundationalism in political theory I call 'architecturalism'. My main suggestion in this section is that writers like Bartelson and Derrida, who believe themselves to be attacking 'foundationalism' are in fact attacking only this perverted form thereof (architecturalism). My key criticism is that by equating the one with the other in the way they do, an aura of illegitimacy falls on earlier theorists who were properly, sensibly and legitimately 'foundational' and who pursued their quest for the ultimate font of authority without being 'architecturalist' in their thinking or 'foundational' in the derogatory sense (the sense in which it is falsely equated with 'architectural') that is now popular. I now propose to compare the overly architecturalised image or understanding of the foundation of authority found in Bartelson and Derrida with that of Thomas Hobbes, whose foundationalism, as we shall now see, is architectural only as and when appropriate.

There is no doubt that for Hobbes the political covenant is foundationalist in the sense that the authority of the political sovereign and the duty of obedience of his subjects clearly stem from this covenant. However, as we noted in chapter ten, even though the covenant is the sole source (more precisely, the sole, immediate source) of the 'formal' authority exercised by the sovereign, yet the political covenant is also a mechanism or medium which enables the eternal laws of nature (their eternal authority as principles of peace and concord) to pass into the definite, temporalised form of the civil law, so that the sovereign only exercises true or 'substantive' authority as the agent of this transmission from eternity into time or, alternatively expressed, as the agent or servant of Hobbes's 'person' of the state. To focus *only* on the political covenant as a process whereby the sovereign is duly authorised (on, that is, the 'how' rather than the 'why' of the political covenant) runs the twofold risk of making it look (i) as if 'time' is the sole origin of 'eternity', as if the 'eternal' authority of the sovereign issues solely from a founding moment in time and (ii) as if the foundation of the authority of law and government is something apart from and independent of, rather than the spiritual heart and ethical essence of, law and government. The 'substantive' ethical foundation of authority (its 'why' and 'what') is foundational in the sense of thoroughly permeating law and government and of (eternally, always) making them what they are. Thus the relation between law and its true, substantive, authoritative foundation is more akin to the relation between matter and its constitutive form than it is to the relation between a superstructure and its physical foundation. In the case of Hobbes, then, we may speak of a founding act or even of a founding moment (at the 'time' of the political covenant), so long as it is understood that we are not speaking of historical time. He uses the device of an imaginary state of nature and an imaginary foundation of the state to highlight what he takes to be the real, ongoing, substantive relation between sovereign and subject. There is, for Hobbes, no magical historical moment when the authority of law and government originated, though there well may be a 'mystical moment' when we each imaginatively re-enact the foundation of the state within ourselves, that is, when, by reflecting upon and grasping for ourselves the rationale of sovereignty, we in a sense become part of the ongoing or perpetual foundation of political authority. Let us now see how all of this differs from Derrida's account.

In the case of Hobbes we may say that the political covenant is the immediate source of formal and institutional authority, that the laws of nature prescribing peace are the ultimate source of substantive authority, and that the vital role performed by the political covenant is to open up definite, formal channels for the flow of substantive authority from its ultimate source, that is, from God (the author of the laws of nature) through the 'person' of the state into everyday government. In contrast, for Derrida, there is only a single, one-dimensional founding act; it is a mysterious 'how' (an originary violence) without a 'why'. Concerning the 'force of law of a legitimate power', he speaks of 'the supposedly originary violence that must have established this authority and that could not itself have been authorised by any anterior legitimacy'.[18] This founding act does not, as in the case of Hobbes, facilitate the flow of authority from its mystical source but is deemed to be the ultimate, self-founding source of authority itself.

---

18. J Derrida, 'Force of Law: The Mystical Foundation of Authority', 927.

As he says, '[s]ince the origin of authority, the foundation or ground, the position of the law can't by definition rest on anything but themselves, they are a violence without ground'.[19] Interestingly, both for Derrida and Hobbes, the final sources of authority 'exceed the opposition between founded and unfounded'[20] but whereas for Hobbes, the final font of authority is neither founded nor unfounded because it is perpetual or eternal, for Derrida it 'exceeds' this distinction because it is, as he says, a 'violence without ground'.[21] Thus when Derrida, with an overly architecturalised image of foundationalism in mind, asks himself the question 'upon what does the foundation of authority itself rest?', his unsurprising answer is that it rests on nothing at all, or, in the vacuum of nothingness, sheer violence. In this way, a distorted understanding of foundationalism leads to a warped understanding of the founding act of authority as a violence that rushes in to fill the vacuum of nothingness. Again, we should note that Hobbes' vacuum of disorder and lawlessness (which, in the state of nature, violence rushes in to destructively fill) bears a certain resemblance to Derrida's vacuum of nothingness, his foundation without foundation, but there the resemblance ends, for Derrida holds the view that the originary violence that fills this void is internally linked[22] to the force of law of a legitimate power, whereas Hobbes has attempted to indelibly impress on our minds

---

19. *Ibid*, 943.
20. *Ibid*.
21. *Ibid*.
22. *Ibid*, 927 and 941.

for all time the fact that law and government are, in their essence, the very antithesis of violence and that whilst violence may well be the foundation, in the sense of the historical source or empirical cause of a political regime, it can never be its ethical foundation or the font of its authority and legitimacy. Thus, whereas Derrida founds the authority of law counter-intuitively on that which legitimate authority is actually designed to counteract (that is violence, originary or otherwise), Hobbes, in contrast, leaves us in no doubt that law is the 'other' of violence, not in the sense of being 'its other' (that is, somehow integral to its essence) but as the instrument or medium of everything positive that issues from the womb of life (development, growth, fulfilment) and as the arch-protector that stands firmly against the anti-being, anti-matter, anti-life, 'vacuum' of violence and disorder.

In the recent work of Jens Bartelson, we also find the distorting influence of an overly architecturalised image of foundationalism. In broad terms, Bartelson is convinced that in modern political discourse, there is a 'discursive prohibition against questioning the ultimate origin of authority'.[23] He regards Kant's insistence that the origin of supreme power 'is *not discoverable* by the people who are subject to it' and that 'the subject *ought not* to indulge in *speculations* about its origin with a view to acting upon them'[24] as an early example and classic statement of this 'discursive prohibition'. Reflecting on this prohibition, he

---

23. J Bartelson, *The Critique of the State* (Cambridge: Cambridge University Press, 2001), 4.
24. I Kant, 'The Metaphysics of Morals',*Kant's Political Writings*, 143.

holds that since it would 'take authority to enforce the prohibition against questioning authority',[25] we face a curious paradox, for 'in order for authority to remain authoritative, it must be unquestionable, yet authority itself lacks the authority to impose such an unquestionability'.[26] The difficulty we encounter here, he believes, is all the greater when authority is understood as 'constituting', that is 'as without foundation outside itself';[27] in this case—and here he invokes Derrida—'it is nothing but an unfounded act which has been rendered foundational by the imposition of a certain forgetfulness as to its divine or violent origin'.[28] However, the difficulties posed by this paradox, he points out, do not disappear when we conceive of authority in a more mundane, democratic fashion as 'constituted', that is, by basing it on 'the imagined will and identity of a given political community, which effectively precedes and constitutes authority by virtue of itself being posited as a constituting force'.[29] The reason why a conception of authority as (democratically) constituted does not allow us to escape from the paradox is explained by Bartelson (again, following Derrida closely) as follows:

> On the one hand, the fact that constituting authority has no foundation outside itself makes it both tempting and *prima facie* easy to criti-

---
25. J Bartelson, *The Critique of the State*, 4
26. Ibid.
27. Ibid, 7.
28. Ibid, 7.
29. Ibid, 7.

cise, since the act that founds it cannot be justified and appears mysterious or illegitimate to the modern and democratically disposed political philosopher. On the other hand, it is difficult, if not impossible, to criticise that same founding act without simultaneously invoking it oneself, since there is no other presumably constituted authority there to validate or justify those acts of criticism.[30]

In the end, only a theological understanding of authority can help us to resolve this paradox or the apparent conflict between the poles of what O'Donovan calls the 'the authority-dialectic in the modern tradition: state sovereignty on the one hand, popular sovereignty on the other'. He points out that those poles are 'best understood as residual fragments of an original theological whole, which owe their opposition and their arbitrariness to the loss of their common centre of attraction'.[31] Certainly, the authority of the state and the authority of popular sovereignty are penultimate expressions of the final or ultimate authority of God. They draw their vitality, force and political significance from the same source, namely this enveloping 'original theological whole' and are thus deeply compatible. Hobbes draws our attention precisely to the coherent unity of this 'original theological whole' by acknowledging God's commanding presence in the

---

30. Ibid, 7
31. O O'Donovan, *The Desire of the Nations: Rediscovering the Roots of Political Theology*, 81.

political: he insists that authority is to be understood as 'substantively constituting', and as 'formally constituted' in a way which avoids the Derridean paradox outlined by Bartelson. It would, for example, be perfectly true to say that in the *Leviathan* God's laws of nature prescribing peace, and the authority they convey into the life of civil society, are constitutive of the civil law in the sense that they constitute its essence and ethical foundation. They are also constitutive in the sense that Hobbes's 'person' of the state is embryonically present in the minds of men in the state of nature in the form of a divinely implanted desire or yearning for peace and in the sense that their collective will for peace and concord (the essence of natural law) motivates, flows into and constitutes the rationale (the truth or substance) of the political covenant. Considered as *acted upon* by the collective will for peace and concord or by the embryonic presence of the 'person' of the state, the acts of men in entering a political covenant may be considered as its medium, that is, as the medium of the constituting authority of the laws of nature/'person' of the state/God. However, when considered as agents *acting in their own right*, making their own free decisions, the law and law-making institutions of the commonwealth are 'constituted' in so far as their formal authority clearly stems from the voluntary acts of men in entering into a political covenant. Thus, if we are primarily interested in the font or ultimate source of authority in the *Leviathan*, then Hobbes would encourage us to direct our attention away from (or behind) the formal processes of authorisation established by the political covenant to the true, substantive constituting authority which is their origin and end. The real point of entering into a political covenant to establish formal authority is to set up the vital civil and institutional arrangements which allow 'authority-in-itself' free passage from its true source or ultimate Author into everyday public life.

Hobbes then is in no doubt that the final font of authority may be discovered; far from being held back by a 'discursive prohibition against questioning the ultimate origin of authority',[32] he actually claims to have found this source in the 'person' of the state or in the commanding presence of God (the Author of Nature) mediated through natural law (the 'informal presence' of God or the 'person' of the state in the desire for peace in each human heart) and the civil law (the 'formal presence' of the sovereign representative). Hobbes regards it as entirely legitimate to engage in a quest for the foundations of authority, for such a quest leads, he believes, to a proper respect for the law and helps ensure the subject's faithful obedience, though he would insist (with Kant) that the subject should not engage in speculations concerning the font of authority 'with a view to acting upon them',[33] for he holds, again with Kant, that the speculations of a rebellious mind are 'a menace to the state'.[34]

With regard to Bartelson's point about the unquestionability of the font of authority in modern political discourse, it would be helpful, I think, to distinguish

---

32. J Bartelson, *The Critique of the State*, 4.
33. Kant, I 1991 'The Metaphysics of Morals', in H Reiss, editor, *Kant's Political Writings*, Cambridge University Press, Cambridge, 143.
34. *Ibid*, 143.

between what we might call the 'theoretical unquestionability' of authority-in-itself or in its origin (or Author), and the 'empirical questionability', aided by theoretical insight, of authority as it is actually exercised in the name of the state. Authority, simply by virtue of what it is or as it issues in its original purity from its font, is indeed unquestionable and beyond reproach. However, it must pass through the sullied human hands of the sovereign power before it arrives with 'the force of law' in the mind of the citizen, so that it becomes quite possible, in the case of apparently evil or improper enactments by a sovereign, to inquire into whether these acts or laws may be genuinely or realistically said to bear the presence of the state into public life. Thus authority as it issues from its source has a profound, even sacred, 'unquestionability' whereas it has a less than total unquestionability as it issues from the mouth of an actual, empirical sovereign or from the government of the day. Perhaps it would be helpful to think in terms of the 'flow' of authority from its source, or of authority as an active, author-ing, author-ising movement and as the process whereby political life is permeated by its true form. If so, then far from seeing authority as 'without foundation outside itself',[35] we would see authority as always having its true foundation outside or beyond itself, as always and only being genuinely authoritative as it issues from its source (so that its origin is 'beyond') and bears the presence of its source, its Author, into the heart or centre of political life (so that its origin is also 'within'). It is when considered in this way as a flow

---

35. J Bartelson, *The Critique of the State*, 7.

or movement from origin to end—or 'from and to its self' in the sense that the flow of authority from its source is also a movement anticipating its completion—that the architectural image of foundationalism is least helpful and most misleading. It is also this 'pure moment of issuing' from the font of authority, and what it practically intends in our current socio-political situation that political critique always has in mind.

The Condition of All Possible Justice

The kind of counter—intuitive and distorting inversion of the 'law/justice—force' relation in Derrida's work that we earlier noted is paralleled by a similar inversion of the kind of 'self—(external) other' or 'I (we)—(external) Thou' relation that is involved or presupposed in what Derrida calls 'the condition of all possible justice'[36] and in what I would call the transition from implicit to explicit justice, from largely unselfconscious to fully conscious justice, from untheorised to theoretically illuminated justice or, finally, from justice understood as a merely local imperative to an appreciation of justice as our universal humanity concretised. Consider the following quote from Derrida:

> To address oneself to the other in the language of the other is, it seems, the condition of all possible justice, but apparently, in all rigor, it

---

36. J Derrida, 'Force of Law: The Mystical Foundation of Authority', 949.

is not only impossible (since I cannot speak the language of the other except to the extent that I appropriate it and assimilate it accordingly to the law of an implicit third) but even excluded by justice as law (*droit*), in as much as justice as right seems to imply an element of universality, the appeal to a third party who suspends the unilaterality or singularity of the idioms.[37]

In considering this passage, the first point that I would like to draw attention to is that justice in its inception, or at least at the moment of its birth in our minds or our collective experience (or 'conscience'), is an 'egocentric' or a 'socio-centric' affair. Initially, the demands of justice are something that I experience or which 'we' collectively experience in my/our unique situation; as thus experienced, justice is both universal and singular in a symbiotic fusion. At the moment of its birth into our consciousness, justice is *not* addressed to the 'the other in the language of the other' but to me (or to 'us') and it is addressed in my (our) language, a language that I (we) have inherited and that is partly constitutive of who I am (of who 'we are'). The implicit (subconscious) universality of this justice only becomes explicit (and consciously recognised) to the degree necessary to provide a suitable justification to the 'external other' of what we do. The latter's questioning of the justice or propriety of what we do brings fully into consciousness the fact (presuming for the moment that it

---
37. Ibid.

is a fact) that 'our ways' are a local sedimentation of our universal humanity and draws the universal justice that is tacitly or implicitly present in 'our ways' (God's 'sedimented presence') into the clear light of day. Once having grasped the pure universality of justice, as the 'voice' or form of our common humanity modulated into our world, we are then in a position to become 'external others' ourselves and to criticise the ways of other societies and traditions, as we have been criticised.

It is important to bear in mind this whole movement of thought, this series of transitions from implicit to explicit justice, when considering what Derrida has to say in this passage. Given the egocentric or socio-centric origins of justice, it is not, I think, correct to say that to 'address oneself to the other in the language of the other is . . . the condition of all possible justice'; it is, rather, I would submit, the condition of 'just criticism'. The possibility of addressing oneself 'to the other in the language of the other' *and of being understood* is the condition, or ground of intelligibility, of a real dialogue or sharing between 'self' and '(external) other' (or at least the 'other' initially experienced as 'external' before the moment when a shared humanity and a shared sense of universal justice is mutually acknowledged) concerning the true meaning of justice in their respective situations. For Christians of course, God (more specifically, the Holy Spirit immanent in humanity) is this ground or condition, and the ultimate source of the imperative language of justice at the heart of our common humanity. Now when Derrida speaks of 'addressing oneself to the other', he assumes that the inevitable singularity, uniqueness and particularity of this address is incompatible with the universal presence of justice in different minds, with justice as a universal which simultaneously envelopes the one who addresses and the one who is addressed. 'An address' he states, 'is always singular, idiomatic and justice, as law (*droit*), seems always to suppose the generality of a rule, a norm or a universal imperative'.[38] Derrida seems to be almost perplexed that this is the case but this apparent perplexity, surely, could be easily dissolved by recognising that the imperative language of justice (or at least of 'just criticism') is the imperative language of our common humanity (Derrida's 'law of an implicit third'). Indeed, Derrida's reference in this passage to the 'law of an implicit third' almost seems like just such a recognition on his part, and even a recognition of God's presence in our universal humanity (the divine criterion operative in humanity as a whole).

Unfortunately, Derrida seems to both explicitly deny, and yet to also implicitly assert, the condition of all possible justice, namely, that it *must be* possible to 'address oneself to the other in the language of the other' or, alternatively expressed, that there must be an 'implicit third' or 'universal presence' that pervades or envelopes humanity as a whole; for, on the one hand, he says that 'in all rigor' this is impossible but that, on the other hand, it *is* possible to the extent that I appropriate (Is this always or inherently illicit?) the language of the other and 'assimilate it according to the law of an implicit third'. My own view is that, despite the 'indeterminacy of translation' and other difficulties, we can and do speak the lan-

---

38. *Ibid.*

guage of the other to the extent that we humbly submit to 'the law of an implicit third' and because the appeal to a third party does not, as Derrida believes, suspend the unilaterality and singularity of our respective experiences and judgments concerning justice but rather reveals the living presence of the *same* universal (justice) in both 'singularities', that is, in our world (our singular experience) and in the other's world. Sartre, I suggest, offers us the right formula; in legislating for ourselves, we legislate for all humanity and are in turn criticisable by all humanity. Likewise, however, the 'other', the 'they' or the 'not-us', in legislating for themselves, legislate for all humanity in a way that we, stretching our imagination and humanity as far as possible, can understand and criticise in turn. We could perhaps summarise this Sartrean formula by saying that we (individually or collectively) must each act on the same universal, ever itself, spirit of justice, as befits our unique situation, and yet, as we shall see in the following section when discussing the 'ordeal of the undecidable', Derrida himself says something remarkably similar.

What Derrida's account in the 'Force of Law' generally obscures is the simultaneously ordinary and mystical nature of justice and its routine operations in human affairs. Derrida is highly suspicious of what he calls 'an obscure, substantialist, occulto—mystic concept' of justice and warns us of 'the risks of substantialism'[39] but he then finds himself perplexed by the ordinary everyday facts of human ethical experience (the 'possibility' of which he acknowledges or 'half' acknowledges); 'how' he asks, al-

---

39. *Ibid*, 929.

most in wonder, 'are we to reconcile the act of justice that must always concern singularity, individuals, irreplaceable groups and lives, the other or myself *as* other, in a unique situation, with rule, norm, value or the imperative of justice' which necessarily have a general form?[40] Derrida here seems to frankly concede that the singularity of the just act and the universality of justice itself *are*, in fact, almost routinely reconciled but seems to want to argue that what is possible—what is indeed an ordinary fact of experience—is really, upon further theoretical investigation, not really possible at all and hence, presumably, not really a fact at all! It would seem to me that, instead of struggling against the obvious facts of our experience, it is more advisable to acknowledge that just as the spirit of a sports team (or a family, or group, or nation) transcends its individual members but lives only in and through them, so too the idea or spirit of justice (the Holy Spirit that indwells each of us) lives and moves through us and guides the humanity in each of us towards an affirmative, life-enhancing fulfilment of the various aspects of our being.

Likewise, Derrida seems to be blind to, or at least highly resistant to, the routine presence of justice in everyday lawful acts. He fails to see that because justice as 'what is due' is universally present in its many instances and manifestations, it is equally present (an identical presence under different guises) both in justice considered as 'infinite, incalculable, rebellious to rule and

---

40. *Ibid*, 949.

foreign to symmetry, heterogeneous and heterotropic' (for him, 'true' justice or justice in the real sense) and justice considered as 'stabilisable and statutory, calculable, a system of regulated and coded prescriptions' (for him, not justice at all).[41] His insensitivity to what we might call the quiet, implicit presence of universal justice in routine (legal) acts of obedience carried out in an unselfconscious manner is only too evident in the following:

> 'Every time that something comes to pass or turns out well, every time that we placidly apply a good rule to a particular case, to a correctly subsumed example, according to a determinant judgment, we can be sure that law (*droit*) may find itself accounted for, but certainly not justice. Law (*droit*) is not justice. Law is the element of calculation and it is just that there be law, but justice is incalculable; it requires us to calculate with the incalculable [as in those moments] in which the decision between just and unjust is never insured by a rule.[42]

Presumably, however, if it is just and proper that there be law (and customs, traditions, ways of life, etc), this quiet, unreflective obedience (or perhaps 'adherence') to the law is equally just and proper. Justice means 'giving what is

---

41. *Ibid*, 959.
42. *Ibid*, 947.

due' and acting upon this imperative is often an ordinary, unadventurous but at the same time highly commendable affair, as when we routinely and unselfconsciously keep a promise or treat others with respect. Derrida, however, seems to equate—and hence to restrict—the universal requirement of justice to 'give what is due' to the kind of thinking and acting that takes place under circumstances in which precisely what *is* due is incredibly difficult to determine; in the words of Richard Beardsworth, Derrida's person 'is always . . . a legislator and policeman'.[43] We may think here of Sartre's famous example of the young man who wrestled with the issue of whether he should leave home and fight for the French resistance or stay at home to look after his sick mother. Which universal voice should he listen to? Which universal value, patriotism or family loyalty, is most pertinent in *these* circumstances? In such cases, to use Derrida's apt expression, 'the decision between just and unjust is never insured by a rule'. However, it is important to note here that this is due not, as Derrida appears to think, to the absence of, but rather to a kind of 'surplus' or 'saturation' of, universality. It is not that our universal humanity suddenly falls silent in such situations but rather that, if anything, it speaks too loudly and in apparently discordant voices, so that we are faced with the unenviable task of deciding which path true justice dictates. Derrida holds, following Kierkegaard, that a just decision, one made in fear and trembling in the absence of calculability and predictability, is ac-

---

43. R Beardsworth, *Derrida and the Political* (London: Routledge, 1996), 12.

tually a 'madness', a decision that 'must rend time and defy dialectics',[44] but fails, I think, to take properly into account Kierkegaard's belief in the simultaneous presence/absence of the 'universal Divine'. The human soul in such dire cases must stand alone before the vertically descending God, or, rather, I would say, the descending gods, for God is both too forcefully present and entirely absent—present in the cacophony of divine universal voices that claim in this case to be the authentic voice of eternal justice, but yet absent, because hidden in this cacophony. The individual soul must search in the whirling 'tower of Babel' or in the 'babble of descending divinities' for the still point at its centre. Thus, when faced with the 'impossible decision' that needs to be made when one is confronted by the 'heterogeneous and unique singularity of the unsubsumable example',[45] this 'unsubsumable example' that Derrida refers to is in fact the 'infinitely subsumable example' in the sense that it might, with varying degrees of plausibility no doubt, be subsumed under a wide variety of different, competing laws or rules.

The Ordeal of the Undecidable

I have argued that Derrida fails to recognise the presence of universal justice in those difficult cases where we face

---

44. Derrida, J 1990 'Force of Law: The Mystical Foundation of Authority', in *Cardozo Law Review*, 11:5–6 (1990): 921–1045, 967.
45. Derrida, J 1990 'Force of Law: The Mystical Foundation of Authority', in *Cardozo Law Review*, 11:5–6 (1990): 921–1045, 963.

what he calls 'the ordeal of the undecidable'.[46] Do such cases illustrate the 'absence of universality', as Derrida suggests, or a 'surplus/saturation of universality' (a cacophonous presence), as I have suggested? Perhaps we are required to make a choice but perhaps—and this is what I hope to show—further analysis will indicate how the 'absence' of justice in one sense is perfectly compatible with its 'presence' in another.

Let us begin by noting that it is agreed on all sides that it is at least possible to refer to certain human acts and decisions as 'just'. Derrida is rightly cautious about designating any particular decision as just[47] but he acknowledges the possibility in principle of just human actions actually taking place. One might suppose that 'just actions' presuppose the presence, in some sense, of justice in a universal sense that speaks to the heart of humanity and that is readily intelligible cross-culturally, and Derrida does indeed, as we shall see in a moment, actually entertain this presumption. However, before doing so, he remarks concerning the undecidable element in each just decision that it 'remains caught, lodged, at least as a ghost—but an essential ghost—in every decision' and he insists that its ghostliness 'deconstructs from within any assurance of presence'.[48] Given the importance of this latter remark on the 'presence of justice' for our present discussion, it is fortunate that he immediately proceeds to explain that

---
46. J Derrida, 'Force of Law: The Mystical Foundation of Authority', 965.
47. Ibid, 963.
48. Ibid, 965.

by 'presence' in this context he has in mind 'any certitude or any supposed criteriology that would assure us of the justice of a decision'.[49] Clearly, for Derrida, justice considered as 'stabilisable and statutory, calculable, a system of regulated and coded prescriptions'[50] is not operative or present here but, rather, justice considered as 'infinite, incalculable, rebellious to rule, etc.[51] When we face the 'ordeal of the undecidable', we must be guided by the 'spirit of justice'[52] or by justice–in–itself, the 'idea of justice' in the Kantian sense.

Surprisingly, or surprisingly for some, Derrida actually warmly embraces justice in this Kantian sense. It may be broadly characterised as incalculable, as requiring us to act, unilaterally and without reference to rules; we are to act in the spirit of justice, of justice itself, by somehow responding to its insistent demand to give 'what is due' to others, even when 'what is due' is notoriously and agonisingly unclear. However we finally decide to act in such agonising cases or however we resolve the 'ordeal of the undecidable', justice in this fundamental sense requires us to maintain a constant and unconditional commitment to the absolute value of the 'other'. In Derrida's own words:

> [T]he deconstruction of all presumption of a determinant certitude of a present justice itself operates on the basis of an infinite 'idea of

---

49. *Ibid*, 965.
50. *Ibid*, 959.
51. *Ibid*.
52. *Ibid*, 949.

justice,' infinite because it is irreducible, irreducible because owed to the other, before any contract . . . This 'idea of justice' seems to me to be irreducible in its affirmative character, in its demand of gift without exchange, without circulation, without recognition or gratitude, without economic circulation and without rules, without reason and without rationality. And so we can recognise in it, indeed accuse, identify a madness. And perhaps another sort of mystique. And deconstruction is mad about this kind of justice. Mad about this desire for justice. This kind of justice, which isn't law, is the very movement of deconstruction at work in law and the history of law, in political history itself, before it even presents itself as the discourse that the academy or modern culture labels 'deconstructionism'.[53]

It is interesting that Derrida here alludes, in what I would regard as a fairly (for him) unambiguous manner, to the irreducible reality of justice, to its ever ceasing movement and circulation, its infinite concretisations, in our hearts and minds, well before it is subjectively registered in the minds of a few intellectuals here and there under a particular guise and finally surfaces into the discourse of the academy as 'deconstructionism'. (Thus

---

53. *Ibid*, 965.

considered, deconstructionism is simply 'God at work' or the operations of the Spirit in and through the most pressing and difficult human situations.) Perhaps more pertinent, though, in the light of our present purpose, is the fact that Derrida is so wholeheartedly committed, and asks us to be likewise committed, to the idea of justice as an absolute and unconditional requirement that is owed to the other and, because absolutely owed, acknowledges the absoluteness (the absolute dignity and significance of the other as 'end-in-itself') of the one(s) to whom it is owed. We should note at this point that for Derrida the incalculable justice of which he speaks and which requires of us a full, wholehearted (because freely given) acknowledgment of the equality and absolute significance of the other is an ethical counterpoint and challenge to the arche-violence that 'appears with *articulation*'[54] and to the potential violence lurking in our 'egoity', our perspectival conception of the other as an-other-to-oneself. (For Derrida, or at least for the Derrida of *Writing and Difference*,[55] this 'reduction of the other to a *real* moment of *my* life, its reduction to the state of empirical alter-ego, is an empirical possibility, or rather eventuality, which is called violence.') However, the spirit of justice described in the 'Force of Law' or what we might call true, incalculable justice requires of us that we overcome

---

54. J Derrida, *Writing and Difference* (Chicago: University of Chicago Press, 1978), 148.
55. *Ibid*, 128.

or somehow transcend our 'egoity' and recognise the other as real (rather than as a mere moment of my life or consciousness), as equal (rather than an ontologically secondary alter-ego), and as absolute (rather than as merely existing for me).

It is clear then from Derrida's account that one of the things that impresses itself forcefully on the mind—that subjectively 'hits home'—in cases where difficult decisions concerning justice need to be made, is the necessity of recognising at all times the intrinsic value of the other. This requirement is unconditional; it is not dependent upon the recognition by the other of us as intrinsic or absolute ends. As he rightly remarks, to recognise and respect the other as a being endowed with absolute significance is a 'gift without exchange' that we are unconditionally required by justice to give. This interior acknowledgement of the intrinsic value of the other, this prompting of the Spirit, *is* the *presence* of justice in the mind and heart. Even if Derrida refers to it as 'heterogeneous', as always specific and unique in its 'appearance for us' and in its demands of us, still it is always the same (universal) 'idea of justice' or 'spirit of justice'.[56] Is there one 'spirit of justice' or many? Is the 'idea of justice', as it is present in me, different from the 'idea of justice' as it is present in you? My suggestion is that Derrida in the 'Force of Law', despite his highly suspicious attitude towards what he calls 'an obscure, substantialist, occulto—mystic concept' of

---

56. J Derrida, 'Force of Law: The Mystical Foundation of Authority', 949.

justice,[57] speaks in an implicitly metaphysical manner as if the *same* spirit of justice is universally present and universally operative in each of us, though incalculable and singular in its effects. However, what is true of the 'justice of persons' is equally true of the 'justice of political regimes', for presumably (incalculable) justice requires that those involuntarily subjugated should be treated fairly and considerately, as absolute ends, by the victorious founders of a new political regime, and it is certainly hard to imagine such a regime acquiring legitimacy or a willing allegiance on the part of the vanquished, unless the 'spirit of justice' prevails.

Whilst it is easy enough for Derrida to dismiss calculable justice (for him, not justice at all) as the mere application of rules, he can not so easily dismiss—and in fact openly acknowledges—the essential, ghostly presence of true, incalculable spirit of justice and its forceful presence in the mind which, as he says, deconstructs from within any assurance of the presence of calculable justice, any utilitarian formula that mechanically yields a 'just' decision, any certitude or any supposed criteriology that would assure us of the justice of a decision'.[58] He is, then, a true Kantian with regard to the 'idea of justice' and the categorical imperative (for him universal/heterogeneous) to treat others as absolute ends but he is much less enthusiastic about 'regulative ideas' in the Kantian sense. The reason for this, I believe, is not, or at least not so much, because of his dislike for any kind of thinking that looks

---

57. *Ibid*, 929.
58. *Ibid*, 965.

remotely 'metaphysical'; in his remarks on metaphysical or mystical justice, he is explicitly anti-metaphysical but implicitly metaphysical. As we have just seen, behind the phenomenal appearance of each human person, he discerns—succumbing to a metaphysical mode of thinking that he refuses to acknowledge—the noumenal reality of intrinsic irreducible value, of priceless dignity; it is this 'metaphysical recognition' that inspires his understanding of the spirit or idea of justice as a 'gift to the other without exchange.' This unconditional affirmation of the absolute value of each person is implicitly, or unconsciously, metaphysical. His caution and reserve concerning Kantian regulative ideas has, rather, much more to do with his intense dislike of rules and regulations that might be seen as making justice, its spirit and effects, somehow calculable or too easily identifiable with a set of ideologically determined rules. Bearing this in mind, Derrida's position is not quite as vulnerable to critical attack as is often supposed, as we shall see in the concluding section.

Political Critique

Thomas McCarthy holds that if Derrida wants to express himself politically, especially in a critical vein, he can only do so by adopting (metaphysical) terms and codes that are incommensurate with his intellectual project. Derrida's criticism of logocentric thinking means that he must fall silent. The price he must pay for his commitment to deconstruction, McCarthy holds, is the lack of any means, criteria or metaphysical weapons which would enable him to effectively criticise competing political viewpoints and interpretations, or to take a stand in support of those 'genuinely', 'truly', or 'really' oppressed. 'In short', McCarthy argues, 'undercutting the appeal to reason, truth and justice as presently 'coded' without offering alternatives may harbor not so much the 'promise' of a better world as the danger of some monstrous mutation'.[59] Political critique is then deemed by McCarthy to be out of bounds for Derrida. However, as we have just seen, Derrida, despite his ambiguous attitude to metaphysics (explicitly rejecting; implicitly accepting, at least in the case of justice), is able not only to successfully respond to this kind of criticism by pointing to his Kantian convictions (his commitment to the 'idea of justice' and to the categorical imperative) but he is also able to 'counter-attack' by arguing that his eschewal of Kantian regulative ideas and ideologically inspired rules has certain advantages for those seeking the true spirit of criticism—for Derrida, the 'truly incalculable'. He can actually claim to be in a *better* position to carry the banner of the 'emancipatory ideal' than those whose metaphysics is too closely tied to a particular ideology (for example, liberalism or feminism) or a single value/idea (for example, liberty or equality)) and too prone, in terms of practical application, to degenerate into a mechanical system of 'easy-to-apply' rules. (This breaches the 'rule of equality': it is wrong!! This breaches the rule of 'liberty/private property: it is wrong!! etc). The

---

59. T McCarthy, 'The Politics of the Ineffable; Derrida's Deconstructionism', in *Ideas and Illusions; on Reconstruction and Deconstruction in Contemporary Critical Theory* (Cambridge Mass: MIT Press, 1991), 112.

kind of metaphysics that Derrida implicitly endorses is entirely innocent of 'rules', 'system', indeed of homogenising tendencies of any and every kind. He can rightly claim to be able to bring to bear in each unique situation his unconditional (metaphysical) commitment to the absolute value of 'the other'; he carries no ideological baggage and is entirely free of 'formulaic repetitions' as he pursues the emancipatory ideal. He holds that incalculable heterogeneous 'impossible' and 'mad' justice is a kind of epiphany in the mind of the critical ethical observer confronting each unique situation of injustice; it is immediately present to the mind or not present at all. Only by acknowledging that, to be just, our reactions to a specific situation must be as unique as the situation itself can the ideologists (liberal, socialist, feminist, etc) wrestle free from their rule/regulations mentality and allow the unmediated (non rule—dependent) presence of justice full sovereignty and sway in their political thinking.

Likewise, Derrida would no doubt freely concede that the 'Force of Law' exhibits certain 'ecstatic' and 'vitalist' tendencies, or at least to construe certain sections of his work in this way does not seem like an unwarranted interpretation. However, the charge that his work exhibits dangerously ecstatic, vitalistic, proto-totalitarian tendencies, as suggested most prominently by Wolin[60] and

---

60. R Wolin, 'Derrida on Marx, or the Perils of Left Heideggerianism', *Labyrinths: Explorations in the Critical History of Ideas* edited by R Wolin (Amherst: University of Massachusetts Press, Amherst, 1995), 231–240.

Lilla,[61] fails to properly take into account his unconditional commitment to the Kantian 'idea of justice' and to the categorical imperative. These authors might seem to be on stronger ground when they suggest that Derrida, as an advocate of deconstruction, (i) fails to foreground and take a 'principled stand' on pressing issues in ethics and politics and (ii) is guilty of nihilism and 'decisionism' since he makes human choice wholly ungrounded, arbitrary and cut off from reason. However, this may well be a justified charge against deconstructionism in general, but not, I think, against Derrida in the *Force of Law*, for in that work his commitment to the categorical imperative, to the priceless dignity owed to each person, sets powerful ethical side constraints upon human choice. The field of choice is not arbitrarily wide. Derrida cannot be fairly categorised as having an 'anything goes' or 'aesthetic' (in a 'beyond ethics' sense) attitude. Again, too, Derrida can reply that he has no objections to those who adopt a 'principled stand', as long as they acknowledge the uniqueness of the situation upon which their principles are brought to bear and do not succumb to, or allow their principles (or ideologies) to lend a false legitimisation to, a top-down homogenising approach.

Still, at the end of the day, it might seem that Derrida simply has no defence against the charge of 'decisionism', for he denies often enough that human choice is grounded in reason. He points out, for example, that the 'idea of justice' is irrevocable in its demand for gift with-

---

61. M Lilla, 'The Politics of Jacques Derrida', in *The New York Review of Books*, 45/11 (25 June 1998): 36–41.

out exchange and 'without reason and rationality'. It is true that, if we take Derrida at his explicit word, there is nothing more to be said. However, we should recall here the fact that, as we saw earlier, Derrida speaks in almost 'Hegelian-Christian' terms of deconstruction as the permanent, circulating movement of the spirit of justice in human history, 'objectively' going about its business well before it happened to be called 'deconstruction', and this means, surely, that he is separated merely by a word from the western metaphysical view of Reason and Spirit as the font of the critical, emancipatory movement of human history. Does it really matter a great deal that those broadly sympathetic to western metaphysics—I take my stand with them—think of social and political advances in human history as the 'work' of the Spirit, of reason, justice and truth, whereas Derrida sees 'deconstruction' at work? We should also recall here that Derrida asks us to banish from our minds the evil ghost of false presence, the ghost of calculable, rule–associated justice that provides us with the comforting but misleading assurance of its presence and induces in us a sense of illusory certainty, *only* in order to allow the presence of incalculable universal justice, the mystical spirit of justice itself, to exercise a kind of sovereign freedom in our minds. Now how, we may well wonder, does this differ from inviting the Holy Spirit into all aspects of our lives and thoughts? We are, after all, to allow the full, immediate presence of justice (its spirit in us) to determine in and through us what is just and unjust in each unique situation that we face. Is it not, then, the case that Derrida, using the language of deconstruction, is in fact simply doing what the leading proponents of the Christian faith and western metaphysics, using the language of universalism (of reason, truth, justice and freedom), have always done? Is he not, for example, like Oliver O'Donovan in his *Resurrection and Moral Order: An Outline for Evangelical Ethics*,[62] when he regards the obligations of the 'calculable' moral law as issuing from and unified by the 'incalculable' principle of love (and the double command of Jesus to love) and as thereby necessitating a unique 'incalculable' response on our part? Or, again, is he not like the 'chastened secularist' Robert Kane when he holds that we 'simply do not know enough to ground ethics necessarily in human reason and knowledge alone'[63] and that our ethical task (personal and collective) is to endeavour to ' "embody the truth" in the sense of attaining objective worth, without being sure of having attained it'.[64] Is Derrida not in effect using 'incalculable, *universal* justice' (the spirit of justice) as his criterion and inspiration both for self-criticism and for political critique?

What Derrida's work and style obscure but what Hobbes helps us to more clearly appreciate is that the state, strictly speaking, does not 'have' or 'exercise' authority; rather, it *is* the essence or eternal font of the authority wielded by *its* (empirical) government. The state is the 'Author' who 'author-ises' its government and the

---

62. O O'Donovan, *Resurrection and Moral Order: An Outline for Evangelical Ethics* (Grand Rapids: Eerdmans, 1986), 201.
63. R Kane, *Through the Moral maze: Searching for Absolute values in a Pluralistic World* (New York: Paragon, 1994), 97.
64. *Ibid*, 98.

latter exercises its authority properly as the state's representative or as the institutional expression and operational presence of the state (the Holy Spirit or the true Spirit of totality). However, whilst insisting on the paramount importance of the 'moral 'person' of the state' as the ultimate font of authority, Hobbes vigorously denies its equally important role as the ultimate basis of political critique. It is important to note that, *pace* Hobbes, political critique presupposes the unquestionability of authority-in-itself and of the pure moment when authority issues from its author-ial source, for just as to 'negatively' criticise unfair or corrupt practices is to invoke the 'memory' of this pure moment, so too to 'positively' critique one's political landscape with a view to its positive transformation (whole or partial) into a fuller reality is to anticipate its end or final fulfilment. Bartelson concedes as much when he says, as we saw earlier, that 'it is difficult, if not impossible, to criticise that same founding act without simultaneously invoking it oneself',[65] for what, after all, is being invoked here, if not the 'memory' of this pure moment of issuing? Interestingly, whilst Bartelson leaves in limbo (or, perhaps more fairly, in the vagaries of discourse) the question of what is involved in acts of political criticism or what it is more precisely that casts an evaluative light on current political practices, Derrida actually speaks of an infinite 'idea of justice' which is 'irreducible in its affirmative character', and which is 'the very movement of deconstruction at work in law and the history of law, in

---

65. J Bartelson, *The Critique of the State*, 7.

political history and history itself'.⁶⁶ He says that he is here speaking of a 'type' and though he immediately adds that he hesitates 'to assimilate too quickly this "idea of justice" to a regulative idea (in the Kantian sense), to a messianic promise or to other horizons *of the same* type',⁶⁷ he nevertheless insists that we can discern this type through the singularities of our historical experience and attain 'a glimpse of the type itself, as the origin, condition, possibility or promise of all its exemplifications (messianism of the Jewish, Christian or Islamic type, idea in the Kantian sense, eschato-teleology of the neo-Hegelian, Marxist or post-Marxist type, etc)'⁶⁸ and though keeping his distance from these 'horizons', as he calls them, 'or at least from their conventional interpretation',⁶⁹ yet this glimpse is enough to ensure Derrida's commitment to the classical emancipatory ideal. 'Nothing', he says, 'seems to me less outdated than the classical emancipatory ideal'.⁷⁰ All of this, to me, justifies us in speaking of the eternal presence of justice and the state, of their eternal subject and source (God the Father), even though Derrida himself would no doubt decisively reject such a view as exhibiting what he calls an 'ontological logic of presence'.⁷¹ When Derrida is understood in this way, even perhaps against his wishes (though, as we have seen, his wishes in this regard are by

---

66. J Derrida, 'Force of Law: The Mystical Foundation of Authority', 965.
67. Ibid.
68. Ibid, 967.
69. Ibid, 67.
70. Ibid, 971.
71. Ibid, 973.

no means clear), his deconstructive (and divisive) wall of 'universal suspicion and separation' becomes instead, as I suggested in chapter one, both a bridge to, and an instrument of, the kind of common philosophical dialogue which Habermas and Ratzinger believe to be possible and which, I believe, their shared 'Munich moment' has dramatically shown to be possible against all the odds.

Invariably, political criticism is directed towards the adequacy or inadequacy of a government's representation of the state. Bartelson remarks that 'the state is usually thought to be *the* institutional expression of political authority'[72] but in the history of political thought, it has rarely been thought of in that way at all; rather, ordered or constitutional government has been seen as the ideal institutional expression of the state, as the public visible face of the invisible self of civil society (its general will). As a kind of moral or collective person or as the 'own self' of civil society, the state is a collective subject of whom it can be truly said both that it has no agency, in so far as the capacity to act, or at least to directly and immediately act, in the public world is restricted to empirical governments, and yet that it does in a certain sense exercise agency, in the sense that it acts through the medium or agency of its government. The state, as actor or agent, could be said to 'use' its government as its operative medium in the public world but we need to be careful not to lose sight of what we might call 'the active autonomy' of government, for otherwise political critique would of course be futile. On the other hand, there is a danger in regarding government

---

72. J Bartelson, *The Critique of the State*, 3.

as alone active or as exercising 'sole agency', for we then lose sight of government as servant of the state and as the medium of its higher will (the general will or the public interest) and forfeit the power to engage in political critique which involves, as we have seen, evoking a higher criterion (the ethical substance of the state or its purity as it flows from its divine source). Perhaps the best way to express the state/government relationship is to say that the state is present in the institutional acts of its government, as the 'own self' of a natural person is present in the person's physical acts in the world. However, the key point to be stressed here is that the single most important question to be asked of any government concerns the adequacy (or the degree of inadequacy) with which it represents the state[73] and bears the presence of God into public life. Thoughts of rebellion are only justified when it is believed, in good faith, that a government has seriously abused its formal authority by subverting the true ethical substance of that authority (that is, the state, or *our state, or the Spirit in us as a political community*), that it represents our worst rather than our best selves, that it is reprehensibly and systematically inadequate in its representation of the state (of the Spirit collectively present in us) and that, far from bearing the presence of the state into the affairs of civil society, it actually bars the authori-

---

73. Quite often, at election time, citizens will vote for a major opposition party because they believe that the government seeking re-election is jaded, tired and no longer adequate (or as adequate as it once was) to the task of bearing the presence of the state into public life and that the opposition party is in a position to offer a more adequate, fresher and more alert representation of the state.

tative 'flow' of the state (a movement of the public spirit or Holy Spirit) into public life.

Just as political criticism is invariably directed towards the adequacy or inadequacy of a government's representation of the state, so too radical theological criticism is likewise directed towards a government's success or failure in representing the 'state' in the sense of God's authentic will for the political community–what I earlier referred to as the reflective, attentive and listening will of 'the invisible holy community' in each society. It was to the 'hidden' members of this community that Jeremiah made his appeal in ancient times, and they responded by drawing deeply from their own intimations and hearing their own inner voices; they rejected unreservedly the religio-political institutions of their own people and chose instead to heed God's Spirit issuing from the mouth of the prophet. They alone were the 'last and true' remnant of God's holy people. Reflecting on the cultural and religious achievement of these faithful individuals, Oliver O'Donovan comments:

> [W]hen the mediating institutions of government collapse, then the memory and hope which single members faithfully conserve provide a span of continuity which can reach out towards the prospect of restructuring. The fractured community which fashioned the individual's conscience is sustained within it and renewed out of it. And having been preserved through single members' memory and hope, Jeremiah anticipates, it will be the

stronger, for it will incorporate that direct knowledge of Yhwh's ways which each has won by his, or her, faithfulness.[74]

What Jeremiah 'anticipates' for God's holy people, for the true community God gathers to Himself, so too must we. Admittedly, we have to regretfully acknowledge that, viewed empirically, the visible, institutional, sinful church at any particular time stands in a problematical relationship to God's 'invisible holy community', hoping that it wholly falls within it but living in fear that it may well be outside it, and yet, viewed ontologically, this true and holy spiritual community is the 'truth' of the church, the ideal that ever animates and inspires it. As Stanley Hauerwas reminds us, Christians must gather regularly together to place themselves humbly in the presence of God and, in worship and supplementation, ask for the grace to truly love each other and to love 'Jesus in all humanity'; only in this way can they *be* God's holy community and *make* it visible, a light to their own nation and to all the nations. The church must ever be what Christ called it to be, the visible community which is ever approximating and ever falling short of, ever running away from in sin and ever rushing towards in grace, the holiness of God. Although empirically, at any particular moment in sinful time, God's invisible holy community spread out across the nations of the world comprises fewer members than the numbers present in its visible political communities,

---

74. O O'Donovan, *The Desire of the Nations: Rediscovering the Roots of Political Theology*, 80.

yet since God's redemptive call goes out to all, and since all human hearts are restless until they at last know the Lord, may we not dare to hope that, in the end, this community is destined to envelop and include the whole of humanity?

Bibliography

Aquinas T 1974, *Summa Theologica*, Eyre and Spotiswoode, London.

Allen, JL, 1963, 'A Decisive Influence on Protestant Ethics', in *Christianity and Crisis*, 23, Nov, 25.

Ankersmit, F 1996, *Aesthetic Politics: Political Philosophy beyond Fact and Value*, Stanford University Press, Stanford.

Athanasius, 1971, 'Discourses', in *The Nicene Creed and Post Nicene Fathers of the Christian Church*, abbreviated in main text as NPNF, 4:2.57, edited by, Philip Schaff and Henry Wace, Eerdmans, Grand Rapids.

Augustine, 1953, *St Augustine Letters 131-164* in *The Fathers of the Church, Vol 20*, New York.

Augustine, 1972, *De Civitate Dei*, Penguin, Harmondsworth.

Augustine, 1991, *The Trinity*, New City Press, Brooklyn.

Augustine, 1990, *Sermons*, translated by E Hill, edited by JE Rotelle, in *The Works of Saint Augustine*, Volume 3, Parts 1–10, New City Press, New York.

Augustine, 1843–, *Enarrationes in Psalmos* (*Expositions on the Book of Psalms*) Volumes 1–6 in *Library of the Fathers*, Oxford.

Basil, 1971, 'On the Spirit', in *The Nicene Creed and Post Nicene Fathers of the Christian Church*, abbreviated in main text as NPNF 8:8.20, edited by, Philip Schaff and Henry Wace, Eerdmans, Grand Rapids.

Barker, E 1915, 'The Discredited State: Thoughts on Politics before the War', in *The Political Quarterly*, 7, (5): 101–121.

Bartelson, J 2001, *The Critique of the State*, Cambridge University Press, Cambridge.

Barth, K 1933, *The Epistle to the Romans*. Oxford University Press, Oxford.

Barth, K 1962, *Theology and Church*. Translated by LP Smith, SCM Press, London.

Barth, K 1968 *Community, State and Church: Three Essays*, Peter Smith, Gloucester, Mass.

Barth, K 1975, *Church Dogmatics*, T&T Clark, Edinburgh.

Beardsworth, R 1996, *Derrida and the Political*, Routledge, London.

Beckley, H 1992, *Passion for Justice: Retrieving the Legacies of Walter Rauschenbusch, John A Ryan and Reinhold Neibuhr*, Westminster/John Knox Press, Louisville.

Bennett, J, 1960-1961, 'Ethical Principles and the Context', in Presidential Address, *Yearbook of the American Society of Christian Social Ethics*.

Berlin, I 1969, *Four Essays on Liberty*, Oxford University Press, London.

Berlin, I 2002a, 'Two Concepts of Liberty', in H Hardy, editor, *Liberty: Incorporating Four Essays on Liberty*, Oxford University Press, Oxford.

Berlin, I 2002b, 'From Hope and Fear Set Free', in H Hardy, editor, *Liberty: Incorporating Four Essays on Liberty*, Oxford University Press, Oxford.

Berlin, I 2002c, 'Introduction', in H Hardy, editor, *Liberty: Incorporating Four Essays on Liberty*, Oxford University Press, Oxford.

Bernauer, J 1990, *Michel Foucault's Force of Flight*, Humanities Press International, London.

Bevir M 1999, 'Foucault and Critique: Deploying Agency against Autonomy', in *Political Theory*, 27, (Feb): 65–84.

Blondel, M 1964, *Letter on Apologetics and History and Dogma*, trans. Alexander Dru and Illtyd Trethowan, Harvill, London.

Blondel, M 1984, *Action: Essay on a Critique of Life and a Science of Practice*, translated by Olivia Blanchette, Notre Dame University Press, Indiana.

Boff, L 1988, *Trinity and Society*, Orbis, New York.

Bonhoeffer, D 1955, *Ethics*, Macmillan, New York.

Bosanquet, B 1913, *The Value and Destiny of the Individual*, Macmillan, London.

Bosanquet, B 1917, *Social and International Ideals: Being Studies in Patriotism*, Macmillan, London.

Bosanquet, B 1917, *Social and International Ideals: Being Studies in Patriotism*, Macmillan, London.

Bosanquet, B 1927, *The Principle of Individuality and Value*, Macmillan, London.

Bosanquet, B 1917–1918, 'Do finite individuals possess a substantive or an adjectival mode of being?', in *Proceedings of the Aristotelian Society*, volume, 18 (1917–1918): 479–506.

Bosanquet, B 1965, *The Philosophical Theory of the State*. Macmillan, London.

Bounds, E 1993, 'Why Have We gathered in This Place?; A Critical Evaluation of Selected Theories of Community', PhD dissertation, Union Theological Seminary, New York.

Bradley, FH 1988, *Ethical Studies*, The Clarendon Press, Oxford.

Bramhall, J 1658, *The Catching of Leviathan*, J Crook, London.

Brettler, MZ 1989, *God is King*, Sheffield, JSOT Press

Brunner, E 1952, *The Christian Doctrine of Creation and Redemption*, Lutterworth Press, Westminster.

Brunner, E 1957, *The Divine Imperative: A Study in Christian Ethics*, Westminster Press, Philadelphia.

Burchell, D 1994, 'Civic Virtue, Civil Advice: Genealogies of Citizenship and Modernity', in *Political Theory Newsletter*, 6/1 (April 1994): 19–31.

Burke, E 1900, *The Works of Edmund Burke*, George Bell and Sons, London.

Butler, J 1990a, *Gender Trouble: Feminism and the Subversion of Identity*, Routledge, New York.

Butler, J 1990b, 'Gender Trouble, Feminist Theory and Psychoanalytic Discourse' in LJ Nicholson, editor, Feminism/*Postmodernism*, Routledge, New York.

Butler, J, Laclau, E, and Zizek, S 2000, *Contingency, Hegemony, Universality*, Verso, London.

Calvin, J 1961, *Institutes of the Christian Religion*, JT Neill, editor, SCM, London.

Carens, JH 2000, *Culture, Citizenship and Community: A Contextual Exploration of Justice as Evenhandedness*, Oxford University Press, Oxford.

Catechism of the Catholic Church (1995), Ligouri Publications, Missouri.

Cone, JH 1975, *God of the Oppressed*, Harper Collins, San Francisco.

Connolly, W 1993, 'Beyond Good and Evil: The Ethical Sensibility of Michel Foucault', in *Political Theory*, 21 (Aug 1993): 365–389.

Connolly, W 1995, *Political Theory and Modernity* Cornell University Press, Ithaca.

Copp, D 1980, 'Hobbes on Artificial Persons and Collective Actions', in *The Philosophical Review*, Volume 89 (1980): 579–606.

Crowder, G 2002, *Liberalism and Value Pluralism*, Continuum, London.

Dearlove, J 1989, 'Bringing the Constitution back in', in *Political Studies* 37, (4): 521–539.

Deleuze, G 1988, *Foucault*, University of Minnesota Press, Minneapolis.

Derrida, J 1978, *Writing and Difference*, University of Chicago Press, Chicago.

Derrida, J 1990 'Force of Law: The Mystical Foundation of Authority', in *Cardozo Law Review*, 11:5–6 (1990): 921–1045.

Dewey, J 1988, *The Public and its Problems*, Ohio University Press, Athens Ohio.

Domhoff, GW 1967, *Who Rules America?*, Prentice Hall, Englewood Cliffs, NJ.

Dorrien, G 1995, *Soul in Society: The Making and Renewal of Social Christianity*, Fortress press, Minneapolis.

Doyle, R. 2004, 'Are we heretics? A review of *The Trinity and Subordinationism* by Kevin Giles', in *The Briefing* (April 2004): 11–19.

Duchrow, U 1970, *Christenheit und Weltverantwortung. Traditionsgeschichte und systematische Struktur der Zweireiche-lehre*, E Klett, Stuttgart.

Duncan, G and Lukes, S 1970, 'Democracy Restated', in HS Kariel, editor, *Frontiers of Democratic Theory*, Random House, New York, 188–213.

Dunn, J 1999, 'Situating Democratic Political Accountability', in A Przeworski, SC Stokes and B Manin, editords, Cambridge University Press, Cambridge.

Easton, D 1953, *The Political System: An Inquiry into the State of Political Science*, Kropf, New York.

Ebeling, G 1975, *Wort und Glaube* 111, JCB Mohr, Tubingen.

Erickson, M 1995, *God in Three Persons: A Contemporary Interpretation of the Trinity*, Baker, Grand Rapids.

Esquivel, AP 1983, *Christ in a Poncho*, Orbis, Mary Knoll.

Evans, B, Rueschemeyer, D, and Skocpol, T, editors, 1987, *Bringing the State Back In*, Cambridge University Press, Cambridge.

Feinberg, J 1970, *Doing and Deserving: Essays in the Theory of Responsibility*, Princeton University Press, Princeton.

Flax, J 1992, 'Beyond Equality: Gender, Justice and Difference', in G Bock and S James, editors, *Beyond Equality and Difference*, Routledge, New York.

Fossedal, GA 1989, *The Democratic Imperative: Exporting the American Revolution*, Basic Books, New York.

Foucault, M 1977, *Discipline and Punish: The Birth of the Prison*, Harmondsworth: Penguin, London.

Foucault, M 1980a, 'Truth and Power', in C Gordon, editor, *Power/Knowledge: Selected Interviews and Other Writings 1972–1977*, Harvester Wheatsheaf, New York.

Foucault, M 1980b, 'Two Lectures' in C Gordon, editor, *Power/Knowledge: Selected Interviews and Other Writings 1972–1977*, Harvester Wheatsheaf, New York.

Foucault, M 1985, *The Use of Pleasure*, Random House, New York.

Foucault, M 1986, *The Care of the Self*, Pantheon, New York.

Foucault, M 1988 'An Aesthetics of Existence', in L Kritzman editor, *Politics, Philosophy, Culture: Interviews and Other Writings, 1977–1984*, Routledge, London.

Foucault, M 1990, 'Truth and Power', in C Gordon, editor, *Power/Knowledge: Selected Interviews and Other Writings, 1972–77*, Harvester Wheatsheaf, London

Foucault, M 1991a, *Remarks on Marx: Conversations with Duccia Trombadori*, translated by RJ Goldstein and J Cascaito, Semiotexte, New York.

Foucault, M 1991b, 'Governmentality', in G Burchell, C Gordon and P Miller, editors, *The Foucault Effect: Studies in Governmentality*, Harvester, London.

Frame, J 2002, *The Doctrine of God: A Theology of Lordship*, P&R, Phillipsburg, NJ.

Frank, J 2002, *Ever Against the Stream; The Politics of Karl Barth, 1906–1968*, Eerdmans, Grand Rapids.

Gadamer, H 1976, *Philosophical Hermeneutics*, University of California Press, Berkeley.

Gadamer, H 1980, 'The Universality of the Hermeneutical Problem', in J Bleicher, editor, *Contemporary Hermeneutics*, Routledge and Kegan Paul, London.

Gadamer, H 1989, *Truth and Method*, Sheed and Ward, London.

Geisler, N 2003, *Systematic Theology*, Volume 2, Bethany, Minneapolis.

Gerhard, J 1979, quoted in Thielicke, H, *Theological Ethics, Volume 2: Politics*, Eerdmans, Grand Rapids.

Germino, DL 1959, 'Two Types of Recent Christian Thought', in *The Journal of Politics*, Volume 21 (1959): 455–486.

Gierke O 1938, *Political Theories of the Middle Ages*, translated by FW Maitland, Cambridge University Press, Cambridge.

Giles, K 2006, *Jesus and the Father: Modern Evangelicals Reinvent the Doctrine of the Trinity*, Zondervan, Grand Rapids.

Grant, J 1989, *White Women's Christ and Black Women's Jesus; Feminist Christology and Womanist Response*, Scholars Press, Atlanta.

Grasso, KL 1996, 'Man, Society and the State: A Catholic Perspective', Comments, in M Cromartie, editor, *Caesar's Coin Revisited: Christians and the Limits of Government*, Eerdmans, Grand Rapids.

Gray, J 1993, *Post-Liberalism; Studies in Political Thought*, Routledge, London.

Gray, J 1995a, *Berlin*, Harper Collins, New York.

Gray, J 1995b, *Enlightenment's Wake: Politics and Culture at the Close of the Modern Age*, Routledge, London.

Gray, J 2000a, 'Pluralism and toleration in Contemporary Political Philosophy', in *Political Studies*, 48 (2000): 323–33.

Gray, J 2000b, *Two Faces of Liberalism*, Polity, Cambridge.

Grenz, SJ 1997, *The Moral Quest; Foundations of Christian Ethics*, InterVarsity Press, Downers Grove, Illinois.

Grudem, W 1995, *Systematic Theology: An Introduction to Biblical Doctrine*, Zondervan, Grand Rapids.

Grudem, W 2004, *Evangelical Feminism and Biblical Truth*, Multnomah, Sisters, Ore.

Gustafson JM 1974, *Theology and Christian Ethics*, Pilgrim Press, Philadelphia.

Habermas, J and Ratzinger, J 2006, *Dialectics of Secularization: On Reason and Religion*, Ignatius Press, San Francisco.

Hare, RM 1955, 'Universalizability', in *Aristotelian Society*, 55 (1955): 295–312.

Hare, RM 1981, *Moral Thinking*, Clarendon Press, Oxford.

Hauerwas, S 1983a, *The Peaceable Kingdom: A Primer in Christian Ethics*, Notre Dame Press, Notre Dame Indiana

Hauerwas, S 1983b, 'On Keeping Theological Ethics Theological', in S Hauerwas and A MacIntyre *Revisions: Changing Perspectives in Moral Philosophy*, University of Notre dame Press, Notre Dame, Indiana.

Hauerwas, S 1988, 'A Christian Critique of Christian America', in C Reynolds and R Norman, *Community in America: The Challenge of Habits of the Heart*, University of California Press, California.

Hauerwas, S and Williamson, M 1989, *Resident Aliens: Life in the Christian Colony*, Abingdon Press, Nashville.

Hegel, GWF 1989, *The Philosophy of Right*, in Great Books of the Western World, William Benton, Chicago.

Herberg, W 1968, 'Introduction' to K Barth, 1968 *Community, State and Church: Three Essays*, Peter Smith, Gloucester, Mass.

Hirschman, AO 1982, 'Rival Interpretations of market society: Civilizing, destructive or feeble?', in *Journal of Economic Literature*, 20 (1982): 1463–84.

Hobbes, T 1839–45 *De Cive* in *The English Works of Thomas Hobbes*, Volume 2, W Molesworth, editor, J Bohn, London.

Hobbes, T 1839–45 *Leviathan* in *The English Works of Thomas Hobbes*, Volume 3, W Molesworth, editor, J Bohn, London.

Hobbes, T 1839–45 *Elements of Law* in *The English Works of Thomas Hobbes*, Volume 4, W Molesworth, editor, J Bohn, London.

Hobbes, T 1839–45 *Behemoth* in *The English Works of Thomas Hobbes*, Volume 6, W Molesworth, editor, J Bohn, London.

Hobbes, T 1996, *Leviathan*, R Tuck, editor, Cambridge University Press, Cambridge.

Hobhouse, LT, 1918, *The Metaphysical Theory of the State*, Allen and Unwin, London.

Hoffding H 1955 *A History of Modern Philosophy*, translated by BE Meyer, Dover Publications, New York.

Hood, RE 1980, 'Karl Barth's Christological Basis for the State and Political Praxis', in *Scottish Journal of Theology*, Volume 33 (1980): 223–238.

Honig, B 1993, *Political Theory and the Displacement of Politics*, Cornell University Press, Ithaca and London.

Huntington, S, 1997, *The Clash of Civilisations and the Remaking of World Order*, Touchstone, New York.

John Paul 11, 1988, 15 August, *Mulieris Dignatem*, Apostolic Letter.

Kane, R 1994, *Through the Moral Maze: Searching for Absolute Values in a Pluralistic World*, Paragon, New York.

Kant I 1972, *Groundwork of the Metaphysic of Morals* in *The Moral Law*, translated by HJ Paton Hutchinson University Library, London.

Kant, I 1991 'The Metaphysics of Morals', in H Reiss, editor, *Kant's Political Writings*, Cambridge University Press, Cambridge.

Kekes, J 1993, *The Morality of Pluralism*, Princeton University Press, Princeton, NJ.

Kekes, J 1997, *Against Liberalism*, Cornell University Press, Ithaca.

Kekes, J 1998 *A Case for Conservatism*, Cornell University Press, Ithaca.

Kirk, R 1982, *The Portable Conservative Reader*, Penguin, Harmondsworth.

Kliever, L 1977, *H Richard Niebuhr*, Word, Waco.

Knight, G 1977, *New Testament Teaching on the Role Relationship of Men and Women*, Baker, Grand Rapids.

Knox, J 1644, *The History of the Reformation of the Church of Scotland*, 2, Robert Bryson, Edinburgh.

Krauthammer, C 1991, 'The Unipolar Moment', in *Foreign Affairs*, 70 (1991): 22–33.

Laclau, E 1990, *New Reflections on the Revolutions of Our Time*, Verso, London.

Laclau, E 1996, *Emancipation(s)*, Verso, London.

Laclau, E and Mouffe, C 1985, *Hegemony and Socialist Strategy*, Verso, London.

La Cugna, C 1991, *God for Us*, Harper, San Francisco.

Laski, HJ 1917, *Studies in the Problem of Sovereignty*, Yale University Press, New Haven, CT.

Laski, HJ 1919, *Authority in the Modern State*, Yale University Press, New Haven, CT.

Lasswell, HD and Kaplan, A 1950, *Power and Society: A Framework for Political Inquiry*, Yale University Press, New Haven, CT.

Lebacqz, K 1986, *Six Theories of Justice*, Augsburg Press, Minneapolis.

Letham, R 2004, *The Holy Trinity in Scripture, History, Theology and Worship*, P&R, Phillipsburg, NJ, Letham.

Lewis, CS 1977, *Mere Christianity*, Fount Paperbacks, Glasgow.

Lilla, M 1998, 'The Politics of Jacques Derrida', in *The New York Review of Books*, 45/11 (25 June 1998): 36–41.

Lindbeck, GA 1984, *The Nature of Doctrine*, Westminster Press, Philadelphia.

Longwood, M 1975, 'Niebuhr and a Theory of Justice', in *Dialog*, 14 (Fall 1975): 253–262.

Lugo, LE 1996, 'Man, Society and the State: A Catholic Perspective', Comments, in M Cromartie, editor, *Caesar's Coin Revisited: Christians and the Limits of Government*, Eerdmans, Grand Rapids.

Lugo, LE 1996, 'Caesar's Coin and the Politics of the Kingdom: A Pluralist Perspective', in M Cromartie, editor, *Caesar's Coin Revisited: Christians and the Limits of Government*, Eerdmans, Grand Rapids.

Luther, M 1967, *Against the Robbing and Murderous Hordes of Peasants* in HT Lehmann and RC Schultz, editors, *Luther's Works*, Volume 46, Fortress Press, Philadelphia.

Luther, M 1979, *The Freedom of a Christian*, in HT Lehmann and HJ Grimm, editors, *Luther's Works*, Volume 31, Fortress Press, Philadelphia.

MacIntyre, A 1985, *After Virtue*, second edition, Duckworth, London.

MacIntyre, A 1988, *Whose Justice? Which Rationality?*, University of Notre Dame Press, Notre Dame, IN.

Maitland, FW 1839, in O Gierke, *Political Theories of the Middle Ages*, translated by FW Maitland, Cambridge University Press, Cambridge.

Manin, G 1997, *The Principles of Representative Government*, Cambridge University Press, Cambridge.

Marshall, P 1984, *Thine is the Kingdom: A Biblical Perspective on the Nature of Government and Politics Today*, Eerdmans, Grand Rapids.

Marshall, P 1996, 'Man, Society and the State: A Catholic Perspective', in Comments, in M Cromartie, editor, *Caesar's Coin Revisited: Christians and the Limits of Government*, Eerdmans, Grand Rapids.

Maududi, SAA 1992, 'Suicide of Western Civilisation', in *West Versus Islam*, translated by Gardezi, S, and Khan, A, International Islamic Publishers, New Delhi.

Maududi, SAA, 2002, 'The Political Theory of Islam', in M Moaddel, and K Talattof, editors, *Modernist and Fundamentalist debates in Islam: A Reader*, Palgrave Macmillan, New York.

Maurice, FD, 2001, quoted in Niebuhr, HR 2001, *Christ and Culture*, Harper Collins, New York.

McCann, D 1980, *Christian Realism and Liberation theology: Practical Theologies in Creative Conflict*, Orbis Books, Maryknoll.

McCarthy, T 1991, 'The Politics of the Ineffable; Derrida's Deconstructionism', in *Ideas and Illusions: On Reconstruction and Deconstruction in Contemporary Critical Theory*, MIT Press, Cambridge.

McLaren, B 2004, *A Generous Orthodoxy*, Zondervan, Grand Rapids.

Milbank, J 1995, *Theology and Social Theory: Beyond Secular Reason*, Blackwell, Oxford.

Miliband, R 1973, *The State in Capitalist Society: the Analysis of the Western System of Power*, Quartet Books, London

Moltmann, M 1981, *The Trinity and the Kingdom*, Harper and Row, New York.

Moltmann, J 1984, *On Human Dignity; Political Theology and Ethics*, SCM Press, London.

Montaigne, ME de 1990, in Derrida, J 'Force of Law. The Mystical Foundation of Authority', in *Cardozo Law Review*, 11:5–6 (1990): 921–1045.

Montesquieu, C 1989, *The Spirit of the Laws,* translated and edited by AM Cohler, BC Miller and HS Stone, Cambridge University Press, Cambridge.

Mouffe, C 1993, *The Return of the Political*, Verso, London.

Mouffe, C, editor, 1999, *The Challenge of Carl Schmitt*, Verso, London.

Mouffe, C 2000, *The Democratic Paradox*, Verso, London.

Mouffe, C 2005, *On the Political*, Routledge, London.

Muravchik, J 1991, *Exporting Democracy: Fulfilling America's Destiny*, American Enterprise Institute, Washington.

Murray, JC 1960, We *Hold These Truths: Catholic Reflections on the American Proposition*, Sheed and Ward, New York.

Murdock, GP 1968, 'The Universality of the Nuclear Family' in NW Bell and EF Vogel, editors, *A Modern Introduction to the Family*, Free Press, New York.

Musk, B 2003, *Holy War: Why do some Muslims become fundamentalists?*, Monarch Books, London.

Nasstrom, S 2006, 'Representative Democracy as Tautology; Ankersmitt and Lefort on Representation', in *European Journal of Political Theory*, 5/3 (2006): 321–342.

Neuhaus, RJ 1984, *The Naked Public Square: Religion and Democracy in America*, Eerdmans, Grand Rapids.

Neuhaus, RJ 1988, 'Nihilism without the Abyss: Law, Rights and Transcendent Good', paper delivered at a conference on Religion and Law in 1985 at the Catholic University Law School and cited in Stanley Hauerwas, 'A Christian Critique of Christian America', in *CH* Reynolds and RV Norman, editors, *Community in America: The Challenge of Habits of the Heart*, University of California Press, Berkeley.

Neuhaus, RJ 1992, 'The Real John Dewey', in *First Things* (January 1992).

Newbiggin, L 1986, *Foolishness to the Greek:; The Gospel and Western Culture*, Eerdmans, Grand Rapids.

Newbiggin, L 1990, *The Gospel in a Pluralist Society*, Eerdmans, Grand Rapids.

Niebuhr, HR 1929, *The Social Sources of Denominationalism*, Meridian Books, New York.

Niebuhr, HR 1932a, 'Faith, Works and Social Salvation', in *Religion in Life*, 1 (1932): 426–30.

Niebuhr, HR 1932b, 'The Only Way into the Kingdom of God', in *Christian Century*, 49.

Niebuhr, HR 1936, 'The Attack upon the Social Gospel', in *Religion in Life*, 5/2 (1936): 176–181.

Niebuhr, HR 1944, 'Towards a New Otherworldliness', *Theology Today* 1/1 (1944): 78–87.

Niebuhr, HR 1946, 'The Responsibility of the Church for Society', in KS Latourette, editor, *The Gospel, the Church and the World*, Interseminary Series, book 3, Harper, New York.

Niebuhr, HR 1956, *The Purpose of the Church and its Ministry*, Harper, New York.

Niebuhr, HR 1960, *Radical Monotheism and Western Culture*, Harper, New York.

Niebuhr, HR, *The Responsible Self; An essay in Christian Moral Philosophy*, Harper, New York.

Niebuhr, HR 1967 *The Meaning of Revelation*, Macmillan, New York.

Niebuhr, HR 1988, 'The Social Gospel and the Mind of Jesus', in *Journal of Religious Ethics*, 16/1 (1988): 115–27.

Niebuhr, HR 2001, *Christ and Culture*, Harper Collins, New York.

Niebuhr, R 1944a, The *Nature and Destiny of Man; A Christian Interpretation*, Volume 2, London, Nisbet & Co Ltd.

Niebuhr, R 1944b, *The Children of Light and the Children of Darkness: A Vindication of Democracy and a Critique of its Traditional Defence*, Scribner, New York.

Niebuhr, R 1966, Man's *Nature and his Communities*, Geoffrey Bles, London.

Niebuhr, R 1989, quoted in P Stallsworth, 'The Story

of an Encounter', in RJ Neuhaus, editor, *Reinhold Niebuhr Today*, Eerdmans, Grand Rapids.

Niebuhr, R 1990, quoted in JC Bennett, 'Tillich and the "Fellowship of Socialist Christians",' *North American Paul Tillich Society Newsletter* 16 (October).

Novak, M 1972, 'Needing Niebuhr Again', in *Commentary* 54 September.

Novak, M 1980, 'Changing the Paradigms: The Cultural Deficiencies of Capitalism', in *Democracy and Mediating Structures: A Theological Inquiry*, American Enterprise Institute, Washington DC.

Novak, M 1981, *Towards a Theology of the Corporation*, American Enterprise Institute, Washington DC.

Novak, M 1982, *The Spirit of Democratic Capitalism*, New York, American Enterprise Institute/Simon & Schuster.

Novak, M 1984, 'The Revolt against our Public Culture', in *National Review* 36 May 4.

Novak, M 1990, 'The Left Still Owns American Culture', in *Forbes* 145, March 5.

Novak, M 1993, *The Catholic Ethic and the Spirit of Capitalism*, Free Press, New York.

Nussbaum, M 1990, 'Aristotelian social democracy', in RB Douglass, G Mara and HS Richardson, editors, *Liberalism and the Good*, Routledge, New York.

Nussbaum, M 2000, *Women and Human Development: the Capabilities Approach*, Cambridge University Press, Cambridge.

Oakeshott, M 1975 *On Human Conduct*, Clarendon Press, Oxford.

O'Brien, C 1999, *Contested Territory: Sexualities and Social Work*, in AS Chambon, A Irving and L Epstein, editors,

Reading Foucault for Social Work, Columbia University Press, New York.

O'Donovan, O 1986, *Resurrection and Moral Order: An Outline for Evangelical Ethics*, Eerdmans, Grand Rapids.

O'Donovan, O 2003, *The Desire of the Nations; Rediscovering the Roots of Political Theology*, Cambridge University Press, Cambridge.

Offe, C 1974, 'Structural Problems of the Capitalist State, Class Rule and the Political System', in Klaus von Beyme, *German Political Studies*, Volume 1 (1974): 31–57.

Pannenberg, W 1988-97, *Systematic Theology*, Volumes 1–3, T&T Clark, Edinburgh.

Pascall, B 1990, in Derrida, J 'Force of Law. The Mystical Foundation of Authority', in *Cardozo Law Review*, 11:5-6 (1990): 921–1045.

Pettersen, A 1996, *Athanasius*, Morehouse, New York.

Pitkin, HF 1967, *The Concept of Representation*, University of California Press, Berkeley.

Pius XI, Pope 1931, *Quadragesimo Anno* (Reconstruction of the Social Order) May 15.

Poulantzas, N 1969, 'The Problems of the Capitalist State' in *New Left Review*, 58 (1969): 67–78.

Poulantzas, N 1973 *Political Power and Social Classes*, New Left Books, London.

Rahner, K 1997, *The Trinity*, Herder and Herder, New York.

Ranciere, J 1995, *On the Shores of Politics*, London, Verso.

Ransom, JS 1997, *Foucault's Discipline: The Politics of Subjectivity*, Duke University Press, London.

Ratzinger, J 2005, *On the Way to Jesus* Christ, Ignatius, San Francisco.

Rawls, J 1985, 'Justice as fairness: political not metaphysical', in *Philosophy and Public Affairs*, 14 (1985): 223–51.

Rawls, J 1971, *A Theory of Justice*, Oxford University Press, Oxford.

Rawls, J 1993, Political *Liberalism*, Columbia University Press, New York.

Raz, J 1986, *The Morality of Freedom*, Clarendon Press, Oxford.

Ricouer, P 1976, 'Philosophical Hermeneutics and Theology' in *Theology Digest*, 24/2 (1976): 154–164.

Ricoeur, P 1981, 'Hermeneutics and the Critique of Ideology' in JB Thompson, editor, Hermeneutics *and the Human Sciences*, Cambridge University Press, Cambridge.

Rowland, T 2008, *Ratzinger's Faith: The Theology of Pope Benedict XVI*, Oxford University Press, Oxford.

Rousseau, JJ 1973, *The Social Contract and Discourses* translated by GDH Cole, Everyman's Library, London.

Runciman D 1997, *Pluralism and the Personality of the State*, Cambridge University Press, Cambridge.

Sandel, M 1982, *Liberalism and the Limits of Justice*, Cambridge University Press, Cambridge.

Sacks, J 1997, The *Politics of Hope*, Johnathon Cape, London.

Sandel M, 1982, *Liberalism and the Limits of Justice*, Cambridge University Press, Cambridge.

Scheeben, MJ 1979, quoted in Thielicke, H, *Theological Ethics, Volume 2: Politics*, Eerdmans, Grand Rapids.

Schlier, H, 1968, quoted in K Barth, *Community, State and Church: Three Essays*, Peter Smith, Gloucester, Mass.

Scriven, C 1988, *The Transformation of Culture*, Herald, Scottdale.

Simmons, J 1995, *Foucault and the Political*, Routledge, New York.

Skinner, Q 1988, 'Warrender and Skinner on Hobbes: A Reply', in *Political Studies*, 36 (1988): 692–95.

Skinner, Q 1999, 'Hobbes and the Purely Artificial "person" of the state', in *The Journal of Political Philosophy*, VII/1 (1999): 1-29.

Skocpol, T 1987, 'Bringing the State back In' in Evans, B, Rueschemeyer, D, and Skocpol, T, editors, *Bringing the State back in*, Cambridge University Press, Cambridge.

Smail, T 2005, *Like Father, Like Son: The Trinity imaged in our Humanity*, Paternoster, Milton Keynes, Bucks.

Smith, VE 1996, *Science of Nature*, Bruce Publishing Company, Milwaukee.

Stauffer, E 1955, *Christ and the Caesars*, translated by K and R Gregor Smith, Westminster Press, Philadelphia.

Stassen, GH, Yeager, DM and Yoder, JH, 1996, *Authentic Transformation: a New Vision of Christ and Culture*, Abingdon Press, Nashville.

Sydney Anglican Diocesan Doctrine Commission Report, 1999 'The Doctrine of the Trinity and its bearing on the Relationship of Men and Women', in *Year Book of the Diocese of Sydney* (2000), Diocesan Registry, Sydney.

Sweet, W, 'Absolute Idealism and Finite Individuality', in *Indian Philosophical Quarterly*, xxiv/4 (October 1997): 431–462.

Taylor, AE 1961, *Elements of Metaphysics*, Methuen, London.

Taylor, C 1989a, 'Cross-purposes; the liberal-communitarian debate', in N Rosenblum, editor, *Liberalism and the Moral Life*, Harvard University Press, Cambridge, MA.

Taylor, C 1989b, *Sources of the Self: The Making of the Modern Identity*, Harvard University Press, Cambridge, MA.

Thielicke, H 1979, *Theological Ethics, Volume 2: Politics*, Eerdmans, Grand Rapids.

Thiele, LP 1990, 'The Agony of Politics: The Nietzschean Roots of Foucault's Thought', in *America Political Science Review*, 84 (1990): 907–925.

Tillich, P 1956, 'The Church in Contemporary Culture', in *World Christian Education*, second quarter, 41–43.

Tinder, G 1996, 'Man, Society and the State: A Catholic Perspective', in Comments, in M Cromartie, editor, *Caesar's Coin Revisited: Christians and the Limits of Government*, Eerdmans, Grand Rapids.

Torrance, A 1996, *Persons in Communion: An Essay on Trinitarian Description and Human Participation*, T&T Clark, Edinburgh.

Torrance, T 1996, *The Christian Doctrine of God; One being, Three Persons*, T&T Clark, Edinburgh.

Trainor, B 1988, 'Warrender and Skinner on Hobbes', *Political Studies*, 36 (1988): 680–91.

Trainor, BT 1998a, *Justice and the State: On Liberal Organicism and the Foundations of Emancipatory Politics*, World Heritage Press, Quebec.

Trainor, BT 1998b, *The Origin and End of Modernity: Reflections on the Meaning of Post-modernism*, World Heritage Press, Quebec.

Trainor, BT 1998c, *Gender, the Marriage Contract and the State; he Role of Promise Keeping in the Conjugal Body Politic,* World Heritage Press, Quebec.

Trainor, BT 2002a, 'Pluralism, Truth and Social Democracy', in *Dissent,* Fall 2002): 69–72.

Trainor, BT 2002b, 'Statism and Anti-juristic Moralism in Bosanquet's Political Philosophy', in *Animus,* 7.

Trainor BT and Jeffreys H 2003a, *The Human Service Disciplines and Social Work: the Foucault Effect,* World Heritage Press, Quebec.

Trainor, BT 2003b, 'Asylum Seekers, Colonialism and the de-legitimization the Australian State', in *Australian Quarterly,* 18–24.

Troeltsch, E 1957, 'The Place of Christianity among the World Religious' in *Christian Thought: Its History and Application, Meridian Books,* New York.

Troeltsch, E 1960, *The Social Teaching of the Christian Churches,* Volume 2, Harper, New York.

Troeltsch, E 1991, 'Das Wesen des modernen Geist', in in JL Adams, editor, *Religion in History,* Minneapolis.

Van Acker, E 2002, 'The role of Government in a Global World', in E Van Acker and G Curran, editors, *Business, Government and Globalization,* Longman, French Forest, 1–11.

Van Til, C 1955, *The Defence of the Faith,* Presbyterian and Reformed, Philadelphia

Walker, JL, 1970, 'Normative Consequences of Democratic Theory', in HS Kariel, editor, *Frontiers of Democratic Theory,* Random House, New York, 227–247.

Von Balthasar, HU, 1997, 'The Fathers, the Scholastics and Ourselves', in *Communio: International Catholic Review*, 24 (1997): 347–396.

Wallis, J, 1976, *Agenda for a Biblical People*, Harper & Row, New York.

Wallis, J, 2005, *God's Politics*, Lion Hudson, Oxford.

Walzer, M 1981, 'The Distribution of Membership', in P Brown and H Shue, editors, *Boundaries: National Autonomy and its Limits*, Rowman and Littlefield, Totowa, NJ.

Walzer, M 1983, Spheres *of Justice: A Defence of Pluralism and Equality*, Basic Books, New York.

Walzer, M 1988 *Company of Critics*, Basic Books, New York.

Walzer, M 1994, *Thick and Thin: Moral Argument at Home and Abroad*, University of Notre Dame Press, Notre Dame, Indiana.

Walzer, M 1998, 'Pluralism and Social Democracy', in *Dissent*, Winter.

Ware, BA 2002, 'How shall we think about the Trinity?', in DS Huffman and EL Johnson, editors, *God Under Fire: Modern Theology Reinvents God*, Zondervan, Grand Rapids: 253–277.

Wattenberg, BJ 1991, *The First Universal nation: Leading Indicators and Ideas about the Surge of America in the1990s*, Free Press, New York.

Wenman, M 2003, 'Laclau or Mouffe? Splitting the Difference', in *Philosophy and Social Criticism*, 29/5, (2003): 581–606.

Wolin, R 1995, 'Derrida on Marx, or the Perils of Left Heideggerianism', in R Wolin, editor, *Labyrinths:*

Explorations in the Critical History of Ideas, University of Massachusetts Press, Amherst, 231-240.

Yeager, DM 1996, 'The Social Self in the Pilgrim Church', in Stassen, GH, Yeager, DM and Yoder, JH, *Authentic Transformation: A New Vision of Christ and Culture*, Abingdon Press, Nashville.

Yeatman, A 1994, *Postmodern Revisionings of the Political* Routledge, New York.

Yoder, JH, 1972, *The Politics of Jesus*, Eerdmans, Grand Rapids.

Yoder, JH 1996, 'How H Richard Niebuhr Reasoned: A Critique of *Christ and Culture*' in GH Stassen, DM Yeager and JH Yoder, *Authentic Transformation: a New Vision of Christ and Culture*, Abingdon Press, Nashville.

Young, I 1990, *Justice and the Politics of Difference*, Princeton University Press, Princeton.

Zylstra, B 1982, 'The Bible, Politics, and the State', in JW Skillen, editor, *Confessing Christ and Doing Politics*, Association for Public Justice Education Fund, Washington DC.

Index

Ankersmit, F, 311-312
Aquinas, T, 27, 77, 85, 429, 473-474, 494-498, 514, 524
Augustine, St., 5, 147-148, 153, 375, 379, 420, 498, 506, 525, 527
Bartelson, J., 29, 307, 318, 331-332, 355-357, 543, 547-551, 574, 576
Barth, K., 17, 24-27, 56, 83, 108, 159, 163, 166-171, 186, 232, 254, 326, 360-363, 399-401, 423-425, 473-525, 538
Beckley, H., 4, 107
Bernard, St., (of Clairvaux) 4, 6
Blondel, M, 14, 127-128, 512-513
Bosanquet, B., 17, 21, 25-26, 61-64, 75, 200-203, 213-224, 296-297, 302, 329-3312, 401-420
Bradley, F., 95, 417n., 542
Brunner, E., 83, 85, 391-392, 425
Culture wars, 226-227; attempt to address, 240-257
Derrida, J., 28-31, 35, 52, 526-575
Deleuze, G., 177-178
Esquivel, A., 59-60
Feinberg, J., 462-466
Foucault, M., 14-17, 128, 157-165, 169-204, 218, 309-310, 316, 318
Gadamer, H-G 59, 70-74
Gray, J., 23, 261-265, 272-273, 289

Grenz, 38-39, 517
Gustafson, J., 136, 196, 511
Habermas, J., 1-3, 18, 31, 231, 359, 576
Hare, RM, 88, 183-184
Hauerwas, S., 8, 97-99, 117, 120-123, 129-137, 143, 579
Hobbes, T. 26-29, 81, 319-320, 402, 426-473, 530, 543-551, 573-574
Hobhouse, L., 304-305
Horizons, fusions of, 70-74
Huntington, S., 23, 36, 261, 278-281
Kung, H., 55
Lewis, C. S., 90, 147, 484n.
Liberalism, classic and modern, 18-22
Lilla, M., 571
Lindbeck, G., 56
Lubac, de, H., 11, 14, 38, 127, 498
Lugo, L., 19, 304, 324
Luther, M., 6, 14, 138-148, 427-428
Marshall, p., 20, 321
McCarthy, T., 568-569
Metanarratives, 14, 16, 158-159, 191-194, 206
Milbank, J., 14, 125-129, 321, 512-513
Mouffe, C., 310-311

Murray, JC., 235
Neuhaus, R., 18, 233-234, 251, 253
Niebuhr, Reinholt, 27, 80-87, 132-133, 284-286, 394, 424-425, 450
Niebuhr, Richard, 9-12, 40, 44-51, 64, 67-70, 75-80, 89n., 91, 101-104, 107, 111, 114-118, 120, 142, 142-149, 512-513, 163-164, 494-495
Novak, M., 252, 283-285
Nussbaum, M., 254-255
Oakeshott, M., 403, 409
O'Donovan, O., 7, 18, 63, 101, 109, 129, 333, 345, 350-353, 397-398, 424, 503, 517, 525, 533, 549, 573, 578
Pannenberg, W., 326-329, 426, 502-504, 507-508, 516
Rahner, K., 11-14, 38, 51, 54, 58, 125-128, 196, 328-329, 378, 426, 512
Ratzinger, J., 1, 11, 31, 38, 87, 231, 314-315, 333, 359, 498, 506, 527, 576
Ransom, J., 159, 172, 177-189
Rawls, J., 20, 23, 254-255, 261, 265-271, 289-292
Runciman, D., 402, 414-415
Sacred, secular and, 3-9, 109, 126-127, 138-143, 231-232, 325, 333, 397, 424, 482
Schmitt, C., 300
Scriven, C., 117-119
Secular, sacred and, 3-9, 109, 126-127, 138-143, 231-232, 325, 333, 397, 424, 482
Skinner, Q., 458-468
Stassen, G., 11, 38-41, 45-47, 50, 54-58, 61, 65
Thielicke, H., 83n, 135-136, 178, 428, 485, 497-500, 505-506, 509, 515, 518n, 519-523

Tillich, P., 251
Tinder, G., 21
Troeltsch, E., 11, 42, 57-59
Truth, servants of, masters of, 16-17, 158-159, 194-197, 202, 206
Universal(ity), the 'real presence' of, 11, 37-38, 86, 372; horizontal, external, 61-62, 66, 68, 89-90, 209-213, 280-284; vertical, internal, 11, 43, 52, 62, 64, 67-68, 73, 77, 90, 99, 115, 120, 209-213, 282, 309, 317
Von Balthasar, H., 53, 106, 498
Wittgenstein, L. 215, 218
Walzer, M, 12, 17, 40, 44, 48-50, 64-66, 70, 75, 200-213, 217, 221, 276-277, 281n, 541n
Wolin, R., 570
Yeagher, D., 75, 118-119
Yeatman, A., 310, 313-314
Yoder, J., 47, 135

Lightning Source UK Ltd.
Milton Keynes UK
UKOW04f2155220917
309708UK00001B/91/P